SEXUAL PERVERSIONS AND PARAPHILIAS: AN A-Z

DR MARK GRIFFITHS

Edited by Dr Mike Sutton

Curtis Press

© 2024 Mark Griffiths

ISBN (pbk) 978-1-8381280-9-8

Published in 2024 by Curtis Press Ltd, UK

This work is subject to copyright. All rights are reserved, whether the whole or part of the material is concerned, specifically the rights of translation, reprinting, reuse of illustrations, recitation, broadcasting, filmmaking, audio production, electronic reproduction of any kind, and digital storage of any kind. Duplication of this publication or parts thereof is permitted only after permission has been obtained from Curtis Press.

The use of general descriptive names, registered names, trademarks, etc., in this publication does not imply, even in the absence of a specific statement, that such names are exempt from the relevant protective laws and regulations and therefore free for general use.

Cover design: Miblart

Typeset by Falcon Oast Graphic Art Ltd, *www.falcon.uk.com*

Printed and bound by CPI Group (UK) Ltd, Croydon, CR0 4YY

Distributed in North America by SCB
Distributed in the United Kingdom by Gazelle Book Services

Visit Curtis Press at *www.curtis-press.com*

Sexual Perversions and Paraphilias: An A-Z

About the Author and Editor

Dr Mark Griffiths is a chartered psychologist and Distinguished Professor of Behavioural Addiction at Nottingham Trent University. He is also Director of the International Gaming Research Unit. He has spent over 37 years in the field and is internationally known for his work on gambling, gaming and other behavioural addictions (sex addiction, social media addiction, exercise addiction and work addiction). He has published over 1600 peer-reviewed research papers, 7 books, over 200 book chapters and over 1500 other articles. Dr Griffiths has appeared on over 3500 radio and television programs and has written over 400 articles for national and international newspapers and magazines.

He has received fellowships from the British Psychological Society for "exceptional contributions to psychology" (2006), the Royal Society of Arts for "achieving eminence in their chosen profession or calling" (2007) and the Academy of Social Sciences for "significant achievements and contributions to the social sciences" (2013).

Dr Griffiths has won over 25 national and international awards during his career including the John Rosecrance Prize for "outstanding scholarly contributions to the field of gambling research" (US Institute for the Study of Gambling and Commercial Gaming, 1994), the Joseph Lister Prize for "outstanding scientific communication in the social sciences" (British Association for the Advancement of Science, 2004), the Excellence in Teaching of Psychology Award for "distinguished contributions in the teaching of psychology" (British Psychological Society, 2005), the Lifetime Research Award for "exceptional long-standing achievement in the field of research to assist problem gamblers and their families" (US National Council on Problem Gambling, 2013), the Research Award for "exceptional research contribution to the field of sexual health and problematic sexual behavior" (US Society for the Advancement of Sexual Health, 2018) and the Lifetime Achievement Award for the Study of Behavioral Addictions for "outstanding contributions to and a lasting impact on the study of behavioral addictions over the course of their career, demonstrating a lifetime commitment to the field" (International Society for the Study of Behavioral Addictions, 2023).

Dr Mike Sutton has a first in law and a PhD in criminology. He is co-founder and Chief Editor of the *Internet Journal of Criminology*, an author and editor. He describes himself as a criminologist, dysologist, academic discoverer and entrenched mythbuster.

Dr Sutton was for 14 years Senior Research Officer at the Home Office in Queen Anne's Gate, London and for 16 years a senior university academic. He is joint winner of the *British*

Journal of Criminology Prize for his groundbreaking work on hackers. He is the originator of the market reduction approach to crime and the supermyth concept.

Since 2014 Dr Sutton has published his BigData discovery that busts the myth that no single person read Patrick Matthew's (1831) prior publication of the complete theory of evolution by natural selection before Darwin and Wallace (1858–1859) claimed, decades later, to have each discovered the same concept. His research on this topic is published by Curtis Press in *Science Fraud: Darwin's Plagiarism of Patrick Matthew's Theory*.

His current research interests include looking at applying his market reduction approach to reduce sex crime offending.

Introduction

Sexual perversions and paraphilias

In 1986, during the second year of my undergraduate psychology degree at the University of Bradford, the psychiatrist Alex Oswald gave a guest lecture on paraphilias. That lecture was better and more interesting than any I have ever heard. Whilst I had always taken some interest in human sexual behaviour, Oswald's lecture was the stimulus for my enduring academic interest in extreme sexual behaviours.

The *Oxford English Dictionary* claims that the term "paraphilia" was coined in 1925 by Stekel and van Teslaar (1925). However, Diederik Janssen (2014) originally unearthed the fact that it was apparently coined by Kraus (1903). Moreover, van Teslaar (1922, p. 156) tells us that he and Stekel used it the same way as Kraus to mean "inverted instinct". As for the psychological concept, the German psychiatrist von Krafft-Ebing (1886) is generally credited with first identifying it in his book *Psychopathia Sexualis* (Sexual Psychopathy).

Paraphilias (from the Greek "beyond usual or typical love") are uncommon types of sexual expression and often more commonly described as sexual deviations, sexual perversions or disorders of sexual preference. They are typically accompanied by intense sexual arousal to unconventional and/or non-sexual stimuli. To many people paraphilias may appear bizarre and/or socially unacceptable, representing the extreme end of the "sexual continuum". In some cases paraphilic behaviour may occur only sporadically, whereas for others it may be compulsive and/or addictive.

Generally, it is thought paraphilias are rare and affect only a very small percentage of adults. However, unlike many known types of offending and victimization, we have no nationally representative statistics on the topic. Furthermore, it is difficult for researchers in the field to estimate the proportion of the population who experience paraphilic behaviours, with much of the scientific literature based on self-reported case studies. As paraphilias typically offer pleasure many individuals affected do not seek psychiatric treatment. Furthermore, reliable statistics are compounded by the fact that numerous paraphilic acts are illegal. As a result of the combination of illegality and sexual deviance, paraphiliacs can experience high levels of shame and guilt and, like those who experience pleasure from the behaviour, may not seek medical or psychiatric help. For those who do their disorders are often difficult to treat. Therapeutic success is more likely to be related to curbing or suppressing the behaviour rather than eliminating it.

Although the statistics are biased there is general agreement among the psychiatric community that all paraphilias are male dominated, with 90% of all those affected being men and some estimates suggesting the male-to-female ratio is as high as 30 to 1. Research also indicates that some paraphilias appear to be more common than others. For instance, the most common paraphilias reported in the scientific literature appear to be masochism, sadism and fetishism. Within clinics that treat sex offenders the most common paraphilias are paedophilia, voyeurism and exhibitionism.

Atypical sexual behaviours often cluster and/or overlap either simultaneously or sequentially. For instance, some research has reported that paraphiliacs commonly experience two to three concurrent paraphilias, with around 5% experiencing up to 10 concurrently. The onset of paraphilic behaviour is typically initiated during early adolescence through a complex biopsychosocial network of causes. The behaviour usually reaches its full development by the age of 20 years. Some of the causes of paraphilic behaviour are known to include various genetic and hormonal abnormalities, prenatal neurodevelopmental factors, neurocognitive and brain dysfunctional, maladaptive learning and dysfunctional family life during childhood (Griffiths, 1999a).

Paraphilias are rarely described as addictions. Most of the debate surrounds whether they are impulse control disorders, or whether they fall within the spectrum of obsessive–compulsive disorders. Arguably, the best criteria for diagnosis of a paraphilia is found in the latest fifth (text revision) edition of the American Psychiatric Association's (2022) *Diagnostic and Statistical Manual of Mental Disorders* (DSM-5-TR). In the DSM-5-TR a paraphilic disorder is *"a paraphilia that is currently causing distress or impairment to the individual or a paraphilia whose satisfaction has entailed personal harm, or risk of harm, to others. A paraphilia is a necessary but not a sufficient condition for having a paraphilic disorder, and a paraphilia by itself does not necessarily justify or require clinical intervention"* (p. 780).

The essential features of a paraphilia are recurrent intense sexually arousing fantasies, sexual urges or behaviours generally involving (i) non-human objects, (ii) the suffering or humiliation of oneself or one's partner, or (iii) children or other non-consenting persons that occur over a period of at least 6 months (American Psychiatric Association, 2022). The DSM-5-TR also distinguishes between paraphilias and paraphile disorders, particularly because some paraphilic behaviours have no negative consequences. More specifically:

"The term paraphilia denotes any intense and persistent sexual interest other than sexual interest in genital stimulation or preparatory fondling with phenotypically normal, physically mature, consenting human partners. In some circumstances, the criteria 'intense and persistent' may be difficult to apply, such as in the assessment of persons who are very old or medically ill and who may not have 'intense' sexual interests of any kind. In such circumstances, the term paraphilia may be defined as any sexual interest greater than or equal to nonparaphilic sexual interests. There are also specific paraphilias that are generally better described as preferential sexual interests than as intense sexual interest." (p. 779)

The element of coercion is another key distinguishing characteristic of paraphilias. Some paraphilias (e.g., sadism, masochism, fetishism, hypoxyphilia, urophilia, coprophilia and klismaphilia) are engaged in alone or include consensual adults who participate in, observe or tolerate the particular paraphiliac behaviour. These atypical non-coercive behaviours are considered by many in the psychiatric community to be relatively benign or harmless because there is no violation of anyone's rights. Atypical coercive paraphilic behaviours, such as exhibitionism, voyeurism, frotteurism, necrophilia and zoophilia are considered much more serious and almost always require therapeutic intervention.

Finally, it is also worth noting that some practitioners working in the field have made distinctions between what are referred to as optional, preferred and exclusive paraphilias. An optional paraphilia is a behaviour that provides an alternative route to becoming sexually aroused. For instance, a male with otherwise fairly normal sexual interests might occasionally enhance his sexual arousal by wearing women's high-heeled shoes and fishnet stockings while having sex. In preferred paraphilias a person prefers the paraphilia to conventional sexual activities, but is still able to engage in conventional sex. For instance, a male might prefer whenever possible to wear women's high-heeled shoes and fishnet stockings during sex. In exclusive paraphilias a person is unable to become sexually aroused in the absence of the paraphilia. In this case a male would be unlikely to get sexually aroused during sex unless he was wearing high-heeled shoes and fishnet stockings.

Sexual fetishes

Although the term "fetish" was used frequently in 19th-century English literature to refer to specific aspects of traditional African religions (Bowditch, 1819), some of which have been associated with sex slavery and child sex abuse (Bilyeu, 1998), the origin of contemporary psychological understanding of particular types of sexual attraction is widely accredited to the French psychologist Alfred Binet (1887) who is arguably best known for inventing the earliest IQ tests.

Fetishes refer to obtaining sexual excitement primarily or exclusively from a non-living (inanimate) object or a particular part of the body that is not conventionally viewed as being particularly sexual in nature. A sexual attraction by males to feet, for example, is more likely to be viewed as a sexual fetish than a sexual attraction towards breasts. Attraction to a very particular body part is typically classed as "partialism". Empirical research by Gosselin and Wilson (1980) indicated that the most prevalent body fetishes are for feet, hands and hair, and that the most prevalent fetish objects are shoes, gloves and (soiled) underwear. However, there may be differences in relation to sexual orientation. Most fetishism research concerns heterosexual men who have fetishistic desires for feminine items, such as high-heeled shoes, lingerie and hosiery. Among homosexual men the fetishistic objects tend to be highly masculine.

Fetishes rarely develop into an offence that harms anyone, although offences may include things like theft of underwear or cutting hair from an unwilling victim. Fetishes may also involve some kind of enhancement of a sexual act, such as a person being asked to wear a particular piece of clothing by the fetishist during sex (e.g., a leather outfit or fishnet stockings). Fetishists (usually male) are often unable to orgasm without the fetish present.

Fetishes can be established in those as young as 4 years old and are not considered to be disorders of sexual preference unless the fetishistic behaviour causes significant negative detriment and/or psychosocial distress for the individual. If the fetish does cause significant distress it would be diagnosed as a paraphilia in the DSM-5-TR (American Psychiatric Association, 2022). Psychological research has shown that many fetishes appear to be the result of early imprinting and conditioning experiences in childhood or adolescence (e.g., where sexual excitement and/or orgasm is paired with non-sexual objects or body parts) or as a consequence of strong traumatic, emotional and/or physical experience. Fetishes may in part be influenced by rejection of the opposite sex and/or by youthful arousal being channelled elsewhere deliberately or accidentally. Some children have been said to associate sexual arousal with objects that belong to an emotionally significant person like a mother or older sister. Such sexual arousal is known as "symbolic transformation". However, there is also evidence that some fetishes have more biological origins, such as people whose fetish results from conditions like temporal lobe epilepsy.

Sometimes it is difficult to draw the line between normal and paraphilic behaviours. Kafka (2010) explains in a review about the DSM criteria that fetishes can be "non-clinical manifestations of a normal spectrum of eroticization or clinical disorders causing significant interpersonal difficulties." The etiology of fetishes is also complicated by the fact that empirical research, such as that conducted by Gosselin and Wilson (1980) reports some fetishists (e.g., those engaging in some form of fetishistic transvestism) view their behaviour as relaxing rather than arousing.

As with many other sexual disorders there is very little reliable epidemiological data on fetishism. In a study from the 1950s only 0.1% of 4,000 patients in private practice were recorded as having fetishism as a primary problem (Curren, 1954). Another study carried out among 561 non-incarcerated sex offenders all of whom were paraphiliacs by Abel *et al.* (1998) reports that only 3.4% were diagnosed with fetishism. Abel *et al.* (1992) investigated the comorbidity rates of various paraphilic behaviours among a group of 859 male paraphiliacs. Of the 859 participants only 12 were diagnosed with fetishism as either a primary or a secondary diagnosis. In a review of fetishism, Darcangelo (2008) noted that fetishism, transvestic fetishism and homosexuality have often been linked. Her review notes that fetishism has also been linked with psychiatric behaviours including kleptomania, borderline personality disorder, obsessive–compulsive personality disorder and attention-deficit/hyperactivity disorder.

My favourite study in this area is Scorolli *et al.* (2007). The authors studied the relative prevalence of different fetishes and used an online methodology to collect large amounts of data. By comparison most studies on fetishistic behaviour are either case studies or small-scale surveys where sample sizes are rarely above 100 participants. To repeat the point already made, data from the studies examining rare fetishes are typically from psychiatric patients, sex offenders and/or those who have sought or have been referred to a therapist.

Scorolli *et al.* (2007) examined the content found in fetish discussion groups. Via a search of Yahoo! groups online the research team located 2,938 groups whose name or description text contained the word "fetish". They then applied a number of inclusion and exclusion criteria.

First, they identified groups who dealt with sexual topics and discarded groups who used "fetish" in a non-sexual context (e.g., fetish for a rock band). Second, they excluded groups who used "fetish" to deny that the group was about sex (e.g., a support group for pregnant women stated explicitly that the group did not discuss "pregnancy fetish"). Third, some groups were excluded because the sexual nature of the topic could not be established with confidence (e.g., there was no description text of what the fetish was). Fourth, groups were excluded if the group discussed "sex" or "fetishism" generically and therefore could not be categorized. Fifth, groups who had no identified members were excluded.

Following application of the inclusion and exclusion criteria, 381 fetish discussion groups were available for analysis. The average number of posts per month within the groups was over 4,000. That included over 150,000 members. The authors argued that figure was inflated because many fetishists would likely be subscribed to more than one group. It was estimated very conservatively that their sample size comprised at least 5,000 fetishists, but was likely to be a lot more. A classification scheme was devised whereby fetish preference was assigned to one or more categories. The three main categories were body, objects and behaviours and these were then further subdivided to describe:

- A part or feature of the body (e.g., feet and fat people) and body modifications (e.g., tattoos).
- An object associated with some part of the body (e.g., shoes).
- An object not associated with some part of the body (e.g., candles).
- A person's own behaviour (e.g., biting fingernails).
- A behaviour of other persons (e.g., smoking).
- A behaviour requiring interaction with others (e.g., humiliation roleplay).

Approximately 70% were assigned to just one of these categories. The relative frequency of each fetish was estimated by taking into account (a) the number of groups devoted to the particular fetish, (b) the number of individuals participating in the fetish groups and (c) the number of messages exchanged within the group forum. Their results showed that body part fetishes were most common (33%), followed by objects associated with the body (30%), preferences for other people's behaviour (18%), own behaviour (7%), social behaviour (7%) and objects unrelated to the body (5%). Feet and objects associated with feet were by far the most common fetishes.

Overall, research in this area is biased towards small-scale studies with biased samples. Therefore, as Darcangelo (2008) concludes, in order to increase understanding surrounding fetishistic behaviour, future empirical research needs to focus on large, population-based, representative samples.

The following chapters of this book provide a simple yet detailed A–Z guide to sexual perversions and paraphilias. It does not include every single paraphilia, as many lists of alleged paraphilias that can be found online include references to paraphilias that are either hypothetical or have no empirical evidence that they even exist. Also, this book does not include a separate entry for paedophilia, simply because there are numerous books dedicated to this area of sexual behaviour. However, I do make reference to it a number of times in relation to other paraphilias.

Abasiophilia

Later in this book I examine medical fetishism, which includes those sexually aroused by medical procedures, people wearing medical accessories and various forms of amputee fetishism. Medical fetishism includes acrotomophilia and apotemnophilia, which are dealt with in more depth in their own entries in this book. Respectively, these names are used to classify individuals sexually aroused by amputees and includes those sexually aroused by the thought of being an amputee as well. Abasiophilia is a paraphilia that intersects both. In non-academic writing the only reference I am aware of to this paraphilia is in *The Scarecrow*, a novel in which the fictitious serial killer Wesley Carver is motivated by abasiophilia. Two of the characters discuss it (Connelly, 2009).

There is relatively little research on abasiophilia. This is because most academic literature on the topic is focused upon sexual amputee fetishes and paraphilias. According to Aggrawal (2009a) abasiophilia is defined as a "love of, or sexual attraction to, people who use leg braces or other orthopaedic appliances." However, there are a number of slightly different definitions depending upon which source is consulted. Butcher (2003) defines abasiophilia as "a psychosexual attraction to people with impaired mobility, especially those who use orthopaedic appliances such as leg braces, orthopaedic leg braces, orthopaedic casts, and/or wheelchairs." Twinn (2007) writes that it is a "sexual attraction to people with mobility facilitators, especially equipment such as braces or wheelchairs." Finally, Pranzarone (2000) notes that abasiophilia is a "paraphilia of the eligibilic/stigmatic type in which sexuoerotic arousal and facilitation or attainment of orgasm are responsive to and contingent on the partner being lame, with a limp, or crippled [from Greek *abasios* (lameness) + -philia]."

The term "abasiophilia" was coined, as were many other paraphilias that I cover in this book, by Money (1990a). Money's definition is that abasiophilia refers to an erotic focus on a partner who is "lame, crippled, or unable to walk". Money's paper describes two case study reports in which the subjects were women. The first was a 42-year-old woman with an amputee paraphilia (i.e., acrotomophilia). The second was a woman in her thirties with a lameness paraphilia (i.e., abasiophilia).

Although the name for the condition was obviously new in its coining, the condition itself was not. Case studies dating back more than 50 years exist, most notably a paper by Fleischl (1960) describing "a man's fantasy of a crippled girl" categorized as "orthopedic fetishism". Contrastingly, Milner *et al.* (2008) in a review of paraphilias not otherwise specified (PNOS) note that: "[Abasiophilia] ... does not appear to qualify as fetishism, because fetishism requires a sexual focus on a nonhuman object."

As we try to make sense of the world we should remember that typologies do not exist in nature like physical objects or laws of nature, such as gravity. They tell us as much about the people who create them as they do the things classified to distinguish one from another. Consequently, the degree to which a distinction should be made between abasiophilia and other similar PNOS categories, such as morphophilia and partialism, is less clear. For example, abasiophilia may be considered a subtype of morphophilia (defined by Milner et al. [2008] as referring to "an erotic focus on one or more of the body characteristics of one's sexual partner") rather than a separate paraphilia.

Although predominantly reported among males, abasiophilia also has been reported among females (Money, 1990a). Even though the etiology of abasiophilia is unknown, psychodynamic interpretations suggest that for a male the deformed limb of a woman partner represents a female penis, as noted by Fleischl (1960). According to psychoanalytic theory a man may be attracted to a crippled woman because his anxiety and hostility relate to "the shock of threatened castration at the sight of the female genital are reduced when the deformed limb (representing a penis) is present."

Pranzarone (2000) also notes the reciprocal paraphilic condition as autoabasiophilia in which individuals are sexually aroused when they focus on their own condition of being lame, crippled or unable to walk, which may involve fantasies of being disabled and/or wearing/using orthopaedic assistive devices. Milner et al. (2008) note that "the vast majority of cases appear to involve males" but, citing the case studies of Money, it has also been reported among females.

Abasiophilia is part of a wider attraction to disability. There is clearly a lot of psychological crossover between abasiophilia and acrotomophilia as well as between autoabasiophilia and apotemnophilia. Both abasiophiles and acrotomophiles are described in the academic literature as "devotees" who are aroused by disability. In relation to autoabasiophiles and apotemnophiles, Bruno (1997) describes such individuals as having a "factitious disability disorder". However, there is a large overlap between these paraphilias. Consequently, Bruno has described individuals with these types of paraphjlia as "devotees, pretenders, and wannabes" (DPWs).

Acnephilia

The word "acnephilia" is a made-up term and does not appear in any books on sexual perversions and paraphilias. The only operational definition of the condition I have come across is from the online Urban Dictionary, which defines acnephilia as:

> "Deriving pleasure from popping pimples or zits on either one's own face or someone close to them. Acnephilia is usually common among girlfriends as they find enjoyment in popping their boyfriend's pimples, despite the pleas and groans from their mates. Symptoms of acnephilia could arise anywhere. From one's own personal home to the public streets. Once acnephilia takes over a young woman's body she is not content until every single one of her boyfriend's pimples are popped and done with."

Before examining the alleged sexual nature of squeezing spots, I did come across an interesting article (Holmes, 2003) in which the author interviewed a number of scientists about why women happily squeeze their sexual partner's spots. Most of those interviewed conceptualized such behaviour as "grooming". For instance, Robin Dunbar is quoted by Holmes as saying:

> "The chief manner in which primates regulate their relationships with one another is through grooming, whereas we more evolved humans rely on verbal and written language."

The article also features an unnamed female psychoanalyst who speculated there may be a ritualistic or purification element at play and implied that the activity was sadomasochistic. She argued that in the same way that those with obsessive–compulsive disorders engage in rituals in order to overcome their anxiety, picking spots may be something soothing in a frenetic life. She then went on to speculate that spot-squeezers may be just transferring "the pleasure of picking at themselves to some other person in a sort of sadistic fondling."

I do not see this at all, and neither did psychologist Fred Penzel (an expert on dermatological obsessive–compulsive disorders) who said in his interview with Holmes:

> "The field of psycho-dermatology has gone nowhere. It's just a bunch of people trying to come up with psycho-sexual interpretations of why people do this sort of stuff."

If you type "acnephilia" or "zit fetish" into any online search engine, there is one webpage that almost every other article mentions and that is an undated online essay entitled "Acnephilia: More commonly known as the zit fetish" on the Backwashzine (BWZ) website. The article claims that, as the pornography market has expanded, there are an increasing number of fetish videos and films being produced to cater for every sexual fetish and sexual niche imaginable. Almost every seemingly non-sexual fluid that can come from a human body has a corresponding paraphilia and/or fetish. This includes urine (urophilia), faeces (coprophilia), vomit (emetophilia), blood (menophilia, clinical vampirism), saliva (spit fetish) and breast milk (lactophilia). So what about pus and the acnephilia market? The BWZ article gave a detailed overview of an acnephilia film called *Pus Poppin' Forefingers*. Here is just the start of the description:

> "For 90 minutes this film follows the adventures of Pizza Face Joe and Polly, whose breasts are covered with zits ... A romance is budding."

After reading the article I did a bit of my own research on the topic and can confirm (a) that there are online forums out there that genuinely appear to cater for acnephiles (such as The Pimple Erotic), and (b) there are dedicated "spot squeezing" websites where dozens of videos have been uploaded for acnephile pleasure (such as the "zit lovers community").

Another online article by San-Joyz (2004) on acne fetishes argues that squeezing spots – even if there is no sexual focus – can be a fetish and that it can be real or imagined. I do not agree that this is fetishistic in the way that I conceptualize fetishes, but this is not a reason to omit competing viewpoints.

Acomophilia

According to various published sources including print books and online articles, acomophilia is a paraphilia in which individuals derive sexual pleasure and arousal from bald people or those with shaved heads and/or shaved genitals. Aggrawal (2009a) makes passing reference to being "acomoclitic". However, it should be noted that this term refers only to being sexually aroused by hairless genitals. Love (2001) mentions it in her encyclopaedia entry on sexual "depilation". But, again, this only relates to hairless genitals and not bald or shaved heads.

One unscientific survey (Music Banter, no date) asked a self-selected sample what their favourite fetish was. Acomophilia accounted for 1.53% of all respondents. The problem is the actual number of respondents is not reported and so it is hard to evaluate how representative those findings are. Other than this survey, I know of no research on the topic of acomophilia.

Acousticophilia (ecouterism)

Aggrawal (2009a) refers to ecouterism as deriving sexual pleasure and arousal "by listening to stories of sexual encounters of others or to sounds of others produced during intercourse either live or recorded." Other slightly different definitions of the behaviour have been noted. For instance, the Right Diagnosis website (2012d) says that ecouteurism refers to "intentionally listening to other people having sex without them being aware of it or consenting to it." The *Dictionary of Psychology and Allied Sciences* (2009) notes that it refers to the "sexual pleasure obtained from sounds or listening to sexual or toilet activities of others."

Intimate Medicine (2010) claimed there was no scientific literature on ecouterism. In fact, that is not quite true. There is a case reported by Mai (1968) concerning a 32-year-old single man who derived sexual satisfaction from covertly tape-recording and then playing back the sounds from female lavatories. Over a 1-year period he amassed 13 hours of toilet recordings of females all of which were made at night and only when he was feeling lonely and depressed.

Mai, who coined the term for this condition "ecouterism", argues that it is phenomenologically and psychopathologically similar to voyeurism (i.e., the deriving of sexual pleasure from watching other people typically engaged in sexual behaviour). Intimate Medicine (2010) concurs by asserting that "ecouterism is the same for the ear as voyeurism is for the eye."

Over a 12-month period the individual in question had regularly frequented female toilets and placed microphones through the windows to record all the sound activity inside the cubicles. He would then go home and listen to the recordings he had made but strenuously denied that he masturbated while the sound recordings were being played. The furthest that the man would go was to say he "got something out of it."

Mai (1968) notes that, despite there being no admission of using the recordings as masturbatory material, there seemed little doubt in his mind "… that this man derived sexual gratification from recording and later listening to the sounds emanating from female toilets."

Mai claims the roots of the behaviour are the man's sexual inadequacy, at least in part caused by his dysfunctional relationship with his overtly aggressive father, who had high hopes for his son's future. However, the son could not live up to those ambitious plans because of his relatively low intellectual ability. Ultimately, this led to him seeking alternative forms of sexual expression manifested in his desire to listen to women going to the toilet.

According to the *Encyclopedia of Unusual Sex Practices* (as well as the online Sex Dictionary and Fetish Freedom, 2012) acousticophilia is defined as "being sexually aroused by any auditory stimulus including music, songs, poetry, verbal abuse, speaking in a particular foreign language, screaming, panting, moaning, groaning and heavy breathing." The key to defining it as acousticophilia appears to be that the stimulus itself is not necessarily sexualized.

Gillette (1989) notes also that he knows of very few women who are ecouterists, the vast majority being men. The lack of empirical research in the area may be due to the fact that auditory aspects of sex have become so commonplace within traditional sexual practice that they are not considered in any way "abnormal" unless the person engages in such activity without the consent of the other individual(s).

Acrophilia

Acrophilia is defined as "sexual pleasure and arousal from heights, high altitudes or being in high places" (Aggrawal, 2009a). Love (2001) has briefly overviewed acrophilia in both her *Encyclopedia of Unusual Sex Practices* and a book chapter (Love, 2005). She writes:

> "Skydiving and bungee-cord-jumping are high-altitude activities that elevate one's adrenalin[e]. This excitement can then be transferred to passion and sex. Both of these activities include a form of bondage, vertigo, and suspension."

My own peer-reviewed research on bungee jumping (Larkin and Griffiths, 2004) suggests it is a "risky but rewarding" behaviour that some people view as potentially addictive. In interviews with bungee-jumpers, my co-author and I did not find any crossover to their sex lives. However, we did not specifically ask because that was not the focus of our research at that time.

Love writes that another acrophile behaviour is having sex at a high altitude. The most obvious example being where people have sex on aeroplanes and thereafter become members of the "Mile High Club". Although some people are likely to want to engage in such an activity just to say they have done it, others may be genuinely sexually aroused by doing the act at altitude.

Others may be sexually excited at the thought of being caught having sex on a plane, whilst others may have sexual fantasies about the people who work on planes (i.e., the pilots and flight attendants). Lovegrove (2000) notes that some people actually develop a fetish for the planes themselves. Such people are into "objectum sexuality", which is used to describe romantic and/or sexual feelings towards inanimate objects or structures (and covered later in this book).

Acrotomophilia and apotemnophilia

Some of the most bizarre paraphilias occasionally make their way into reputable scientific journals. Those involving sexual gratification from amputation of some description are a good example.

Since the late 1800s the medical literature has described men and women who are sexually attracted to amputees, those who limp or use crutches, braces and wheelchairs, as well as individuals who pretend to be or who actually want to become disabled. References to such individuals can be found in the books of Stekel (1952), von Krafft-Ebing (1886) and Hirschfeld (1944) as well as in published case studies, such as Fleischl (1960) and London (1952).

The relationship between amputated limbs and sexual desire was little known outside particular academic circles, but was (Money, 1988) first brought to public attention in the letters pages of *Penthouse* in 1972 (see below). Although it has been reported that some thought these letters were a joke or hoax (Persaud, 2003), it became clear that for a small minority of people this was a rare but *bona fide* paraphilia. One letter published in *Penthouse* in May 1973 informed its readership:

> *"... Sexually I feel I can compete with any two-legged girl. Because my husband is so turned on by the sight of my stump, I usually begin our lovemaking by undressing slowly at the foot of the bed. Once I have my clothes off, I lift my stump so that it points towards my husband and I begin to massage it. This excites my husband greatly, so he takes over and we go from there."*

One development in the world of amputee paraphilias has been the advent of the internet. This has brought global attention to people with disabilities and their admirers. Most of these sites are chatrooms and home pages for male devotees of female amputees. However, there are lots of other sites that include female devotees of male amputees, particular sexual orientations (heterosexual, homosexual) and particular attractions (e.g., crutches, plaster casts, crutch and neck braces). One specific bulletin board posting entitled "Bunion Love" requested "photos, videos, or correspondence of girls with deformed/crippled feet, or toe/toes amputated or who have severe bunions on their feet. The more severe, the better."

Money (1977) was the first to coin the term "apotemnophilia". Apotemnophilia is Greek for "amputation love". The term refers to being sexually excited by the fantasy or reality of being an amputee. As in the case study recorded by Money (1977, 1988), discussed earlier under abasiophilia, this behaviour is often accompanied by obsessive scheming to convince a surgeon to perform a medically unnecessary amputation. This might seem to most people to be a type of masochism, but reported case studies suggest that there is no erotization of pain itself – only of the healed amputated stump. To give you an inside look into the world of the apotemnophiliac, here is a real-life case account from Money's published files:

Case study: *The man, a professor of architecture, telephoned Professor Money's sex research unit asking if he could have his leg amputated. He was told that this would not be possible but he continued to phone and write to the unit for the next 4 years.*

12 Acrotomophilia and apotemnophilia

Later it was discovered that he had made many attempts to self-inflict serious injury to his left leg. His obsession had been present since he was 13 years old in the form of self-amputee fantasies. On one notable occasion he hammered a stainless steel rod into his left leg and then tried to infect the open wound by smearing it with facial acne mixed with anal and nasal mucus. When his leg showed serious signs of infection he reported it to the hospital. Unfortunately, his attempt failed as antibiotic treatment cleared the infection up. Looking into his childhood background, the most prominent early recollection was his left leg being severely burned by an overturned pot of boiling oatmeal at the age of 2 years. This left him unable to walk for a year.

According to Money there was little else in his family history to suggest the origins of such bizarre behaviour. However, Money (1988) does offer a complex and apparently Freudian explanation, based on information about the man's sexuality and thoughts on the matter.

Given the unconventional desires of the apotemnophiliac, it is perhaps unsurprising that self-mutilation occurs. To some extent, the condition resembles Munchausen's Syndrome in that MS patients are obsessed with self-inducing symptoms repetitively for the sake of being a patient, whereas the apotemnophiliac is obsessed with the symptom itself for the sake of being an amputee.

Acrotomophilia is a slightly different paraphilia from apotemnophilia and refers to being sexually aroused by a partner who is an amputee. They are excited by the stump or the stumps of the amputee partner and are dependent upon them for sexual arousal and attainment of orgasm.

The first survey of male acrotomophiles was published in the early 1980s (Dixon, 1983). The 195 acrotomophiles in the study were all customers of AMPIX (a company providing stories about and pictures of amputees) and were described as white, college-educated professional males. The results indicated that 75% had been aware of their interest in amputees by the age of 15 years. It was also reported that 55% of respondents had dated amputees, 40% had had sex with an amputee, and 5% had married an amputee. A total of 53% of the respondents had pretended to be an amputee (11% having done so publicly) and 71% had fantasized about being an amputee.

Another study (Nattress, 1996) surveyed 50 acrotomophiles. The participants were again white, college-educated professional males. Of these, 96% had been aware of their interest in amputees by their teens. In this sample, 41% had been married to or lived with an amputee, more than 43% had pretended to be amputees and 22% desired to become amputees. Using psychometric tests the acrotomophiles were found on average to have high scores on self-esteem, but low scores on social interest, emotional stability and personal relationships.

Such tendencies have become a concern of people with disabilities since acrotomophiles demonstrate problematic behaviours. These include collecting names, addresses and phone numbers of disabled people, making obsessive and intrusive phone calls, sending letters and emails to individuals with disabilities, attending and sometimes organizing disability-related events, lurking in public places to watch, take covert pictures of, talk to and touch disabled people and even engaging in predatory stalking.

A variety of explanations have been offered for devotee, pretender and wannabe (DPW) attractions, desires and behaviours. The most appealing explanation involves the pairing in childhood of a disability-related stimulus with sexual arousal. For example, one plaster cast devotee reported by Bruno (1997) had his first sexual experience with a girl who was wearing a leg cast. However, only 19% of participants in the AMPIX survey related their interest in amputees to any kind of direct contact with a disabled person, and the overwhelming majority of devotees reported their interest in disabled people began long before puberty.

Apotemnophiles need only one, albeit very extreme, medical intervention that leaves them with a lasting and obvious stigma of disability that they believe will permanently satisfy their need for love and attention. If the common psychological foundation of these conditions is that disability in and of itself will satisfy unmet needs for love and attention, then there are only two factors that differentiate between DPWs and those with a factitious physical disability: the awareness of a desire to appear or actually become disabled and physically appearing to be disabled.

Aelurophilia

Shaffer and Penn (2006) developed a comprehensive paraphilia classification system. They defined aelurophilia as "deriving sexual gratification from cats". The same definition was also provided by Aggrawal (2011a) in his classification of zoophilia. Before I take a closer academic look at the clinical literature on aelurophilia I would like to share the following story reported in the Russian newspaper *Pravda* in March 2004:

> "Two women attempted to experience sexual pleasure from intimate contact with a cat. The weird endeavor ended rather sadly for one of the women [Svetlana]: she was hospitalized with severe genital injuries. Doctors arrived to hospitalize the woman, who had suffered from unexpected bleeding ... They saw the woman lying on the sofa ... Streaks of blood could be seen on her legs. The woman's friend was speechless to explain what had happened. The woman was taken to the gynecological department of the local hospital where doctors determined the unusual character of the genital injuries ... When the woman recovered, she confessed that she had been injured during her love act with a cat ... Svetlana was bored and she decided to visit her friend Vera. The two women had some wine and started talking about intimate matters. Vera was the first to suggest trying something totally unusual ... Vera brought in a cat [called Timka] ... Vera took her clothes off, put the light out and played an adult movie on the video recorder. She lied down, took a bottle of valerian and poured some on her most intimate body part. When the cat smelled valerian, he started licking it away, putting Vera in a state of ecstasy. Vera told Svetlana ... there is nothing better than the cat's little tongue. When the cat started licking valerian off Svetlana, something happened to the animal. Timka probably took too much of the medication: he started licking the liquid away but all of a sudden he seized the genitals of the poor woman with his claws and teeth. Svetlana screamed and tried to push the fierce pet away from her, but the cat wouldn't let go. Vera hurried to help her friend: she emptied a bucket of water on the cat and threw the animal out of the house. When she saw that Svetlana

was bleeding, she called an ambulance. [Svetlana's husband] Boris could not take the fact that his wife preferred having oral sex with a cat [and] kicked Svetlana out of the house ... It is noteworthy that lonely women often use their pets (cats or dogs, regardless of sex) to satisfy their sexual needs. Such pet adventures often lead to lamentable consequences – not for pets, but for orgasm-craving women, as a rule. An overdose of valerian can make the loveliest cat become a fierce and aggressive animal."

Munro and Thrusfield (2001) reported they had collected data on animal abuse from over 400 British vets. They reported that 6% of their cases involved sexual abuse based on their observations of injuries in the animals' genital and anal areas. Of these, 21 cases referred to dogs and 3 to cats.

Beetz (2007) in a study of 32 male zoophiles reported that sex had occurred with dogs (78%), horses (53%), cats (13%) and farm animals (19%). She also reported that many of the zoophiles (including the cat-lovers) had a very close emotional attachment to their animals and that they loved their animal partner as others loved their human partners (and are devastated when their animal partner dies). In a later paper (Beetz, 2004) she also noted:

"Besides the whole range of sexual practices with more or less common mammals of a suitable size and anatomy, including deer, tapirs, antelopes, and camels (Massen, 1994), sexual contacts with more unusual species were mentioned in the literature. Insertion of fish – eels seem to be preferred – and snakes into the vagina and sexual stimulation through the movements of the animal (Dekkers, 1994), masturbation of male or female cats and letting cats lick the human genitalia or eat food from the penis or the vagina (Miletski, 2002) are further practices."

Miletski (2002) conducts one of the largest studies in this area examining 93 zoophiles (82 men and 11 women). Her study finds that most of her sample had sexual contact with dogs (90%). However, she also reports that 19.5% of her participants admitted to having had sexual contact with female felines (large cats or domestic cats) and 17% with male felines (large cats or domestic cats). Large cats presumably referred to lions, tigers, panthers, etc. although this was not made explicit.

Agalmatophilia

Strauss (2012) reported the story of Reighner Deleighnie, a 40-year-old woman from London, who claimed that she had fallen in love with a three-foot statue of the Greek god Adonis that she bought for £395:

"She enjoys reading and talking to her companion, and keeps him close by when she watches television and eats dinner. She also kisses and caresses him, imagining the pair of them walking through meadows of wildflowers or at the seaside. She shares the condition with Amanda Whittaker, a 27-year-old shop assistant from Leeds who has fallen head over heels for the Statue of Liberty."

Agalmatophilia is a paraphilia in which individuals derive sexual arousal from an attraction to (usually nude) statues, dolls, mannequins and/or other similar body-shaped objects. It is also part of a wider condition known as "object sexuality" (i.e., individuals who develop deep emotional and/or romantic attachments to specific inanimate objects or structures). The behaviour can manifest itself in many forms including actual sexual contact with body-shaped objects, fantasies of having sexual encounters with body-shaped objects, the act or sexual fantasy of watching encounters between body-shaped objects themselves and/or sexual arousal from thoughts of being transformed or transforming into a body-shaped object.

Arguably the first academically documented case was by von Krafft-Ebing (1877) who recounted the case of a male gardener who fell in love with a statue of the Venus de Milo and was discovered attempting to have sexual intercourse with it.

Alien egg fetishism

When I originally started researching material for this topic, I thought it was going to be about "insertion fantasy fetishes", which refer to the sexual desires or fantasies of having something inserted into a person via any means in the pelvic region (vaginally, anally), with the insertion object typically being something out of the ordinary, such as specifically shaped foods, abnormal objects or even whole people. Moreover, I expected that to relate closely to paraphilias, such as macrophilia and microphilia. However, that is not the case. When I googled "alien egg fetishism", one article I came across was in the online magazine Vice entitled "The emerging fetish of laying alien eggs inside yourself" by Toby McCasker (2015).

Individuals who derive sexual pleasure and arousal from extraterrestrial, robotic, supernatural or otherwise non-human lifeforms are known as exophiles. Most of them never claim to have had sex with an alien, but claim to be sexually excited and aroused by the thought of doing so. Although the topic of this particular entry does not fall under exophilia, it does comprise an activity that could be said to be part of an "insertion fetish".

After reading this entry you may come to the conclusion that it is a thinly disguised advert for Primal Hardwere (PH), but I can assure you that it is not. It just happens that the focus of this article (sexual arousal from the insertion of "alien eggs" into the vagina or anus) uses a product that is only available (as far as I am aware) from PH. The article by McCasker starts in much the same way as a number of my own:

> "Recently, while on the Internet looking at weird sex things, I came upon the gushing testimony of a young woman who had just discovered Primal Hardwere's patented Ovipositor; one of the most unusual and confronting sex toys I've ever heard of. The Ovipositor is basically a big dildo that lays goopy eggs molded from gelatin in the body cavity of your choice. Fans of the Ovipositor say that the sensation of mushy extraterrestrial ovum slopping back out of them is a real treat. The owner of Primal Hardwere is a man who insisted I refer to him only as LoneWolf. A Native American of indeterminate age, he apparently worked as a builder, fast food dude, fashion model, church organist, butcher, and pursued veterinary medicine at the University of New Hampshire."

16 Alien egg fetishism

For those who are unaware, an ovipositor is an organ used by insects for the laying of eggs. The most infamous ovipositor I can think of is the fantasy fiction one belonging to the alien queen xenomorph in the sci-fi film *Alien Resurrection*.

McCasker asked the developer of the Ovipositor dildo to explain the product and the thinking behind it:

> "The idea is to replicate the act of being impregnated with eggs. Usually from an alien or insect. If you've seen the Alien movies, you'll get the picture. Many people find this sort of thing very arousing. The toys are simply phallic-shaped hollow tubes that can be used to insert gelatin eggs into oneself. There is a funnel-shaped hole in the bottom to receive the eggs, which are inserted one by one, forcing them up the tube and out the top … Let's face it, there are three things that will always sell: Food, death, and sex. I tried food service and decided after managing three restaurants and owning one that it was the same thing, day in and day out, and it didn't look like that was going to change much. Death didn't really interest me. I wanted something more fun. Something that breaks the monotony of people's days and makes them spit out their coffee when you tell them what you do … I wanted to push the boundaries of people's comfort levels, make them question their own erections and wet panties, and let them know their fantasies do not have to go unrealized."

Obviously PH did not start making Ovipositor dildos on a whim, but it all began after LoneWolf had created some one-off customized commissions prior to setting up PH. Unsurprisingly, no other company was (or is) making such products and LoneWolf saw a gap in the market (or created a new market depending upon your perspective). There are also a number of different types of Ovipositor including the Splorch and the Krubera.

It is hard to know whether using such niche sex toys is a genuine fetish, but PH are making money from selling such products. Therefore, it would appear that some people out there are at least experimenting with alien imagery and alienlike artefacts as part of their sex lives.

Altocalciphilia

According to Belk (2003), individuals in the USA "buy approximately a billion pairs of footwear a year and 80% of these are estimated to be purchased for purposes of sexual attraction." Belk's figures come from Rossi (1990a, b) who has been writing scientific papers on shoes for decades. I have no idea whether these figures are accurate, but there is little doubt that, when it comes to sexual fetishism, shoes – and particularly high-heel shoes – are one of the most common types of object for which people develop fetishes. Individuals with a shoe fetish derive sexual arousal from shoes and footwear. Shoe fetishism is also referred to as retifism (named after French novelist Nicolas-Edme Rétif).

People with shoe fetishism can be erotically interested in either men's or women's shoes. Although shoes may appear to carry sexual connotations in mainstream culture (e.g., women's shoes are commonly sold as being "sexy"), this opinion refers to an ethnographic or cultural context, and is likely not intended to be taken literally. Another fetishism, which sometimes is seen as related to shoe fetishism, is boot fetishism.

Scorolli et al. (2007) studied the relative prevalence of different fetishes using online fetish forum data and estimated that their sample comprised at least 5,000 fetishists, but was likely to be a lot more. Their results showed that there were 44,722 members of online fetish forums. Of these, people preferring objects related to body parts and footwear (shoes, boots, etc.) was the second most preferred among 26,739 online fetish forum members. A total of 32% of all objects related to body parts, which was just behind (no pun intended) objects worn on the buttocks, legs and/or both (33%).

As the opening quotes to this entry highlight, high-heeled footwear is often associated with sexiness. Those who find the allure of high heels sexually arousing are said to have altocalciphilia (a subtype of shoe fetishism). The online medical website Right Diagnosis says that the defining features of altocalciphilia are: (i) a sexual interest in high heels, (ii) an abnormal amount of time spent thinking about high heels, (iii) recurring intense sexual fantasies involving high heels, (iv) recurring intense sexual urges involving high heels and (v) sexual preference for high heels.

I am not aware of any empirical research specifically into altocalciphilia, but in researching this topic I did come across an interesting Master's Thesis by Sancaktar (2006), who provided an analysis of shoes within the context of the social history of fashion, and which included a chapter on shoe fetishism.

There is no doubt that high-heel fetishism exists and of all fetishes it appears to be one of the most common. Unfortunately, whilst there is much speculating and theorizing there is very little data. Once again, much of the academic material on this topic is at best anecdotal.

Alvinophilia

According to Aggrawal (2009a) alvinophilia is a paraphilia in which individuals derive sexual pleasure and sexual arousal from navels and bellies, although he refers to it as "alvinolagnia". I have yet to come across a proper definition, but some sources say it includes any sexual pleasure or arousal from any aspect of a belly or a navel.

Scorolli et al. (2007) made specific reference to alvinophilia in a study comprising more than 5,000 fetishists. They reported that 3% of the sites featured references to belly and/or navel fetishes. However, there is no further information as to whether the belly/navel fetish was connected to piercing, pregnancy and/or belly inflation.

Belly size is obviously one of the most important aspects of a fat fetishist's sexual focus. Many fat admirers are "feeders" who deliberately overfeed their sexual partners (i.e., "feedees") on their way to becoming a "big beautiful woman" (BBW). Within the context of their sexual relationship, feeders obtain sexual gratification from encouraging excessive food eating and the actual gaining of body fat of their sexual partner. For many it is the increasing stomach size that becomes the primary sexual focus. The bigger the stomach the more sexually aroused the feeder becomes. There are also fat fetishists who are turned on by "gut-flopping". This involves masochistic elements involving female domination ("femdom").

18 Alvinophilia

A related sexual fetish is belly inflation, which I would argue is subsumed within alvinophilia. Belly inflation, part of the wider practice of body inflation, involves the practice of inflating or sometimes pretending to inflate a part of one's body, typically for sexual gratification. For some this may be connected with sexual arousal from receiving enemas (i.e., klismaphilia). A number of sites are dedicated to this practice, such as the Body Inflation website.

Given the lack of research into alvinophilia, online accounts are all that academic theorizing has to go on. Once again, this is another area that the research community would benefit from knowing more about.

Amaurophilia

"I have a blindness fetish. It's something I've been obsessed with all my life. Also, I would consider my sexual orientation to be asexual. I'm really not at all turned on by guys and I have no interest in sex – in fact, it honestly disgusts me. However, when indulging in my fetish, I do masturbate." (Susan at All Experts, 2012)

According to Aggrawal (2009a) amaurophilia is a paraphilia in which the individual derives sexual pleasure and arousal "by a partner who is blind or unable to see due to artificial means such as being blindfolded or having sex in total darkness." A similar definition of amaurophilia is provided by Love (2001) as "a preference for a blind or blindfolded sex partner". She also added one exclusion criterion wherein if both partners are blind, then it would not be classed as amaurophilia.

Love also makes reference to a similar paraphilia called "lygerastia", which refers to individuals who derive sexual pleasure and arousal only in darkness. The critical similarity in both of these is that the individuals in question are sexually aroused by sexual partners who are unable to see them.

Amaurophilia is yet another paraphilia where there has been no academic and/or clinical research, most probably because the focus of sexual arousal is fairly innocuous. It is highly unlikely people would come forward wanting any kind of treatment since amaurophiles are likely to live with their sexual preference without any problem.

Online sources note that amaurophilia is extremely rare and that, for some people, the simulation and/or roleplaying of having sex with someone who is blind is also a sexual turn-on. This can be achieved with a wide range of accessories including sleep shades, blindfolds, eye patches and/or vision-restricting contact lenses. Furthermore, partners may swap roles. One short online article claimed that:

"Some amaurophiliacs may even extend this play outside of sex through the use of blindfolds or contact lenses in conjunction with a white cane for mobility. Some amaurophiliacs may choose to learn Braille in order to enhance their experience during play sessions."

This type of behaviour (if true – and I have yet to find any empirical evidence that it is) is very similar to the psychology and behaviour of "pretenders" of the DPW typology (i.e., devotees, pretenders and wannabes) that I wrote about previously in relation to apotemnophilia (i.e., those who derive sexual pleasure and arousal from the thought of being an amputee). Much of the psychology here is about the one-to-one attention that being disabled can bring and has been linked to factitious disability disorders such as Munchausen's Syndrome.

As with most other "niche" fetishes and paraphilias, online communities of like-minded individuals have developed, such as websites like the Blind-Fetish Live Journal and Blind One. The former's page is "devoted to those with an interest in blindness and blindfolds from an erotic point of view." The site's founder informs readers that if they think amaurophilia "is weird or sick, you don't have to look at this page. I feel a bit weird about it myself, but for some reason I am really turned on by blind or blindfolded women."

Unfortunately, very few of the accounts I have come across give any real indication as to how their blindness fetish developed. Should empirical research be carried out, the etiology and motivations for blindness fetishes would certainly be an obvious place to start.

Anaesthesiophilia

Later in this book I examine medical fetishism, which refers to an umbrella group of related sexual fetishes in which individuals derive sexual pleasure and arousal from medical and/or clinical practices and procedures (e.g., undergoing rectal examinations or urethral swabs, having temperature taken rectally), objects (e.g., stethoscopes, hypodermic needles), situations (e.g., waiting to see a nurse) and environments (e.g., being in a hospital waiting room). One specific form of medical fetishism is anaesthesia fetishism in which individuals derive sexual pleasure and arousal from either administering and/or receiving some kind of anaesthetic, such as chloroform, ether or butane.

My first ever article on paraphilic behaviour was published back in 1999 (Griffiths, 1999a). The article was on autoerotic deaths and featured the cases of 10 people who died in strange sexual circumstances. One of the cases was originally reported by McLennan et al. (1988). The case concerned a single 59-year-old white US male antiques dealer. He was found dead in his locked apartment, seated in front of a dental anaesthetic machine, with an anaesthetic mask over his face. In his mouth was a rubber teat similar (but much bigger) than the kind used for a baby's feeding bottle. There were other anaesthetic machines around the apartment along with a lot of sexual literature (magazines, photographs, paintings and manuscripts all concerned with his elaborate fetish and some included photographs of himself in these situations). The deceased was wearing a rubber-type apron, three woollen cardigans, a woman's blouse, two pairs of women's trousers and a pair of women's bloomers. This appeared to be a genuine case of anaesthesiophilia. A similar case was also reported in Leadbeatter (1988). The lethal method used to induce cerebral hypoxia was inhalation of nitrous oxide (a.k.a. "laughing gas") from a dental anaesthetic machine.

In the same article I also feature the case of a single 32-year-old white US male computer programmer, which was originally reported by Cordner (1983). The man was found dead in bed with a cassette recorder next to him. He was covered in dry semen stains, was wearing headphones and had been listening to "snorting" horse sounds. There was also a can of aerosol propellant. At the end of the bed was a large painting of a male strapped to the hind legs of a horse who was being anally penetrated by the horse (yes, a horse!). The horse was ridden by a leather-clad woman. He was also wearing some kind of homemade masturbatory device. His death was recorded as cardiorespiratory failure consistent with aerosol propellant abuse (death by misadventure).

Although this case was not technically anaesthesiophilia, it did involve self-administration of a chemical agent to modify the sensations of masturbation. However, Rogers (2009) seems to suggest that the case I have just described would be classed as anaesthesiophilia in line with her definition of such a paraphilia because it involves the person using a volatile substance (e.g., chloroform, ether or butane) as a source of sexual arousal. She also points out the commonalities between anaesthesiophilia, hypoxyphilia (sexual arousal and pleasure from oxygen deprivation) and electrophilia (sexual arousal and pleasure from electricity and electric stimuli).

Clearly, much of what we know about anaesthesiophilia appears to be based on case reports where the use of an anaesthetizing agent during the sexual act has gone horribly wrong. Most of the deaths occurred because the individuals involved appeared to have been on their own and were presumably performing a masturbatory act. Engaging in such an act when more than one person is present, of course, significantly reduces the chances of anything untoward happening for the anaesthesiophile.

Anthropophagolagnia

Later in this book I examine the psychology of sexual cannibalism and erotophonophilia (a.k.a. "lust murder"). One very rare subtype of both sexual cannibalism and erotophonophilia is anthropophagolagnia. This particular type of paraphilia has been defined by Aggrawal (2009a) as "rape with cannibalism", and by the Right Diagnosis website as "sexual urges, preferences or fantasies involving raping and then cannibalizing the victim." The Listaholic website goes so far as to say that anthropophagolagnia is one of the 10 "most bizarre sexual fetishes on earth" claiming that the serial killer is the "poster boy" for these "twisted" individuals. Other serial killers who might be classed as anthropophagolagniacs include Albert Fish, Peter Kirsten, Ottis Toole and Ed Gein.

The case of 40-year-old preacher Stephen Tari, leader of a 6,000-strong cannibal rape cult in Papua New Guinea, is an interesting one. He was in prison following his conviction for a brutal rape, but escaped only to be killed by people from his village in retaliation for the cannibalistic rape murders he had committed. As reported in the press:

"[Tari] had previously been accused of raping, murdering and eating three girls in front of their traumatised mothers ... The charismatic cult leader, who wore white robes and is said to have regularly drunk the blood of his 'flower girls', quickly returned to his home village of Gal after [a prison] escape, but could only manage 6 months

before killing yet again ... It has not yet been established if the murdered woman was killed as part of a blood sacrifice, but it is considered likely as Tari was said to have been attempting to resurrect his cult following the spell in prison."

Hickey (2010) noted that paraphilic behaviour is very common among those who commit sexual crimes and that more than one person is often present, but that sex offending and paraphilias may be two independent constructs meaning that one does not necessarily affect the other.

Along with anthropophagolagnia, other "attack paraphilias" that have been associated with serial killers include amokoscisia (sexual arousal or sexual frenzy from a desire to slash or mutilate other individuals who are typically women), anophelorastia (sexual arousal from defiling or ravaging another individual), biastophilia (sexual arousal from violently raping other individuals; a.k.a. "raptophilia"), dippoldism (sexual arousal from abusing children, typically in the form of spanking and corporal punishment), necrophilia (sexual arousal from having sex with dead individuals), paedophilia (sexual arousal from having sex with minors, typically via manipulation and grooming) and sexual sadism (empowerment and sexual arousal derived from inflicting pain and/or injuring other individuals).

The "preparatory paraphilias" that typically precede serial killing and attack paraphilias, such as anthropophagolagnia, include agonophilia (sexual arousal caused by a sexual partner pretending to struggle), altocalciphilia (sexual arousal from high-heeled shoes), autonecrophilia (sexual arousal by imagining oneself as a dead person), exhibitionism (exposing genitals to inappropriate and/or non-consenting people for sexual arousal), frottage (sexual arousal from rubbing up against the body of a sexual partner or object), gerontophilia (sexual arousal from someone whose age is older and belongs to a different generation), hebephilia (men who are sexually aroused by teenagers), kleptolagnia (sexual arousal from stealing), retifism (sexual arousal from shoes), scatophilia (sexual arousal through making telephone calls, using vulgar language and/or trying to elicit a reaction from the other party), scoptophilia (a.k.a. voyeurism; sexual arousal by watching others typically engaged in sexual behaviour without their consent) and somnophilia (sexual arousal from fondling strangers in their sleep). The multiplicity of co-existent paraphilias (including anthropophagolagnia) is highlighted by the case of the notorious serial killer Jeffrey Dahmer (Purcell and Arrigo, 2001).

Almost nothing is known empirically about anthropophagolagnia except that it is very rare and that almost all information about it comes from serial killers who have been caught. Explanations for the development of anthropophagolagnia can only be speculated, but are likely to be no different from the development of other paraphilic behaviours.

Aquaphilia

In a later entry in this book I write about psychrocism and sexual arousal from ice. Such work got me wondering what other sexual behaviours might involve water. In a comprehensive list of paraphilias in Aggrawal (2009a) and Love (2001) a number of water-related paraphilias and sexual behaviours were listed. The list included:

22 Aquaphilia

- Aquaphilia: Sexual arousal from water and/or watery environments including bathtubs or swimming pools (a.k.a. "hydrophilia").
- Albutophilia: Sexual arousal from water.
- Ablutophilia: Sexual arousal from baths or showers.
- Antiophilia: Sexual arousal from floods.
- Coitobalnism: Sex in a bathtub.
- *Coïtus à unda*: Sex under water.
- Bidetonism: The use of water spray from a bidet as a genitosexual stimulant for women while masturbating.

Love (2001) has a section in her book devoted to having sex in and/or under water (i.e., *coïtus à unda*). Such a paraphilia can include masturbation, oral sex and/or penetrative sex in any number of water-based situations (e.g., bath, shower, swimming pool, lake or ocean). She also says that such activities can include fellatio where the partner holds hot water in his or her mouth. She also highlights a number of other activities that come under the generic banner of "water sex" including:

- Sexually based "entertainment" hosted in pubs, bars and/or restaurants (e.g., wet T-shirt or jock-strap competitions or naked women swimming inside large aquariums).
- The use of water as a lubricant to facilitate insertion of body parts (e.g., fingers and toes) or sex toys into various body orifices.
- The use of baby baths along with the addition of a child's bath toys for those who derive sexual pleasure from being an adult baby (i.e., infantilism).

She also claimed that Tiberius Caesar had a passion for aquatic sex. She claimed Caesar trained young boys (whom he called "minnows") to swim after him and come up from below to nibble and suck on his genitals. Other cultures are not so liberal. For instance, Aggrawal (2009a) noted that in Hinduism, according to the Laws of Manu (i.e., the words of Brahma, the Hindu god of creation), "A man who has committed a bestial crime, or an unnatural crime with a female, or has had intercourse in water, or with a menstruating woman shall perform a *Samtapana Krikkhra*" (i.e., a 24-hour fast where no food can be consumed whatsoever).

Another more unusual water-related paraphilia is hypoxyphilia. Here autoerotic asphyxiates use a variety of methods to restrict their oxygen supply including partial hanging, placing plastic bags or masks over the face, chest compression and submerging under water (a.k.a. *aqua eroticum* in the clinical and forensic literature). Reports of water-related hypoxyphilic deaths are exceedingly rare, but have been documented.

The term "aqua-eroticism" was first used in a paper by Sivaloganathan (1984). However, the use of the term in that paper solely related to hypoxyphilia (i.e., autoerotic asphyxiation). While there have been many papers and articles about hypoxyphilia, to my knowledge only two papers have been published involving submersion under water. These very rare occurrences have come to light when things have gone drastically wrong (i.e., death for the person engaging in the activity). As with hypoxyphilic activity more generally, underwater submersion while holding one's breath produces the same effects of oxygen deprivation as other methods (e.g., hanging and self-strangulation).

In the case documented by Sivaloganathan, a man was found drowned with a stone tied to his ankle to weigh him down in the water. He was also assumed to have transvestite tendencies as he was found dressed in women's clothes. It was assumed to be an example of autoerotic asphyxia given that it seemed to be a very peculiar way to be swimming or committing suicide. The act of swimming in the opposite sex's clothes with a weight tied to his leg also had many key features of deliberately induced danger as a method of increasing the arousal level. There is always the possibility that other similar types of incident may have occurred, but have been labelled as suicide rather than death by misadventure.

The second case in the academic literature was reported by Sauvageau and Racette (2006a, b). Here, the evidence for autoerotic asphyxiation is more clear-cut. One summer, a 25-year-old man was found dead in a lake submerged underneath his boat. Despite being the height of summer, he was wearing a hockey helmet, a snowmobile suit and ski boots. However, underneath these clothes he was found to be wearing a self-constructed plastic bodysuit that extended over his naked body from head to toe with a separate plastic tube wrapped around his genitals. Furthermore, there were clear bondage elements. Around his wrists, ankles, knees and waist he was tightly bound in a mixture of mesh and chains (all of which were padlocked to his groin). The only air supply was a black tube joined to his mouth and sealed to the suit by silicone. The man's air supply system comprised an open plastic container floating on the lake and connected to his mouth.

The only other sexually related water fetish or paraphilia that I have come across is liquidophilia. Various online articles, such as the not-so-imaginatively titled Dirty Mag website (2011), mention this behaviour and all define it as "a paraphilia in which individuals derive sexual pleasure and arousal from immersing their genitals in some kind of liquid."

Most liquidophiles use water, which means taking a bath would be highly erotic for such people. Indeed, any liquid can apparently be used. It has been claimed that some liquidophiles have a preference for liquids that resemble body secretions, such as breast milk.

Arachnephilia

Later in this book I examine paraphilias involving individuals who derive sexual stimulation and arousal from ants and/or other insects (formicophilia), as well as individuals who derive sexual stimulation and arousal from bees (melissophilia) and bee stings (as a radical and painful way of increasing penis size). Sexually paraphilic interest by humans in insects is also known as entomophilia.

One specific insect-related paraphilia is arachnephilia, which is sometimes spelled "arachnophilia". Aggrawal (2009a, 2011a) defines arachnephilia as "[sexual] ... arousal from spiders". Holmes and Holmes (2009) have an identical definition. The only difference being they spell it "arachnophilia", although I am not quite clear how it is a "nuisance sex behaviour". Love (2001) defines arachnephilia as referring to individuals who "are aroused by sex play involving spiders".

There are no statistics on the incidence or prevalence of arachnephilia. In fact, at the time of writing there is not a single published case study. Nevertheless, in my exhaustive search for papers on academic databases I did come across a few references to arachnephilia (not including the many papers that referenced a piece of software called "arachnophilia"). The first academic paper to mention "arachnophilia" was Adams (1981). The paper analysed the tendency to equate female sexual desire, a woman's love, that which is female and femininity with a "voracious spider".

The Right Diagnosis website (2013a) claims that treatment for arachnephilia "is generally not sought unless the condition becomes problematic for people in some way and they feel compelled to address their condition. The majority of people simply learn to accept their fetish and manage to achieve gratification in an appropriate manner."

I certainly cannot deny this may be the case as there is a complete lack of any reference to treatment in any academic book or journal.

Autassassinophilia

Autassassinophilia is a paraphilia in which an individual derives sexual pleasure and arousal by the thought and/or risk of being killed. The paraphilia may on occasion overlap with other paraphilias, such as autoerotic asphyxiation (i.e., sexual suffocation) where there is a risk to their life. In some instances the autassassinophile may also derive sexual pleasure and arousal from planning his own death. Given these facts it is clear that autassassinophilia is exceedingly rare and very dangerous. The condition was first written about in a clinical (and academic) context by Money (1986).

Some of you reading this might think that autoassassinophilia is more of a theoretical rather than an actual paraphilia. However, there are a number of documented cases of two lovers in a consensual "murder pact". The most high-profile heterosexual case is that of Sharon Lopatka and Robert Glass.

Lopatka (from Maryland, USA) was strangled and killed consensually by Glass whom she met online at an "extreme fantasy" website. Over a number of months in 1996 they exchanged 1,000s of emails (discovered by the police after she was found dead) fantasizing about – and planning – her own murder. Glass eventually pleaded guilty to manslaughter claiming he never actually intended to kill her.

The most high-profile homosexual case was that of two Germans Armin Meiwes and Jürgen Brandes – a case that I examine in this book in relation to vorarephilia, the paraphilia in which people are sexually aroused by the idea of being eaten, eating another person or observing this process for sexual gratification and indulging in autosarcophagy (i.e., self-cannibalism). Meiwes, a computer technician, gained worldwide media attention as the "Rotenburg Cannibal" for killing and eating a fellow German male victim, who also was a computer technician. The one aspect of this case that shocked most people was not the fact that Meiwes ate a lot of Brande's body, but that Brande appeared to consent to being eaten.

In court, Brande's consent to being killed was accepted by the jury and Meiwes was given an 8½-year prison sentence for manslaughter. This and other cases raise some interesting and controversial ethical questions that were discussed at length in Downing's (2004) excellent and thought-provoking phenomenological paper on autassassinophilia. She clearly makes the point that being killed for sexual pleasure "problematizes commonplace assumptions about the legitimacy to consent."

Avian bestiality

Some years ago my friend and colleague Belinda Winder asked me if I knew anything about paraphilias involving birds. She is no stranger to paraphilias as they feature quite a lot in a book she co-edited entitled *A Psychologist's Casebook of Crime: From Arson to Voyeurism* (Winder and Banyard, 2017). Her request piqued my interest on the topic enough for me to have a quick look at what has been written.

Aggrawal (2009a) noted that bestial acts involving birds are commonplace in mythology and folklore. For instance, the Greek god Zeus was said to assume the shape of various animals as part of his seduction technique. He transformed into a swan in order to seduce Leda (the mother of Troy), and became an eagle to carry off a young Ganymede. Elsewhere in his book, Aggrawal (2009a) writes about bestiality being commonplace in ancient Rome. Examples cited include bestial acts with chickens. He notes that professional people supplied animals specifically for bestial purposes. For instance, the Belluari supplied dogs and monkeys, the Caprarii supplied female goats and the Anserarii supplied geese.

The Marquis de Sade, whose name famously gave rise to the term and concept "sadism", wrote about avian sex in a Parisian brothel where they employed a turkey. de Sade claimed:

> "The girl holds the bird's neck locked between her thighs, you have her ass straight ahead of you for prospect, and she cuts the bird's throat the same moment you discharge."

Academically, von Krafft-Ebing (1886) was arguably the first to write about bestial acts with birds. In a chapter on zoosadism he wrote about a male poet who "became powerfully excited sexually whenever he saw cows slaughtered" and another male who "committed sodomy with geese, and cut their necks off, *tempore ejaculationis!*" This latter practice is called "avisodomy" and is listed as one of the many acts of zoophilia (Aggrawal, 2011a). The practice typically involves breaking the neck of a bird and then penetrating it. Mantegazza (2001) claimed that:

> "... the Chinese are famous for their love affairs with geese. Just when they are at the point of ejaculation they wring off the birds' necks in order that they may get the pleasure of the last spasms of the anal sphincters of the dying geese."

Ornithophilia is a subclass of zoophilia and specifically refers to those individuals who are sexually aroused by the thought and/or the act of having sex with birds. As far as I have been able to establish there are no specific case studies in the literature that refer to the condition. The only specific mention of "ornithophilia" I have come across in

26 Avian bestiality

the academic literature is in the writings of Aggrawal (including his 2011a paper mentioned earlier). Munro (2006) noted that sexual contact with birds exists.

A case reported by Ene and Sasaran (2011) described the late onset of zoophilia in a 42-year-old man who suddenly started engaging in zoophilic behaviour following an aneurysm in the posterior cerebral artery. More specifically, he developed a sexual interest towards the hens in his garden, and his wife found him several times having sex with them. Unfortunately, the man died a few weeks later following an aneurysm.

Balloon fetishism

Unsurprisingly, balloon fetishes are sexual fetishes that feature balloons as the source of sexual arousal and pleasure. Those who use balloons in this way are known as "looners". David Kerekes (2010) noted that some balloon fetishists "revel in the popping of balloons and [others] may become anxious and tearful at the very thought of popping balloons." Gates (2000) noted that other looners enjoy particular aspects of balloons, such as blowing them up and/or interacting with them by way of rubbing up against them, sitting and/or lying on them.

I visited a few balloon fetish websites which show that some looners like watching people inflate balloons until they burst. Others like gigantic balloons that they can stick their head inside. For some the smell or the colour of the balloon may be an important part of the fetish.

There has been very little empirical research carried out on looners. Much of what is known is anecdotal and hearsay. Anecdotal case studies suggest that the etiology of the fetish varies from one person to the next. Nevertheless, some claim that the behaviour can be explained by sexual imprinting where specific sexual preferences may be acquired through exposure to particular stimuli during a specific period early in life. Some looners recall that in childhood they remember being sexually aroused when they saw balloons being popped by the opposite sex or anyone for whom they had a crush. It has also been alleged that – somewhat paradoxically – looners may have phonophobia (i.e., a fear of loud sounds) as a result of being in the vicinity of balloons popping loudly.

Brundage (2002) interviewed self-confessed looner Mike D about his balloon fetish. Quite simply, Brundage wanted to know why looners are so sexually aroused by balloons. Mike D, who now runs the balloon fetish video site Mellyloon that has sent over 1,000 balloon fetish films to the Middle East, Asia, South and North America, said:

> "I'm not sure I have the answer to that. There's always something that goes back to your childhood. Like your babysitter blew up a balloon or your mother popped your balloon. Then along comes puberty and these things that made such an impression on you as a child turn into something erotic … I'm still phobic [about balloons]. That's where my whole fetish derived from, that fear."

McIntyre (2011) interviewed another male looner Shaun who was particularly aroused by balloons because of their smell. Shaun said:

"The smell of a room that has a lot of balloons, especially after they have oxidized over a period of a couple days, is nearly indescribable. Each brand possesses a smell as distinct to looners as perfume. The odor is subtly sweet with a hint of rubber. One sniff can identify a Rifco brand product because its latex smells slightly of chocolate chip cookies. The aroma adds to the experience, as does the feel and sound of balloons. The sensation of swimming through hundreds of balloons in my bedroom was overwhelming and amazing."

McIntyre also noted that some looners care more about the balloon's size, colour and brand. Some prefer solid-coloured balloons and others prefer transparent balloons. One looner said that size was crucial ("the bigger the better"). This particular looner claimed he could orgasm simply by blowing up a balloon until it popped.

McIntyre also claimed in her article that most looners grew up ashamed with the belief that no one else in the world had their sexual fetish. It was only when they found other like-minded people online that they realized they were "not alone". This helped eliminate looners' feelings of isolation. This then makes it easier to tell potential partners about their fetish and helps looners to keep their behaviour under control.

Belonophilia

Belonophilia concerns sexual arousal from needles. Fuller (2012) reported the case of 58-year-old Australian facial surgeon Arthur Bosanquet. The surgeon was disqualified from practising as a dentist after admitting to the Dental Tribunal of New South Wales that he had a "needle fetish" with an underlying homosexual/bisexual interest that led to the sexual abuse of three teenage patients. He was initially jailed for 9 months for both indecent and common assaults. On appeal these were downgraded to suspended sentences. As Fuller (2012) noted:

"[Bosanquet] devised a bogus university study which tricked the young men into masturbating in front of him ... The surgeon blamed his behaviour on his needle fetish, sexual interests and too much work ... The tribunal heard evidence that, in several cases, Bosanquet offered the young men money to complete the study, which focused on taking blood pressure readings and blood samples before and after masturbation. The incidents, which spanned an 8-year period, included two occasions where he conducted the 'study' at the patients' homes."

Asia One News (2012) reported the case of a 40-year-old man from Kuala Lumpur who had pricked "scores of needles into his lover's body" claiming that he had been performing acupuncture on her. His lover was forced to endure his fetishistic use of needles and was threatened with stabbing if she did not agree to her becoming his human pin cushion. The news report further noted:

"The woman was startled from her slumber by a sharp piercing feeling on her body. The man pointed a knife at her and threatened to kill her, saying he was going to perform acupuncture on her. Afraid, she gave in to the agonizing 'treatment'. The man told her that he, too, needed the treatment and wanted her to prick needles into

his body. The victim, worried that the matter could get out of hand, told her boyfriend she needed to wash up and prepare for work. She pleaded with him to remove the needles and pins from her face, hands and body. During the brief respite, the frightened woman stealthily left the house and fled to the Sungai Besi police station to lodge a report."

Later in this book I examine piquerism, which is sexual arousal from penetrating another person's body with sharp objects, such as pins, razors and knives. The sexualization of pins and needles has long been part of sexual sadomasochistic practices and is known as "needle play". Whether "needle play" can really be classed as a "needle fetish" as part of belonophilia is debatable. The online non-academic needle play literature appears to be more rooted in erotic piercing than needle fetishes *per se*. There have certainly been a growing number of academic papers on sexual piercing since Buhrich's (1983) research. At the time of writing, genuine "needle fetishism" appears to be very rare.

Breast fetishism

Where does normal love of breasts end and abnormal love of breasts begin? When it comes to male sexual arousal, female breasts are at the top of many men's lists as the body part they find most sexually attractive. According to Aggrawal (2009a) the paraphilia of being aroused by female breasts is mammagymnophilia (a.k.a. "mazophilia") and consists of "a pronounced fetishistic sexual interest in female breasts, their shape, movement and especially their size."

While studying for my undergraduate degree, as part of my studies I undertook a project on the psychology of female orgasm. During the literature research stage I read almost every paper and book that I could on sexuality and female sexuality. I read Desmond Morris's book *The Naked Ape* (Morris, 1967) and was very interested in his theories on sexual signalling. Morris argued that women's breasts had evolved to look like female buttocks as humans had slowly changed the way they had sex from males mounting females from the rear to face-to-face sex. Crawford and Krebs (1998) theorized that female humans' permanently enlarged breasts allows them to "solicit male attention and investment even when they are not really fertile."

I am still surprised that there has been little empirical research on the role of breast and nipple stimulation in influencing sexual arousal during sex. Levin and Meston (2006) claimed there had never been a study that questioned people about breasts and sexual arousal. Therefore, they surveyed 301 "sexually experienced undergraduates" (148 males and 153 females mostly between the ages of 18 and 22 years). The authors reported:

"81.5% [of women] reported that stimulation of their nipples/breasts caused or enhanced their sexual arousal, 78.2% agreed that when sexually aroused such manipulation increased their arousal, 59.1% had asked to have their nipples stimulated during lovemaking, and only 7.2% found that the manipulation decreased their arousal. In regard to the men, 51.7% reported that nipple stimulation caused or

enhanced their sexual arousal, 39% agreed that when sexually aroused such manipulation increased their arousal, only 17.1% had asked to have their nipples stimulated, and only 7.5% found that such stimulation decreased their arousal."

Aggrawal (2009a) describes sexual gratification from any of several erotic BDSM (bondage and discipline, dominance and submission, sadism and masochism) activities focusing solely on inflicting pain on the breast, nipples and areola as "tit torture". This brief overview again highlights a major recurring theme in this book: namely, when it comes to breast fetishism and its many variants there is surprisingly little scientific research.

Bride fetishism

While researching other paraphilias – namely, harmatophilia (i.e., individuals who derive sexual arousal from those who are sexually incompetent), parthenophilia (i.e., individuals who derive sexual arousal from virgins), cuckold fetish (i.e., individuals who derive sexual arousal from the knowledge that their wives are having sex with other men) and veil fetishism (i.e., individuals who derive sexual arousal from those who wear veils) – I came across various references to bride fetishism. This fetish does not appear in books by either Aggrawal (2009a) or Love (2001). Nonetheless, Harwood (2011) mentions in passing something called the "virgin bride fetish", as do a number of novels. Three different ones are by Jayne Blye, all of which are easily discoverable by searching Google Books and inputting the term "bride fetish".

As far as I am aware, there is no academic research on bride fetishism, but there is plenty of anecdotal evidence to suggest that (a) it exists and (b) that there are specific subvarieties. For instance, there are dozens of bespoke webpages devoted to bride fetishism including Deviant Art's website page on "bridal fetish", Behance's website page on "fetish bride", Goddess Narcissa's webpage on "black fetish bride", Hot Wife Allie's website (with a myriad of bride fetish postings, such as "the great wedding porn gallery" and "wedding night cuckold") and Jim Roe's webpage on "nude bride fetish".

I also came across dedicated webpages on "fetish vampire brides", "mature bride fetish", "bondaged brides" and "bride face-sitting fetish". Be warned, though, most of these sites contain very sexually explicit material. In addition to this there are dedicated sites that make fetish bridal wear, such as the Adixxtion website and provide online-dating services to match up fetish brides and grooms. I am the first to admit that none of this is in any way academic, but it does at least point to the fact that there appears to be a niche (sexual) market for bride fetishism.

In my research, I have to admit that I did not come across a single dedicated online bride fetish forum group, although I did come across discussions on fetish sites where some individuals claimed they had bride fetishes, even though they were few and far between.

My own (online) research relying on non-academic and anecdotal sources suggests that bride fetishism is a niche sexual market that appears to have at least a handful of genuine adherents. I cannot really see this subject ever being the topic of serious academic research, but I would be happy to be proved wrong.

Burping fetishes

I have examined some idiosyncratic fetishes over the past 15 years. Up there with the strangest, and perhaps one of the least commonplace, is burping fetishism. My assertion here that it is one of the least commonplace comes from the fact there is, perhaps unsurprisingly, absolutely nothing in the academic or clinical literature on burping fetishism. Furthermore, I was only able to locate one online forum that appeared to be solely dedicated to the sexual side of burping. You could do worse than check out the Burp Fetish Forum's website if this topic intrigues you. I should also mention that on YouTube there are dedicated collections of people burping on camera. Although these collected clips may be sexually arousing to a burp fetishist, I guess most people who watch them do so because they find them amusing.

While I was researching sneeze fetishes, which in itself is a strange and rare fetish, I came across written sources about a few people also admitting that they were sexually aroused by the thought and/or sight of someone burping and belching.

I am not sure if there is really any difference between burping and belching, although from what I have read in a fetishistic sense, belching is very loud burping, whereas ordinary burping is not necessarily loud. Anecdotally, the "loudness" aspect appears to be an important element to burp fetishists. In this sense, it is the noise made rather than the action itself that appears to be what is sexualized and/or interpreted by the fetishist as sexually pleasurable and arousing. In sexual behaviour more generally, hearing quite clearly influences sexual arousal and response. However, this is typically in the form of music that facilitates people's mood in readiness for sex and/or the sounds that people make while engaging in sexual activity (e.g., "talking dirty" and/or moaning and groaning while having sex).

Candaulism and cuckold fetishes

Later in this book I examine exhibitionism, which in this context typically means individuals who expose their genitals to other people. There I cover a subtype called "candaulism", which I define as "a term referring to people who expose themselves to their sexual partners (e.g., a wife or husband) in a sexually explicit way." On this theme, I once received an email saying that the definition I provided was not as detailed as it could have been. In response to my (friendly) critic I decided to take a more detailed look.

The first place I looked was the *Encyclopedia of Unusual Sex Practices* (Love, 2001). Interestingly, she defined candaulism as "a group of three people where only two of them engage in sex and the other watches, sometimes from a closet." Love then discusses troilism, which is where three people typically comprise a sexual couple and a third person where one of the three (typically the husband or male partner of the couple) watches the other two have sex. Nothing of what was written was based on anything I would call empirical and research based, although it was an interesting read.

Next, I turned to my favourite book on sexual deviation (i.e., Aggrawal, 2009a). He describes candaulism as a "variation of exhibitionism [where] persons do not exhibit themselves but their spouses – usually a male exhibiting his wife." He further cites Marten's (1986) case study on candaulism. On the basis of this, Aggrawal says that candaulism also involves "getting sadomasochistic pleasure when the husband exposes his wife, or pictures of her, to other voyeurist people." I have no idea how representative Marten's case study is of candaulism as his paper appears to be not only the sole academic case study that has ever been published but also was published in the author of the case study's native language (Polish), so all I have to go on is Aggrawal's second-hand account.

Aggrawal also researched the origin of the word "candaulism". He reports that von Krafft-Ebing (1886) coined the term and that it came from the obscure history of Candaules, king of the ancient kingdom of Lydia (735–718 BC). Aggrawal claimed that "husbands" (a term I am assuming covers all male sexual partners within a heterosexual couple) take the "paraphilia to the extreme and enjoy other people having sex with their wives" (which I am similarly assuming includes any female partner within a heterosexual couple). Aggrawal then adds that "this practice can take the form of swinging, in which husbands exchange wives for sexual intercourse and watch each other. In certain cases the relation evolves into a stable union of these persons, known as troilism." Finally, Holmes and Holmes (2009) discuss candaulism and likewise link it to "swinging" (i.e., the swapping of sexual partners).

Capnolagnia

Watch any film or television programme made before 2000 featuring a post-coital couple in bed and, odds on, one if not both of them will be smoking a cigarette. I start with this anecdotal observation to establish that sex and cigarette smoking are quite literally no strange bedfellows.

For a small minority of people, smoking can be sexually arousing. For some it may even be a paraphilia called "capnolagnia". Aggrawal (2009a) defines capnolagnia as "a paraphilia in which individuals derive sexual pleasure and sexual arousal from watching others smoke." According to an article on smoking fetishism on the Collar 'n' Cuffs website (2010), smoking can include normal cigarettes or marijuana spliffs.

The defining features of capnolagnia are outlined on the Right Diagnosis website (2012a). It is claimed that people who experience one (or more) of the following symptoms are considered to have a smoking fetish: (i) sexual interest in watching other people smoke, (ii) recurring intense sexual fantasies involving watching other people smoke and (iii) recurring intense sexual urges involving watching other people smoke.

As far as I am aware, there is almost no empirical or clinical research on capnolagnia. Given that there are no treatment papers in the clinical and medical literature it suggests that either capnolagnia is rare and/or people who have the fetish live with it happily without feeling the need to seek treatment.

Arguably, it was not really until the advent of the internet and the formation of online forums that people were even aware that smoking fetishes existed. As with many other fetishes, like-minded people began to meet at online newsgroups, such as alt.smokers.glamour and alt.sex.fetish.smokers. Online groups grew in number and content, trading stories, pictures, videos and DVDs.

A short article on "bizarre" fetishes on the Religious Sex website (2012) claimed that there was a "darker and more extreme version" of capnolagnia found among BDSM communities as well as in the female domination subcultures, in which submissive partners may be treated like a human ashtray and forced by their dominant partner to swallow cigarette ash, have cigarette smoke blown continually into their face and/or have cigarettes stubbed out on their naked flesh. The use of "submissive" here as an inanimate item has overlaps with the humiliating and masochistic world of forniphilia (i.e., use of people as human furniture for sexual pleasure), which I examine later in this book.

Car-cranking and pedal-pumping fetishes

While researching both podophilia (sexual arousal from feet) and stuck fetishism (sexual arousal from being stuck and/or stranded), I came across lots of online references to "car cranking" and accelerator "pedal pumping". Almost all the online articles and videos that I have come across appear to indicate that the fetish is primarily male based with females doing the pedal pumping and car engine cranking.

As you may have gathered during my research on this topic, I came across nothing academic whatsoever – not even a case study. So we know nothing about incidence, prevalence or etiology. However, there is clearly a niche market for those into car accelerator "pedal pumping" – not just based on the number of YouTube videos and specialist videoclip sites, but also evidenced by pedal pump fiction and online discussions of the topic.

Whether motor vehicle pedal pumping will ever be the topic of serious academic research remains to be seen. However, given the empirical research base on podophilia, there certainly seems to be some scope to look at the psychological and behavioural overlaps.

Catheterophilia

Later in this book I examine medical fetishism in which individuals derive sexual pleasure and arousal from medical procedures and/or something medically related. Both Aggrawal (2009a) and Love (2001) define catheterophilia as "sexual arousal from the use of catheters". The Right Diagnosis website (2012b) goes a little further and reports that catheterophilia can include one or more of the following: (i) sexual interest in using a catheter, (ii) abnormal amount of time spent thinking about using a catheter, (iii) recurring intense sexual fantasies involving using a catheter, (iv) recurring intense sexual urges involving using a catheter and (vi) sexual preference for using a catheter.

Catheterophilia is also a subtype of urethralism. It may share some overlaps with other paraphilias, such as paraphilic infantilism in which individuals derive sexual pleasure and arousal from pretending to be an adult baby (Maddy's Mansion, 2010).

Pranzarone (2000) also provided a little information on catheterophilia and noted that it is a paraphilia of the "… fetishistic and talismanic type in which the sexual arousal and facilitation or attainment of orgasm are responsive to and contingent on having a catheter inserted up into the urethra."

Catheterization is nothing new and according to Love (2001) has been practised for at least 4,000 years. She also provided a lengthy entry in her sexual encyclopaedia, although most of it was devoted to describing different types of catheters. Her perspective on catheter use is related more to sexual masochism and sexual sadism. More specifically, she claims that:

> "Catheters are used in sex play as a symbol of total control over a partner. This type of sex play is similar to the catheterization found in healthcare facilities. The sterilized catheter is inserted up through the urethra and into the bladder which allows the flow of urine to be controlled by the dominant partner. The stimulation seems to trigger the brain's pleasure center that ordinarily responds to urination or ejaculation … the urethra is often sore and burns for half an hour afterward."

Apart from definitions of catheterophilia and short summaries that argue the condition exists, there has been little in the way of academic or clinical research. I could not even find a single case study. Alison *et al.* (2001) reported that enduring the insertion of a catheter is one of the activities engaged in by sadomasochists, particularly those involved in "hyper-masculine pain administration". Other associated activities by such practitioners included rimming, dildo use, cock binding, being urinated upon, being given an enema, fisting and being defecated upon. Gay men were more likely than heterosexuals to engage in these types of activity.

The Right Diagnosis website (2012b) also claimed that treatment for catheterophilia is generally not sought unless the condition becomes problematic for the person in some way, and the individual involved feels compelled to address the condition. The site also claims that the majority of catheterophiles learn to accept their fetish and manage to achieve gratification in an appropriate manner.

Childbirth fetishism

Later in this book I examine maieusiophilia, a paraphilia and/or fetish in which an individual derives sexual pleasure and sexual arousal from particular aspects of human female pregnancy. Aggrawal (2009a) defines maieusiophilia as "gaining sexual arousal from pregnant women and/or female childbirth". However, other sources define maieusiophilia more broadly to include sexual attraction to women who also appear pregnant, attraction to lactation and/or attraction to particular stages of pregnancy from impregnation through to childbirth. It is this latter aspect (i.e., childbirth) that I examine here.

As far as I am aware, there is no empirical research on the fetishized aspects of childbirth. However, I did come across an interesting paper on the pornography of childbirth (Longhurst, 2006). The paper focuses on the moral issues surrounding the case of New Zealand "adult actress" and former stripper Nikki Devi's desire to give birth as part of a pornographic film called *Ripe*. In New Zealand the Department of Child, Youth and Family Services wanted to separate the mother and child if the film was ever completed, but New Zealand's laws were not clear on whether the act of giving birth in a pornographic film was a form of child abuse.

From everything that I have read sexual arousal from either experiencing and/or watching childbirth appears to be very rare. However, it does seem to be prevalent in a minority of individuals. Whether it ever becomes the topic of scientific research remains to be seen, although I am sure more academic articles about morality issues may appear in philosophy-minded journals in the years to come.

Choreophilia

The association between dancing and sex has long been known. Many forms of dancing including belly dancing, pole dancing, lap dancing and (obviously) striptease are erotic and/or sex based. Furthermore, there are specific types of dance that are thought to be "sexy" in and of themselves (e.g., salsa, rumba, tango and cha-cha).

For some people the desire to dance may form the basis of a paraphilia (i.e., choreophilia). Both Aggrawal (2009a) and Love (2001) define choreophilia simply as "sexual arousal from dancing". This does not, however, necessarily seem to indicate that the behaviour is in and of itself a paraphilia.

The Right Diagnosis website (2012c) says that choreophilia refers to sexual urges, preferences or fantasies that involve dancing including (i) sexual interest in dancing, (ii) recurring intense sexual fantasies involving dancing and/or (iii) recurring intense sexual urges.

In her entry on belly dancing, Love also unearthed an interesting nugget from an 1898 book by Jacobus X called *Untrodden Fields of Anthropology*, which outlined another form of sexual dancing performed by Senegalese people in Africa:

"In the anamalis fubil, the dancer in his movements, imitates the copulation of the great Indian duck. This drake has a member of a corkscrew shape, and a particular movement. The woman, for her part, tucks up her clothes, and convulsively agitates the lower part of her body by the motion of her haunches; she alternately shows her partner her vulva, and hides it from him, by a regular movement, backwards and forwards, of the body."

In more contemporary times, Love claimed that modern dance halls had their roots in sexual practices. The first US dance halls were founded by bar owners who hired females to dance with their clients (as a way of attracting new clients and more of them). Some of the hired women were prostitutes who then used the opportunity provided by the bar owners to offer additional sexual services.

An interesting article (Lovatt, 2012) examines the relationship between sex and dancing. It reported that Charles Darwin believed dance was part of the mate selection process. As empirical evidence of this, Lovatt also noted that:

"Two groups of researchers (Brown et al., 2005 and Fink et al., 2007) suggest that the way we dance might be influenced by our hormonal and genetic make-up, such that we use dance to communicate the quality of our genes to potential mates. In my own lab I have observed similar findings. I filmed people dancing naturally in a real nightclub and I found that men with high levels of the sex hormone testosterone dance differently to men with low levels of testosterone and, most importantly, women prefer the dancing of high-testosterone men. Now, if we couple this with the finding that the female sexual partners of high-testosterone men report having more orgasms during sex than the sexual partners of low-testosterone men we can see how dancing style is well worth looking at when we are looking for a mate."

As far as I am aware, there is no empirical research on choreophilia, although there would appear to be some overlap with other little-researched paraphilias, such as melophilia (individuals who derive sexual pleasure and arousal from music), podophilia (i.e., foot fetishism in relation to high-heeled dancing shoes) and various types of clothing fetishes (Fetipedia, 2012).

Chremastistophilia and symphorophilia

Later on in this book I examine hybristophilia, a paraphilia in which an individual derives sexual arousal and pleasure from having a sexual partner who is known to have committed serious crimes, such as rape, murder or armed robbery. Another criminal-focused paraphilia is chremastistophilia, in which the individual derives sexual arousal and pleasure from being robbed, conned, cheated, blackmailed and/or being held up by the individual's sexual partner (or, in a few cases, a complete stranger). Some websites, such as kinkify.com, colloquially refer to it as the "hold-up kink".

Some have speculated that the strong emotions of frustration, fear, annoyance, rage and/or submission are subconsciously drawn upon by chremastistophiles and then focused into sexual arousal/gratification. This could be viewed as edgeplay (i.e., rough and deviant sexual play enjoyed by sexual masochists and sexual sadists) as the behaviour can be life threatening for chremastistophiles actively seeking out someone to steal from them purely for sexual kicks.

The reciprocal condition where the sexual focus is on robbing one's sexual partner has not been given a name. People who derive sexual pleasure and arousal from breaking and entering a property and then stealing is known as kleptophilia, which I overview later in this book. In my research into chremastistophilia I have yet to come across a single piece of empirical research on the topic

Gordon and Elias (2012) claim that chremastistophilia is accepted as potentially lethal alongside other criminally related paraphilias, such as hybristophilia and autassassinophilia, in which the individual derives sexual arousal by the risk of being killed. Unfortunately, I cannot find a single academic or clinical study that has ever been published in a peer-reviewed journal, so this is clearly an area that is in need of empirical research.

Another strange paraphilia with a potentially criminally based sexual focus is symphorophilia. This is a paraphilia that Money (1986) says relates to individuals who derive sexual arousal and pleasure from witnessing and/or stage-managing a "disaster, such as a conflagration or traffic accident, and watching it happen." Again, I have yet to come across any empirical research on the topic, although I do briefly examine this paraphilia in relation to sex and cars later in this book. It has been alleged that in very rare cases an accident that may injure or even kill someone may bring the symphorophile to the point of orgasm quicker. The condition is probably better known in popular culture than in academic terms. For instance, the main characters in Ballard's (1973) novel *Crash* and the subsequent 1996 film adaptation of the same name were symphorophiles.

As with chremastistophilia I have been unable to find a single clinical or academic study published in a peer-reviewed journal. So it would appear that this paraphilia is incredibly rare.

Chronophilic behaviours

Most of you reading this will probably be thinking that, when it comes to age preference, the world is broadly split into the minority of individuals who are involved in paedophilia (i.e., individuals who derive sexual pleasure and arousal from children) and those whose sexual preference is geared towards sex with adults. In fact, in researching this entry I was surprised to learn that I am a teleiophile.

Teleiophilia (a.k.a. "adultophilia") refers to adult individuals whose primary sexual focus is other adult individuals. As Aggrawal (2009a) reassuringly notes in his book, "teleiophilia is not a sexual paraphilia." However, individuals whose primary sexual preference is for elderly adults are said to be engaging in gerontophilia (Kaul and Duffy, 1991), which is sometimes called "graeophilia". But who qualifies as elderly? Apparently, it is quite widely agreed in Western industrialized nations to be anyone 65 years or older, although opinions do differ.

According to the DSM-5-TR (American Psychiatric Association, 2022), paedophilia is described as a form of paraphilia whereby individuals experience intense sexual urges towards a prepubescent child or children (typically aged under 13 years), and experiences recurrent sexual urges towards (and fantasizes about) children that the individual has acted upon and/or causes distress and interpersonal difficulty. Technically, many child-abusers would not be defined as paedophiles according to the DSM criteria as the behaviour may not be causing the abusers any psychological problems themselves. However, in day-to-day language most people would define any adult who engages in any form of sexual behaviour with a minor as paedophilia.

One of the most disturbing and horrific cases that I am aware of involved two children who were systematically abused by their grandfather and their grandfather's friends. The grandfather had sexually abused his daughter throughout her childhood and then began abusing his daughter's children from an early age. After the grandfather died a video was played at the reading of the will that the family thought contained the grandfather's verbal reading of his last will and testament. What the video actually contained was a short film of the grandfather having sexual intercourse with his 2-year-old granddaughter and his 4-year-old grandson.

The reason I recount this story is that this is an example of what is known as nepiophilia (a.k.a. "infantophilia") and refers to individuals who have a sexual preference for very young children (usually up to 3 years old). The term paedohebephilia refers to the expansion and reclassification of paedophilia into subgroups, such as distinctions made between paedophiles who prefer pubescent or post-pubescent children. More specifically, hebephilia refers to individuals who have a sexual preference for pubescent youths (i.e., typically adolescents around 11 to 14 years of age). However, some authors, such as Aggrawal (2009a), claim that hebephilia is a preference for pubescent children between 11 and 14 years for females and 11 to 16 years for males.

Ephebophilia refers to individuals with a sexual preference for post-pubescent youths (mid-to-late adolescents aged around 15 to 19 years of age). Other researchers in the sexual studies field, such as Freund (1990a, b), have used the term "adolescentophilia" as referring to individuals who have a sexual preference for pubescent and/or adolescent youths.

Claustrophilia

According to Aggrawal (2009a) claustrophilia is a paraphilia in which individuals derive sexual pleasure and arousal from being confined in small places. The online Urban Dictionary defines claustrophilia slightly differently as "individuals deriving sexual gratification from sexual intercourse in tight spaces." There are other sources who use the word "claustrophilia" simply to mean "a love of small spaces" without any sexual element attached to it.

Some years ago the print and broadcast media were full of reports about the inquest of Gareth Williams, the British spy who was discovered dead in his rented London flat (Littlejohn, 2012). In August 2010 his naked body was found padlocked inside a duffel bag. However, some of the reports concentrated on whether the fact he was found dead in a small bag was an indication that he was a claustrophile. The inquest heard that he had an interest in bondage websites, but this was only a very small part of his internet-browsing history. The coroner Fiona Wilcox declared his death as "unnatural".

Another closely related paraphilia to claustrophilia would appear to be taphephilia. Aggrawal (2009a) defines taphephilia as "deriving sexual pleasure and arousal from being buried alive." I have to say that when I first read about this paraphilia I had major doubts about its existence; that is, until I came across groups, such as the Six Feet Under Club and the Buried Stories website. As the home pages of these sites assert:

Extract 1: *"Buried or burial whilst still alive is a nightmare to some but a joy or fetish to others. The desire to be boxed, bagged and buried is a great turn-on for many. The feeling of utter helplessness as the sounds of the first shovel of dirt hits the top of their coffin. The fantasy may also involve being placed in a casket, bodybag or other enclosure before being buried either on the beach, in dirt or even in quicksand. Encased or entombed, enclosed or just bagged, Buried Stories contains stories of people being buried, sunk in quicksand or encased within an enclosure. Some may have acted out their desires whilst others have written about their fantasy to share with you."*

Extract 2: *"Even though a sexual nature is one of the few things most humans share in common, our social convention is to push all trace of it out of the public sphere. The Six Feet Under Club offers attendees a unique opportunity to experience the warping of public and private intimate space. At [a Monochrom] conference, couples can volunteer to be buried together in a casket beneath the ground. The space they occupy will be extremely private and intimate. The coffin is a reminder of the social norm of exclusive pair bonding 'till death do us part."*

Apart from Howie (2009) I know of no academic who has written or examined either claustrophilia or taphephilia. Furthermore, despite the many academic merits of Howie's research, I would not describe it as in any way empirical, particularly as most of the source material is from English, French and Italian readings from the 13th and 14th century – interesting but hardly contemporary.

Climacophilia

In this book I mention a number of paraphilias that appear to have been derived from the opposite phobic behaviours. Some examples include defecaloesiophilia (sexual arousal from painful bowel movements), lockiophilia (sexual arousal from childbirth), categelophilia (sexual arousal from being ridiculed) and rupophilia (sexual arousal

40 Climacophilia

from dirt). Another one that I could add to this list is climacophilia, which is sexual arousal from falling down stairs. This particular paraphilia received considerable media attention a few years ago when Baring (2013) was plugging his book *Perv: The Sexual Deviant in All of Us*, which I will return to below. Paul Bloom of Yale University went so far as to describe Baring as the "Hunter S. Thompson of science writing".

Climacophilia appears to be the opposite of climacophobia. In Aggrawal's (2009a) book, climacophilia is given a seven-word entry between "clinical vampirism" (arousal by drinking human or animal blood) and "coitobalnism" (having sex in the bath) and is simply defined as "deriving pleasure from falling down stairs." There is no mention of it at all in Love's (2001) encyclopaedia. Various websites provide definitions including the Pro Boner website that states "Climacophilia is an intriguing paraphilia characterised by sexual arousal to falling down the stairs. Climacophiles have their best orgasms when they're falling down the stairs." The Buzz IO website tells us that "Climacophilia is being sexually stimulated by seeing someone fall down a flight of stairs." When reviewing Baring's book, the *New York Times* defined it as "the erotic compulsion to tumble down stairs."

All of these definitions and snippets imply slightly different things relating to the same alleged behaviour. While all involve some kind of sexual arousal from falling down stairs, the *New York Times* says the behaviour is an "erotic compulsion" whereas most others describe the behaviour as arousing, stimulating and pleasurable (without being compulsive). One definition states "orgasm" is involved while the rest do not. However, there is no evidence that this paraphilia actually exists.

Clothing fetishes

The Huffington Post published a story (Hazell, 2012) that got me thinking about the relationship between clothing and sexual arousal. The news item reported that an "intimacy dress" designed by Daan Roosegaarde detects when the person wearing it is feeling sexually aroused. It was reported that:

> "The futuristic 'Intimacy 2.0' design is made of hi-tech fabric, leather and opaque e-foils and becomes transparent when it 'detects' a quickening heartbeat. The technical dress, dubbed 'techno-poetry' by the designer himself, operates with the help of wireless technology, LEDs and various electronics. Talking about his saucy design, Roosegaarde told the Daily Mail that 'Intimacy 2.0' is a fashion project exploring the relation between intimacy and technology. Technology as used here is not merely functional but also is a tool to create intimacy as well as privacy on a direct, personal level which in our contemporary tech society is becoming increasingly important."

Whether the dress serves any real practical purpose is debatable, but clothes have long been a source in and of themselves of sexual arousal and fetishization. In fact, the term "fetish fashion" has permeated into popular usage to become associated now with any style or appearance in the form of a type of clothing and/or accessory that has been created to be deliberately extreme and/or provocative.

Clothing fetishes are sexual fetishes in which individuals derive sexual arousal and pleasure from either (i) viewing or imagining very specific items of clothing, (ii) viewing or imagining a set of clothes (e.g., a particular uniform or fashion look) and/or (iii) individuals themselves or others wearing the clothing item or uniform. As with other fetishes, the item the individual has fixated upon normally has to be present for sexual arousal to occur. The source of the arousal may also depend on the material from which the clothing items are made and/or the function of the clothing on the person wearing them (e.g., clothes that may restrict a person's movement or may accentuate a particular attribute of the body). Some clothing fetishists also collect particular clothing items.

Clothing fetishes are known to overlap with other paraphilias including transvestite fetishism, sexual sadism and sexual masochism. Restrictive types of clothing are most associated with sadomasochistic activity and are often made from PVC or latex. They include very narrow skirts that impede movement. They are often referred to as "hobble skirts", some of which are ankle length to make walking almost impossible. Similarly, the highest of high-heel shoes are used because they too make it difficult to walk.

Another popular item of restrictive clothing is a tight corset. Individuals playing sexually submissive roles are often forced to wear a bondage corset (a.k.a. "a discipline corset") as a form of punishment. This is associated with the masochistic sexual practice of "tightlacing" (a.k.a. "corset training" and "waist training") where submissive partners, typically female, are forced to wear a tightly laced corset that results in extreme body modifications to the submissive partner's figure and posture, such as "hourglass" figures, in which the woman looks as though she has an incredibly small waist.

Excluding footwear fetishes (which are very prevalent), there are many other particular types of clothing fetishes. Arguably, the most well known are stocking and suspender fetishes and uniform fetishes (e.g., a woman dressing up as a nurse or a man dressing up as a fireman). However, there are other less reported clothing fetishes including sock fetishes, denim jean fetishes and coat/jacket fetishes.

Yet again, therefore, here is another area in this fascinating field that would benefit from more empirical research to further our understanding of human behaviour. On which note there is much in need of our understanding following a posting on China's leading auction site *Taobao* for the sale of Beijing Olympics cheerleaders' uniforms including their unwashed bras and panties. The advert whipped up a minor storm on China's internet. An agent claiming to represent one of the many international teams of Olympics cheerleaders put up the intimate innerwear items (presumably underwear) for auction and "guaranteed their authenticity" and "unwashed" status. In language intended to appeal to panty fetishists the agent wrote, "They are sure to excite you. When you hold them up to your nose and sniff, you'll smell the youthful fragrance of the young girls" … the auction listing has been further inflamed by incensed Chinese netizens as a "vulgar, shameless insult to the Olympics spirit …" From all accounts the "panty donors" (or perhaps more accurately "owners") may have been cheerleaders from Japan, where there exists a thriving market for used innerwear that are utilized in autoerotic practices. In fact, so-called *burusera* shops in Japanese cities and towns cater for the kinky needs of hormonally driven men to this day (Vembu, 2008).

In Japan *burusera* shops sell second-hand clothes and undergarments as well as items (including sanitary towels and tampons) that are soiled with body fluids from the owner of the original items (e.g., urine, faecal matter and menstrual blood). Typically the merchandise sold is accompanied by a photograph of the girl wearing or holding the item, which acts as a "certificate of authenticity". The buyers of such items typically smell the items as a source of sexual stimulation and gratification. In Japan, there was even a film *Burusera: Shop of Horrors*, released in 1996 and directed by Takeshi Miyasaka, about three high-school girls from Tokyo who make extra pocket money selling their underwear to a *burusera* shop, but do not actually realize that they are facilitating the latest Japanese fetish craze.

A short article about *burusera* at the Heaven 666 website (Morana, 2008) provides pictures of Japanese vending machines that were once used to sell prepacked and "ready-to-sniff" used panties. The same article also makes reference to *namasera*, a variation of *burusera* that means "fresh". Apparently, the *namasera* concept is the same as *burusera*, but in this case "the goods are still being worn by the girl who then removes them and hands them over directly at the point of sale."

As many clinicians have noted, there is a well-known crossover relationship between fetishism, sadomasochism and other paraphilias where the wearing of "uniforms" plays a critical role. However, Bhugra and De Silva (1996) conclude:

> "The relationship of uniforms in fantasy and fetish is a complex one. Often in clinical situations it becomes impossible to ascertain when fantasy leads to fetish in reality and how much of a role fantasy plays in arousal related to a fetish. From a preliminary pilot study with a small number of rubber fetishists it appears that the distinction between fetish and fantasy is difficult even for the individual."

Coimetrophilia

According to the English Word Information website, coimetromania is defined as "(i) an abnormal attraction to and desire to visit cemeteries, (ii) a compulsion to examine the various graves and other burial aspects of cemeteries and/or (iii) in some situations in psychiatry someone who has a morbid attraction to graves and cemeteries." The name comes from the Greek word *koimeterion* which roughly translates to "sleeping room, burial place; grave, graveyard; final resting place".

Given that coimetrophilia does not make an appearance in the books of Aggrawal (2009a) or Love (2001), this suggests that if such a paraphilia exists then it is incredibly rare. It would also seem to be related to placophilia, which is where individuals derive sexual pleasure and arousal from tombstones (which does make it into Aggrawal's book but not Love's encyclopaedia). As I repeat later in this book, after finding out what placophobia was, the musician and author Julian Cope claimed he must be a placophile on a post at his Head Heritage website (although my guess is that his love for tombstones is not sexual).

Literature on coimetrophilia (and placophilia) is almost non-existent and, to date, there has certainly been no academic or clinical research on the topic. Given that coimetrophilia is yet another word that was derived from the opposite phobia (i.e., coimetrophobia, a morbid fear of cemeteries and graveyards), it could well be that coimetrophilia is a hypothetical paraphilia rather than a real one.

Coprophilia

Coprophilia (a.k.a. "coprolagnia") is a paraphilia in which people get sexual pleasure from viewing, smelling or handling faeces (Arnone *et al.*, 2024). However, the sexual excitement can also come from either (i) fantasizing about someone engaging in these activities, (ii) watching somebody defecate on somebody else or (iii) they themselves defecating on somebody else. In rare instances some people may become sexually aroused when they are defecated upon by somebody else. The act of being defecated upon has been termed "brown showers" and for some individuals may result in orgasm (Janus and Janus, 1993). Milner *et al.* (2008) write:

> *"Although some authors have defined the focus of coprophilia as the act of elimination (McCary, 1967), others have defined it as the act of consumption of excrement (Allen, 1969). To complicate the definition further, it appears that some individuals may have an interest in eliminating on one's partner or in playing with the fecal matter. According to Smith (1976), a common analytic interpretation is that the excrement symbolically represents the penis and that the presence of the fecal matter serves as a defense against castration anxiety."*

In the American Psychiatric Association's DSM-5-TR (2022), coprophilia is classified under "other specified paraphilic disorder" (OSPD) along with other paraphilias, such as urophilia, necrophilia, zoophilia, klismaphilia and telephone scatophilia. As with all paraphilias in the paraphilias not otherwise specified (PNOS) category, diagnosis is made only:

> *"... if the behavior, sexual urges, or fantasies cause clinically significant distress or impairment in social, occupational, or other important areas of functioning ... Fantasies, behaviors, or objects are paraphilic only when they lead to clinically significant distress or impairment (e.g., are obligatory, result in sexual dysfunction, require participation of non-consenting individuals, lead to legal complications, interfere with social relationships)."*

Penix (2008) says there are no data indicating successful treatment of coprophilia. Surprisingly little scientific research has been carried out on coprophilia, probably because it is so rare. Lake (2008) noted that both coprophilia and coprophagia are traditionally considered characteristics of schizophrenia. However, there are case reports in the literature of non-psychotic coprophiliacs with normal intelligence (Wise and Goldberg, 1995).

Sandnabba *et al.* (1999) surveyed 164 Finnish male sadomasochists and reported that 18% of them had engaged in at least one coprophilic act (6% as a masochist, 3% as a sadist and 9% as both). There was no difference in sexual orientation with 18% of heterosexual sadomasochists and 17% of homosexual sadomasochists having engaged in at least one coprophilic act. The results also showed that the sadomasochists were socially well adjusted and that their sadomasochistic behaviour was mainly a facilitative aspect of their sexual lives. Moser and Levitt (1987) reported a prevalence rate of 12.5% for coprophilic behaviour among 225 sadomasochists. More recently, Rehor (2015) conducted an international survey among 1,580 females from the "kink" community. This included questions relating to "faeces play". The survey found 10.57% had watched coprophilic activity, 3.99% had been defecated upon, 3.35% reported they had defecated on others and 13.7% had engaged in some form of coprophilic activity.

The origins of coprophilic behaviour certainly appear to be a result of both classical and operant conditioning. However, other people suggest different etiological factors may contribute to the development of coprophilia. For instance, Hingsburger (1989) reported the case of an institutionalized and mentally handicapped man in Canada who engaged in coprophilic acts approximately three times a week. It was argued that the cause of his coprophilia was the patient's maladaptive response to a severely limited institutional environment rather than any behavioural conditioning. A review of the coprophilia literature by Arnone *et al.* (2024) summarized the scant theorizing and noted that:

> *"Smith (1976) offered an analytic interpretation of coprophilia – mainly that the excrement symbolically represents the penis and the presence of the fecal matter acts as a defense against castration anxiety. According to Gardner (1996), coprophilia is a product of childhood perversity in which a young child must learn that touching their fecal eliminations and then placing their fingers (or feces) in the mouth is viewed by society as a disgusting practice ... Researchers are uncertain about the exact causes of paraphilias in general and coprophilia in particular, although these disorders probably develop from a combination of factors that come into play in specific ways for particular persons. One biological explanation holds that some people are simply "wired" to have paraphilias (Moser, 1992). Another holds that some men have stronger and more pervasive sex drives, possibly due to increased amounts of or sensitivity to the male sex hormone testosterone. As a result, such men are more prone to seek out other sexual outlets when more traditional outlets are not readily available. Their increased sexual reactivity may also facilitate learning a paraphilia like coprophilia (Lang et al., 1989)."*

Whatever the origins, it is evident that compared with many other paraphilic behaviours there is a dearth of empirical and clinical data relating to the acquisition, development and maintenance of coprophilia (Omasiali, 2011).

One of the most bizarre sex-related stories I have come across concerns an Englishman named David Truscott from Pengegon Parc, Camborne, Cornwall, UK (Crazy News, 2011). When I wrote about this on my blogsite some years ago I asked whether this might be an unusual case of zoocoprophilia.

Truscott was 41 years old when he was imprisoned for 2 years after he had harassed and terrorized one particular family over a 6-year period near Redruth, Cornwall, UK. He repeatedly covered his naked (or scantily clad) body in cow manure and would roll around on the ground masturbating inside the family's farm. When he was not completely naked he just wore underpants, although on one occasion he was apprehended by police wearing shiny red shorts and latex gloves. He had already received a court order preventing him from going anywhere near the family, but breached his restraining order on 26 February 2011 when he was caught by farmer Clive Roth's 16-year-old son pleasuring himself while covered in cow manure.

Jill Wilson, the crown prosecutor in the case at Truro Court, told the court that there was "… a history of [Truscott] visiting this particular farm seeking sexual gratification while immersed in cow dung and mud." Mark Charnley, the lawyer defending Truscott, told the court that his client was a "… sad, vulnerable, socially inadequate man … He does show remorse for what he did and had a realization of the harm he was doing to the family." The defence lawyer asked for leniency because his client had no close family and had learning difficulties. He also suggested that Truscott was suffering from a form of autism that led him to engage in his sexual behaviour while under stress. However, Judge Christopher Elwen said Truscott had to be jailed for his "perverted activities [and because he had] made the home life of the Roth family absolute hell through your bizarre fetish and disgusting behaviour." The judge concluded "The family members live in fear of what you might get up to from time to time. They have constantly to look over their shoulders. Any untoward activity on the farm brings your disgusting behaviour to mind."

It was back in 2004 that Truscott was first spotted by the family when he was found masturbating in the faeces of the farm's muck spreader. As the behaviour was not an isolated incident, the family tried to keep their manure-spreading equipment clean as a deterrent. Nevertheless, Truscott still found ways to make himself a nuisance to the family. When the manure became harder to come by, Truscott took his revenge on the family by setting fire to an animal pen containing the family's cows and calves, which resulted in one of the cows dying. The family's 3-year-old son was traumatized by the incident and lived in fear that the house where he lived was going to be burned to the ground. Mr Roth's mother also lived in fear that the farmhouse was going to be the subject of an arson attack. As a consequence, Truscott received a 3-year prison sentence, which took into account his guilty plea.

When he was released from prison in 2009, Truscott returned to the family's farmhouse and was found naked in a pile of manure. He received yet another prison sentence (20 weeks) and a restraining order preventing him from stepping foot on the family's farm. However, this proved ineffective and was broken on a number of subsequent occasions including one where he immersed himself almost naked inside a large vat of manure inside the farm's milking parlour. It was also revealed in court that Truscott owned 360 pairs of women's knickers and usually slept in women's pyjamas. In 2014 Truscott received another 5-year prison sentence.

Although I have only the various news reports to go on, I would make a number of observations. First, the primary sexual attraction appeared to be towards animal faeces. Therefore, he could possibly be classed as a coprophile. Although I have never come across a case of anyone in the academic and clinical literature deriving sexual pleasure from anything other than human faeces, definitions of coprophilia never specify that the faecal matter has to be human. Maybe Truscott's behaviour could therefore be classed as "zoocoprophilia" (my own word to describe individuals who derive sexual pleasure and arousal from animal faeces).

Second, and I admit this is highly speculative, it could perhaps be argued that Truscott would classify as a "Class V zoosexual" in Aggrawal's (2009b) new classification of zoophiles (outlined later in this book). The Class V zoosexual type comprises what Aggrawal calls fetishistic zoophiles. These individuals keep various animal parts, especially fur, which they then use as an erotic stimulus as a crucial part of their sexual activity. Such individuals have been reported in the clinical literature, such as the case of a woman (Randall *et al.*, 1990) who used the tongue of a deer as her primary masturbatory aid. Given that animal manure appeared to be a critical component in Truscott's masturbatory activity maybe he could arguably be classed as a Class V zoosexual. Third, there is some empirical evidence supporting an overlap between coprophilia and zoophilia.

An earlier study on a sample of paraphiliacs reported that zoophiles appear to engage in many paraphilic behaviours including coprophilia. In a survey of 561 non-incarcerated paraphiliacs seeking treatment, Abel *et al.* (1988) reported that all of the 14 zoophiles in their sample reported more than one paraphilia and seven of them reported at least five other paraphilas including coprophilia, urophilia, paedophilia, exhibitionism, voyeurism, frotteurism, telephone scatophilia, transvestic fetishism, fetishism itself, sexual sadism and/or sexual masochism. This also supports the observation that when someone has a paraphilia, he or she often has others. In the case of Truscott there was some evidence that he engaged in transvestite sexual behaviour by the fact that he often wore women's knickers and slept in female nightwear.

Finally, the fact that Truscott's lawyer suggested his client had a form of autism may be an important element in the behaviour displayed. As noted earlier in this entry, various medical and psychological disorders have been identified that are associated with coprophagia including mental retardation and autism.

Coulrophilia

There are various websites that list hundreds of different types of paraphilia, many of which are simply the names of specific phobias wherein the suffix "-phobia" is replaced by the suffix "-philia". Examples of this include agoraphobia and agoraphilia (fear of the outdoors; sexual arousal from the outdoors), cremnophobia and cremnophilia (fear of steep cliffs and precipices; sexual arousal from steep cliffs and precipices) and kynophobia and kynophilia (fear of getting rabies; sexual arousal from getting rabies). Another paraphilia that often appears in these lists is coulrophilia (sexual arousal from clowns), which I assumed was just based on the opposite phobia (i.e., coulrophobia – fear of clowns) and did not really exist, especially as it does not appear in the books of either Aggrawal (2009a) or Love (2001). Furthermore, there is not a single reference to coulrophilia in any academic article or book of which I am aware.

I had all but given up writing on coulrophilia until by chance I came across an online forum where a group of people were discussing their respective clown fetishes. I have picked out some of the more interesting admissions and have attempted to provide a little commentary on each extract and then a more general summary. Obviously, I have no way of knowing how truthful any of these accounts are, but they appeared genuine to me, particularly given the detail into which some of them go.

Case 1 *(gay male):* "I think my fetish started out as more of a fetish for face painting, which has turned me on [for] as long as I can remember ... Until I found this [paraphilia] site I always thought I was pretty much alone. Most of the comments I've seen elsewhere revolve around scary clowns. Not for me. My face paint interest has always been about silly, the sillier the better! That goes for clowns too, the clown face always seemed like the goofiest, silliest face paint you could possibly put on. One thing led to another and I went from painting my face to buying a clown nose, to the whole deal, costume, paint, wig, gloves, bow tie, shoes, you name it. I think for me the turn-on comes from the willingness to look silly. I've always been very stoic and uptight to a fault. I find it very hard to let my hair down and relax. So, I think it's the fear of being silly in front of other people that gives me a rush. To see someone not only look goofy in front of other people, but to actually want to do it, and enjoy it, is overwhelming to me ... Although most people don't find this stuff sexual and would never know the difference, in my mind I'd be doing something private out in the open. My partner has been wonderful with this. I got up some incredible courage one day and put on a clown nose in front of him and to my surprise he wasn't the least bit put off. I eventually felt him out a bit more here and there and then just told him everything. Since then he's been very supportive and helped me embrace my fetish and the happiness it brings me."

This person noted that his initial sexual arousal dates back (presumably) to childhood and was for face painting rather than clowns. It appears there was a gradual generalization process that changed the sexual focus from face painting to clowns. In addiction terminology, this individual seems to have developed a kind of tolerance over time as the sexual focus went from just buying a clown nose to gradually buying the whole costume to satisfy his sexual needs. The high or buzz came from the silliness associated with wearing clown's clothing, although I am unsure as to whether it is genuinely just the silliness or whether it might be some sort of feeling of being humiliated, but that is pure speculation on my part. Given his partner supported the fetish there is no problem with the behaviour. The fetish only appeared to manifest itself when he wore the clown outfit himself.

Case 2 *(heterosexual male):* "I am a very lucky man. Roughly 10 years ago, I completely opened up to my then girlfriend of a few months, admitting everything to her ... That I loved seeing girls get pied in the face and have buckets of slime dumped on their heads. And that what I promoted as an irrational fear of clowns was to hide the fact that I actually was heavily aroused whenever I saw a female clown. That I really just wanted to dress in baggy pants, wear greasepaint and a big red nose, hurl pies, spank with rubber chickens and have a good silly fuck. She said 'okay'. It was no big deal. Years of repression and guilt and I had nothing to fear. She loved me and was willing to indulge in my fetish sparingly. I felt like the luckiest guy in the world."

As with Case 1, the partner was supportive of the fetish (following an "opening up" conversation) and therefore there is no problem. Interestingly, the person pretended to be afraid of clowns as a way of masking his true feelings and that is something not unusual in the more general fetish literature. The most interesting observation is the fact that there was also a crossover with "pie fetish" (the throwing of pies at people), which is a form of salirophilia (sexual arousal for messiness). The reference to spanking with "rubber chickens" may also suggest at least in part a spanking fetish. The fetish appears to be located in the visual attraction to women in clown's clothing rather than wearing it himself.

> **Case 3** *(bisexual male):* *"I have always had a clown fetish as long as I can remember. Even before I knew what arousal was, or fetishes for that matter, any of it, I have been strangely interested in clowns. I used to think of clowns before I went to sleep at night … I honestly thought it was because I hated clowns and wanted to fight them, but I realize it was the other way around. I would imagine myself at an entire circus surrounded by clowns and going on adventures to fight them … So I don't remember thinking about clowns that much after I was really young until puberty hit … Throughout my teens and beyond, I've fantasized about clowns. I've also always liked both sexes of clowns, male and female. My fetish can work with both, honestly … I've always been into a classical clown look, circus type, hilarious and silly … In my late teens and early adulthood, when the Internet was becoming more common, I would talk to others that had clown feelings like me. It was a shock, at the time, to log online to look up pictures of clowns and suddenly realize that others had your fetish. As tame as my fetish is, it honestly takes up the primary desire of my sexuality, and to meet others that felt the same way it was cool. Clowning also introduced me to the pie fetish, which I like as well but honestly, it's the clowning that does it for me."*

This person's clown fetish again began at an early age and appears to have grown through thinking about clowns before going to sleep every night (and therefore sexualizing the content even if the individual was unaware that the content was sexual). There appears to be what Sigmund Freud would call a latent period, the years before puberty, when the sexualization of clowns all but disappeared only to reappear in his teenage years (i.e., an adolescent "awakening"). Like Case 2, it appears the individual was sexually aroused by watching clowns irrespective of gender rather than dressing up as a clown himself. Also like Case 2, he mentioned an associated "pie fetish" (i.e., a possible salirophilia crossover fetish). He describes his love of clowns as his "primary desire" indicating that it may well be a true fetish rather than just a strong sexual liking for clowns.

On the whole, coulrophilia seems to originate from a young age, is mostly male based and arguably appears to have associative pairings from this young age between sexual arousal and clowns, resulting in classically conditioned behavioural responses (i.e., sexual attraction to clowns). There also appeared to be overlaps with other sexually paraphilic behaviours (i.e., salirophilia in the form of "pie fetishes" and transvestic dressing up). Although not mentioned in these cases, Halloween appears to be a time that some enjoyed as an annual opportunity to engage in their preferred sexual behaviour. There did not seem to be any association between coulrophilia and sexual orientation as even among such a small number of cases there were homosexual, bisexual and heterosexual orientations. Whether any empirical or clinical research into coulrophilia will ever be carried out remains debatable, but these few cases at least suggest the paraphilia may exist.

Crush fetishism

Crush fetishism is a sexual fetish in which an individual derives sexual arousal from watching or fantasizing about someone of the opposite sex crushing items (e.g., toys, cigarettes, mobile phones and laptops), food (e.g., fruit), small animals and insects in extreme cases and/or being stepped on, sat upon and/or crushed by a person. The latter variant is a type of sexual masochism. There are also dedicated phone sex services that cater for crush fetishism suggesting overlaps with telephonicophilia (i.e., getting sexually aroused by telephone sex talk).

Another similar fetish appears to be "trampling fetishism". This comprises paraphilic fantasies and/or practises of being trampled underfoot by another person and is found in both homosexual and heterosexual activities. As trampling often produces pain, trampling fetishes are considered a variant of sadomasochism.

Crush fetishism has also been associated with formicophilia, a paraphilia in which individuals derive sexual arousal from insects. For instance, Pearson (1991) describes a fetishistic behaviour in which people get sexual pleasure from watching insects, worms and spiders being squashed, particularly men watching women doing it. If the fantasy or behaviour involves giant people it is often considered a variant of macrophilia (i.e., a paraphilia in which individuals derive sexual arousal from a fascination with giants and/or a sexual fantasy involving giants). As Biles (2004) notes in an essay on crush fetishists:

> "Among the many obscure and bizarre sects of fetishism, few remain so perplexing or so underexamined as that of the 'crush freaks'. At the cutting edge of the edgy world of sexual fetishistic practices, the crush freaks are notorious for their enthusiasm for witnessing the crushing death of insects and other, usually invertebrate, animals, such as arachnids, crustaceans, and worms. More specifically, crush freaks are sexually aroused by the sight of an insect exploded beneath the pressure of a human foot – usually, but not necessarily, a relatively large and beautiful female foot."

Crush fetishes in relation to insects and animals comprise two types: hard crush and soft crush. Soft-crush fetishes are apparently more common and typically refer to the crushing of invertebrates (e.g., spiders, beetles and worms). Hard-crush fetishes typically refer to the crushing of larger (vertebrate) animals (e.g., reptiles, birds and mammals). Some crush fetishists are very specific about how they like to see insects and/or animals crushed. Some prefer the person doing the crushing to be wearing particular types of footwear, such as high heels and flip-flops, or no footwear at all.

Hard-crush fetish videos have attracted worldwide media attention and have prompted criminal actions in a number of jurisdictions. For instance, back in August 2011 police in the Philippines arrested Vicente Ridon and Dorma Ridon, a married couple who had filmed dozens of "crush fetish" videos (a.k.a. "animal snuff" films). These films showed six female teenagers (aged between 12 and 18 years) torturing and killing animals before being posted onto online "crush fetish" websites all over the world. The case was initiated by PETA (People for the Ethical Treatment of Animals) who helped track the couple down over the course of a year's detective work. The Ridons were eventually charged with animal cruelty, child abuse and human trafficking.

This is by no means an isolated incident and is not the product of mentally ill people. In April 2012 in Milan a 40-year-old mother of three Anna B was given a €5,400 fine and a 4-month suspended prison sentence after being found guilty of being sexually aroused by crushing animals while wearing stockings and stiletto heels. She had posted dozens of online videos of herself crushing rabbits, mice and chicks. Following the banning of crush videos in 2010 this case was the first prosecution under the new law in Italy. Paolo Iosca, the lawyer representing the Italian Anti-Vivisection League, said:

> "This case was brought to our attention following a tip-off to us and we acted immediately to bring this woman to justice. The videos she posted showed her semi-naked, wearing tights and high heels and crushing innocent animals such as rabbits, chicks and mice to death. They were particularly crude and offensive. This woman, who is a mother of three children, was clearly enjoying herself as she was slaughtering these animals and filming their agony."

The legality of erotic crush films and the actual practice of crushing animals vary by region and country. For instance, China does not have any animal cruelty laws and, therefore, no criminal acts are being committed in that jurisdiction. In the UK, crush videos are illegal. However, as far as I have been able to ascertain there are currently no laws forbidding the crushing of insects in any country. In November 2010 a Chinese crush fetish video was posted online featuring a young attractive girl sitting on a rabbit and crushing it to death. In a journalistic investigation by China Hush an online user with the pseudonym "Sound of Heaven" said that:

> "People who like crush fetish are not promoting and encouraging violence and murdering people, but it is an extension to [sadomasochism] a state, crushed to death by a woman, a spirit of sacrificing oneself for her."

Other similar videos including the abusing and killing of cats and dogs have also appeared online. Although these acts of killing could be viewed as acts of zoosadism because of the sexual element, the person doing the killing of the animals is usually paid for his/her "services" and does not appear to get any sexual satisfaction from the act itself. It is the person watching hard-crush videos who typically derives the sexual pleasure from it.

There has been little empirical research into either crush fetishism or zoosadism and most academically published papers are case reports. One of these is my own case study (Griffiths, 2013) of "Brad" whose main paraphilia was eproctophilia (i.e., sexual arousal by flatulence). Brad was also a crush fetishist. Brad claimed he had had this fetish "since birth" and went on to explain further:

> "[I have another fetish that] I am not proud of, but it exists and may help your study. I have a crush fetish, which is essentially arousal from seeing people step on objects or insects. This particular one has had a lot of bad publicity. As for this one, I can't tell you where it originated. I remember rubbing myself in my crib as a baby to such thoughts, leading me to believe I may have literally been born with it. I could have been no older than 2½ years old. Keep in mind, these are very primal memories which are mostly a blur. All I recall is that around the time of those memories, I would also rub myself to the thought of someone stepping on an insect, or sometimes a machine

made to crush up children like myself. Come to think of it, that last one may have been caused by seeing an apple cider press as a toddler. I also seem to recall that, and being afraid of it because of how it 'hurt' the apples."

I also asked Brad if he thought there was any connection between his crush fetish and his eproctophilia. He responded that, if there was any connection, then it concerned "the idea of the duality" in that he would not expect to see a woman fart in front of him and, similarly, he would not expect a woman to kill an insect in front of him for no real reason. In relation to his crush fetish he also reported:

"It's my oldest fetish with no known origin, and I like it for about the same reason as eproctophilia. Maybe that I also disliked seeing people kill bugs as a kid, while also finding it arousing. I was quite the pacifist. Also, when I first discovered ejaculation, I made the connection that ejaculating was somewhat like when a bug is stepped on. I thought about a bug squirting under pressure and then I would do the same. May or may not be relevant, but it was a connection I made as a kid."

Clearly, this is just one case study and Brad is unlikely to be representative of the entire eproctophile and/or crush fetish community. Further research is needed to assess the extent to which the case study I reported is representative and whether the etiological and developmental pathways are more complex than I initially described in my case study account.

Cynophilia

Shaffer and Penn (2006) developed a comprehensive paraphilia classification system. They listed various types of zoophilia and report that cynophilia referred to sexual arousal from having sex with dogs and that canophilia was sexual arousal from dogs. I made the assumption the latter means that the person being aroused may not have had actual sexual contact with a dog.

Jamison and Morel (2012) reported the case of Eric Antunes, a 29-year-old man who was accused of having oral sex with a dog. As it turned out the Pinellas-Pasco State Attorney's Office in Florida, USA "declined to pursue a charge of animal cruelty under the state's new bestiality law," but it was confirmed that Antunes, an employee at the Pinellas County Humane Society, had six photographs on his mobile phone of himself performing sexual acts with his girlfriend's three-legged dog Ruby. The case was dropped because there is no law in Florida forbidding people having oral sex with animals. Jamison and Morel (2012) further reported that:

"Assistant State Attorney Beverly Andringa said her office declined to prosecute Antunes for bestiality because, out of the six photographs found on his cellphone, only one would meet the strict criteria of the statute. Officials also aren't certain when all the photos were taken. Some might have pre-dated the new law."

In Georgia, USA 19-year-old Bernard Archer was arrested after being caught on camera having sexual intercourse with pitbull dogs and charged with two counts of bestiality. A newspaper report said that:

> "Home owners witnessed a young black male having sexual intercourse with two dogs. WGCL-TV reports that Archer was hired to clean the cages of several pitbulls by Dr. Cathryn Lafayette, a local resident who owned the dogs. [On] Saturday [March 3], Lafayette was woken up from a nap by the Newton County police, who informed her of Archer's crimes against her animals. Though initially skeptical of the claims, she was convinced when authorities showed her video evidence."

I mention these cases by way of making it clear that sexual contact between human beings and dogs not only occurs but is reported on a fairly regular basis. There are also cases of what Aggrawal (2009a) classes "cynophilia by proxy" in which one person forces another, typically a man forcing his wife or partner, to have sex with a dog:

> "In R v. Tierney (1990) 12 Cr. App. R(S) 216, the defendant took photographs of his wife having intercourse with his Alsatian dog for his own continuing satisfaction. In this case, 3 months' imprisonment was given to the accused, but not to his wife because she consented to perform the act in desperation in order to retain her husband's affections."

Zoophiles may well otherwise be kind and respect the dogs concerned. However, since animals cannot give informed consent such sexual activity is in my view morally wrong.

Dacryphilia

Dacryphilia (a.k.a. "dacrylagnia") is a paraphilia in which an individual derives sexual arousal from the sight of tears or seeing someone crying. However, some definitions appear to have widened the definition of dacryphilia to include (i) sexual arousal from someone displaying strong emotion and/or (ii) sexual arousal from the emotional release that accompanies crying (i.e., an "emotional catharsis").

When I wrote my first blog on this topic there was nothing in the academic literature. However, it was clear that this paraphilia existed given the dedicated online websites, such as Sad Little Girls. Based on what I found on online websites, I speculated there were two fundamentally different types of dacryphiles that I called (i) sadistic dacryphiles and (ii) voyeuristic dacryphiles.

Sadistic dacryphiles: Watching someone else cry is not something that people want to see as we do not usually gain gratification from seeing others psychologically suffer. Therefore, one particular paraphilia with which dacryphilia is closely associated is that of sexual sadism. Here, the dominant partner's sexual arousal often results from seeing a submissive who may or may not be a sexual masochist in emotional distress. The emotional distress may result from psychological humiliation by the sexual sadist who may verbally taunt the submissive into crying. It is the elicitation of the tearful response by the submissive that results in the greatest sexual arousal for the dominant partner. In extreme cases sexual sadists may physically torture their partners into crying. For sadists, psychological reinforcement lies in the power and control they have over their submissive and compliant partner (referred to as "power play"). Knowing that their direct (verbal and/or physical) actions have directly caused someone to break down and cry is highly rewarding and reinforcing to the sadistic dacryphile.

Voyeuristic dacryphiles: There are also non-sadistic dacryphiles who get sexual pleasure by being a third-party bystander who watches "power play" leading to the submissive breaking down and crying. There are also voyeuristic dacryphiles who are sexually aroused by someone crying whatever the cause.

The origins of dacryphilia are unknown, but are likely to be rooted in early conditioning experiences both classical and operant. As with other paraphilic behaviours, it would also appear that some people are very specific in how they are sexually aroused by someone crying. As one male confessing to an online fetish discussion group said:

> "I'm turned on by women who cry with their bottom lip stuck out. I've had this weird fetish since I was five. When the bottom lip sticks out, gets bulgy or curls downwards and the chin goes upwards and wrinkles – that's an immediate turn-on. I've come across dacryphiliacs who are turned on by tears or by submission – but for me, it's about the bottom lip. I'm starting to think I'm the only person on this planet with this problem."

This quote clearly shows how very specific the sexual focus in dacryphilia can be (i.e., crying having to be accompanied by a protruding bottom lip). This would certainly be indicative of a powerful classically conditioned response as the stimuli for sexual arousal are so very specific. Given there was nothing in the academic literature on this paraphilic behaviour, the area (if you excuse the bad pun) was crying out for research. I have now published a number of academic papers on this specific paraphilia (Greenhill and Griffiths, 2014, 2015, 2016, 2022).

The potential contrast between sadomasochistic and emotional dacryphilic interests is particularly fascinating as both of these interests occupy differing and almost opposing aspects of human sexual experience. Likewise, the potential existence of sadistic vs masochistic and active vs passive interests within dacryphilia suggest that it is a non-normative sexual interest with enough variety for an interesting dataset and analysis.

The most interesting study I have published comprised interviews with eight dacryphiles (Greenhill and Griffiths, 2015). The sample comprised six females and two males aged 20 to 50 years (five from the USA and the others from the UK, Romania and Belgium). We proposed a new typology of dacryphilia based on these interviews. Our participants were recruited via recruitment posts on one specific dacryphilia forum (i.e., CryingLovers), one general fetish forum (i.e., FetLife) and one BDSM forum (i.e., collarchat.com). Based on the interviews, the three types of dacryphile we identified were (i) compassionate dacryphiles, (ii) dominant/submissive dacryphiles and (iii) "curled lip" dacryphiles. The possibility that dacryphilia represents an extension of normative human behaviour towards crying and tears raises the question of why some individuals might find sexual arousal in crying and tears.

Damsel-in-distress fetishes

While researching sexual sadism, sexual masochism and knismolagnia (all examined later in the book) I kept coming across references to damsel-in-distress (DiD) fetishes all of which involve the basic concept of a helpless female victim who may (but sometimes may not) need rescuing from a captor and/or some kind of perilous situation.

It is mostly males who have DiD fetishes, which can be very specific and include such things as (i) kidnap and rescue fetishes (sexual pleasure from watching or engaging with women being kidnapped and/or rescued from potentially life-threatening scenarios where they are cuffed, bound and/or controlled by another person or persons), (ii) tickle bondage fetishes (sexual pleasure from watching or tickling women while they are tied up), (iii) quicksand fetishes (sexual pleasure from watching women sink in quicksand) and (iv) pedal pumping and cranking fetishes (sexual pleasure from watching women stranded in their cars with repeated pressing of the gas pedal and revving up – which also has elements of foot fetishism – while turning the key in an attempt to get the engine to start).

A quick internet search reveals there is a dedicated DiD fan community who host a range of online forums and discussion groups, such as the Staked Damsels website "for anyone who finds burning at the stake, bondage and damsels in distress erotic" or the Danger Island website where "you'll find all your 'damsel in distress' fetish needs met", as well as a wide range of YouTube videoclips (type "pedal pump cranking" into an online search engine and you will see what I mean). There are also websites that provide lists of films and television shows that feature DiD scenarios, such as the 1981 made-for-television film *Terror Among Us* and links to YouTube clips just showing the relevant DiD video capture (a.k.a. "vidcap") scenes from films (a.k.a. "Didcaps" by the DiD fan community).

It remains to be seen whether any academic or clinical research ever gets carried out on this particular subdomain of sadomasochism, but I will not be holding my breath.

Delphinophilia

Brenner (2009) wrote a book (*Wet Goddess*) which has to rank as one of the strangest books ever written about zoophilic activity. It is based on his 9-month sexual relationship with a dolphin held captive at the Floridaland Amusement Park. Back in 1970, while studying at the New College of Florida, Sarasota, Brenner had a relationship with a dolphin called Dolly. Brenner claims the dolphin made the first moves in their relationship.

In an interview with the Huffington Post (McCormack, 2011), Brenner said that Dolly became "more and more aggressive. She would thrust herself against me. I found that extraordinarily erotic. It's like being with a tiger or a bear. This is an animal that could kill you in two seconds if it wanted to." Brenner claimed the relationship ended when Dolly was moved to an oceanarium following the closure of the amusement park in Florida where Dolly was being held captive. In this interview Brenner further added:

> "I had every intention of going to visit the dolphin when I got back to the South, but it didn't work out that way. I learned the hard way that dolphins are chattel, and much more emotionally vulnerable than I had ever imagined … Some people find it hard to imagine that I wasn't abusing the animal. They didn't see me interacting with the dolphin. They weren't there. These creatures basically have free will. What is repulsive about a relationship where both partners feel and express love for each other? I know what I'm talking about here because after we made love, the dolphin put her snout on my shoulder, embraced me with her flippers and we stared into each other's eyes for about a minute. This was not some dog trying to hump my leg, okay. This was a 400-lb wild-born female dolphin. She was an awesome creature … As self-aware mammals, dolphins are capable of making profound emotional attachments to other dolphins and, apparently, to selected humans as well. A dolphin can die of loneliness, of a broken heart, of separation anxiety."

Brenner's story may not be as unique as one might first imagine. In 1991 a 38-year-old Briton named Alan Cooper was accused of masturbating a tamed dolphin called Freddie in front of a number of swimmers in Northumbria, England (McGuigan, 2023). He was charged with performing a "lewd act". At Cooper's trial expert witnesses testified that male dolphins use their penile erections socially as well as sexually. As a consequence, Cooper was acquitted as it could not be proved that the act was sexual.

However, there are a range of websites that give practical advice on how to have sex with a dolphin and how to tell if they want sex, such as the Sexwork site. There are also websites devoted totally to dolphin lovers, such as the Delphinophile site. Furthermore, there are dozens of online confessions about either having sex or wanting to have sex with dolphins on the Beast Forum website. Be warned, though, these are very sexually explicit and all involve zoophilic activity.

So, what do academics have to say about delphinophilia? The most recent studies of zoophilia (i.e., since 2000) have typically collected their data online from non-clinical samples. This has included studies by Andrea Beetz (32 zoophiles), Colin Williams and Martin Weinberg (114 zoophiles) and Hani Miletski (93 zoophiles). In all three studies the most commonly preferred animals were dogs and horses. However, sex with dolphins was not unheard of among these samples.

My own brief look at delphinophilia certainly comes to the conclusion that it exists among a small minority of zoophiles. This has been confirmed by academic researchers in the zoophilia field. However, since animals cannot give informed consent such sexual activity is morally wrong. I am in agreement with Denise Herzing (of the Wild Dolphin Project in the USA) who was reported as saying:

> "Glorifying human sexual interactions with other species is inappropriate for the health and wellbeing of any animal. It puts the dolphin's own health and social behavioral settings at risk."

Dendrophilia

The word "dendrophilia" has now been adopted by some in the sexology field to refer to those who have a fetishistic or paraphilic interest in trees (i.e., individuals who derive sexual pleasure, sexual arousal and/or are sexually attracted to trees). This may involve actual sexual contact with trees and/or venerating them as phallic symbols, something noted by Corsini (1999). Aggrawal (2009a) defines dendrophilia as "arousal from trees or fertility worship of them". However, Pranzarone (2000) writes that it is the love of trees, but categorically states without giving us any reason that "it is not a paraphilia."

A British case of dendrophilia came to light when a 21-year-old Scot named William Shaw received a lifetime ban from Airdrie's Centenary Park for attempting to have sex with one of its trees (with *The Sun* winning the best headline with "Fancy a tree-some?"). He dropped his trousers and underpants and simulated sex with a tree while in the visitor attraction area in September 2009. He was subsequently charged at the town's sheriff court with an act of public indecency. The sheriff (Frank Pieri) released Shaw on bail on the condition that he did not set foot in Centenary Park again. I also feel duty bound to point out that there was also a YouTube video posted in March 2012 showing a very intoxicated woman trying to have sex with a tree. However, as far as I am aware, there is not a single academic or clinical study published on this topic – not even a case study.

Dental brace fetishism

While researching medical fetishism, I came across a number of subforms of medical fetishism including dental brace fetishism. There are certainly dedicated online websites that specialize in dental brace pornography, such as Fetish Braces, Beauty and Braces and E-Hotsex. Be warned, though, these are sexually explicit sites. Most of these sites feature scantily clad and/or naked women with braces, which seems to indicate that such sexual penchants and fetishes are male based. There are also online discussion websites about how having braces affects people's sex lives, such as the Metal Mouth Forum. There are also various online articles about having sex if you wear braces, such as Archwired (no date). The article notes:

> "Having braces doesn't have to mean the end of certain sexual pleasures. It might mean tweaking your technique … or just plain being more careful. In the words of one enlightened Archwired reader, 'practice makes perfect'. And if you decide to abstain … well, as they say, absence … or maybe in this case abstinence … will make it all the fonder until the braces are off."

Given that many dental brace wearers are adolescents it does raise suggestions or at least perhaps some telling questions with paedophilic undertones. Although that is pure speculation on my part, I cannot see this area of fetishistic interest ever being seriously researched in an academic context (but stranger things have happened).

Depilation fetishes

Depilation fetishes involve those who derive sexual pleasure and arousal from lack of body hair. The fetish appears to take many different forms and might include being sexually aroused by (i) the sight of a shaved area of the human body such as a bald pubic area, (ii) the sight of someone actually shaving an area of their body (e.g., their pubic region) and/or (iii) the actual act of shaving someone's body parts. The fetish may overlap with other paraphilias, such as olfactophilia (i.e., deriving sexual arousal and pleasure from specific smells) since those individuals with a depilation fetish may find the odour of shaving cream or aftershave products additionally attractive.

Love (2001) devoted a reasonably large section of her book to sexual depilation and claimed that in some countries the origins of sexual depilation preferences were conditioned by early pre-adolescent experiences. She writes:

> "Shaving or removal of the pubic hair was practiced in Rome, the Middle East, Japan, China, India, and North Africa. Sex in many of these countries began during

pre-pubescence before either partner had developed pubic hair. The male and female became conditioned to respond sexually to bald genitals. Some later in life became impotent at the sight of pubic hair on a partner."

She also referred to the act of pulling out clumps of pubic hair to produce an orgasm in some men. Her research indicated that this particular type of sexual service was offered in Moorish baths in North Africa by women who were skilled at this art.

Love further observed that depilation or shaving is used in sexplay as part of body worship and bondage. She reported that dominant partners "shave their slaves to put them into a psychological role of submission, exposure, humiliation and shame." She also notes that depilation may be necessary when it comes to aesthetics in transvestism, infantilism and/or body painting.

As far as academic research goes I have only managed to find one study that specifically examined depilation practices. Martins *et al.* (2008) compared body hair removal practices among gay and heterosexual men. The authors invited a sample of gay (n = 106) and heterosexual men (n = 228) to participate in a survey assessing "whether they had ever removed their back, buttock or pubic hair, the frequency with which they did so, the methods used and their self-reported reasons for removing this hair." The results showed that most men had engaged in hair removal practices, but that heterosexual men (33%) were much less likely than gay men (63%) to have removed their back and/or buttock hair at least once in their lives. In relation to the removal of pubic hair, heterosexual men (66%) were again much less likely than gay men (82%) to have done so at least once. However, as far as I can ascertain no case studies have been published specifically examining depilation fetishes.

Doll fetishism

Doll fetishism is a type of sexual fetishism in which individuals are sexually aroused and attracted to dolls and/or doll-like objects (e.g., figurines). The attraction can take many different forms and can include one or more of the following: (i) actual sexual contact with a doll, (ii) sexual fantasies involving an animate or inanimate doll, (iii) sexual fantasies about two or more dolls having sex with one another and (iv) sexual fantasies from thoughts about being transformed or transforming someone else into a doll, the latter being part of a wider set of transformation fetishes that also includes furries (i.e., people who identify as anthropomorphic animals) and technofetishists (i.e., people fixated on technology). There is also a virtual form of doll fetishism in which such fantasies can be acted out online and in virtual worlds via self-created doll avatars. In addition, some doll fetish sites feature films and/or animated pictures of humans being sexually gratified by the use of dolls. Such animated films have some crossover with people into toonophilia (i.e., individuals who derive sexual pleasure from cartoon characters). Aggrawal (2009a) noted that doll fetishism can be a transformation fetish:

"Examples are animal transformation, fantasies, and doll fetish ... Doll fetish is a transformation fetish of being transformed into a doll or transforming someone

else into a doll. It is often played out as roleplay between two or more people. One partner – often the female – is dressed to look like a Barbie Doll in shape with bold hair, enhanced breasts, small waist, high heels, and a very revealing outfit made from rubber, latex or spandex."

For doll fetishists the doll in question can be either male or female, but is more often female. For those into female dolls there appears to be a preference for such dolls to have "Barbie"-type figures, long blonde hair, large breasts, ultra-thin waist and shapely buttocks. For adults who dress to look like a doll there are a number of accessories that might have to be used including blonde wigs, padded bras, tight corsets (to minimize waist size), skimpy dresses (typically latex, leather or spandex), buttock pads and a strap-on vagina if the individual is male.

There are also clear sadomasochistic elements for those who wish to transform into a doll (a.k.a. "dollification"). Lewis (2011) not only dealt with "age play" between adults but also included a paragraph on doll fetishes. She wrote that:

"Dollification is about the process of a woman evolving mentally and physically into a 'living doll' and the partners enjoying the process of objectification and transformation. The nature of this interest means it is very much based on a master/slave or dom/sub relationship. The man is known as the owner or dollmaster, as he directs the way the woman transforms into a doll. Accessories include but are not limited to corsets for a tiny waist and accentuated hips, heavy mask-like make-up (if not an actual mask), doll-like wigs, false eyelashes and the use of rubber, vinyl or plastic outfits. The role also requires the woman to have no ability to speak and no free will in how she moves or positions her body, so the dollmaster acts somewhat like a puppetmaster. The doll also commonly shows no emotion, pain or enjoyment during play and is expected to remain silent."

In 1996 life-size sex dolls called "RealDolls" were sold commercially for the first time. Made by Californian company Abyss Creations they are now sold globally and currently cost around $5,000 per doll. RealDolls (as you can guess from the name) are incredibly lifelike thanks to having a PVC skeleton, steel joints, and being covered in lifelike silicone skin. They are advertised as "the state-of-the-art for lifelike human body simulation". They come armed with three "realistic" orifices – mouth, vagina and anus. The company also makes male dolls to order based on what the customer wants. In 2007 the BBC made a really good television documentary directed by Nick Holt called *Guys and Dolls* that followed the lives of four men who lived with RealDolls. Many other types of dolls have been created including Boy Toy and Wicked Real Dolls. In 2001 The Doll Forum, an online discussion site for individuals who use RealDolls, was created (Boiteau, 2011).

Doorknob licking

When I first came across the Art-Sheep website featuring many photographs of young Japanese women licking doorknobs I thought it was some kind of spoof site. Further research revealed it was not a joke. For instance, Ntumy (2013) claims the reason for the existence of such sites was "straightforward" because Japanese pornography censorship laws were so draconian that they obliged Japanese people "to be more creative about what they masturbate to."

A number of online articles claim that the strict censorship laws of Japan have made the country "infamous for using a wide variety of stand-ins" for penises as there is a "crackdown on the depiction of genitalia." This has led to swords, fish, vegetables and tentacles being used as substitute phallic images (Sumitra, 2012; Ashcroft, 2011a, b; Artsheep, 2015). Later in the book there is a separate entry on tentacle erotica fetishism.

Doraphilia

Most definitions of doraphilia are fairly consistent. Aggrawal (2009a) defines doraphilia as the "love of animal fur, leather or skins". Love (2001) writes that doraphilia is "the attraction [is] usually for animal skin or leather, which has been used as clothing throughout human existence. It is considered a fetish when it has to be present during sex." Other online definitions claim doraphilia is "abnormal affection towards fur or skins of animals." I have also come across online definitions that subsume doraphilia to a type of dermophilia in which individuals derive sexual pleasure and arousal from the skin. However, I think it is more logical to view dermophilia as a subtype of doraphilia (or not a subtype at all if it does not include the love of animal skin). Somewhat confusingly, Love (2001) in her account of doraphilia devotes much of the entry to the sexual aspects of human skin rather than animal skin.

The wearing of leather is, of course, commonplace in many sexual practices, such as sexual sadism and sexual masochism. In fact, it has arguably become uniform or even stereotypical, such as "The Gimp" character in the film *Pulp Fiction*. As Love (2001) notes in her encyclopaedia entry:

> *"Erotic leather apparel can be purchased at some lingerie and leather shops or ordered from Europe. Leather jock straps (some with chrome studs), bikini panties with zippered crotches, body suits, bras, corsets, dresses, skirts, pants exposing the rear, costumes, and accessories are all available."*

She also speculates about the psychology of wearing leather and fur and mentions Harlow's (1958) classic study into maternal attachment on rhesus monkeys as evidence at least in part for her claims:

> *"The feel and smell of leather gives many people a feeling of power. Some explain this as subconsciously taking on the character of the animal with whose skin they cloak themselves. This was a common belief of holy men during their ancient religious ceremonies. The Roman emperor Nero dressed in an animal skin and then emulated the beast's ferocious behavior as he sexually assaulted the people he had tied to stakes. An explanation for the continued appeal of leather or fur is that some people feel secure and nurtured by being wrapped in skin, a sort of surrogate mother effect. Clinical studies showed that rhesus monkeys who had their mothers replaced by inanimate objects responded better or clung to the ones that were wrapped in some type of fur."*

For sexual leather enthusiasts the colour black appears to be especially important. Although I have carried out research on the importance of colour in gambling (e.g., Griffiths, 2010), I have never thought about it from a sexual clothing perspective. Again, examining the paraphilia literature it could perhaps be argued that doraphilia has overlaps with some types of zoophilia. Aggrawal (2011a) proposed a new classification of zoophilia comprising 10 different types of zoophile based on their primary erotic focus one of which is what Aggrawal calls "fetishistic zoophiles". These are individuals who keep various animal parts, especially fur, that they then use as an erotic stimulus and a crucial part of their sexual activity. Such individuals have been reported in the clinical literature including the case of a woman (Randall *et al.*, 1990) who used the tongue of a deer as her primary masturbatory aid, which the authors described as a case of "xenolingual autoeroticism".

Ear fetishes

Most of the body parts examined in this book on fetishes are arguably devoid of any sexual sensitivity and would not be described as erogenous zones. However, the earlobe is a sensitive area because it contains many nerve endings. Paget (2002) notes that one of the most stimulating spots on the female body is "the pyramid from the front and back of the shoulder blades, up to the apex of the ear lobe. It's a fabulous area to play with, second only to a woman's mouth in terms of getting her motor running."

As far as I am aware there has never been any academic research on ear fetishism. The only remotely scholarly thing I learned from researching this topic was that "gynotikolobomassophilia" refers to sexual pleasure from nibbling on a woman's earlobe (Aggrawal, 2009a). According to the One Look webpage at least four websites list this as a *bona fide* sexual activity, although other definitions include slight variations, such as "a proclivity for nibbling on women's earlobes" and "a love of biting a female's earlobes".

There is wide variation in what the arousing factor is. It may be concerned with either the shape or size of the ear, a particular part of the ear and/or something that adorns the ear. Some of the fetishes may be subtypes of other fetishes (e.g., piercing fetishes) rather than a true body part fetish. Moreover, most of the fetishes appear to involve heterosexuals, although one account did mention being aroused by ears from someone of the same sex. However, ear fetishism can be experienced by both men and women. Finally, there appear to be other by-products of sexual earplay that may also be arousing (e.g., the taste of earwax – see next section).

Earwax obsession and fetishes

Brown (2008) investigated ridiculous and obscure facts by typing various phrases into Google to discover what came back as the Number 1 result, something he termed "the completely pointless Google experiment". One of the phrases he typed in was "What is the weirdest earwax story ever?" He writes:

> "Now I'm not one of these people that have a fetish for earwax (and yes, they DO exist!) but this seemed like a rather innocuous question. According to the #1 result on Google, it's using earwax as a remedy for cold sores, as found on the Remedicated website, under '15 of the weirdest home remedies as folk treatments ever'."

In Japan they have a specific word *mimikaki* to describe the act of picking earwax out of one's or someone's ears. Moreover, I read that the removal of earwax in Japan is often done in the context of lovers' grooming customs and rituals. One website went so far as to claim that "as with practically every aspect of Japanese culture, *mimikaki* is often fetishized." The *Sportsman's Daily* (2010) claimed that Bill Belichick, head coach of the American football team New England Patriots, had an earwax fetish. He is reported to have said:

> "I'm into Q-Tips. Any kind of swab basically. I enjoy sniffing earwax. The hard of hearing really get my juices flowing. And I've got a headphone collection that would make the folks at Sony sit up and take notice."

In the same news item, sex therapist Clifton Hamels claimed that ear fetishes are among the rarest of fetishes. There is absolutely no academic or clinical research on the topic of earwax fetishes and there is not likely to be since no problems seem to be associated with such behaviour.

Edgeplay (extreme sexual behaviour)

In this book I examine a wide variety of different, but potentially dangerous sexual fetishes and paraphilias including sexual masochism, autoerotic asphyxiation (breathplay/hypoxyphilia), enema play (klismaphilia), scatplay (coprophilia), watersports (urophilia) and electricity play (electrophilia). All these sexual behaviours could arguably be classed as edgeplay. The online Urban Dictionary defines edgeplay as "sexual play that is very extreme in nature. Said to be on the edge of safety and sometimes even sanity. Can be very dangerous if not practiced correctly. [Examples include] breathplay, bloodplay, humiliation play, total power exchange (TPE), [and] rape roleplay."

Aggrawal (2009a) noted that edgeplay is dangerous in many different ways as the activities may involve (i) increased risk of spreading disease (e.g., through cutting or bloodplay), (ii) psychological danger (e.g., humiliation play, incest fantasies and rape roleplay), (iii) challenging social taboos (e.g., ageplay, scat fetishism and racial slurs) and (iv) even permanent harm or death (e.g., gunplay and breathplay). Such activities can be done alone, with a partner or with a group of people. From what I have been told anecdotally and read online, edgeplay enthusiasts claim they know the human body better than most medical professionals. They further claim to exercise as much safety as is humanly possible when going to the point of near death and then resuscitating themselves (London Fetish Fair, 2014).

White (2012) confirmed in one of the few articles on edgeplay that what is considered "edgy" has changed over the past three decades. She claimed that in the 1980s and 1990s sexual activities, such as scatplay, ageplay, puppyplay and suspension by skin hook piercings, were not allowed at BDSM sex conventions. However, all of these can now be found at such events. This is because "attitudes about what should be forbidden seem to have shifted thanks to people getting better [sexually] educated." Much of this has run in tandem with the rise of the internet where there are now numerous "how to" guides on almost every type of "adult" sexual activity as well as articles on sexual ethics. One of the interviewees for her article (Madeline) describes edgeplay somewhat paradoxically as "consensual non-consent" where activities like "rapeplay" do not involve "safewords", typically used by BDSM practitioners to signal the activity to cease. Madeline "talks lovingly" about the rapeplay between her and her husband and claims it keeps "their long-term relationship tender and fresh and, likewise, their trusting relationship allows them to do rapeplay."

Electrophilia

As noted earlier in the book, the first article I ever got published on paraphilic behaviour was an article on autoerotic deaths (Griffiths, 1999a) and featured the cases of 10 people who had died in strange sexual circumstances. One of the cases was that reported by Sivaloganathan (1981).

The case involved a 36-year-old gay male who was an ex-television engineer. He was found dead with a wire cradle enclosing his scrotum attached to another loop of wire (with the end folded over) inserted into his anus. Some researchers writing on this topic have noted that rectal application of electricity is a common practice for obtaining semen from bulls and may be the basis behind this uncommon method of masturbation. The wires were connected to two terminals that supplied electricity to the loudspeaker within the television set. When switched on these wires carried a current of 0.6 amps at 2.2 volts (a quarter of the current needed to light a small torch). The dead man was found with two significant injuries. The first was on the right side of his face (entrance mark of the current) and the second was over the left side of his scrotum (where the loop of wire had been). While masturbating, one of the wires had broken off resulting in a cessation of stimulating activity. It was assumed the man must have looked inside the back of the open television set where his face came into contact with an exposed metal cap that zapped 2,500 volts through him. The metal cap was the only live part of the television set and it was this that killed him. A similar case was reported in Klintschar et al. (1998) who noted:

> "A plausible reconstruction of the accident involves attachment of one electrode to the anus and accidental touching of the other electrode with hand and chest when attempting to attach it to the penis. Death was caused by myocardial fibrillation. Both the cable and pornographic literature were obviously hidden by the parents of the deceased to conceal the actual cause of death."

Schott et al. (2003) reported an accidental electrocution during autoeroticism. This case involved an 18-year-old male who was found dead by his brother in his bedroom wearing two brassieres. The authors reported that:

> "Two wet green terry cloths were under the brassiere cups, connected to the house current via two metal washers and a bifid electrical cord. Literature depicting nude women was found near the victim. Autopsy revealed second-degree and third-degree burns of the mammary regions. Death was attributed to accidental self-electrocution."

I mention these three cases by way of introduction to electrophilia. Both Aggrawal (2009a) and Love (2001) define electrophilia as "sexual pleasure and arousal from electricity (or electric stimulus)". Greenspan (2011) briefly looked at the death in 2008 of Kirsten Taylor who died as a result of electrophilic sexplay (death by electric nipple clamps). As Greenspan reported in his online paper:

> "When 29-year-old Kirsten Taylor of Craley, Pennsylvania, died from electrocution, her husband Toby initially told the cops she'd been shocked by her hair dryer. This was not true. He'd later admit that they were into weird sexual behaviors. The night she died, they'd put electric clamps on her nipples and Toby was administering shocks to her by turning on and off a power strip … Something went wrong and one of the shocks killed her. Which was a surprise since he said they'd 'been engaging in electric shock sex' for about 2 years."

Her husband Toby Taylor was charged with involuntary manslaughter. All these behaviours have the potential to result in a well-recognized mode of accidental death and come under the general rubric of sexual masochism. Most of what is known about electrophilia is based on published case studies in the forensic pathology literature and is typically based on those who have died from the practice. Little is known about the prevalence of the behaviour either as a standalone masturbatory aid or as part of sadomasochistic sexual play.

Emetophilia

Emetophilia (a.k.a. "vomerophilia") is a rare paraphilia in which individuals are sexually aroused either by self-induced vomiting or watching others vomit (i.e., there is an erotic focus on the regurgitated contents of a person's stomach). More specifically, emetophiliacs are reported to love vomiting on their sexual partners. This practice is sometimes referred to as a "Roman shower" based on the often-quoted stories of Romans throwing up between courses so that they could eat even more, and Roman "vomitoriums".

Adams (2002) highlighted what vomitoriums really were. Vomitoriums existed but were actually passageways in amphitheatres that opened into a tier of seats from below or behind. Adams claims that "the vomitoria deposited mobs of people into their seats and afterward disgorged them with equal abruptness into the streets – whence therefore, presumably, the name." Adams goes on to say that although the Romans were no strangers to vomiting, they never did so on purpose. Vomiting does appear to have been part of the fine-dining experience, but was not done between courses to make room for more food.

To my knowledge, there is only one academic paper in the sex literature on the topic. This was by the renowned American psychiatrist and psychoanalyst Robert Stoller. Stoller (1982) claimed it to be "a previously unreported aberration". Although Stoller claims that vomiting paraphilias can occur in both males and females, the three case studies he outlined were all female. He suggested that emetophilia may manifest itself in a variety of ways (real vs imagined; self vs others; facilitative vs obligatory).

If individuals have a sexual attraction to the vomit itself (rather than the vomiting process), then the diagnosis would be fetishism.

The first case described a woman who did not actually vomit herself, but claimed she could reach orgasm "by imagining someone vomiting in a hard, humiliating fashion." The second woman experienced an orgasm every time she vomited. The third woman said that "vomiting for me is like an orgasm in that I'm tensed, I feel the intense flood of good feelings almost continually throughout the vomiting and experience relief and quiet warmth in my body when I'm finished. It is not identical to an orgasm. I do not feel it intensely in my genitals alone, but I do feel it there as well as the rest of my body and in my mouth."

Stoller (1982) noted the problem with this particular paraphilia is that the accounts are not based on those requiring treatment and that the stories take on an almost mythic-like quality rather than being "true-to-life". He went on to say that "concentrating on exact, naturalistic data collecting would show us how much we do not know ... erotic impulses are a never-ending source of ingenious, even wondrous constructions [and] almost every object or body function can be eroticized."

No one knows empirically how widespread the practice is and whether it is restricted to people from specific countries.

Eproctophilia

Olfactophilia (a.k.a. "osmolagnia", "osphresiolagnia" and "ozolagnia") is a paraphilia in which an individual derives sexual pleasure from smells and odours. Given the large body of research on olfaction it should not be surprising that in some cases there should be an association with sexual behaviour. The erotic focus is most likely to relate to body odours of a sexual partner including genital odours.

One bizarre subtype of olfactophilia is eproctophilia. This refers to a condition in which people are sexually attracted to flatulence. Therefore, eproctophiles are said to spend an abnormal amount of time thinking about flatulence and have recurring intense sexual urges and fantasies involving flatulence. There are also examples of this practice on sites on YouTube where some people have uploaded their videos of farting on their partners' faces. Based on such anecdotal evidence it would appear to be the domain of heterosexual men being farted upon by females.

Like most paraphilias, eproctophilia appears to be found mainly among men. More specifically, anecdotal evidence suggests it is mainly found among heterosexual males who are particularly attracted to female flatulence. The accounts that I initially came across suggested that farts are typically targeted at the face, but sometimes more specifically at the mouth, the ear or the nose. Some claim it is a "softer form" of coprophilia in which people are sexually aroused by faeces. Treatment for eproctophilia is generally not sought unless in some way it becomes problematic for the person. It appears that the majority of eproctophiles accept their fetish, particularly as there are no published treatment case studies in the sexology literature. Somewhat unsurprisingly, it may be the case that men who have this type of fetish cannot get their partners to engage in it, even though they are in a stable relationship.

However, in one of my most infamous published case studies (Griffiths, 2013), I reported the first ever academic case study on this topic, which concerned a 22-year-old single man "Brad" (a pseudonym) from Illinois, USA. Brad first contacted me after he had read one of my blogs on eproctophilia. I asked Brad about his first experience(s) of eproctophilia. He claimed that, compared with other eproctophiles who had "colourful first experiences", his experience was "a bit more tame than most, which is disappointing in a way." Brad recalled that in middle school he had a crush on a particular girl. He thought "she was the most beautiful thing [he] had ever seen." When talking with his friends, Brad recalled that one of them mentioned that the girl he had a crush on had farted in her science class. As Brad said:

"This blew my mind. Prior to that, I'd never really considered it. I knew by simple biology that girls farted, but hearing that the girl I had been fawning over was capable of such a thing sparked a strange interest in me."

Brad first engaged in an eproctophile act at around the age of 16 or 17 years. He was with a male friend and up to that point he had considered himself as heterosexual. However, this changed when he heard his male friend fart in front of him. Brad recalled:

"It was rather appealing in sound, and I found myself fixating on it. At first, I didn't want to admit I was into his farting, but eventually I decided to experiment. I set up a bet at some point and intentionally lost, with the wager being the right to fart in the loser's face for a week. I continued to lose such bets once every few weeks for about 2 years."

I asked about his thoughts surrounding eproctophilia. He claimed to "enjoy everything about it" now that he had experienced it directly:

"I'm not sure how graphic you would like the details to be, but I have had my face farted on by both men and women, at point blank range. I like the sound and the smell. The worse, the better. In terms of sound, I prefer a deep bubbling sound. In terms of smell, I like acrid sulfur. I prefer the farter to be clothed. I don't particularly like seeing the anus open. It's not revolting to me, I just prefer fabric for three reasons. First, the sound tends to be better with fabric, particularly jeans or nylons. Second, the smell lingers in cloth, whereas in the nude it is a relatively quick blast of smell. Third, I like the look of butt cheeks better when they are defined by fabric."

I asked why he preferred sulphurous farts. He said that:

"The more disgusting, the more I like it as it heightens the sense of duality. The more disgusting the fart and the prettier the lady, the more of a schism it is between the societal expectation and the reality. As for men, it's simply more dominating for it to be a really gross fart than a mild poot."

I asked Brad whether he was more sexually aroused when engaged in eproctophile sexual activity than when engaged in "normal" sex. He then said he might be "technically asexual" as he had no desire for actual sex (as he preferred masturbation to sexual intercourse). I further questioned him about the extent to which he considered eproctiphile acts as masochistic. He responded:

"Sometimes one of my more common fantasies is receiving a fart as a reward for completing a task. I play videogames, for instance, and one includes me helping a girlfriend solve a puzzle in a game. Then, while still playing, she tells me to get ready for my reward and lets one rip. There's an idea of subservience, not necessarily masochism. An idea of being there without being the focal point, where she lets me smell her farts and rub her feet and cuddle up and such, without fussing too much over me. I enjoy all aspects, really, from the S/M standpoint in which someone dominates me by farting on me, to the subservient aspect of being like a pet or article of furniture in which she isn't particularly dominating, just coexisting, to the aspect of dominance for myself in which I learn her closely guarded secret of what her farts sound and smell like."

One of the more interesting things that came from interviewing Brad was his forthrightness on what he believed about eproctophilia and other people's perceptions of it. Brad's account of his early eproctophile experiences are suggestive of behavioural conditioning and/or sexual imprinting. In this case it is classical conditioning where being sexually aroused by an attractive woman is paired with something that is not inherently sexual (i.e., flatulence). It then starts to become an erotic focus in and of itself. Brad also had very specific criteria for the behaviour to be sexually arousing (i.e., the person had to fart while fully clothed as it sounded better, the smell was longer lasting, and the farts themselves had to be acrid smelling).

Brad saw clear similarities between his interest in eproctophilia and being sexually aroused by watching females defecate. He specifically noted his coprophilic tendencies in his desire to watch women on the toilet. The co-occurrence of Brad's eproctophilia and elements of sexual masochism, such as deliberately losing a bet resulting in Brad being farted upon all week by his male friend, demonstrates that the behaviour has other paraphilic elements. Brad mentioned the sadomasochistic elements of the eproctophilic behaviour a number of times.

Erotic wrestling fetishes

In a later entry on sthenolagnia (i.e., sexual pleasure and arousal from "muscle worship") I mentioned an overlap with erotic wrestling. In fact, Love (2001) specifically refers to sthenolagnia in her entry on "wrestling" for erotic purposes. If you type in "wrestling fetish" to an online search engine, the first dozen or so pages display hundreds of dedicated websites that feature pornographic videoclips of erotic wrestling.

With regards to sthenolagnia and muscle worshippers I noted that such individuals can derive sexual arousal from simply touching people with highly visible muscles, typically a fitness instructor, bodybuilder or wrestler. The various tactile activities that can facilitate sexual pleasure include rubbing, massaging, kissing, licking and/or other more diverse activities including lifting, carrying and engaging in wrestling moves. A paper by Slade (1984) was the first academic paper I located to even mention erotic wrestling fetishes. Slade examined the history of violence in hardcore pornographic films. The reference is only a passing one about film content and noted:

"Men 'punish' a female for teasing or flirting, for masturbating, or for copulating with another man or woman. Women may spank other women (a bow to the women-wrestling fetish) or humiliate men, taunting their impotence or ordering them to perform acts of submission."

There is some crossover between muscle worship and wrestling fetishes (and appears to have good face validity). However, from everything that I have read there appears to be almost no psychological overlap between wrestling fetishes and mud wrestling as the latter is rooted far more in "wet and messy" fetishism and salirophilia, as opposed to muscle worship and sthenolagnia, although in the absence of empirical data I might be completely wrong. However, as with many paraphiliac and fetishistic behaviours I have examined, nothing is known about the prevalence or etiology of this particular behaviour.

Erotophonophilia

Erotophonophilia (a.k.a. "lust murder") is a paraphilia in which individuals derive sexual pleasure and arousal from murdering (or imagining they are murdering) someone. Many academics in the forensic field refer to such killings as "lust murder". However, there are countless slightly different definitions of sexual murder depending on which academic text you read. For instance, Schlesinger (2004) notes all the following slightly different terms and definitions for sexual killing:

- **Lust murder**: *"The connection between lust and desire to kill and the sadistic crime alone becomes the equivalent of coitus"* (von Krafft-Ebing, 1886). *"A sexual factor is clearly apparent ... or deeper study will sometimes reveal that sexual conflict underlies the act of aggression"* (MacDonald, 1986).
- **Sadistic lust murder**: *"After killing the victim, the murderer tortures, cuts, maims, or slashes the victim ... on parts [of the body] that contain strong sexual significance to him and serves as sexual stimulation"* (De River, 1958).
- **Sadistic murder**: *"Distinguished from sadistic homicide by the involvement of a mutilating attack or displacement of the breasts, rectum or genitals"* (Hazelwood and Douglas, 1980). *"The offender derives the greatest satisfaction from the victim's response to torture"* (Douglas et al., 1992).
- **Sex murder**: *"Murder with evidence or observations that indicate[s] that the murder was sexual in nature"* (Ressler et al., 1986).
- **Sexual murder**: *"The killing may also be closely bound to the sexual element of an attack ... the offender's control of his victim, and her pain and humiliation become linked to his sexual arousal"* (Grubin, 1994).
- **Erotophonophilia**: *"Murder associated with sexual sadism as defined in Diagnostic and Statistical Manual of Mental Disorders"* (Money, 1990b).
- **Sexual homicide**: *"Involves a sexual element (activity) as the basis for the sequence of acts leading to death"* (Douglas et al., 1992).
- **Lust killing**: *"The primary goal is to kill the victim as part of a ritualized attack ... the motivation ... is the enactment of some type of fantasy that has preoccupied him or her for some time"* (Malmquist, 1996).

Erotophonophilia

For many people, erotophonophilia (or whichever definition you care to choose from the list above) is the most heinous of all paraphilias. Erotophonophiles have extreme violent fantasies and typically kill their victims during sex and/or mutilate their victims' sexual organs (the latter of which is usually post mortem). Most erotophonophiles are male, although females with the paraphilia are known to exist. Lust murderers are known to be psychologically and behaviourally different from those who kill out of revenge or anger displacement.

Complete fantasy fulfilment is rarely achieved and the fantasy continually evolves based on experiences with prior victims. This is one of the reasons that behaviour may be repeated continually until they die or are caught by law enforcement agencies. Erotophonophilia may overlap with other paraphilias including necrophilia, sexual sadism and/or sexual cannibalism. Such behaviour may be fuelled by use of extreme pornography and/or psychoactive drug use (e.g., alcohol and cocaine). Unsurprisingly, the group of people most likely to be erotophonophiles are serial killers. Such people utilize sexual torture as a mechanism to degrade, humiliate, subjugate and ultimately control their victims. However, some scholars have argued that not all sex murderers are sadists (see, e.g., Grubin, 1994).

Erotophonophiles typically choose their victims on the basis of sexual attractiveness, although there might be one particular physical attribute that is sexualized by the killer, such as a particular body shape, hair style and skin colour. This is referred to as an erotophonophile's "ideal victim type" (IVT). After a victim has been selected and prior to the killing the erotophonophile may engage in a range of predatory behaviours, such as stalking.

Influential research carried out by Brittain (1970) and followed up by the US Federal Bureau of Investigation (FBI) in the 1990s describes a number of characteristics of typical lust murderers. They are characterized as over-controlled, timid, introverted, sexually inexperienced, highly deviant and having violent sadistic fantasies. However, more recent research has not necessarily supported the early claims made by Brittain. Grubin's (1994) work suggests much of this early work was a composite picture of a lust murderer based more on clinical impressions than systematic research.

One of the most cited studies in the area of lust murder is that by Dietz et al. (1990). They examined 30 sexual sadists most of whom were sexual murderers. They found that the majority were employed white males (75%), married (50%), had a history of homosexuality (43%) and cross-dressed (20%). They further reported that they had parents who had divorced or had marital infidelities (50%), suffered physical abuse (23%), suffered sexual abuse (20%) and abused drugs in addition to being addicted to alcohol (50%). Almost all the sample had planned their offences (93%) and the majority had no prior knowledge of the victim (83%). The victims were typically abducted, held against their will for over 24 hours, blindfolded, bound and gagged. All victims were tortured and were forced to endure oral sex, rape and/or the insertion of foreign objects vaginally. Many subsequent studies have reported similar findings. However, the main problem with many of these studies was that there was no (non-sadistic) control group against which the results could be compared.

Studies carried out by the FBI have reported that sexually sadistic murderers exhibit psychopathy and narcissism. However, other more recent studies have not found any relationships with psychopathy. Therefore, it has been suggested that the FBI samples may represent a particularly extreme group of sadistic sex murderers compared with other published studies. Research by Grubin (1994), comparing 21 men who had murdered women during a sexual attack with 121 rapists who did not kill their victims, found that sexual murderers had significantly higher rates of social isolation and difficulties within sexual relationships. However, sexual murderers and rapists did not differ in their utilization of pornography and deviant sexual fantasy.

Exhibitionism

Exhibitionism typically refers to an intense desire or compulsion to expose sexual parts of the body (i.e., genitals, buttocks and breasts) to unwilling observers in public or semi-public places (Hocken and Thorne, 2017; Murphy and Page, 2008). If the behaviour is antisocial or threatening it is typically defined as indecent exposure and becomes a matter for the law. Non-threatening exposure of sexual body parts, such as women showing their breasts during Mardi Gras, is usually termed "flashing" as opposed to indecent exposure. However, there is a whole range of different terms used to describe various exhibitionist acts including (in alphabetical order):

- **Anasyrma**: Typically refers to the lifting of a skirt or dress by a woman when not wearing any knickers and exposing her genitals.
- **Candaulism**: Specifically refers to individuals who expose themselves to their partners in a sexually explicit way.
- **Flashing**: Typically the brief display of bare female breasts or the brief showing of genitals by a man or woman.
- **Martymachlia**: Specifically refers to a paraphilic behaviour that involves being sexually aroused by having others watch the individual performing a sexual act.
- **Mooning**: Typically refers to the displaying of bare buttocks by pulling down trousers and/or underwear. Evidence suggests that when performed by women the primary motivation may be sexual whereas for males it may be done for the sake of mockery or humour.
- **Streaking**: Typically refers to running naked (usually men) or topless (usually female) in a public place (e.g., a cricket pitch or a football stadium).

In DSM-5-TR, the American Psychiatric Association (2022) defines exhibitionistic disorder as "sexual arousal from the exposure of one's genitals to an unsuspecting person, as manifested by fantasies, urges, or behaviors … The individual has acted on these sexual urges with a nonconsenting person, or the sexual urges or fantasies cause clinically significant distress or impairment in social, occupational, or other important areas of functioning" (p. 784). Exhibitionism is not necessarily a compulsive or impulsive behaviour, but in its most extreme and compulsive form it is called "apodysophilia".

The prevalence of individuals with exhibitionistic disorder is unknown, although it is much more likely to occur among males (American Psychiatric Association, 2022). It is also a disorder that typically begins before the age of 18 years (Hocken and Thorne,

2017). The American Psychiatric Association's (2022) DSM-5-TR also made reference to a couple of prevalence studies and reported the lifetime prevalence to be 4.1% among Swedish males (compared with 2.1% among females). Much higher prevalence rates were reported in a study from Canada where the lifetime prevalence of exhibitionism (as opposed to exhibitionistic disorder) was reported to be 30.9% (32.6% among males, 29.4% among females), although the prevalence for persistent exhibitionism was much lower (4.8% males and 0.8% females). The incidence is also lower among those aged above 40 years (Hocken and Thorn, 2017).

Exophilia

Exophilia refers to individuals who derive sexual pleasure and arousal from extraterrestrial, robotic, supernatural or otherwise non-human lifeforms. However, it should be pointed out that the only academic reference to exophilia I have found is by Aggrawal (2009a), who defines exophilia as "a fetish for the bizarre and unusual".

In many ways, these types of sexual preference could be described as totally impractical as the chances of making love to a ghost/spirit (i.e., spectrophilia), aliens, demi-gods and/or a robot are arguably negligible. Although the sexual focus is non-human and the shape of the desired form is typically humanoid, it would not include people who are sexually attracted to statues, dolls and/or mannequins (i.e., agalmatophilia).

Online sources claim that the overwhelming majority of exophiles never claim to have had sex with an alien (unsurprisingly), but are sexually excited and aroused by the thought of doing so. I was surprised about how many alien fetish sex sites there are, which partly shows just how popular this type of paraphilic and/or fetishistic interest is. An online essay on alien sex by Necromagickal (no date), who chooses not to reveal his name for fear of being arrested, notes that:

> "The only 'official' reports of sex between humans and aliens derive from the lore of alien abductions. The first credited abduction sex story came from 1957 in Brazil. Antonio Boas was plowing the fields of his family farm when a UFO showed up. He was taken inside and prepped to meet a fair-haired alien."

In January 2011 news reports surfaced that a male Chinese farmer called Meng Zhaoguo claimed to have had mid-air sex for 40 minutes with a levitating alien. Meng said, "She was three metres tall, had 12 fingers and braided leg hair." According to Meng the intergalactic coupling actually took place in 1994 in Heilongjiang's Wuchang county when a female humanoid visited him. He told the *China Daily* newspaper: "I didn't believe in aliens before I actually met them. Seeing is believing." He then passed a lie detector test conducted by the police. He also claimed that the aliens told him that the offspring of the sexual union would appear 60 years after they had sex.

Obviously I do not believe these incidents (or any other alien abduction stories) because they totally lack any verifiable empirical evidence. However, I do know that many people believe in aliens and believe they regularly visit earth. Some people genuinely believe they have been abducted by alien lifeforms and have had sex with them either with their consent or against their will. Supervert (2001) argued:

"Exophilia should be understood as an abnormal desire for that which is outside earth … It is characterized by arousal in the presence of aliens or, less directly, representations of aliens … The exophile is rarely apprehended in the very act of satisfying his fetish. Evidently the reason for this is not the scarcity of exophiles but the lack of extraterrestrials themselves."

Faunoiphilia

According to Aggrawal (2009a) faunoiphilia is a paraphilia in which individuals derive sexual pleasure and arousal from watching animals mate. Aggrawal notes that faunoiphilia is therefore a form of zoophilic voyeurism (a.k.a. "mixoscopic zoophilia"). Aggrawal (2011a) proposed a new zoophilia typology. In this typology he classes zoophiles according to 1 of 10 different types (Class I to Class X).

In Aggrawal's typology faunoiphiles come under Class III, which comprises individuals whom he describes as zoophilic fantasizers. Aggrawal claimed these people fantasize about having sexual intercourse with animals, but do not actually have sex with animals. He claimed that this type of zoophile may masturbate in the presence of animals and that both zoophilic voyeurs and zoophilic exhibitionists are subsumed within this particular zoophilic type. Prior to this paper, Masters (1962) noted that interest in (and sexual excitement at) watching animals mate may be an indicator of latent zoophilia.

There is clearly a difference between being interested in and watching animals mate, on the one hand, and being sexually aroused by such behaviour, on the other. For instance, while researching arachnophilia (individuals who derive sexual pleasure and arousal from spiders), I came across the amazing fact that the orb spider has a detachable penis. I mention this because the same article revealed that the argonaut octopus also has a detachable penis (in this case one of its tentacles) that actually separates and swims over to the female. I would certainly like to see this, but obviously not for sexual pleasure. While researching delphinophilia (individuals who derive sexual pleasure and arousal from dolphins), I read that dolphins' penises are major sense organs that they use to feel objects. Again, this is something I would like to see, but not for sexual pleasure.

Most of the evidence for the existence of faunoiphilia comes from case studies. McNally and Lukach (1991) reported a case study of a white 33-year-old "mildly mentally retarded man" they called "Mr. Z". He was the only child of separated parents (an alcoholic father and a schizophrenic mother who also suffered from epilepsy). She died when he was 12 years old. Mr Z had engaged in a series of "satisfactory sexual relationships with women" and had even married. However, his 3-year marriage had ended. Mr Z's preferred sexual behaviour was to expose himself and masturbate in front of large dogs of either sex. He also liked to rub his penis against large dogs. However, Mr Z also engaged in zoophilic voyeurism, which in Mr Z's case involved not only sexual arousal from watching dogs engage in sexual behaviour but also getting sexually aroused just watching dogs. Various publications have noted situations in which people have had voyeuristic fantasies about sexual contact with animals without actually wanting to have sex with them. Friday (1973) included 190 fantasies from different women, 23 of which involved zoophilic activity. Friday argued that zoophilic fantasies have the capacity to provide an escape from cultural expectations, restrictions and judgments in relation to sex. Given the scarcity of academic literature on faunoiphilia nothing is known about the incidence, prevalence or etiology of the behaviour.

Fat fetishes and feederism

Online letter from "Jill" to "Dr. Feeder":

> "I am a feedee from Boston in desperate need of a feeder. I have tried dieting and I know my mission is to be fat. I feel I can't do it alone. I fantasize about meeting a dominant man who is a feeder ... How do I get fat on my own? What foods? Can you give me a sample daily diet?"

Response to Jill's letter from Dr Feeder:

> "See my article 'How to Get Fat'. The kinds of foods don't matter so much. Eat what you enjoy the most, especially if it's fattening. The more you enjoy overeating, the more you will overeat. A lot of variety is also important."

Many years ago when I was just entering my teens (well, 1979 since you ask), I heard a song by Adam and the Ants called *Fat Fun*, which I had no idea at the time was all about fat fetishes. I should have guessed given that so many songs written by Adam Ant at the time were about fetishes and paraphilias – something I have written about in essays at length elsewhere (Griffiths, 1999b, 2003).

Over the last few years fat fetishism and fat admiration have come more into the public domain through national press and television documentaries. I was interviewed by *The Times* newspaper on the topic back in June 2010. Fat fetishists (a.k.a. "chubby-chasers") are mostly heterosexual and have an overwhelming and often exclusive sexual attraction towards very obese individuals of the opposite sex. As a number of researchers point out, there is no widely held consensus about how to define a fat-admirer (FA), but the term is typically used in relation to individuals who find attractive someone considered clinically overweight. However, Monaghan (2005) noted and described aspects of the small gay fat admiration community through the use of qualitative data he collected online.

Fat fetishism also includes "feederism" and "gaining" in which sexual arousal and gratification is stimulated through the person (the "feedee") gaining body fat. Feederism is a practice carried out by many FAs within the context of their sexual relationships and is where the individuals concerned obtain sexual gratification from the encouraging and gaining of body fat through excessive food eating. Sexual gratification may also be facilitated and/or enhanced by the eating behaviour itself and/or from the feedee becoming fatter ("gaining") in which either one or both individuals in the sexual relationship participate in activities that result in the gaining of excess body fat. This may not only involve eating more food but also engaging in sedentary activities that leave the feedee immobile. Some FAs may also derive pleasure from very specific parts of the body becoming fatter. Terry and Vasey (2011), working at the University of Lethbridge, Canada, claimed feedees are individuals who become sexually aroused by eating, by being fed and by the idea or act of gaining weight.

Even if FAs do not have direct sexual access to someone grossly overweight, there are other activities that they can encourage their sexual partners to engage in, such as "padding" (where individuals wear padded or layered clothing in a way that makes them appear to have a distended abdomen) and inflation (where individuals inflate their abdomen with air or liquid such that their abdomens are distended).

There has been a lot of psychological research showing that the attractiveness of women is related to their having both a low body mass index (BMI) and a low waist-to-hip ratio (WHR). However, there has been a great deal of debate about the universality of the findings and a lot of research into whether body shape attractiveness is determined by other factors, such as cross-cultural differences and gender role stereotyping. There has also been research into physical attractiveness among subcultures, such as people with eating disorders or in relation to sexual orientation. For instance, Swami and Tovee (2006) reported that lesbians appear to idealize a heavier body weight in a potential partner than do heterosexual women or men.

I have briefly written about feederism in two of my academic papers on paraphilias: Griffiths (2013) on fart fetishism (eproctophilia) and Griffiths (2012b) on how the internet has facilitated scientific research into paraphilias. I was also interviewed for the Discovery Channel's television series *Forbidden* about American Gabi Jones from Colorado ("Gaining Gabi") who appeared in the episode "Pleasure and pain".

At the time the television programme was being recorded, Gabi weighed 490 pounds and her sole aim was to get even fatter and heavier (before she became a feedee she was 250 pounds). Being a feedee is also her career and her thousands of online fans pay $20 a month to watch her eat in addition to sending her food to eat. She also claimed that she becomes sexually aroused when eating excessively. By 2014 she weighed 600 pounds.

Felching

I apologize for what I am about to write as some of you may be disturbed by what you read concerning the alleged practice of felching. Love (2001) defines felching as "a sexual practice in two very different ways. The first variant is said to refer to the act of sucking semen from the anus of a sexual partner following anal sex. The second variant is said to refer to the stuffing of small animals, typically rodents (e.g., gerbils, hamsters, mice and rats), into the vagina or anus for sexual stimulation." No-one doubts the existence of the first variant. However, there are countless online debates about whether the practice of inserting small animals into body orifices really exists.

If the second variant of felching does exist, then it could possibly be a subtype of musophilia, which Aggrawal (2009a) defines as "an act involving sexual arousal from mice" despite making no reference as to how this sexual arousal might actually occur.

The most infamous felching story involves US actor Richard Gere. An untrue story started circulating in the mid-1980s that Gere had checked into the Cedars-Sinai Medical Center in California for an emergency "gerbilectomy". In fact, the Gere story has become so well known that it has been alluded to in popular mainstream films (e.g., *Scream* in 1996 and *Urban Legend* in 1998) and television comedy programmes (e.g., *The Vicar of Dibley* when Dawn French's character, commenting on the sex appeal of Richard Gere, says she would not have minded being the hamster). In 2006 US actor Sylvester Stallone stated in public that he believed Richard Gere personally blamed him for starting the rumour. Before this, Philadelphian KYW TV newscaster Jerry Penacoli was rumoured to have visited an emergency room to dislodge a gerbil from his colon – same story, different person.

Brunvand (2001) cited Vorpagel's (1988) paper entitled "A rodent by any other name: Implications of a contemporary legend." This paper said the "gerbilling" story began in 1984 and started out as a story involving an unknown gay man and a mouse. Over subsequent years, the unknown gay man became Richard Gere and the mouse became a gerbil.

I carried out a full literature search on academic databases and could not find a single example of somebody seeking treatment to remove a rodent from his or her rectum. However, Lo *et al.* (2004), working at the Kwong Wah Hospital in Hong Kong, reported the case of a 50-year-old man who had to have a live eel removed from his rectum. The authors specifically stated that the insertion of a live animal into the rectum causing rectal perforation had never been reported in the medical literature previously. At this point, it is also worth mentioning Eckart and Katchis's (1989) paper on anorectal trauma. They commented on felching and said, more specifically, "a sexual practice has been mentioned recently where living rodents, including gerbils and mice, have been inserted into the rectum; the animal's futile efforts to claw its way to safety result in mucosal tears in the rectum." However, they did not present any evidence for its existence.

Mike Walker from the *National Enquirer* strove in vain to document any instance of gerbil stuffing by anyone anywhere. A promising lead popped up in a book edited by Matson and McNamara (2012) published by the American Hospital Association (AHA) entitled *The Hospital Emergency Department: A Guide to Operational Excellence*. The book has an entry "rectal mass – gerbils" under the category of emergency room procedures that require 25 minutes to perform. However, when an investigator contacted John A. Page, the author of the entry in question, the latter claimed that "the proofreader at the AHA obviously had a sense of humor."

My research into the topic came across a story in the *Sydney Morning Herald* (2010) about convicted cocaine smuggler Douglas Spink who was arrested for running a "bestiality farm" in Washington State. State officials found dozens of dogs, horses and pet mice along with thousands of images of bestiality. The report said the mice were euthanized, had their tails cut off, were smothered in petroleum jelly and had string tied around them. The fact the mice were covered in petroleum jelly and had string tied around their bodies suggests this facilitated ease of insertion into body orifices and easy retrieval. A case of "necrofelching" perhaps?

Figging

While researching sexual urtication and sexual arousal from stinging nettles (see entry later in this book), I came across the sexual practice of figging. For the uninitiated, figging in the broadest sense refers to the act of inserting something, typically ginger, into a body orifice, such as the anus, vagina and/or urethra that subsequently causes a stinging and/or burning sensation for sexual pleasure and arousal. Figging would appear to be a relatively rare sexual activity as it does not appear in either book by Aggrawal (2009a) or Love (2001). Furthermore, there is not a single reference to figging in any academic article or book of which I am aware. According to an online article at the London Fetish Scene website (2009):

> *"The word [figging] is likely to be a derivative of 'feague', the practice during Victorian times of putting a piece of peeled ginger into a horse's anus to make it appear more sprightly and hold its tail up (for shows and selling). Mostly, figging is still used to mean putting a peeled, shaped piece of ginger root into an anus, but in a BDSM context the anus would be that of a [submissive]."*

In my research I have come across a number of websites espousing the joys of figging. Figging and Anal Discipline (2005) has a surprisingly diverse set of articles, such as "Why figging enhances sex". Furthermore, there are a number of websites providing "how to" guides for figging. For instance, one detailed guide on the LiveJournal website (2007) by a BDSM practitioner provides a full description of the "theory and practice of ginger figging" and asserted:

> *"Figging is a fairly rare practice that seems to have declined in popularity recently, which I think is a shame because it's so easy and the effects are so interesting. It's a lot of fun, and I encourage people to experiment with it."*

Although there are many academic articles on sadomasochism and sadomasochistic practices, not one of them mentions figging. Therefore, absolutely nothing is known about the prevalence of the practice.

Findoms and "wallet rape"

Chris Summers, a journalist at the *Daily Star*, was writing an article on exophilia (sexual arousal from aliens) and looking for some academic input for his story. He found my blog on the topic. This resulted in him sending me some of the tabloid tales he had published on paraphilias including one published a week or so earlier on "wallet rape". Most definitions of "wallet rape", such as the one in the online Urban Dictionary, describe it as paying "way too much for something" resulting in "feelings of victimization, embarrassment and guilt". However, this was not the focus of the *Daily Star* article. According to Summers' story, wallet rape refers to men who get a sexual kick out of giving money to women. More specifically:

> *"Hundreds of men in Britain and thousands more worldwide enjoy being under the*

control of a financial dominatrix or 'findom'. These guys are not 'sugar daddies' who shower young lovers with expensive gifts in return for a sexual pay-off. In most cases they don't even get to meet the "goddess" they worship. They just enjoy being 'paypigs' or 'slaves' ... [most findoms] never [have] sex with [their] clients."

Summers interviewed a number of individuals for his article including "Goddess Haven" (a 21-year-old female findom), "Bill" (a 60-year-old businessman who worked up to 14 hours a day and is a lifelong "submissive") and Canadian sexologist and author Jess O'Reilly (O'Reilly, 2012). According to Goddess Haven:

> "I've learned so much about my clientele in the 3 years that I've been on this journey. When I first started if you asked me whether these men were just completely weird and out of their mind, but why would I care? I was getting what I wanted out of it. As my journey progressed I realised that a lot of these people are just looking to escape their boring everyday lives. A great deal of these men that serve me are 'high powered' businessmen who just want to come home and not be the centre of attention. Some of these men don't even have time to spend the money they make for themselves and just want to see a beautiful woman enjoy it with no strings attached. I've realised that most of my clientele are turned on by losing their sense of control and being taken advantage of by a powerful woman. I'll usually meet clients that pay well and can afford to session with me in reality. I have clients all over the world. I've had requests to kidnap people, tie them up and leave them in the woods. There are some findoms out there who give it a bad name, especially as it becomes more popular. There are a lot of women who are just hopping on the bandwagon and have no idea what they're doing."

As with any fetishistic or paraphilic behaviour, if it is carried out by two consenting adults and is legal, then there is nothing problematic about engaging in such activity. However, given that money is involved this could (in a minority of cases) end up being a behaviour akin to problem gambling in that the person enjoys engaging in the behaviour despite it becoming problematic when the activity goes beyond the individual's disposable income and causes problems elsewhere in his life.

Fingernail fetishes

The one thing about sexual fetishes that always amazes me is how specific some people's sexual likes and interests are. One such fetish is fingernail fetish. According to McCallum (1998) this fetish is a specific subtype of hand fetishism (other subtypes include finger fetishism and palm fetishism). They can include non-sexual specific actions done by the hands, such as washing-up or drying the dishes. We can be pretty certain the fetish exists because there are dedicated websites catering to all sexual fingernail needs, such as the Fingernail Fetish website (which boasts "a collection of soft-core image galleries and videos catering to those with a long-nail fetish") and the one run by the Pinterest website.

Fingernail fetishes are certainly referenced by leading academics and clinicians in the sexology field, although most references to them point out their existence, but give little information with respect to incidence, prevalence or etiological development. For instance, Stekel (1952) noted:

> "The true fetish lover dispenses with a sexual partner and gratifies himself with a symbol. This symbol can be represented by a piece of clothing, a part of the partner's body (pubic hair, nails, braid or pigtail) or any object used by the other person."

Similarly, Kafka (2010) made reference to the fetishization of fingernails without giving any detail. Aggrawal (2009a) reported a truly bizarre case involving necrophilia and fingernails. Citing Masters and Lea (1963) he briefly described the case of a man who derived sexual gratification from eating the nail trimmings of corpses. I have no idea if this would count as a genuine case of fingernail fetishism, but it is certainly a case of someone who gained sexual gratification from fingernails, albeit from dead people.

Most fingernail fetishist accounts that I have read indicate the individuals involved were happy living with their preferred fetish. This is certainly an area where the amount of clinical and academic research is limited.

Formicophilia

Another paraphilia that has been conceptualized as a subtype of zoophilia is formicophilia (i.e., being sexually aroused by insects crawling and/or nibbling on one's genitals). There also appear to some cultural variations, such as *Genki Genki* in Japan. *Genki Genki* is a style of erotic art and pornography that features women with various creatures mostly from the ocean, but does also include insects.

To date, only two academic papers have been published directly concerning formicophilia (Dewaraja and Money, 1986; Dewaraja, 1987). Dewaraja and Money (1986) were the first to publish a paper on this topic, and defined formicophilia as "a paraphilia in which the focus of sexual arousal was on small creatures, such as snails, frogs, ants, or other insects creeping, crawling or nibbling on the body, especially the genitalia, perianal area or nipples." Love (2001) pointed out that formicophilia should only technically refer to sexual arousal from ants and that paraphilias concerning insects more generally should be named "entomophilia". There are other specific insect-related paraphilias, such as arachnophilia (i.e., sexual arousal from spiders). However, spiders are arachnids – not insects. If you are unconvinced that formicophiliacs even exist, you should check out the lovebugz website, which has to be seen to be believed (you have been warned!).

Forniphilia

Forniphilia is a form of sexual objectification and is viewed by many as a form of sexual bondage in which the human body is typically contorted by being tightly bound into the shape of a piece of furniture where the person has to stay still for extended periods of time. The first time I came across the word was in an article on paraphilias in *The Times of India* that reported forniphilia as:

"A seemingly sexist wish to see the opposite sex being installed as pieces of furniture (the person is tightly bound and made to remain immobile in a particular position for a period of time)."

The term "forniphilia" was allegedly coined by Jeff Gord, the man behind The House of Gord (a website that considers itself to be "The Home of Ultra Bondage"). The submissive person who is made to look like a piece of human furniture typically has to wear a gag and runs the risk of being smothered. It is then up to the dominant person to regularly check on the psychological and physical wellbeing of the submissive. The House of Gord's website notes:

"The act of turning a woman into nothing more than a piece of functional furniture is the ultimate goal for many bondage enthusiasts. Often completely immobile the woman finds that she is at least useful to her owner, perhaps performing the role of a table, chair or even hat stand. Many find this type of sexual objectification highly erotic, especially if the subject is in some way vulnerable … Knowing she cannot move she can only hope she will be of some use. Awaiting use, she is forced to wait and obey until needed."

A quick look at the House of Gord's FAQ page shows the many types of furniture that women have been temporarily turned into including many types of tables, lamps, pedestals, various types of chairs (office chairs, rocking chairs, etc.), footstools, ceiling decorations (chandeliers), lawn sprinklers and bird tables.

Perhaps unsurprisingly, I did not manage to locate a single piece of empirical research on the topic of forniphilia. Norris (2010) gave it little more than a passing reference in a section on "Dominant/submissive relationship styles" under the categories "objectification" and "dehumanization". Other than that, I do not think the word "forniphilia" has until now made it into hard-copy print. It certainly looks like an area in need of some research and/or feminist critique.

Frotteurism

Frotteurism (a.k.a. "frottage" as it was originally called) is a paraphilia in which individuals, typically male but occasionally female, derive sexual pleasure and arousal from non-consensually rubbing up against other people, typically but not always female strangers. Such behaviour results in male frotteurs gaining an erection, which they then use, sometimes along with their pelvis, to rub up against women. Given that frotteurs like to carry out their activity undetected by their victims, they frequent public places where individuals are crowded close together, such as in underground tube trains, lifts and anywhere there are crowds (music gigs, sporting events, etc.). Most acts of frotteurism are carried out from behind the selected victim and without eye contact. The act itself is viewed as a criminal offence (i.e., a sexual assault) in most Westernized cultures, but is more typically classed as a misdemeanour. Frottage now tends to indicate consensual rubbing between two individuals.

Frotteurism was first recognized as a specific paraphilia in the Revised Third Edition of the American Psychiatric Association's *Diagnostic and Statistical Manual of Mental*

Disorders (DSM-III-R, 1987). The current DSM-5-TR criteria used to diagnose frotteurism are: (i) having, over a period of at least 6 months, recurrent, intense sexually arousing fantasies, sexual urges or behaviours involving touching and rubbing against a non-consenting person, and (ii) acting on these sexual urges, or such sexual urges or fantasies causing marked distress or interpersonal difficulty (American Psychiatric Association, 2022).

The prevalence of those who meet the full criteria for frotteuristic disorder is unknown (American Psychiatric Association, 2022). However, acts of frotteurism are reported to occur in up to 30% of North American adult males in the general population. The prevalence among females is thought to be significantly lower. It has also been reported that among men with paraphilic disorders and hypersexuality in outpatient settings, approximately 10%–14% meet the diagnostic criteria for frotteuristic disorder.

Frotteurism (dancing)

In this book I have examined both choreophilia (sexual arousal from dancing) and frotteurism, outlined in the previous section (Lussier and Piche, 2008). However, while researching these areas I came across a number of academic papers on "dancing frotteurism". For instance, Krueger and Kaplan (2008), in a book chapter on frotteurism, outlined four case studies of frotteurs in treatment, one of which was a 58-year-old male who had engaged in various types of frotteuristic behaviour over a 40-year period (an estimated 20,000 acts of frotteurism). This included "dirty dancing" where he would go to nightclubs and deliberately rub himself up against women while dancing with them. He estimated that he engaged in this type of frotteuristic behaviour on approximately 100 nights of the year and other frotteuristic behaviour, such as rubbing himself against women on buses and in train subways, on approximately 200 days a year.

In a short online article concerning frotteurism on the Anxiety Zone website (Anxiety Zone, 2013), the term "dry humping" (a.k.a. "grinding") is viewed as a form of modern dancing style. The same article also noted that frotteurism may not always be non-consensual:

> *"Frotteurism carries a connotation of 'anonymous and discreet rubbing' in a public place – like on a crowded train. The contact may be mutual or a one-way perpetration ... As with most other sexual practices, frottage with a non-consenting person is regarded as a form of sexual assault in most jurisdictions ... Frot is a term used among homosexual men to refer to penis to penis rubbing in a conventional private context. It is also known as 'phrot', 'swordfighting', 'cockrub', 'penis fencing', 'bumping dicks', 'frication' and 'the Princeton rub'. Advocates of this practice represent it as a safer and more erotic alternative to anal sex. Two people engaging in clothed frottage in a manner that simulates intercourse is known in the vernacular as 'dry humping'. A modern dancing style which involves partners rubbing their clothed bodies on one another is called 'grinding'."*

Frýdiphilia

In this book there are many entries on different body part fetishes and paraphilias including a number involving human hair (or the lack of it). These include individuals who are sexually aroused by (i) human hair, in general, but usually head hair (trichophilia/hirsutophilia), (ii) female body hair fetishism, (iii) beard fetishism (pogonophilia), (iv) haircut fetishism, (v) armpit hair fetishism (maschalagnia), (vi) depilation and shaving fetishism and (vii) baldness fetishism (acomophilia).

However, I once got an email from a man asking if I had ever come across individuals with a fetish for eyebrow hair. He claimed he had a fetish for women with "big bushy eyebrows" and gave the example of Cara Delevinge, the model and actress who played the Enchantress June Moone in the film *Suicide Squad*. I wrote back and told him that I had never come across anyone with such a fetish, but would look into it.

As far as I am aware, not only is there no academic or clinical research on the topic of eyebrow fetishes, but also there are not even any articles. There was nothing in the books by Love (2001) or Aggrawal (2009a). Eyebrows were not even mentioned in the list of fetishized body parts in the study by Scorolli *et al.* (2007) that I have cited a number of times in this book.

Even through there is a complete lack of scientific studies relating to eyebrow fetishes I have designated it a new paraphilia as there is anecdotal evidence that it exists. Based on traditional nosology I use the Greek words for "eyebrow" (*frýdi*) and "love" (*philia*), and this "new" paraphilia is therefore called "frýdiphilia".

On the internet I was unable to locate a single online forum dedicated to people who have eyebrow fetishes. However, I did locate a few individuals claiming to have eyebrow fetishes (or at least some behaviour indicative of some kind of eyebrow fetish). None of the information I found gave any clue as to the etiology of their love for eyebrows. Moreover, no-one found their fetish in any way problematic. Two of the individuals said their fetish for eyebrows was not their only focus of sexual attraction (with noses and beards also being cited as an additional source of sexual arousal). Given the apparent rarity I doubt that this type of fetish or paraphilia will ever be the topic of academic or clinical study.

Furniture fetishism

What is the first thing that comes into your head when you hear the words "furniture sex"? Maybe you think about people having sex on particular items of furniture? Maybe you think of specially designed "sexy furniture", such as the items featured on the Pinterest website? Maybe you think about people displayed and used as pieces of human furniture (see the entry on forniphilia if you have no idea about what I am talking). There are also those who design bespoke furniture to enhance sexual pleasure. For instance, Angelowicz (2012) examined the "sex furniture" designed by Josh and Jasmine, a couple whose entire house is furnished with sex furniture (and who were featured on a 2012 episode of the US TV show *Strange Sex* entitled 'Erection Correction: Sex Furniture'). According to the article "each piece [of furniture] supposedly accommodates multiple positions and enhances orgasm."

Rigney (2012) recounted a story about American married man 46-year-old Gerard Streator who was accused of having sex with a yellow sofa that had been abandoned on the pavement in Waukesha, Wisconsin, USA. At 11 p.m. on September 3, 2012, Streator was spotted by off-duty policeman Ryan Edwards copulating with the sofa while the police officer was out on a late-night run. The police officer was quoted as saying:

> *"A subject leaning over the couch facing down and it looked like he was having sexual relations with someone on the couch. [I] could see the male's hips thrusting up and down on the couch [and] could see that the defendant's penis was erect. [He] had been thrusting his pelvic area against the cushions and trying to sexually gratify himself by rubbing his penis between the two cushions. [He was] thrusting his hips as if he was having sex with a person."*

The officer chased Streator back to the man's apartment. Streator was arrested the following day for a criminal misdemeanour at the County Springs Hotel where he worked. The article describes Streator as a "couch fetishist" who engaged in "bizarre sexual conduct with the abandoned couch".

Another strange case involved a man in Hong Kong who late one night attempted to have sex with a local park bench. He penetrated one of the holes in the park bench, but his penis got stuck and the emergency services had to be called out to try and cut him free. There is now a video posted on YouTube of the emergency services cutting the man free, which has already been seen by tens of thousands of viewers.

Hazell (2008) reported that an American married man and father of three 40-year-old Art Price had been observed on four separate occasions in Bellevue, Ohio, USA having sex with a picnic table, the most recent being March 14, 2008 when a neighbour filmed the incident to show the police. The neighbour had observed Price "in his garden turning over a round metal table before performing a sex act upon it." A spokesman for the local police, Police Captain Matt Johnson, said: "He was completely nude. He would use the hole from the umbrella and have sex with the table. Once you think you've seen it all, something else comes around." Price was charged with four counts of public indecency because his sexual frolics with the picnic table occurred near an elementary school.

As far as I am aware, there is no specific paraphilia associated with getting sexual pleasure and arousal from furniture items. So once again I decided to designate it a new paraphilia based on this and other similar cases I have read about. There are three ways in which paraphilias appear to derive their names:

- The paraphilic word can be derived from two or more Greek words relating to the focus of the sexual desire and then appending the Greek word for "love" (*philia*). For instance, Money (1986) coins the word "acrotomophilia" (sexual arousal from a partner who is an amputee) from the Greek *akron* ("extremity"), *tome* ("cutting") and *philia* ("love") and "stigmatophilia" from the Greek *stigma* ("mark") and *philia* ("love").
- The paraphilic word can be derived from the opposite of an existing word for some kind of phobia. For instance, the fear of clowns is known as coulrophobia and the love of clowns is coulrophilia.

- The paraphilic word can be simply derived from the English word for the focus of sexual desire followed by the Greek suffix *-philia*. For instance, "acnephilia" (sexual pleasure and arousal from someone with acne) derives from the English "acne" and the Greek word "*philia*".

Therefore, I could perhaps refer to this sexual behaviour as "furniturephilia", which certainly has an alliterative ring to it, but is not very original. As far as I am aware, there is no named phobia for fear of furniture, so this avenue is closed. Finally, I tried to track down the Greek word for furniture. The word "furniture" is derived from the French word *fourniture* (which means "the act of furnishing") and cannot be historically traced back to Greek. However, one of my research colleagues (from Greece) informed me that *epiplo* is the singular for furniture and that *epipla* is the plural. Therefore, I am going to name those with a furniture sex paraphilia as engaging in "epiplophilia". Additionally, given that some individuals seem only to like seated furniture, such as a "throne" from the Greek *thronos*, in the absence of any other names for paraphilias involving seated furniture I hereby name this as "thronosphilia", which I will operationally define not just as "the gaining of sexual pleasure and arousal from furniture but also chairs and seating".

Furries

Back in early 1995 a good friend of mine (who knew I had an academic interest in paraphilias) asked me if I knew of any psychological research on "furries". He told me that his girlfriend preferred to have sex with him when she was dressed up in animal clothing (in this case, a fox). At the time I knew absolutely nothing about the "furry fandom" community, but I always kept an eye out for academic research on the topic. It was not until I read Gurley's (2001) paper that I got to know about the phenomenon. Gurley proclaimed that "this is no hobby. It's sex; it's religion; it's a whole new way of life."

Although I did not know anyone personally in the furry community, I was led to believe that they were not very happy with the way Gurley had portrayed them. My next memory of furries in the mainstream was when I watched a 2003 episode of *CSI: Crime Scene Investigation* entitled "Fur and loathing". Furries were the main focus of the episode when a man was found dead fully dressed as a raccoon.

Despite the furry fandom community being around for a number of years, it was not until 2008 that the first peer-reviewed academic paper was published that included some primary data on furries.

For me the most interesting part of the published research (Gerbasi *et al.*, 2008, 2011) was the creation of a "furry typology" based on participants' responses to furry identity questions. Basically, being furry means different things to different furries. More specifically, furries were asked to respond "yes" or "no" to the following two questions: (i) "Do you consider yourself to be less than 100% human?" and (ii) "If you could become 0% human, would you?"

These questions gave rise to two independent dimensions of (i) self-perception (undistorted vs distorted), and (ii) species identity (attained vs unattained).

86 Furries

Approximately 25% of furries responded positively to both these questions. The research team claimed that these responses meant furries in this particular grouping had "distorted and unattained" identities (i.e., what could possibly be termed a "species identity disorder").

The implication of this finding has led to some debate, as Gerbasi *et al.* (2008, 2011) did, on whether this particular type of furry may suffer "species identity disorder" with specific characteristics that parallel individuals who have gender identity disorder.

Gastergastrizophilia

One of the weirdest sounding paraphilias that I have ever come across is gastergastrizophilia in which individuals allegedly derive sexual pleasure and arousal from bellypunching. I use the word "allegedly" as I have never seen this paraphilia listed in any reputable academic source. It does not appear in either of the books by Aggrawal (2009a) or Love (2001). The lengthiest article that I have come across on gastergastrizophilia is on *Full Wiki* (2013).

The fact that someone has written about sexual bellypunching in no way proves that the behaviour exists. In an article I wrote on my personal blog site, I examined a hoax paraphilia called "emysphilia" (sexual arousal from turtles). In researching that blog I came to the conclusion that the paraphilia simply did not exist as there was no evidence of any kind except the originally published article (plus the fact that the author later admitted it was a hoax). Sexual bellypunching as a fetish or paraphilia is something that I do not think can be so easily dismissed. I managed to collect a few first-hand accounts of sexual bellypunching on the Dark Fetish website.

Based on the research I have done, it would appear that there used to be a Wikipedia entry on sexual bellypunching, but was removed back in 2006. Some people claimed that the information provided in the original webpage could not be verified and that it might even have been made up by the person who created the original Wikipedia entry. As one person noted in the Wikipedia discussion the original author of the bellypunching article had:

> "... added a bunch of links, but they consist of Yahoo! groups, personal websites, and a couple [of] porn sites which themselves are non-notable. None of these are reliable sources, none of them help with the fact that this article still violates Wikipedia's verifiability. Unverifiable content can't stay on Wikipedia, no matter how much some people might like said content."

Comments were also made along the lines that Wikipedia does not need to have a separate page for every single obscure fetish. Personally, I do not see this as an argument for not having a *Wikipedia* entry. However, the original author of the page countered by saying:

> "It's not about liking (or in your case, disliking) [the bellypunching] entry, but about showing diligence in mapping out within Wikipedia all these various concepts that exist in the world. Some concepts are better cited than others, it's true. However, that

doesn't mean that some things, which are perhaps more ephemeral, or which came into their own with the rise of the Internet, can't be listed ... I suggest that if one can prove that a lot of people are involved in a concept, and that this concept exists as such, then the concept must surely merit some inclusion, even if that inclusion is limited only to what one can source ... I have shown that thousands of people have taken it upon themselves to join public groups around this [bellypunching] fetish; and found any number of websites, most of which have been around for years, creating a sort of community ... It would be a mistake to make an article called bellypunching videos on the basis of the fact of such videos existing, because that would ignore the evident existence of the concept of the fetish."

I have to admit that, having done my own online search, I can certainly vouch for the fact that there are hundreds of sexual bellypunching videos available online (e.g., websites such as Belly Punching Fetish, Heroine Movies and Teen Bellypunch – be warned, though, these are sexually explicit sites), and there are online discussion groups that discuss bellypunching as a sexual preference and/or sexual fetish. Personally, I think there is enough to suggest that the activity exists and that there is no reason a separate *Wikipedia* page should not exist. The fact that sexual bellypunching videos are for sale online suggests there is a market for it. I also came across some Japanese anime that featured sexual bellypunching along with anecdotal evidence that bellypunching is part of Japanese sexual culture. However, I am the first to admit that such videos might appeal to sadists and masochists who are simply sexually turned on by the giving or receiving of pain rather than being sexually aroused by bellypunching *per se*. My guess is that the original article on sexual bellypunching was removed because the evidence base did not fulfil *Wikipedia's* purported minimum evidence threshold.

Gas mask fetishism

Elsewhere in this book I examine mask fetishism, which involves individuals who derive sexual pleasure and arousal from either wearing masks and/or seeing others wearing masks. This entry takes a more detailed look at gas mask fetishism. As with mask fetishism more generally, there is little in the way of academic or clinical research on gas mask fetishism and much of what is known can best be described as anecdotal.

Gas mask fetishism appears to have potential overlap with other types of paraphilic and/or fetishistic behaviour, particularly hypoxyphilia (i.e., deriving sexual pleasure and arousal from oxygen deprivation). For instance, Skugarevsky *et al.* (2011) examined a couple of deaths due to hypoxyphilia one of which involved someone who was wearing a gas mask at the scene of death. They noted:

"[Hypoxyphiliacs] use a variety of techniques to produce the hypoxia like strangulation, suffocation or reduction of the oxygen in the inspired air that may be achieved with plastic bags or gas masks that may allow inhaling some anesthetic gases (chloroform, nitrous oxide) and volatile chemicals (isopropyl nitrite and isobutyl nitrite or 'poppers')."

In an interesting paper by Marshall *et al.* (2011) the authors examined the entertainment value of gas masks. The authors argued that a range of popular entertainments clearly demonstrated that there was "widespread and growing public appetite for extreme, visceral, and horrifying experiences." Their idea of a gas mask interface emerged out of a long-term project "to develop interactive entertainments using biological sensing, which led to the idea of exploring the aesthetics of respiration monitoring as a form of engaging spectacle and gaming interaction." Reflecting on their experiences with gas masks as part of the entertainment experience, they identified six key dimensions (i.e., cultural, visceral, control, social performance and engineering) in designing fearsome interactions some of which I think are applicable to the use of gas masks in sexual play and gas mask fetishism. However, I have yet to come across any focused empirical research on gas mask fetishes and/or sexuality.

Genital bisection

One of the most noticeable trends over the last few years has been body modification. According to Veale and Daniels (2012):

> "Body modification is a term used to describe the deliberate altering of the human body for non-medical reasons (e.g., self-expression). It is invariably done either by the individual concerned or by a lay practitioner, usually because the individual cannot afford the fee or because it would transgress the ethical boundaries of a cosmetic surgeon. It appears to be a lifestyle choice and, in some instances, is part of a subculture of sadomasochism. It has existed in many different forms across different cultures and ages."

Body modification can range from the relatively minor to the extremely major. At the minor level this may include such modifications as tattooing and minor body piercings to the nipples and genitalia. At the more extreme level it may include branding of the skin, pearling (i.e., permanent insertion of small beads beneath the skin of the labia or foreskin), major scarification (through controlled skin burning) and tongue splitting (so that it is similar to that of a snake).

Other body modifications to the genitals can include the removal of the clitoral hood in women or penile subincision in men (i.e., splitting of the underside of the penis; there is a photograph on *Wikipedia*'s page on subincision should you want to see the final result). Some people have gone as far as to have their whole faces modified including the infamous examples of Dennis Anver (The Tigerman) and Erik Sprague (The Lizardman).

According to Veale and Daniels (2012) there has been little research into the psychological aspects of body modification. They cite the work of Lemma (2010), a psychotherapist, who suggested that, for some individuals, body modification is a way of trying to modify those parts of the self that the individual feels to be unacceptable. Arguably, one of the most gruesome and extreme forms of body modification is "genital bisection" (the total splitting of the penis in which the penis is literally cut into two symmetrical halves).

Photographic evidence of "genital bisection" can be found on the genital bisection page at the Body Modification E-zine (BME) encyclopaedia website, which gives five examples of real split penises (of men who are pleased with the results).

90 Genital bisection

The practice of genital bisection has also been outlined by Love (2001). She wrote about the practice from a more historical and anthropological perspective and reported that Australian Aborigines used to ritually split their penises from the glans towards the penis base in worship of a totem lizard that had a split penis. She then described the account of an Englishman who had carried out the procedure over a period of several years and described the results:

"My decision to surgically remodel my genitals was deliberate, of deep satisfaction to me, highly exciting, sexually adventurous, and erotically exhilarating … Full erections were maintained as previously but now in two complete, separate halves. The erotic zones of my penis are still the same, with orgasms and ejaculations functioning perfectly. Entry into the vagina requires a little extra effort for insertion, but once my penis is inside, its opened effect on the vagina's inner lining is more pronounced, giving better female orgasmic feelings."

A possible downside of extreme body modification including genital modifications is the association it has with increased risk of suicide. Hicinbothem *et al.* (2006) surveyed a large sample of individuals who subscribed to a website for body modification (e.g., piercings, tattoos, scarification and surgical procedures). They reported that people who had undergone body modification had a higher incidence of prior suicidality (i.e., suicidal ideation and attempted suicide) than those who had not undergone body modification. However, they also noted that controlling for self-reported depression weakened the strength of the association.

I will end this entry with a glossary of terms (all taken – almost verbatim – from the BME website):

- *"Head splitting is the bisection of the glans of the penis. The procedure is usually carried out using a scalpel or surgical scissors (although cauterizing, electronic cauterizing or laser may also be used). The wound often needs to be cauterized, either with silver nitrate or with heat. Post-procedural bleeding is relatively heavy and tends to last several days.*
- *Meatotomy is incision into and enlargement of a meatus. When the subincision is only underneath the glans it is known as a meatotomy (or, if naturally occurring, a hypospadia).*
- *Hypospadia is a birth defect where the urethra and urethral groove are malformed, causing the urethra to exit the penis sooner than it normally would (i.e., closer to the base, rather than at the tip of the glans).*
- *Subincision is the bisection of the underside of the penis (from the urethra to the raphe; versus a superincision which is the top half).*
- *Superincision is a form of bisection that's opposite to a subincision, splitting only the top half of the shaft and leaving the tissue below the urethra intact.*
- *Inversion is a form of genital bisection that involves a combination of subincision and superincision while leaving the glans intact.*
- *The corpus cavernosum are two areas of erectile tissue which run along the length of the penis, and fill with blood during erection."*

Glasses fetishism

According to Aggrawal (2009a) glasses fetishism refers to a "fetishistic attraction to people wearing prescription glasses, sunglasses, or cosmetic contact lenses or to the act of wearing glasses or the glasses themselves." Other related activities include wearing glasses during sexual acts and ejaculating onto glasses.

Back in 2009 Jerry Lowery of Illinois, USA then aged 38 years was charged with stealing more than 500 pairs of glasses from suburban spectacle shops because of his fetish for eyeglasses. The Associated Press reported that:

> "Prosecutors said Lowery walked into three shops between April and July and said he had a gun. They say he took more than 500 pairs of high-end glasses including Prada and Gucci brands, but didn't take cash. The criminal complaint quotes Lowery as saying he 'really likes to be around glasses'. He told investigators he tries them on in front of a mirror and then discards them."

Scorolli *et al.* (2007) examined the relative prevalence of different fetishes. Fetishes for glasses featured in a small number of the fetishistic groups located. Glasses were then mentioned in their discussion concerning the formation of fetishes and paraphilias. Glasses fetishism was used as an example to argue against genetic and evolutionary biological theories for fetishism.

Glossaphilia (tongue fetish)

If you type "tongue fetish" into an online search engine, you will get a list of hundreds (if not thousands) of websites (mainly in the form of pornographic video-clips). This includes such websites as the Tongue Fetish Organization (which claims to be "the leading tongue fetish site on the net") and Tonguefetish.net as well as dedicated webpages on tongue fetishes at such sites as Dailymotion and Tongue Art. Be warned, though, these are all sexually explicit.

One of the strangest stories about tongue fetishes in recent years concerned Jafny Mohamed Sunny, a young male sex offender from Singapore who had a fetish for young girls' tongues. As was reported in the *Straits Times* (Lum, 2012):

> "[Jafny Mohamed Sunny] used his military police credentials to pass himself off as a police officer. And he did that with the vilest of intentions – so he could frighten and coerce his young, vulnerable victims – as young as 12 years old – into quiet places at HDB [Housing & Development Board] blocks, where he could molest and do horrible things to them. [He] also had a fetish. After cornering some of his female victims, he would ask them to stick out their tongues – just so he could touch them. He later explained to a psychiatrist that he did that because he had an urge to know the length of girls' tongues. He claimed 'voices' in his head compelled him to do it, and said he would get inner satisfaction after checking the lengths of girls' tongues. Jafny had checked the tongues of five girls on different occasions. [He] was sentenced to 8½ years' jail and 12 strokes of the cane for three out of 10 charges that were proceeded against him."

Glossaphilia (tongue fetish)

As I have never seen this sexual behaviour officially listed in any reputable academic source, I decided to give the behaviour a name. The Greek word for "tongue" is *glossa* and the word "glossal" usually refers to, relates to and/or pertains to the tongue. Therefore, I am naming the behaviour "glossaphilia", a paraphilia in which individuals derive sexual pleasure and arousal from human tongues.

I deliberately use the word "human" as I noted in a previous entry that there is a zoophilic classification of people whom Aggrawal (2011a) calls fetishistic zoophiles. They keep various animal parts that they then use as an erotic stimulus and a crucial part of their sexual activity. Such individuals have been reported in the clinical literature including the case of a woman (Randall *et al.*, 1990) who used the tongue of a deer as her primary masturbatory aid.

Gynemimetophilia

In a review of paraphilias not otherwise specified (PNOS). Milner *et al.* (2008) briefly overviewed "gynemimetophilia". The term was coined by Money (1984) from the Greek *gyne* ("woman"), *mimos* ("mime") and *philia* ("love"). Milner *et al.* (2008) defined gynemimetophilia as "a paraphilia in which an individual (usually male) derives sexual arousal and pleasure from sexual partners who are gynemimetic, typically sex-reassigned male-to-female transsexuals." Such people are colloquially known as "transfans" (a.k.a. "tranny-chasers" and "tranny-hawks"). Milner *et al.* (2008) also noted a related condition termed "gynemimesis" that normally refers to a homosexual male who engages in female impersonation without sex reassignment, such as a drag queen. Among females, the paraphilic equivalent (also coined by Money, 1984) is andromimetophilia from the Greek *andros* ("man"), *mimos* ("mime") and *philia* ("love").

The reasons for attraction differ from one person to another, but Escoffier (2011) highlighted that the exoticism of the transgendered individual can be a primary attraction and that such people are "often both hyperfeminine in appearance and sexually aggressive". He claimed the phenomenon was fairly new and that the first known cases occurred in 1953 following the first case of male-to-female sex change (i.e., Christine Jorgensen). Others may be attracted to what transgendered individuals represent and the way they challenge male/female sexual orthodoxy.

Weinberg and Williams (2010) examined men sexually interested in transwomen (MSTW). In their study, transwomen were defined as "genetic males who use estrogen to feminize their body, but retained their penis." They examined the nature of the sexual attraction of MSTWs towards transwomen and then examined how this related to their sexual orientation identity. Their main finding was that those MSTWs who identified as heterosexual tended to gloss over the fact that the transwoman has a penis, while bisexually identified MSTWs were more likely to incorporate the transwoman's penis into the sexual experience.

Haematophilia

If you are in any way prudish or squeamish, then stop reading this particular entry now and skip to the next one. Haematophilia is a paraphilia in which individuals derive sexual pleasure and arousal from the tasting of or drinking blood, and can include the sexualized use of tampons. It was while researching the entry on paraphilic vampirism and menophilia (i.e., a paraphilia in which individuals derive sexual arousal from menstruating females) that I came across various references to tampons as a source of sexual arousal and pleasure. Both menophilia and paraphilic vampirism are arguably subcategories of haematophilia. Hickey (2010) noted that in most countries drinking blood is not a crime. He further noted in reference to haematophilia that:

"The activity is usually done in the presence of others. Most persons engaging in this form of paraphilia also have participated in or have co-occurring paraphilias often harmful to others. In addition, a 'true hematolagniac' is a fantasy-driven psychopath and to be considered very dangerous. According to Noll (1992), such desires are founded in severe childhood abuse. The child may engage in auto-vampirism in tasting his own blood during puberty. These acts are eventually sexualized and reinforced through masturbation. A progressive paraphilic stage during adolescence is sexual arousal from eating animals and drinking their blood (zoophagia) while masturbating. The compulsive, fantasy-driven, sexual nature of this paraphilia creates a very dangerous adult."

Hickey (2010) also included a case study on Peter Kürten (1883–1931), a mass murderer nicknamed the "Vampire of Dusseldorf" who terrified the inhabitants of his home town in Germany. This case study was also written about by Schlesinger (2004). Hickey (2010), citing the work of Prins (1985), wrote that:

"Kürten was raised in a very physically and sexually abusive home where he witnessed his alcoholic father raping his mother and sisters. He also engaged in sexually abusing his sisters ... At age 11 he was taught by the local dog catcher how to torture dogs and sheep while masturbating. He developed multiple paraphilias including vampirism, hematolagnia, necrophilia, erotophonophilia, and zoophagia and was known to drink directly from the severed jugular of his victims. He raped, tortured, and killed at least nine known victims although he was believed to have murdered several others. He used hammers, knives, and scissors to kill both young girls and

women and admitted that he was sexually aroused by the blood and violence. Some victims incurred many more stab wounds than others, and when asked about this variation he explained that with some victims his orgasm was achieved more quickly … Before his beheading he asked if he would be able to hear the blood gushing from his neck stump because 'that would be the pleasure to end all pleasures'."

This brief overview shows that Kürten had multiple paraphilias including necrophilia and was a genuine haematophile. I picked out necrophilia as one of the co-occurring paraphilias because Aggrawal (2009a, 2011b) has written extensively on necrophilia and notes in both his (2009b) paper and his (2011b) book that "some [necrophiles] remove clothes, especially panties or even tampons from corpses to keep as fetish objects … and their paraphilia is known as necrofetishism." This was the first-ever academic reference I had read that related to the sexualized and fetishistic use of tampons.

Not only has sexualized tampon use been associated with haematophilia, menophilia and necrophilia, it has also been associated with mysophilia in which individuals derive sexual pleasure and arousal from filth. I have examined this in more detail in relation to salirophilia. If you want some non-academic proof, then there are a number of online websites catering for tampon-loving mysophiles including Charlotte's Panties, which sells used tampons and sanitary pads for sexual pleasure. Another website you might possibly want to check out is Men in Menstruation (which, perhaps more accurately, should be named "Men into Menstruation"). Another unusual way in which tampon use has been sexualized is in urethral stimulation. A number of medical papers, such as the one by Kochakarn and Pummanagura (2008), have made reference to the fact that tampons have got stuck in the urethra during self-inflicted sexual stimulation.

Although there have been academic and clinical writings on various "blood paraphilias" (most notably paraphilic vampirism), there is nothing to my knowledge specifically on tampon fetishes. Whether empirical research is needed is debatable, but even a quick perusal of various online fetish sites suggests that, while it may be a dubious niche sexual market, there are definitely admirers and adherents out there.

Haemorrhoid fetishism

If there is any subject likely to cause embarrassment (if you have them) and/or laughter (if you do not) it is haemorrhoids (a.k.a. "piles"). I am sure most of you reading this know what haemorrhoids are. However, if you do not, then *Wikipedia* (2013j)'s anatomical description might be helpful, although the website's photographs made me a little queasy:

"Haemorrhoids … are vascular structures in the anal canal which help with stool control. They become pathological or piles when swollen or inflamed. In their physiological state, they act as a cushion composed of arteriovenous channels and connective tissue."

One thing that never ceases to amaze me is what other human beings find sexually attractive. This is evidenced by those who are sexually attracted to ugly people (teratophilia), amputees (acrotomophilia) and those with physical deformities (abasiophilia). The only reason I am including such an entry is because I came across this online snippet:

> "If you find a guy who's not disgusted, sure you can. I had a mate with a hemorrhoid fetish once. He used to brag about how he loved popping them out."

I have to admit I was more than a little suspicious about whether anybody could be genuinely turned on and sexually aroused by somebody else's haemorrhoids. Nevertheless, I decided to look into it (but not at them). One thing that convinced me there is a niche market for almost anything was the number of hardcore pornography videos catering to those with a sexual interest in haemorrhoids or at the very least a penchant for watching those with haemorrhoids having sex, such as the Heavy-R and Muchosucko websites. Be warned, though, such videos are very sexually explicit and may upset some people. These videos are clearly made by individuals who believe they can make money from people who want to watch this type of thing. However, it could always be the case that watching people with haemorrhoids having sex is not done for sexual purposes, but simply viewing out of horrified curiosity or else because they are writing an A–Z guide to paraphilias.

Whilst researching the entry for rectal foreign bodies, I came across a study by Huang *et al.* (2003). Their paper examined 10 cases of males (average age 57 years) who had reported to Taipei Veterans General Hospital because they had got an object stuck inside their rectal passage. The reason I mention this paper is because two of the 10 men (one aged 50 years in a case from 1999 and the other aged 76 years from a case in 1991) had got sexual vibrators stuck inside their rectal passage after using them to "smooth" their haemorrhoids. It is unclear as to whether the smoothing of the haemorrhoids caused sexual stimulation, but the fact that it was a sexual vibrator at least suggests the practice was more than just therapeutic.

It will not surprise anyone that there is absolutely nothing written about haemorrhoid fetishes either academically or clinically. However, the Urban Dictionary (2013) features an online article on "Jarmel Berries" (which I have to admit I had never heard of), but relates to the sexualization of haemorrhoids.

Haircut fetishism

Later in this book I examine trichophilia (a.k.a. "trichopathophilia", "hirsutophilia" and/or "hair fetishism"). According to Aggrawal (2009a) trichophilia is a paraphilia in which individuals derive sexual pleasure and arousal from human hair, most commonly head hair. However, I have come across what appears to be a subtype of trichophilia termed "haircut fetishism", which appears to share some behavioural and psychological similarities with depilation fetishism.

One of my oldest friends with whom I was at university owns a number of barber shops in the Northwest of England. He told me me that haircut fetishism is well known in hairdressing circles and that there is a real niche market for "forced haircut fetishism". As far as I am aware, there is no published academic or clinical research on haircut fetishism, although there is a lot of anecdotal information about its existence. For instance, there are hundreds of online haircut videos, a substantial majority of which catering to those who are sexually aroused from seeing people having their hair cut against their will (i.e., non-consensual coercive "forced" haircuts).

There are (and have been) various hair fetishist magazines most of which are American, such as *The Yankee Clipper*, *The Razor's Edge* and *The Bald Truth* (although the latter may appeal as much to depilation fetishists as to haircut fetishists). There are certainly loads of websites haircut fetishists can visit including CutsCuts, Bald Beauties, Haircut.net, Extreme Haircut and Barber Shop Video (Kesse, 2007). However, given the lack of research, the prevalence of haircut fetishism is unknown.

"Hands on hips" fetish

"Hands on the hip is a type of hand partialism, which means the attraction to a specific action performed by the hands. It's very hard to explain the presence of a fetish site devoted entirely to women posing with their hands on their hips, standing defiantly and angrily in the way so many mothers do when their children misbehave. Somewhere, deep in the psyche of the site's creator, he desperately wants to find a mother figure who will discipline him with nothing harsher than a time-out and denial of television." (Murano, 2009)

Murano's brief description appears to somewhat concur with Wikipedia's brief entry on hand fetishism, which appears to have come, typically without citation, from McCallum (1998). That entry claims hand fetishism

"… may include the sexual attraction to a specific area such as the fingers, palm or nails, or the attraction to a specific action performed by the hands; which may otherwise be considered non-sexual – such as washing or drying dishes. This fetish may manifest itself as a desire to experience physical interaction, or as a source of sexual fantasy."

Handwear fetishism

In an earlier entry in this book I examined clothing fetishes (a.k.a. "garment fetishes"). Clothing fetishes revolve around or fixate upon either specific types of clothing (lingerie, fishnet stockings, etc.), specific fabrics (leather, rubber, fur, wool, etc.) or specific styles (restrictive, skin tight, baggy, etc.). According to Weinberg *et al.* (1995) common clothing fetishes include shoes, stockings, diapers, gloves, underwear and bras. The clothes fetishist is fixated on the specific type of clothing, which becomes an exclusive or recurrent stimulus for sexual arousal and gratification.

A number of academic papers claim that glove fetishes are commonplace. However, in a study by Scorolli *et al.* (2007), on the relative prevalence of different fetishes using online fetish forum data, no data were reported relating to glove fetishism. Their analysis included a breakdown of sexual preferences for objects associated with the body including clothing. Excluding footwear, which is associated more specifically with podophilia (a.k.a. "foot fetishism"), the results of the study showed that the most fetishized items of clothing were underwear (12%; 10,046 fetishists), whole-body wear such as coats and uniforms (9%, 9,434 fetishists), upper-body wear such as jackets and waistcoats (9%, 9,226 fetishists) and head and neckwear such as hats and ties (3%, 2,357 fetishists). From this particular study the authors concluded that the most common clothing fetishes were footwear, underwear (including swimwear) and uniforms, but nothing related to gloves. In fact, there was nothing related to any kind of hand fetishism whatsoever.

My own anecdotal research into glove fetishes suggests that the fetish exists and that it has a higher profile and more online forums than many other fetishes that I have examined in this book. There are many dedicated websites that cater to glove fetishes such as the World Wide Glove Fetish Association, Glove Mansion, Fetish Glove and the Leather Gloves Fetish Facebook page. There are also commercial sites such as Clips 4 Sale that sell dedicated glove fetish videos as well as online sites such as The Experience Project that feature individuals recounting their personal experiences of glove fetishism. There is also the fetishistic use of gloves in Nazi fetishism, based on research by Lopez and Godard (2013) who examined the subculture of erotic evil.

Noguchi and Kato (2004) reported the case of a 22-year-old male glove fetishist. The man became fixated on gloves after watching a television programme in which the heroine in the show conquered her enemies while wearing gloves. This led to the man attaching strong sexual significance to gloves in his late teens when he started watching pornographic films. The paper further noted that he had assaulted women as many as four times in order to steal their gloves. Apart from this paper, there has been little theorizing and little detail on or about the sexual appeal of gloves.

Harmatophilia and parthenophilia

One of the more unusual paraphilias I have come across in my reading is harmatophilia. Aggrawal (2009a) defines harmatophilia as "deriving sexual pleasure and arousal from sexual incompetence or mistakes, usually in a female partner." Other definitions I have come across are similar, such as the Sensual Swingers website that defines harmatophilia as "sexual arousal from a sexually inadequate partner", whereas the Inspire Jessamae website simply says it is a "penchant for partners who are useless in bed." The Right Diagnosis website (2012g) describes harmatophilia more widely as referring to (i) sexual urges, arousal or fantasies involving breaking rules or making mistakes, and (ii) recurring intense sexual fantasies involving breaking rules or making mistakes.

As far as I am aware, there is absolutely no empirical evidence relating to harmatophilia – not even a single case study (although all mentions I have come across assume that it is predominantly male based). Therefore, this appears to be yet another paraphilia that has been created as a theoretical opposite to a legitimately known phobia (i.e., harmatophobia, which refers to people who have an abnormal fear surrounding sin as well as a fear of making errors and mistakes). However, parthenophilia is another paraphilia that might be psychologically and conceptually similar to harmatophilia.

Parthenophilia is defined by Aggrawal (2009a) as "a sexual attraction to and arousal by virgins". Love (2001) noted that, although sex with a virgin is avoided by some people, other individuals "find it novel, feeling honored, enjoy the feeling of power in defiling a virgin, are relieved that they cannot be compared with anyone else, or have a religious ethic that would create prejudice against a partner who was not a virgin." She also cites evidence that some brothels and bordellos often cater to men who pay extra to have sex with a virgin. A brief entry on parthenophilia at the London Fetish Scene website noted that in 18th-century and 19th-century England "there was a somewhat sordid trade in the prostitution of girls or young women who were claimed to be virgins (often involving the attempted reconstruction of the hymen in order to obtain a high price for her deflowering more than once)." There is an implicit assumption that such practices no longer exist. However, I have come across more contemporary anecdotal accounts suggesting that some men who regularly visit prostitutes prefer virgins and are willing to pay extra for such a service.

Headphone fetishism

One of the strangest sites that I have come across in my search for sexual fetishes is the Headph0ne Phet1sh website. Unsurprisingly, it is a site dedicated to "all manner of ladies wearing all kinds of headphones." There appear to be thousands of photographs and videoclips of attractive woman wearing headphones.

I also came across a webpage hosted by The Church of Headphone Fetish that appears to be more geared towards anime-type illustration material than the photographs and videoclips found on the Headph0ne Phet1sh website. A similar selection of headphone fetish illustrations, although not just restricted to anime, can also be found on the Deviant Art website.

Headphone fetishism would appear to be a relatively rare sexual activity as it does not appear in the books by Aggrawal (2009a) or Love (2001). Furthermore, there is not a single reference to headphone fetishism in any academic article or book of which I am aware. Therefore, I went online in search of people who had confessed to this strange fetish. I have to admit the pickings were fairly slim, but I did find a few.

In the absence of scientific research why anyone should be sexually attracted to headphones is anyone's guess. Personally, I think that if headphone fetish really exists, then its etiology is most likely explained by behavioural conditioning in childhood and adolescence.

Herpetophilia

Elsewhere in the book I examine various subtypes of zoophilia. It was not until very recently that I came across an article on herpetophilia, which according to the online Urban Dictionary is "… the sexual attraction to reptiles, commonly dinosaurs or anthropomorphic lizards."

There is a fairly active online community of herpetophiles including herpy.net, which has lots of discussion topics, such as "How to please a reptile." Dinosaur-loving herpetophiles can be found interacting with each other on sites like Lava Dome Five where there is an overt crossover between herpetophilia and macrophilia (i.e., sexual arousal from giants – in this case giant reptiles in the form of dinosaurs).

My own view is that sex should always be consensual and interspecies sexual activity by nature is therefore always non-consensual. People who engage in such sex claim it is "cruelty free" but this does not make sexual activity with animals an acceptable activity.

Another paraphilia related to herpetophilia and a subcategory of zoophilia is ophidiophilia. Aggrawal (2009a) defined this as "a sexual attraction to snakes". There are some really quite bizarre snake sexuality websites including some where there is a crossover with vorarephilia (sexual arousal from the idea of being eaten, eating another person or observing this process for sexual gratification). This seems a logical crossover given that snakes swallow their prey whole (check out the Snake Eats website if you do not believe me).

An act often associated with ophidiophilia is ophidicism. This is where women voluntarily insert a snake (sometimes an eel) tail first into their vaginas to get sexual pleasure as it wriggles free. There are also stories of both men and women allegedly receiving sexual pleasure from snakes wriggling free following anal insertion. Acts of ophidicism have been documented going back to Ancient Greek times.

Hirsutophilia

In this book I examine a number of fetishes and paraphilias related to human body hair including trichophilia (sexual arousal from hair, usually head hair), pogonophilia (sexual arousal from beards) and haircut fetishism (sexual arousal from seeing someone get their hair cut either voluntarily or through coercion). Another subtype of trichophilia is hirsutophilia in which individuals get sexual pleasure and arousal from women who are abnormally hairy (including but not limited to overly hairy pubic hair, underarm hair, hairy arms, hairy legs and hair around nipples). As far as I am aware, there is no academic research on this topic, although typing "hairy women" into an online search engine reveals dozens of websites, presumably catering to men who get their sexual kicks from hirsute women.

Homilophilia

According to Aggrawal (2009a) homilophilia refers to individuals who derive sexual pleasure and arousal from the hearing or giving of sermons. Unsurprisingly, no academic research on this topic has been published (not even a single case study), so I did start to wonder if this paraphilia was theoretical or actually real. Given there is so little written on the topic, I am not surprised that not all academic sources agree on what the paraphilia actually constitutes.

Hooper (2009) described homilophilia as a "public-speaking fetish" and claimed that "some people get turned on by standing up in front of an audience and making a sexually fueled speech. Others become excited by listening and may end up bouncing compulsively on the edge of his or her seat." The Right Diagnosis website (2011) claimed that homilophilia refers to "sexual urges, arousal or fantasies involving listening to or giving a speech or sermon." An online article on the A–Z of paraphilias entitled "A freaky kind of love" defined homilophilia more broadly as referring to individuals who derive sexual arousal from "giving lectures". Love (2001) covers all bases and defines homilophilia as "sexual arousal while listening to or giving sermons and speeches." She also says the condition is known by another name – autagonistophilia. However, in most of the definitions I have come across, very few of them would include being sexually aroused from giving or hearing a sermon or lecture.

Almost all definitions of autagonistophilia concern individuals deriving sexual pleasure and arousal from displaying themselves in a sexual act in front of others, particularly on stage. In this sense it is a form of exhibitionism. Campbell (2004, 2009) defined autagonistophilia as "a paraphilia in which sexual arousal and orgasm are contingent upon displaying one's self in a live show" (i.e., being observed performing on stage or on camera). Aggrawal (2009a) defined it as "sexual arousal and orgasm [being] contingent upon displaying one's self in a live show or while being photographed." Milner *et al.* (2008) in a review of "paraphilias not otherwise specified" noted that the erotic focus in autagonistophilia involves being observed by an audience. Money (1986) also said the source of erotic focus involves being seen on stage or on camera. Both of these latter definitions could technically include those giving a sermon or lecture, but personally I have come to the conclusion that homilophilia and autagonistophilia are two separate paraphilic behaviours.

Hybristophilia

It is hardly surprising that there are many links and associations between criminal behaviour and paraphilic behaviour. Many paraphilic behaviours are of course criminal offences. I have covered many of these elsewhere in this book. There are also criminal activities containing paraphilic elements that are either part of the criminal act itself and/or involve objects left at the crime scene. One such activity is hybristophilia where the source of sexual arousal is the criminal activity.

Hybristophilia was defined by Money (1984) as "a paraphilia in which an individual derives sexual arousal and pleasure from having a sexual partner who is known to have committed an outrage or crime, such as rape, murder, or armed robbery." This type of paraphilic behaviour is sometimes colloquially known as "Bonnie and Clyde Syndrome". In some cases the person who is the focus of the sexual desire is someone who has been imprisoned. In other cases, hybristophiles may urge and coerce their partners to commit a crime.

In yet other cases, the hybristophile may contact someone who is already in prison with whom they are not acquainted except by reputation and/or what they have read or seen in the media. For instance, it is well known that serial killers, particularly those who have received lots of media publicity, get lots of fan mail from female admirers some of whom are likely to be genuine hybristophiles. High-profile murderers and serial killers who are known to have received sexual fan mail include Charles Manson, Jeffrey Dahmer, Richard Ramirez and Ted Bundy. Compared with other paraphilic behaviours, hybristophilia is quite unusual in that it appears to be more common among women than men, and that it varies in both disposition and degree (Vitello, 2006).

Academic research has reported that hybristophiles are often insecure, have low self-esteem and have often been victims of physical and sexual abuse. This brief overview demonstrates that this is an area in which rigorous empirical research is greatly needed since much of what is known is based on interview evidence and populist books.

Hyphephilia

Earlier in this book I briefly examined frotteurism in which a person derives sexual pleasure or gratification from rubbing, especially the genitals, against another nonconsensual person, typically in a public place, such as a crowded train, or in crowded areas, such as malls, elevators, busy sidewalks and public transportation vehicles. Such behaviour is closely related to (or a subtype of) "toucherism" depending on which source you read. Some descriptions of toucherism claim that the individual touches or fondles other people rather than rubbing to gain sexual arousal. For instance, the Psychology Dictionary (2014) defines toucherism as "carnal interest and stimulation gathered from touching a stranger on an erotic area of their body, especially the buttocks, breasts, or genitalia."

Freund (1990) claimed that behaviours such as toucherism, frotteurism and exhibitionism are caused by "courtship disorders". According to Freund, normal courtship comprises four phases: (i) locating a partner, (ii) pre-tactile interactions, (iii) tactile interactions and (iv) genital union. Freund proposes that toucherism is a disturbance of the third phase of the courtship disorder. Similarly, Money (1986) proposed the "lovemap" theory, which suggests that paraphilic behaviour occurs when an abnormal lovemap develops and interferes with the ability to participate in loving sexual intercourse.

The reason I began this entry by mentioning frotteurism and toucherism is that there is a tactile fetishistic behaviour called "hyphephilia", which I would argue is a subtype of toucherism, but not necessarily a subtype of frotteurism suggesting that toucherism and frotteurism may be two separate paraphilias. Aggrawal (2009a) defines hyphephilia as "a paraphilia in which individuals derive sexual arousal from touching skin, hair, leather or fur," although these could be very specific paraphilias, such as trichophilia (i.e., individuals who derive sexual arousal from human hair). This is similar to (but not the same as) the online English Encyclopedia that notes:

"In psychiatry, [hyphephilia is] a sexual perversion in which sexual arousal and orgasm depend upon touching or rubbing the partner's skin or hair, or upon the sensations related to feeling fur, leather, fabric, or other substances in association with sexual activity with the partner."

The Right Diagnosis medical website adds an arguably zoophilic element by claiming that the symptoms of hyphephilia are a (i) sexual interest in the feel and smell of animal skin, fur or leather, (ii) recurring intense sexual fantasies involving the feel and smell of animal skin, fur or leather, (iii) recurring intense sexual urges involving the feel and smell of animal skin, fur or leather and/or (iv) sexual preference for the feel and smell of animal skin, fur or leather. Finally, Pranzarone (2000) is a little more technical and says:

> "Hyphephilia [is] one of a group of paraphilias of the fetishistic/talismanic type in which the sexuoerotic stimulus is associated with the touching, rubbing, or the feel of skin, hair, leather, fur, and fabric, especially if worn in proximity to erotically significant parts of the body."

Hickey (2010) noted that paraphilic behaviour is very common among those who commit sexual crimes, but that the two activities (sex offending and paraphilias) can be two independent constructs in which one does not necessarily affect the other. Hickey asserted that hyphephilia is one of the so-called "preparatory paraphilias" as opposed to the "attack paraphilias". Attack paraphilias are described by Hickey as being sexually violent towards other individuals, including children in extreme circumstances. Preparatory paraphilias are defined by Hickey as those "that have been found as part of the lust killer's sexual fantasies and activities." However, Hickey noted that individuals who engage in preparatory paraphilias do not necessarily go on to become serial killers.

Like many paraphilic and fetishistic behaviours there is no scientific agreement concerning the cause of hyphephilia. This probably depends on the person rather than a single characteristic factor. Most experts would no doubt attribute hyphephilic behaviour to an initially random or accidental touching of a specific item the individual subsequently found sexually arousing. Through processes, such as classical and operant conditioning, successive repetitions of the associative pairings of the behaviour would then reinforce the behaviour and result in the behaviour being repeated.

One of the few references I came across to mention hyphephilia is Gould (1991) who claimed that the field of sex research has been overlooked by consumer research and that Money's (1986) concept of "lovemaps" could be applied. Although hyphephilia is unlikely to be problematic for many, those who seek therapy are likely to receive the same types of therapeutic intervention that are recommended for frotteurism (behaviour therapy, reality therapy and cognitive behavioural therapy), although the most critical thing is that the person seeking such treatment must want actively to change the behaviour.

Hypnofetishism

Back in 1986 when I was still an undergraduate psychology student, an optional part of my degree allowed me and some of my fellow undergraduates to attend a training course on hypnosis. As a consequence of taking the course I became very interested in the clinical applications of hypnosis. Along with one of my fellow students Cheryl Gillett and our supervisor Peter Davies we carried out some research using hypnosis and aversive classical conditioning techniques, which was eventually published (Gillett et al., 1989; Griffiths et al., 1989a, b). Although I stopped researching in the area I never lost my academic interest in all things hypnotic.

Given my personal interest in both hypnosis and paraphilias, this entry examines the relationship between hypnosis and sexual behaviour and, more specifically, hypnophilia and hypnofetishism. According to a short article on hypnofetishism on the Health Explores website (2011), seduction through mind control (i.e., erotic hypnosis) has a long history in Western culture dating back to the sirens of Greek mythology who were portrayed in Homer's *Odyssey* as having a "bewitching" song that lured sailors to their deaths. The article further claimed that witches in the Middle Ages had a "hypnotic aspect" to their sexuality. Despite the long history, the hypnotic aspects of sex have not been widely researched.

Love (2001) devoted a whole entry to sex and hypnosis, but did not mention fetishes or paraphilias. Her entry concentrated on the use of hypnosis for improving sexual health and the treatment of sexual problems, as well as its use as a seduction technique, some of which is non-consensual and would be classed as sexual assault. She noted:

> "There are historical records of cases where hypnotists were able to use hypnotic suggestions to facilitate intercourse. [Dr. Magnus] Hirschfeld was consulted during a trial where an impotent husband filed sexual assault charges against a wife's physician. The doctor confessed that he'd ordered her to 'raise her skirt, lie down, spread her legs, take out his penis, introduce it into her vagina, then, during the act, perform parallel movements until mutual orgasm occurred.' Suspicion was aroused when she became pregnant and a detective was hired by the husband, who confirmed his fears."

Love (2001) also made reference to the fact that hypnosis has occasionally been used in the treatment of sexual problems and dysfunctions. One paper that Love cites a lot is Ringrose (1989). In this paper a young adult male sought treatment for his overwhelming sexual attraction to his mother-in-law. Ringrose used hypnosis and an aversive conditioning technique to pair thoughts of his mother-in-law with both an aversive smell (ammonia) and an aversive taste (castor oil). The treatment was said to be successful because, following the treatment, the man no longer had sexual feelings toward his mother-in-law. I tried to track this paper down, particularly because my own research career began with my work on aversive conditioning. However, it does not appear in any academic databases and the journal's website only has papers dating back to 2002 despite the journal being founded in 1973. Therefore, I can only go on Love's (2001) reading of the paper. Moreover, I have no methodological details of the therapy utilized. Preston (1996) reported that:

> "Over 20% of young adults look at sex as being an opportunity to experience the power of their partner, and over 20% look at sex as an opportunity to exert power over their partner. Clearly hypnosis is one way they can experience this power because hypnosis is explicitly one person taking control of another and using that control."

One thing I know about hypnosis from my own research over 35 years ago is that there is a wide range of hypnotic susceptibilities among humans. Hypnofetishism is always likely to be a minority sexual interest because the degree to which people can be hypnotized depends on many factors including (i) the confidence and trust that someone has in letting someone else hypnotize them, (ii) the general fears people have about being hypnotized in any capacity, (iii) the previous experience someone has of being hypnotized and (iv) the experience of the hypnotist.

There are also many ethical questions. For instance, Gibbons (2011a, b) in short articles on hypnophilia wondered to what extent hypnophilia occurred among professional hypnotherapists, how many in the profession were sexually obsessed by the use of hypnosis and how many use their skill as an instrument of serial seduction? As yet, we simply do not know. There are also ethical questions concerning informed sexual consent. Just because people allow others to perform hypnosis on them does not necessarily mean that they are fully consenting to sexual acts engaged in while in a hypnotic trance

Hypoxyphilia

Hypoxyphilia (a.k.a. "autoerotic asphyxiation" and "asphyxiophilia") is a rare and potentially life-threatening paraphilia in which a person seeks to reduce the supply of oxygen to the brain during a heightened state of sexual arousal. Restricting the oxygen flow causes a build-up of carbon dioxide. This increase in carbon dioxide brings about feelings of giddiness and pleasure that, when accompanied by masturbation, can heighten sexual sensations. Typically, this is achieved by placing a chain, leather belt or rope noose around the neck or a plastic bag over the head. Hypoxyphiliacs generally do it alone but sometimes with a partner. Such activity often results in death. Deaths occur due to the loss of consciousness caused by partial asphyxia. High-profile deaths by hanging include the Australian INXS singer Michael Hutchence, the US actor David Carradine, and the English MP and television reporter Stephen Milligan.

Although asphyxia from hanging has frequently been described, a review of autoerotic asphyxiate deaths by Byard (1994) concluded that a wide variety of other lethal situations have been reported. Other hypoxyphilia variants reported include the use of plastic bags, electrocution, water submersion, and power hydraulics.

There is some disagreement as to how common such deaths are. The American Psychiatric Association estimates that one in a million deaths are caused this way. The FBI estimated there to be a mortality rate of 1,000 deaths per year in the USA. In a review of the literature, Uva (1995) estimated the mortality rate as being anywhere between 250 and 1,000 deaths per year in the USA. Most hypoxyphiliacs are male as evidenced by one Canadian study (Blanchard and Hucker, 1991) reporting that only 1 of 117 accidental hypoxyphilic deaths involved a female. In general, hypoxyphiliacs are white middle-aged males, although there are cases in the literature of women or men up to 87 years of age.

Although there are limited data, the goal seems to be to increase orgasm intensity. This bears some relationship with those who use amyl nitrate, which reduces brain oxygenation. It has been said that this type of behaviour may be a dangerous variant or manifestation of sexual masochism with its ritualized bondage themes. The person often keeps diaries and may watch himself in mirrors or video-record himself. A

German study of 40 accidental autoerotic deaths (Janssen *et al.*, 2005) reported that the bodies of hypoxyphiliacs are typically discovered naked and/or with genitalia in hand. Pornographic and/or other paraphilic material and/or sex toys are often present. Furthermore, the individuals had ejaculated shortly before their death. A study by Hucker (2008) of 100 hypoxyphiliacs shows that hypoxyphilia was associated with other paraphilias and fetushes including masochism (71%), sadism (31%), bondage (44%) and self-flagellation (37%).

Hucker (2011a) recommended that the term "hypoxyphilia" be abandoned in favour of the term "asphyxiophilia" because there is little empirical evidence to indicate that the effects of oxygen deprivation *per se* are the primary motive for the paraphiliac's behavior. He argued that the behaviour is sexual arousal by oxygen deprivation.

Impregnation fetishism

Later in this book I examine maieusiophilia, which according to Aggrawal (2009a) is defined as gaining sexual arousal from pregnant women and/or female childbirth. However, other sources define maieusiophilia more broadly to include sexual attraction to women who appear pregnant, attraction to lactation and/or attraction to particular stages of pregnancy from impregnation to childbirth. This entry briefly examines impregnation fetishes that may (or may not depending upon the definition used) be a subtype of maieusiophilia.

In researching this topic I was unable to locate a single academic paper that had examined impregnation fetishes – not even a passing reference. After spending one Sunday afternoon scouring lots of "adult" websites in the name of research for this topic, I was left in no doubt that there is a niche market for impregnation fetishes. There are a number of dedicated websites that cater specifically to such fetishists, the most popular (at least in terms of number of visitors) appeared to be the ImpregNation site. There are also more general fetish sites, such as the Dark Fetish website that contain dedicated groups like the Breeding and Forced Impregnation group. There are also a number of erotic fiction websites and blogs, such as Kristen Archives and Breeder's Erotica, that are dedicated to publishing impregnation stories. However, be warned, they feature pictures of sexual activity.

Based on the many accounts that I read it would appear that both men and women can have impregnation fetishes, but there was little to explain the etiology. On the Is It Normal? website, 15 of 16 indivduals who participated in a discussion thread on impregnation fetishes said that such fetishes are "normal". In fact, one discussion participant went so far as to claim, "If you look at it from an evolutionary point of view, it's probably the most normal fetish thinkable." That certainly has some face validity. Unfortunately, we can only speculate as to how such fetishes develop. Most fetishistic behaviours begin in childhood or adolescence and many appear to be rooted in early associative pairings (e.g., classical conditioning). There is no reason to suggest that is not the case here, but few of the accounts I came across mentioned early formative experiences. The jury is still out on whether impregnation fetishes are a subtype of pregnancy fetishism. However, my own reading is that, although they may overlap within individuals, they are two separate fetishes.

Infantilism

Infantilism is a rare paraphilia in which individuals typically get sexually aroused from being a baby and, consequently, is commonly referred to as "adult baby syndrome". Some websites claim that the condition also goes under the name of "autonepiophilia". However, Money (1984) who coined this particular paraphilia, described the condition as particularly relating to "diaper fetishism" (i.e., people who get sexually aroused from wearing diapers – "nappies" in the UK). Milner *et al.* (2008) noted in a review of paraphilias not otherwise specified (PNOS) that:

> *"Although infantilism is classified as sexual masochism in DSM-IV it is questionable whether the criteria for sexual masochism are always met. For example, if the infantile role playing does not involve feelings of humiliation and suffering, then the diagnosis of sexual masochism would not be appropriate and a diagnosis of infantilism as paraphilia NOS is warranted."*

Infantilists often wear diapers, drink from a baby bottle, are wet-nursed (sometimes simulated), crawl about the floor, have baby baths, eat baby foods, play with baby toys, are spanked and may roleplay and regress to an infant-like state. There may also be some crossover with other sexually paraphilic behaviour including masochism (as they may enjoy being spanked and/or humiliated), transvestism (as they may like to be dressed in baby clothes of the opposite sex, when it is known as "sissy baby" syndrome), urophilia (as they may enjoy urinating in their diapers), coprophilia (as they may enjoy defecating in their diapers) and lactophilia (as they may enjoy being breastfed).

Up until 1980 there had only been three published case studies on infantilism all of which were in the *American Journal of Psychiatry* between 1964 and 1967. Malitz (1966) reported a case of a 20-year-old college student who had a compulsion to wear diapers underneath rubber pants and defecate in them, although he did not see himself as an adult baby. While defecating he would typically reach orgasm even if he did not masturbate. Tuchman and Lachman (1964) reported the case of a father who was arrested for molesting his young daughters. Like the first case, he wore rubber pants over his diaper and enjoyed urinating and masturbating in it. Dinello (1967) reported the case of a 17-year-old male who in his mid-teens started wearing diapers under his clothing, drank from baby bottles, ate baby food and masturbated while wearing the diaper. He eventually gave up wearing diapers and began dressing in women's clothing. Pettit and Barr (1980) reported the case of a 24-year-old man who began dressing in female clothes at the age of 10 years. By the age of 15 years, he began to dress as a baby and developed a fetish for diapers.

Pate and Gabbard (2003) also presented a case study showing many similarities with earlier published case studies. Their case study was a 35-year-old single man who had wanted to be a baby since the age of 12 years and began wearing diapers aged 17 years. His diaper-wearing had started to compromise his interpersonal relationships. He admitted wearing diapers was "a kind of a sexual thing" and said he masturbated while wearing them. He only ever masturbated while wearing diapers, but also urinated and defecated while wearing them. He wore and used up to five diapers a day.

Pate and Gabbard (2003) concluded that the object of sexual arousal was the wearing of diapers and that the behaviour was a paraphilia. More specifically, they wrote:

> "Adult baby syndrome is still a new entity for psychiatrists, and there are undoubtedly variations within the syndrome. [One of the cases saying] he wanted someone to 'make him be a baby' evokes images of the sadomasochistic scenarios enacted by a dominatrix and her clients. Indeed, a significant number of middle-aged men seek out dominatrices to spank them, punish them, and tell them that they have been 'a bad boy'. The wish to be treated as a baby is probably a spectrum condition that has many manifestations involving men, women, heterosexuals, bisexuals, and homosexuals."

Other case studies have noted different etiological pathways into infantilism with childhood sexual abuse and transgender issues being apparent common factors among a number of published case studies. Lehne and Money (2003) reviewed the case of a man with changing fetishes (transvestic fetishism, paedophilia) who in the final analysis described himself as an adult baby (he was aged 45 years). Croarkin *et al.* (2004) reported a case in which a depressed 32-year-old male engaged in behaviours that included getting sexual arousal and gratification from wearing diapers and becoming a baby. The authors suggested that his infantilism may have been related to obsessive–compulsive disorder. Evcimen and Gratz (2006) reported the case of a 25-year-old male who wished to be a 10-year-old girl, although it is debatable whether this case would really be classed as infantilism.

A more recent case of "adult baby syndrome" was reported by Kise and Nguyen (2011). They outlined in detail the case of a 38-year-old biological male who preferred to be identified as a female, even getting the authors to refer to him as "she" throughout their paper. For 2 years "she" slept in a crib rather than a bed, drank from baby bottles, sucked on dummies and engaged in baby talk. "She" had wanted to be a baby since "her" early thirties, suffered from Guillain–Barré Syndrome (a disorder affecting the peripheral nervous system) and had been a paraplegic since the age of 13 years following a complication that arose from a tracheotomy. "She" had been sexually abused as a child and had attempted suicide 28 times. Kise and Nguyen (2011) concluded:

> "Perhaps desiring the identity of a baby is an entity all in itself, just like major depressive disorder or schizophrenia ... This does not represent a new phenomenon ... In some instances, [adult baby syndrome] seems to represent a paraphilia. [In this case] she specifically denied sexual pleasure ... her primary intent seems to be one of gaining attention and additional care, freeing her from adult responsibilities. Further investigation into the connection and potential co-morbidity between ABS [adult baby syndrome] and gender identity disorder may lead to interesting findings."

Nothing is known about the incidence or prevalence of infantilism and there is no consensus on the etiology of infantilism. However, it has been linked to maladaptive learning in childhood, faulty childhood imprinting and erotic targeting errors. Although for many with infantilism the sexual element may be downplayed, there do seem to be individuals who want to be gently nurtured, seek attention, be cared for and/or surrender their day-to-day adult life responsibilities.

One of the reasons so little is known about infantilism is that adult babies do not

Inflatophilia 109

want to cease engaging in their behaviour. For most adult babies their behaviour does not constitute a medical condition that requires treatment or cause any functional impairment, personal distress or distress to others. Those who do end up seeking psychological or psychiatric help may do so because another individual, such as their sexual partner, encourages or forces them to seek help.

Inflatable rubber suit fetishism

In this book I examine various sexual fetishes that involve sexual arousal from being completely enveloped in some sort of outer garment, such as rubber-dolling and mummification. Another fetish that is arguably related is inflatable rubber suit fetishism (a.k.a. "body inflation fetishism"). However, I think the latter term sounds more like people who actually inflate some parts of their body, such as belly inflation and scrotal infusion. These paraphilias are covered elsewhere in this book.

Gallagher (2015), in an article about his television interview in 2000 with "Mr Blow Up" (MBU) for a documentary he was making about the rise of online fetish websites, described MBU as "one of the more interesting characters I met – alongside representatives from the wet and messy ('sploshing') communities, adult babies, furries and used panty-sellers." According to Gallagher (2015) MBU was a Londoner who talked about "his love of being inside a latex suit that was pumped full of air." MBU first became attracted to the idea of being enveloped in an air-filled rubber suit as a child when playing with a beach ball. MBU often thought about what it would be like to be inside the ball as it bounced everywhere on the beach. Gallagher (2015) then went on to describe what happened in the documentary:

> "Mr Blow Up, with the help of his latex-clad wife, slipped into one of his talcum-sprinkled outfits and sat on the sofa while she used a foot pump to blow up his headdress. Just at the very moment I thought he might explode (like some sort of latex Mr Creosote), Mr B gave a thumbs-up. He later explained how being so constrained made him feel happy, secure and excited."

In my research for this entry, I came across many websites that sell inflatable suits accompanied by in-depth information on how to put on such suits and how they are designed. For instance, the Latex Wiki website (LW) provides pictures and descriptions of inflatable catsuits, ballbody suits and blueberry suits.

Unsurprisingly, there has never been any academic research on inflatable rubber suit fetishism. Therefore, little is known about what fetishists enjoy about the activity so much. Given the potential dangers of this fetish, I am surprised there are no papers from the medical community reporting on accidents from suits bursting.

Inflatophilia

According to Opentopia (2013) inflatophilia refers to a sexual fetish in which individuals derive sexual attraction to and/or are sexually aroused by inflatable objects and/or toys. The fetish appears to have psychological and behavioural overlaps with balloon fetishism. Moreover, like "looners" (a.k.a. "balloon fetishists"), inflatophiles have been categorized into one of three subtypes. According to the entry in Opentopia these three groups are based on the activity preference related to the inflatable object(s) and comprise:

- *Poppers:* Individuals who derive sexual pleasure and arousal from "popping" (i.e., puncturing) inflatable objects and/or trying to reinflate the inflatable that has popped.
- *Inflators:* Individuals who derive sexual pleasure and arousal while sitting or lying on top of inflatable objects that are being filled with air.
- *Deflators:* Individuals who derive sexual pleasure and arousal from releasing the air in inflatable objects while sitting or lying on top of them.

These groups are not mutually exclusive and inflatophiles may belong to one or more of the three subtypes. The act of inflating or deflating may be carried out by the inflatophiles themselves or may be done by others (e.g., their sexual partners). Personally, I feel that the behaviour is best explained through various behavioural conditioning processes that occur in childhood and/or adolescence (most notably, classical conditioning). Rolnik (2012) in a paper exploring inflatable fetishism writes:

> "My discovery of this strange sub-cult [of inflatable fetishism] began when I innocently favorited a photo of an inflatable horse toy on a popular art website. I simply thought it looked hilarious and judging by the user's other pics, it didn't seem like anything 'alt' was going on. But that all changed when I got a message from the photographer featuring a link to the blog Hollow Paws, which had a discrete sentence in the upper right hand corner that made it all clear: A website for furries who love inflatable critters ... I asked the blogger what people exactly did with the inflatables featured in [the featured articles] ... Moments later I received an answer: '... Sometimes they hump them.' Horrified, yet intrigued, I began to uncover a secret world of anonymous patrons who do everything from wear full motocross gear and aggressively hump vinyl Shamu pool rafts until they explode, to fabricators who design prosthetic vaginas for plastic dolphins."

Rolnik (2012) also concurred that inflatophiles can be differentiated into subtypes, such as "poppers" and "non-poppers", but claimed the two types *detest* each other based on the very specific online forums devoted to various inflatable fetishes, such as the Blow To Pop website. Rolnik (2012) interviewed psychiatrist Dr Soroya Bacchus about the psychology of inflatophilia and cites her as saying:

> "When I heard about this fetish, they didn't seem too different from the people who have intercourse with blow-up dolls. They both suffer from a sexual function disorder that is categorized in the realm of paraphilia – meaning a love of some object, whether it's an inanimate one or a non-consenting partner. The basic component is arousal, so sometimes there might be actual ejaculation on the toys, but oftentimes in cases of paraphilia it happens afterwards during masturbation. These kinds of disorders tend to feed on themselves."

Dr Bacchus appears to believe all inflatophiles suffer from sexual function disorder. However, my anecdotal reading suggests that most inflatophiles use inflatables as an adjunct to their "normal" sex life rather than as a replacement. If this is the case, then I personally do not see the person as suffering from a sexual function disorder. As with many idiosyncratic fetishes, there has been no empirical or clinical research on inflatophilia. Therefore, nothing is known about how prevalent the behaviour is. The existence of more than a sprinkling of dedicated online forums and websites certainly suggests there is a small and committed inflatophile community. It would appear that the fetish is relatively benign and of little problem to its participants, which probably explains why there has been little interest from psychologists and clinicians.

Injection fetishes

One of the subtypes of medical fetishism relates to individuals who derive sexual pleasure and arousal from being the recipients of a medical or clinical procedure, typically some kind of body examination. This includes genital and urological examinations (e.g., a gynaecological examination), genital procedures (e.g., fitting a catheter or menstrual cup), rectal procedures (e.g., inserting suppositories, taking a rectal temperature and prostate massage), the application of medical dressings and accessories (e.g., putting on a bandage or diaper, fitting a dental retainer and putting someone's arm in plaster) and the application and fitting of medical devices (e.g., fitting a splint, orthopaedic cast or brace).

Another type of medical fetish is one involving individuals who have "injection fetishes". Such fetishes clearly appear to be very niche sexual behaviours within medical fetishism. However, there are various online forums and websites that cater to individuals who derive sexual pleasure from the giving or receiving of injections (or watching such acts). For instance, there is a dedicated forum within the Voy.com website where individuals share their injection stories. Other sites include the Real Injection website (which features stories and clips from films and news stories where injections are administered), the Needing Needles webpage on Tumblr (which mainly consists of photographic pictures featuring hypodermic needles), the Injection Girls website (which does not appear to be overtly sexual, but would be highly arousing for those with an injection fetish), the Fetish Clinic website (featuring lots of medical fetish videos including injections) and even a dedicated Facebook page on the topic.

Katoptronophilia

Aggrawal (2009a) says that the paraphilia in which someone derives sexual arousal "from looking at oneself in a mirror [and] arousal from images in mirrors" is called "spectrophilia". However, most sources state that spectrophilia relates to those who derive sexual arousal and pleasure from the thought of having sex with a ghost or having sexual thoughts about ghosts.

At first glance, katoptronophilia appears to be a subtype of voyeurism in which the key distinguishing feature is the use of mirrors as part of the voyeuristic act. However, voyeurism is usually defined as the act of gaining sexual arousal from the watching of *others* either naked and/or engaging in sexual behaviour. I stressed the word "others" because katoptronophilia involves individuals watching themselves having sex by means of a mirror. Technically, katoptronophilia is a subtype of scoptophilia (a.k.a. "scopophilia"). According to Pranzarone (2000) scoptophilia/scopophilia is:

> "A paraphilia of the solicitational [and] allurative type in which sexuoerotic arousal and facilitation or attainment of orgasm are responsive to, and contingent on watching others engaging in sexual activity, including sexual intercourse [from Greek, skopein, to view + -philia]. The condition in which a person is dependent on looking at sexual organs and watching their coital performance in order to obtain erotic arousal and facilitate and achieve orgasm. It is not surreptitious, as in voyeurism. The reciprocal paraphilic condition is sometimes also referred to as scoptophilia; or by its own name, autagonistophilia. Synonyms, mixophilia; mixoscopia; scopophilia."

Just to complicate things further, many online definitions of mixophilia, which, as in the definition by Pranzarone (2000), appears to be another word for scoptophilia, often mention mirrors in the definitions. For instance, the Fetish List website defines mixophilia as "gaining sexual arousal and pleasure from watching their partner or themselves engage in sexual activity." Usually, this means watching themselves in a mirror. This is similar to the definition of mixophilia in the online Gay Slang Dictionary, which notes:

> "A person with this fetish [mixophilia] likes to watch his partner or the both of them engage in sexual activity. Usually this means watching themselves perform in a mirror. A common theme in gay porn pictures is the presence of a mirror in which part or all of the action is reflected."

I have yet to come across a single academic article on the topic and most of the theorizing is speculative to say the least. An article on the Forbidden Light (2007) webpage argues that katoptronphilia is evolving and that "technology is also expanding on this fetish; live-stream cameras, multiple cameras, big-screen monitors … the possibilities are limitless."

I am not convinced that evolving technology providing more ways for individuals to watch themselves having sex is actually katoptronphilia because the key distinguishing feature of this paraphilia is the use of mirrors – not individuals watching themselves. I also have some doubts as to whether this is a genuine paraphilic behaviour and whether it will ever be the subject of serious academic research because it is highly unlikely that such behaviour is problematic in any way.

Klismaphilia

Klismaphilia, from the Greek for "enema" (*klisma*), was first coined by Denko (1973, 1976) when she reported two case studies in the early 1970s. It is a very unusual variant of sexual expression in which an individual obtains sexual pleasure from receiving enemas (i.e., the cleansing of the colonic canal via anal douching). Less commonly, some people also get sexual pleasure from the giving of enemas to other people. Although warm water is typically used to clean the lower rectum, other substances have been reported including coffee, yogurt, air, whisky, wine, beer, cocaine, epoxy resin and even cement. For instance, Hemandas *et al.* (2005) reported the unique case of an unemployed 27-year-old patient self-administering epoxy resin, a liquid used as a masonry adhesive, for anal sexual gratification. The American Psychiatric Association's (2022) *Diagnostic and Statistical Manual of Mental Disorders* (DSM-5-TR) classifies klismaphilia under "other specified paraphilic disorder" (OSPD).

Kinsey *et al.*'s (1948, 1953) surveys of the sexual behaviour of males and females in the late 1940s and early 1950s specifically mentioned women using enemas as a masturbatory aid, but no such practice was reported by males. Although Kinsey *et al.*'s research provides evidence that klismaphilia was engaged in by women, as with most paraphilias it is typically males who are more likely to be klismaphiliacs. Published research on klismaphiliacs is rare since it is thought that most keep their engagement in this activity very secret.

The little research into klismaphilia suggests that the act of receiving enemas can cause intense stimulation and produce pleasurable sensations (e.g., gaining pleasure from a large water-distended belly or the feeling of internal pressure). Enemas cause mechanical distension of the rectum that then stimulates the nerve endings supplying the pelvic organs, such as rectal stretch receptors. It has also been reported that drugs that are administered rectally including aqueous and alcoholic solutions are absorbed very rapidly and have a "mainlining effect" similar to that of intravenous drug injection.

Typically, klismaphiliacs retrospectively report discovering these very particular sexual desires after being given enemas sometime in their childhood. Published case studies suggest that klismaphilia most likely arises in children who were given them by a loving and affectionate mother. This association between loving attention and anal stimulation may eroticize the experience for some people such that as adults they may manifest a need to receive an enema as a substitute for or necessary prerequisite to genital intercourse.

Denko (1973) initially reported two case studies on klismaphilia. Then, a few years later Denko (1976) wrote a paper in which she reported a study comprising 15 klismaphiliacs. Based on these limited data, she concluded that klismaphiliacs comprised one of three groups labelled Type A, Type B and Type C:

- *Type A:* Individuals who were unhappy, believed their klismaphilic behaviour to be abnormal but kept the behaviour compartmentalized. The behaviour originated in childhood and the enemas were usually self-administered. Some of the cases in this group also engaged in other paraphilic behaviour (e.g., fetishism, masochism, and coprophilia).
- *Type B:* Individuals who were similar to Type A individuals, but accepted the condition and were more likely to engage in klismaphilia with their sexual partners.
- *Type C:* Individuals who engaged in multiple paraphilic behaviours with other similar like-minded individuals. Their klismaphilia was integrated with a range of other paraphilic behaviours (e.g., transvestism and masochism).

Arndt (1991), after placing advertisements in sex magazines to recruit klismaphiliacs, surveyed 22 individuals, all males except one, who were aged between 25 and 54 years. Although most were homosexual (80%; the other 20% were bisexual), nearly two thirds were married or had been married. They typically engaged in klismaphilia twice a week and half of them reported the enemas were self-administered. The remainder gave and/or received enemas from their sexual partner. Just over one third of the sample (40%) had other paraphilic interests that typically revolved around sexual masochism (e.g., being spanked).

Agnew (1982) provided a physiological perspective on klismaphilia concentrating on the ritualization of inserting, filling and expelling components. He compared the physiological similarities between rectal stimulation and vaginal intercourse and said that the behaviour was reinforcing. This observation, when taken together with the work of Denko, suggests that much of the klismaphiliac's behaviour is maintained by both classical and operant conditioning. Agnew (2000) further noted that some individuals receive such extreme pleasure from the practice that they reach orgasm. He also linked klismaphilia with sadomasochistic activities.

Accidental rectal trauma and the lodging of foreign bodies in the gastrointestinal tract have been widely reported in the medical literature. Arguably, the most notorious case in relation to klismaphilia is that reported by Stephens and Taff (1987). They wrote about a young man who turned up at hospital complaining of rectal pain. After an examination by a doctor it became apparent that there was a stony hard mass lodged in the man's rectum. Upon further questioning, the patient revealed that 4 hours earlier he and his boyfriend had been "fooling around" and that, after stirring a batch of concrete mix, the patient had laid on his back with his feet against the wall at a 45-degree angle while his boyfriend poured the mixture through a funnel into his rectum. The concrete had set and was eventually removed. On removal, a ping-pong ball was found. Klismaphiliacs use a ping-pong ball as a plug to promote retention and increase stimulation. The use of a ping-pong ball also suggests the person was an experienced klismaphiliac. Hemandas *et al.* (2005) claimed that "as the exploration of anal eroticism increases in popularity, more and more cases of complications as a direct result of their abuse are likely to be encountered."

Knismolagnia

There are hundreds of paraphilias about which little is known. One of the most obscure, but which is definitely known to exist, is knismolagnia. According to Aggrawal (2009a) knismophilia is a paraphilia in which individuals derive sexual pleasure and arousal from tickling or being tickled (a.k.a. "titillagnia"). The Right Diagnosis website (2012e) claims the symptoms of knismolagnia are (i) sexual arousal gained from being tickled, (ii) sexual interest in tickling, (iii) recurring intense sexual urges involving tickling and (iv) sexual arousal associated with tickling.

As far as I can ascertain there is almost nothing in the academic literature on knismolagnia. However, there are a number of online articles and writings about the sexual side of tickling, although I have spotted a common mistake that may have arisen from a single source. Many online sources, such as the Acarophilia website and Kinky Sex Questions (2012a, b, c), appear to include tickling as belonging to acarophilia, defined as "the deriving of sexual arousal and pleasure from scratching or being scratched" when in fact it is not. However, there is clearly a fine line between hard tickling and scratching.

Shaffer and Penn (2006) developed a comprehensive paraphilia classification system (as already pointed out in previous entries on "aelurophilia" and "cynophilia"). Shaffer and Penn made specific references to both acarophilia and knismolagnia, although these mentions (despite being academic in context) were part of a wider theoretical point. More specifically, they noted that some paraphilias – specifically acarophilia and knismolagnia (although Shaffer and Penn use the term "titillagnia" for the latter) – are completely *innocuous* and this demonstrates that not all paraphiliacs are sex offenders and vice versa. This appears to be supported by the Right Diagnosis website (2012e) which claimed that treatment for knismolagnia is generally not sought and that individuals with the condition "simply learn to accept their fetish and manage to achieve gratification in an appropriate manner."

According to most online sources the main reason sexual tickling is popular among those in the BDSM community is the person is usually already restrained. The dominant partner may also blindfold his victim to enhance the sexual pain/pleasure. Of all the paraphilias in this book, knismophilia appears to have been one of the least researched (academically or clinically).

Lactophilia

Lactophilia (a.k.a. "breast milk fetishism") is a paraphilia in which individuals, typically male, derive sexual pleasure from watching women lactate, sucking on women's milk-filled breasts and/or having sex with lactating women. Sometimes sexual arousal is enhanced by the woman also being pregnant, although many men prefer lactating women post pregnancy. The paraphilic aspect may also be part of other paraphilias, such as infantilism in which sexual arousal is derived from being an "adult baby". For many infantilists the practice is often referred to as adult nursing, suckling or adult breastfeeding. In fact, some lactophiles describe themselves as being in an adult nursing relationship. Those who suckle and are suckled within the confines of a monogamous sexual relationship are often referred to as a "nursing couple".

There are a number of different methods by which erotic lactation can take place. "Lactation games" typically refer to any kind of sexual activity that includes female breast milk. The activity is thought to be widespread, but can be unintentional post pregnancy since many women who have just had babies release milk as a reflex action when sexually aroused.

Over the last decade there appears to have been an increased demand for lactation pornography with the advent of pornographic magazines, such as *Pregnant Pink and Milking*. Despite it evidently being a specialty market, the internet has increased the opportunity to see such pornography even if the person involved is not a lactophile. Such niche pornography may also be considered taboo, even by those who have no objections to pornography, particularly because of its association with children and incest.

Adult nursing relationships (ANRs) involve a person, typically male, breastfeeding from a woman's lactating breast. It is only considered to be an ANR when the practice is regular rather than a one-off or happens almost accidentally during post-pregnancy sex. Anecdotal evidence suggests that successful ANRs are reliant on trusting and stable long-term relationships. If the practice is not regular, then the woman's milk production ceases. In some cases it is thought that suckling can be a replacement for sex and that the mutual and intimate tenderness involved between consenting couples has a stabilizing influence on such relationships. It has also been noted that some women are capable of achieving orgasm during the suckling process. There may also be a number of inherently non-sexual reasons such behaviour is found within loving couples. For instance, couples who may want to adopt a child may use the context of an ANR to stimulate the production of breast milk pre adoption.

It has also been noted that an apparently small minority of women experience sensual and/or sexual pleasure from expressing breast milk either manually or from a breast pump. The feelings produced may depend on the context (e.g., some women may only get sexual pleasure if their partner is present during expression). Giles (2003) noted that some women feel more "feminine" when breastfeeding and therefore may want to continue with lactation, even after their children have been weaned, for emotional and/or sensual motivations.

Scorolli *et al.* (2007) reported that some websites feature references to lactophiles. However, this particular fetish was included in a "body fluids" fetish category along with coprophilia, urophilia, menophilia and mucophilia. Although this category made up a sizeable minority of all online fetishes (9%), what proportion of these online fetish sites were lactophilic compared with fetishes of other body fluids is unknown.

The rise in interest surrounding lactophilic activity has led to lactation prostitution in which grown adults (including women) pay for the opportunity to be breastfed. This can be part of other activities, such as infantilism, in which having a diaper changed may play a more primary role. It can also be part of an action done is isolation from any other service or activity. Giles (2004) made reference to a New Zealand brothel that offered lactation services to its clients. Giles (2005) further writes:

> "Induced lactation allows for a splitting away of breastfeeding from maternity, opening up possibilities for elaborating on the cultural meanings and uses of breastmilk as a substance, breastfeeding as a practice, and lactation as a process. Finally, by introducing lactation into sexual play, it offers the opportunity for a mutual confluence of bodily flows which may help to disassemble the binaries of sexual difference."

Breastfeeding can also feature in other types of sexual activity, such as sadism and masochism, as part of a wider set of dominance and submission sexual practices. For instance, submissive women may be commanded by their male or female dominant partner to be milked or to produce milk. Alternatively, breastfeeding can be used as a surrogate pleasure reward or surrogate pleasure for male or female submissive partners who have done exactly as they have been told by the dominant partner.

Lactophilia may also be associated with other paraphilias, such as maieusiophilia (i.e., pregnancy fetishism) in which individuals, typically male, but some bisexual or lesbian females also, derive attraction and/or sexual gratification from someone being or appearing pregnant. There is also a very small minority of individuals who develop a sexual fascination with the idea of themselves being pregnant (i.e., gravidophilia). This would appear to be psychologically similar to people who get sexually excited by the thought of being an amputee (i.e., apotemnophilia).

There has been very little empirical research on lactophilia or associated behaviours. Enquist *et al.* (2011) reported the results of a survey designed to investigate whether two specific sexual preferences, one for pregnant women and the other for lactating women, were associated with exposure to pregnant or lactating women early in an individual's life. Their data were collected using an online questionnaire advertised in newsgroups (e.g., alt.sex.fetish and alt.sex.fetish.breastmilk) and Yahoo! discussion groups (e.g., Lactaters and Pregnant Ladies). Individuals in these online communities typically described themselves as fetishists for pregnant and/or lactating women. The research team collected usable data from 2,082 participants. Some of the main findings were:

- The average age of the respondents was 37 years.
- The average age at which respondents became aware of their preference for pregnant and/or lactating women was 19 years.
- Most respondents reported both a pregnancy and a lactation preference (71%; 1,474 individuals).
- A small minority of the respondents reported having a preference for pregnancy fetish only (14%; 296 individuals).
- An even smaller minority of the respondents reported having a preference for lactation fetish only (11%; 224 individuals).
- A total of 4% (87 individuals) had neither preference and were excluded from further analysis.
- The great majority of the sample had younger brothers or sisters suggesting that they were exposed to pregnant women and/or experienced seeing their siblings being breastfed when in childhood.

This final finding led the authors to suggest their results were consistent with the hypothesis that specific sexual preferences may be acquired through exposure to particular stimuli during a period early in life similar to "sexual imprinting" in birds and mammals. In fact, there have been a number of studies offering empirical support for the idea that human partner choice is at least in part determined by parental characteristics. The authors concluded that their study offered new insights into the growing issue of an association between pregnancy, lactation and sexuality.

Lift and carry fetishism

Elsewhere in this book (i.e., on muscle worship and sexual piggybacks), I briefly mentioned that some individuals have lift and carry (L&C) fetishes. To my knowledge there has been no academic research on L&C fetishism, but it did make it on to the Buzzfeed website's "11 most unlikely sexual fetishes" list along with balloon popping, gut flopping, beard rubbing, masking and pedal pushing. According to an article on L&C fetishism (Area Orion, 2011):

> "The fantasy world of female muscle is no stranger to the odd and weird. Another such addition is lift and carry, a fetish where someone is aroused by being lifted and carried away, most often by a woman. She doesn't need to be a bodybuilder or powerlifter, just strong enough to carry the weight of a full grown man. So what is the turn-on with lift and carry? To many, it can be harmless fun or even part of foreplay. Some like the helpless feeling of domination by a powerful woman with no control. Others like the difference in size and enjoy the feeling of having the woman struggle beneath their weight. There are various types of lifts popular to L&C. Piggy-back rides, shoulder rides, over-the-shoulder carries, pony and donkey rides and fireman's carry are just

a few. These obviously depend on the strength of the woman and weight of the man to pull off successfully ... Many men are embarrassed to have this fetish, feeling the gender role reversal makes them appear weak. Fortunate for them, there are websites, videos, stories, forums and even porn for lift and carry where fans can live out their fantasies in private."

The activity, while niche, appears to have a large online following with forums discussing sex and fetishes where seemingly masses of pornographic L&C videos can be bought. There also appears to be a market for men buying the services of strong women. Moreover, bodybuilders can supplement their income by fulfilling the desires of those who wish to be lifted and carried.

Lip fetishism

Lips play an important role in human sexual behaviour. Given how important lips are in traditional courtship rituals and sexual intimacy, it is perhaps surprising that lip fetishes appear to be relatively rare, at least based on the complete lack of published research on the topic. The reason lips are so rarely seen as the objects of fetish desires may be because they are so integral to sexual courtship.

The behaviour in which individuals have a sexual interest concerning a specific and often exclusive body part is known as "partialism". In the DSM-5-TR partialism is now subsumed within fetishistic disorder if (i) it is not focused on the genitals and (ii) causes significant psychosocial distress for the individual or has detrimental effects on important areas of his or her life (American Psychiatric Association, 2022). Partialists will often describe the body part of interest to them as having as much, if not greater, sexual arousal for them as the genitals.

As with other sexual fetishes in this book, especially when there is little written academically, I look for online forums and dedicated websites where lip fetishism is the sole focus. However, there appears to be very little online for lip fetishism. Although those who claimed to have lip or lip-related fetishes can be either male and female, they chose not to provide any details.

In my own research (Greenhill and Griffiths, 2015) we reported perhaps the strangest type of lip-related fetishism. Our paper was actually about dacryphilia (sexual arousal from crying) and comprised data collected from online interviews with 8 dacryphiles (6 females and 2 males aged 20 to 50 years). One of the males expressed his dacryphilia primarily through an interest in curled lips. More specifically, he was aroused by the sight of someone's bottom lip curling while crying. Two subthemes were identified as characteristic of this individual's interest in curled lips: (i) an attraction to lips during crying and (ii) the rarity of such a dacryphilic interest. In the first instance he suggested that his interest was rare or perhaps unique:

"My own dacryphilia focus (lip curling) is pretty much unique, as far as I can tell. I haven't found any dacryphiliacs who focus on this aspect of crying. I have come across a minority of people who like it, but it is still not their main kink ... [I personally like the] protruding, curling, contorting or bulging of the bottom lip when women cry."

Although his fetish focused primarily on the physical (i.e., the lips, a physical part of the body), it differed from other dacryphiles whose focus was either on compassionate or dominant/submissive interests both of which involved emotional components. We claimed in our paper that this "curled lip" dacryphile's lip fetishism was different and was instead linked to one of the secondary products of crying (i.e., movement of the lips):

> *"I'm definitely a big fan of women's lips in general, but I feel there's a definite difference between being attracted to lips and being attracted to lips curled as a result of crying."*

In this extract our participant's interest in curled lips appeared to be a dacryphilic interest rather than a form of partialism. He expressed his interest as being focused on the movement of the bottom lip during crying. Although sexual arousal caused by the movement of the bottom lip would initially appear to be linked with partialism, our participant clearly distanced his dacryphilic interest from this sexual interest by specifically differentiating the two. This suggests that dacryphilia may be concerned not only with the primary product of crying (i.e., tears), but also with secondary products (i.e., how the rest of the face moves during crying).

Given that the love of lips or lip-related behaviours are unlikely to cause problems, it is therefore unsurprising that there has been little academic or clinical literature on the topic. Most sexual fetishes are written about only when the behaviour is problematic, such as when an individual seeks help for his or her problem or a partner discovers the fetish and does not like it, both of which appear to be incredibly rare where lip fetishism is concerned.

Macrophilia

Macrophilia appears to be an increasingly popular paraphilia in which individuals derive sexual arousal from a fascination with giants and/or a sexual fantasy involving giants. Such fantasies may include the macrophiles themselves shrinking in front of a normal-sized person (male or female). Alternatively, macrophiles may fantasize about their sexual partner growing to an abnormal height while the macrophiles themselves remain unchanged.

Although the literal translation of macrophilia is a "lover of large", in this context it does not refer to those in the fat admiration community (i.e., people who are sexually attracted to very fat women). It specifically refers to individuals who are sexually attracted to people much taller than themselves (i.e., it is the height rather than width that is crucial). As the scale between small and tall is not generally found in real human life almost all macrophilic behaviour is sexual fantasy.

The overwhelming majority of macrophiles are thought to be heterosexual males who are sexually attracted to giantesses. However, even non-sexual scenarios involving giants can result in sexual stimulation. Each fantasy situation is different for every macrophile as the behaviour is fantasy based. Even the preferred heights of fantasy giants differ between individuals. For instance, some macrophiles have a preference for people only a few feet taller than themselves whereas others involve giants who are hundreds of feet high.

The reason this paraphilia has increased massively over the last decade is down to the internet playing a crucial role in helping create and facilitate the paraphilia. As a result of the paraphilia being almost totally fantasy based, much of the material from which macrophiles gain their sexual gratification is placed and distributed online. There is a wide range of macrophile artwork, photographs and videos online. Applications, such as Photoshop, are widely used to create collages of fake giants. Photographs are also taken from low angles to make everything in the viewfinder including people seem much bigger. The internet is also full of homemade camcorder films of people trampling and destroying model cities.

Although most macrophilic behaviour is fantasy based, there are some macrophiles who attempt to experience the fetish in real life by dating extraordinarily tall women (a.k.a. "Amazons") even if they have to pay for the privilege to do so. For instance, it was reported that Mikayla Miles, who is nearly 7 feet tall in her fetish boots and 6 feet 4 inches without the boots, provides private sessions with macrophiles to engage in behaviours such as trampling, domination, roleplay and foot worship. Macrophiles can also meet their tall heroines at gatherings, such as the annual Amazon Convention.

I have yet to come across a single academic paper that has been published on macrophilia, although there has been some psychological speculation about its origins. Clinical psychologist Helen Friedman has been reported as saying:

> "[Macrophiles] are playing out some old, unresolved psychological issue. Maybe as a child they felt overwhelmed by a dominant mother, or a sadistic mother. Maybe they were abused. [Macrophilia] is not so much a fetish as a disassociation from reality. It's part of an internal world. The macro's submersion in fantasy serves as a substitute for a more normalized approach to sex. Healthy sexuality is about personal intimacy. It's about feeling good about yourself in a way that expresses caring and feeling a connection to another person."

However, most online accounts by macrophiles that I have read do not seem to match the psychological profile posited by Helen Friedman.

Maschalagnia

Aggrawal (2009a) defines maschalagnia as "a fetish for armpits". According to one gay fetish website the attraction to armpits can be based on a number of factors and senses, but claims it is the olfactory and visual components that are the most common sensory factors when it comes to armpit sexual arousal.

Other armpit-related sexual practices include hircusophilism (a sexual preference for underarm hair) and axillism (the use of the armpit for sex, a.k.a. "bagpiping"). There are a surprising number of fetish websites purely devoted to the sexual allure of armpits, such as Armpit Fetish, Armpit Sex, Armpit Licking, Girl Pits ("the original underarm fetish forum") and Man On Man Armpits. Most of these people enjoy kissing, tasting and smelling their partner's armpits during sexual foreplay. Sometimes they ask their sexual partners not to shower, bathe or wash their armpits so that the smell is as strong as possible. Love (2001) claims that sexual arousal from armpits:

> "... is more common in Europe where women allow their armpit hair to grow. This area is very sensitive to the flicker of a tongue or the warmth of a penis. Unshaven hair is also said to retain pheromones, the sex hormones that cause arousal when inhaled. The advantages of axillism for men are that of a tight fit, friction against the penis, close proximity to the breasts and no risk of pregnancy or disease. Axillism, when engaged in within a day of shaving, produces more sensation but later underarm stubble can cause irritation of the penile skin."

As far as I am aware, there is no empirical evidence suggesting that armpit fetishism is more prevalent in Europe. My feeling is that this is educated guesswork on Love's part. Psychologist (and one of the first sexologists) Havelock Ellis (1905) made many references to armpits and sex. For instance, he noted that:

> "Before coitus the sexual energy seems to be dissipated along all the nerve channels and especially along the secondary sexual routes, the breasts, nape of neck, eyebrows, lips, cheeks, armpits and hair."

He then went on to say how the focus of sexuality can shift:

> "The odour of the body, like its beauty, in so far as it can be regarded as a possible sexual allurement, has in the course of development been transferred to the upper parts. The careful concealment of the sexual region has doubtless favoured this transfer. It has thus happened that when personal odour acts as a sexual allurement it is the armpit, in any case normally the chief focus of odour in the body, which mainly comes into play, together with the skin and the hair."

He also cited a case study from Féré (1902). Féré was arguably the first academic to mention the fetishistic properties of armpits:

> "Sometimes the odour of the armpit may even become a kind of fetish which is craved for its own sake and in itself suffices to give pleasure. Féré has recorded such a case, in a friend of his own, a man of 60, with whom at one time he used to hunt ... On these hunting expeditions he used to tease the girls and women he met ... when he came upon them walking in the fields with their short-sleeved chemises exposed. When he had succeeded in introducing his hand into the woman's armpit he went away satisfied, and frequently held the hand to his nose with evident pleasure. After long hesitation Féré asked for an explanation, which was frankly given. As a child he had liked the odour, without knowing why. As a young man women with strong odours had stimulated him to extraordinary sexual exploits, and now they were the only women who had any influence on him. He professed to be able to recognize continence by the odour, as well as the most favourable moment for approaching a woman."

Ellis (1905) also claimed that some men can detect menstruating women from the smell of their armpits. Although this is not sexual in and of itself, it is more likely for those men who engage in menophilia (a paraphilia where individuals derive sexual arousal from menstruating females) that the armpits may be an indirect sexual stimulus. Ellis argued that the attraction is mostly directed towards the "strong pungent odour of the armpit", because it is the most powerful in the body and sufficiently powerful to act as a muscular stimulant even in the absence of any direct sexual association. As one (now defunct) website's description of armpit fetishism noted:

> "Armpit odour is an aphrodisiac for some people. The smell acts as a muscular stimulant, naturally encouraging arousal, reminding armpit lovers of their favourite part of the opposite sex's body. Compared to other fetishes, it's not that weird. But don't tell that to people in Singapore, where an armpit-loving man was recently sentenced to 14 years in jail and 18 strokes of the cane."

An online essay at an adult site (Wonderland Burlesque, 2011) briefly examined armpit fetishes and had a small section entitled "psychological aspects". However, it really did not give any psychological insight at all. The anonymous author speculated that:

> "I think the act of licking another person's armpit or breathing in their odour are a means of striving for intimacy, on a very base level. A person's musk is very distinctive; very much a product of that individual and how their body processes various consumables ... Or it could be a physical reaction having to do with the taste and

smell of a man's underarms, in their natural form: minus cologne, antiperspirant, and the like. Pheromones, commonly believed to trigger a social response in members of the same species, are produced by the skin's apocrine sebaceous glands, secreted via armpits and found in sweat."

As with many of the paraphilias and fetishes in this book, there is little empirical research on maschalagnia or armpit sexual practices more generally. References to sexual aspects of armpits sometimes crop up in the academic literature on gay sexual preferences. For instance, Moskowitz and Roloff (2007) examined sexual practices in relation to "bug chasing" relating to a small group of gay men who attempt to voluntarily contract HIV. They noted that among gay BDSM practitioners a small but significant minority are into dominant and/or submissive "armpit play".

Maybe the area is just too trivial for academic and/or clinical study since it is not a condition that requires medical, psychiatric and/or psychological intervention. In fact, the only snippet I have come across is Baguley (2006) in a chapter on crab lice (*Pediculosis pubis*) reminding readers that such lice as part of a sexually transmitted disease can be found in armpit hair as well as pubic hair.

Mask fetishism

A news programme broadcast by *BBC News* (2005) reported the case of Norman Hutchins, a 53-year-old man with a fetish for surgical masks. He constantly phoned hospitals and dental surgeries pretending that he needed masks for charity events. For instance, he would tell medical staff he was doing a fun run in fancy dress or that he needed the masks for amateur dramatics. However, he used the masks for his own fetishistic sexual kicks. He was described in court as "a menace to anyone involved in medical or dental institutions."

Mask fetishism involves individuals who derive sexual pleasure and arousal from either wearing masks and/or seeing others wearing masks. There is little in the way of academic or clinical research on the topic and much of what is known can best be described as anecdotal. The masks that form the basis of such sexual arousal are often very specific and may overlap with other types of paraphilic and/or fetishistic behaviour. For instance, individuals into coulrophilia (sexual arousal from clowns) will prefer clown masks; furries will prefer animal masks; sexual sadists will prefer leather, PVC or rubber masks (e.g., "gimp"-type masks as featured in Quentin Tarantino's film *Pulp Fiction*); and those into medical fetishism will prefer surgical masks.

However, there are many other types of mask that may stimulate sexual arousal including gas masks, hangman's masks, Ninja masks, leather masks such as the archetypal rapist's mask, rubber face masks (some of which may represent a famous celebrity), oxygen masks (as popularized in David Lynch's film *Blue Velvet*), porcelain masks and novelty masks (e.g., Halloween characters, alien characters and horror movie characters). There are also individuals who derive sexual pleasure and arousal from women wearing Muslim and harem-type face coverings, although this is usually deemed to be a veil fetish rather than a mask fetish.

Love (2001) has a small section on masks and hoods. Love noted that the first time masks took on a sexual perspective was in Europe during the 18th century. She also reported that prostitutes originally used them "to hide their identity but later they became popular among women of higher social status." In the context of sadomasochistic bondage, Love writes that hoods and masks are used to "depersonalize a partner" and that the anonymity it affords gives the dominant partner more power and results in both parties having fewer inhibitions.

A 35-year-old male Cypriot posted a query on mask and encasement fetishes to Allan Schwartz's Mental Help website because he was on the brink of suicide. The man talked about his mask fantasies dating back to early childhood. He talked about how sexually turned on he was seeing women wearing scarves around their faces. His fiancée tried to share his sexual fetish and wore a catsuit hood for him, but ultimately decided she got little from it. However, it got to the point that the man could not get sexually aroused unless his fiancée was wearing a mask. Schwartz (2009) replied:

> "The human face represents the very essence of a person and most intimate lovers would want to have their face seen while making love and to observe the face of their partner. Yes, a mask sometimes, if that is your wish, but not always. In a way, the mask causes you and her to not really be there together … I suspect that you are conflicted about your sexual feelings and about sexuality as a human means of communication. The mask, something you always must have your partner wear, may hide the real and personal woman, rendering the sex anonymous. This is only a guess but I suspect that something of the kind is going on."

Another paraphilia that is associated with mask fetishism is hypoxyphilia (deriving sexual pleasure and arousal from oxygen deprivation). For instance, Skugarevsky *et al.* (2011) examined a couple of deaths due to hypoxyphilia, one of which involved the victim wearing a gas mask at the scene of death. They noted that:

> "[Hypoxyphiliacs] use a variety of techniques to produce the hypoxia-like strangulation, suffocation or reduction of the oxygen in the inspired air that may be achieved with plastic bags or gas masks that may allow inhaling some anesthetic gases (chloroform, nitrous oxide) and volatile chemicals (isopropyl nitrite, isobutyl nitrite, 'poppers')."

The incidence and prevalence of mask fetishism is unknown, although the ALT Experience website in 2012 claimed that it is "a common paraphilia". However, no statistics or evidence were provided to support the claim of being commonplace. The site also claimed (without any supporting evidence) that:

> "The psychological factors behind this have to do with society's idea of the face as a focal point of beauty. By covering up the face, sexual play not only hides a person's appearance, but creates a degree of anonymity. Without being able to see facial features, it is more difficult to read responses of pain, fear, pleasure and so forth. This, in a sense, creates an aspect of anonymity that goes beyond just the physical features of a person's face. Thus, the mind is more open to imagination and fantasy."

Sandnabba *et al.* (2002) examined the sexual behaviour of sadomasochists. They summarize the results of five empirical studies from a sample of 184 Finnish sadomasochists (22 women and 162 men). More specifically, they examined the frequency with which the participants engaged in different sexual practices, behaviours and roleplays during the preceding 12 months. They reported that 66% had used masks and/or blindfolds at least once. Given the lack of empirical data on mask fetishism, such claims may well be verified as true by future research. However, unlike the case with hypoxyphiliacs, I am not holding my breath!

Masochism

Later in this book I examine the psychological literature on sexual sadism. Many look at sexual masochism and its counterpart sexual sadism as two sides of the same coin. Sexual masochists derive sexual gratification from receiving physical and/or psychological pain. von Krafft-Ebing (1886) first coined the term "masochism" in his sexology book *Psychopathia Sexualis* and named it after the 19th-century novelist Leopold von Sacher-Masoch. The latter's book *Venus in Furs* (von Sacher-Masoch, 2000) is well known to those of us who are big Velvet Underground fans. It depicts a man's humiliation and suffering perpetrated by a female dominatrix. There are other names for the same phenomenon, such as "algolagnia" which refers to people who have a craving for pain. Algolagnia was coined by von Krafft-Ebing (1886), but never caught on in the same way as the term "masochism".

The American Psychiatric Association's (2022) DSM-5-TR acknowledges the overlap between masochism and sadism, but classes them as two distinct entities (i.e., sexual masochism disorder and sexual sadism disorder). DSM-5-TR defines masochism as when an individual experiences "recurrent, intense sexually arousing fantasies, sexual urges, or behaviors involving the act (real, not simulated) of being humiliated, beaten, bound or otherwise made to suffer" over a 6-month period. To distinguish it as a disorder rather than a non-problematic sexual preference, the masochistic sexual urges, fantasies and/or behaviours have to cause "clinically significant distress or impairment in social, occupational or other important areas of functioning." Interestingly, other paraphilic behaviours (such as hypoxyphilia) come under the rubric of sexual masochism.

The true prevalence of sexual masochism disorder is unknown (American Psychiatric Association, 2022). However, most sexual masochism is not disordered. Early empirical studies, such as Kinsey *et al.* (1948, 1953), reported that a quarter of males and females had experienced sexual arousal from being bitten by their partner during sex, although later studies report much lower figures of around 3% to 5%. Person *et al.* (1989) surveyed college students about their sexual behaviours and fantasies. The results showed that around 4% had been tied up or sexually degraded during sex and that 1% had spanked, whipped or hit a consenting partner during sex, although "consenting partner" did not necessarily mean they enjoyed being smacked, whipped or beaten. Moser and Kleinplatz (2007) claimed that about 10% of the adult population engage in sadomasochistic activity. The American Psychiatric Association (2022) estimated that 2.2% of males and 1.3% of females had engaged in BDSM behavior in the past year (based on representative data from Australia).

Masochistic fantasies are not uncommon. For instance, Crépault and Couture (1980) reported that 46% of men had sexual fantasies about being kidnapped and raped by a woman, 12% had fantasies relating to being humiliated and 36% fantasized about being bound and sexually stimulated by a woman.

Although there is a lot of evidence showing that sexually masochistic desires, fantasies and behaviours are relatively common among men, there has been some dispute as to whether women are interested in sexual masochism. Research certainly indicates that consensual sexually masochistic behaviour by females can occur and some authors argue that there is a biologically based tendency towards submissiveness among females. However, some claim that it is very rare in women. Spengler (1977) claimed that almost all women who participate in sadomasochistic activities are prostitutes who have no personal preference for such activity. However, a number of more recent studies into sadomasochists all indicate that a small but significant minority of women engage in both sexually masochistic and sadistic activities (13% to 30%) and that very few of such women are prostitutes. However, compared with male sadomasochists, female counterparts are less likely to need sadomasochistic activity to reach sexual satisfaction.

Research has also indicated that men are more likely than women to experience masochistic desires during adolescence, although a significant minority of male masochists did not express interest in such behaviour until they reached adulthood. Studies into sadomasochists show little difference in sexual orientation. For instance, Spengler (1977) in a study of 245 male sadomasochists reported that 30% were heterosexual, 31% were bisexual and 38% were homosexual. Other studies have found much higher levels of heterosexuality, although amongst female sadomasochists there tends to be higher levels of bisexuality than in the study by Spengler.

Breslow et al. (1985) surveyed 182 sadomasochists (52 of whom were women). One third of the men (33%) were dominant, 41% were submissive and 26% were both. Similar results were found among the females. Spanking and master–slave relationships were the preferred sexual activities for both male and female sadomasochists, although there were some minor differences. More females preferred bondage and restraint, whereas more men preferred pain and whipping. Klismaphilia may also have been a comorbid paraphilia as 33% of men and 22% of females made sexual use of enemas.

A Finnish study (Alison et al., 2001) reported that flagellation and bondage are among the most popular activities of sadomasochists. However, there was a wide range of lesser activities that carried greater risk of physical harm including piercings, hypoxyphilia, fisting, knifeplay and electric shocks. There were also major differences depending upon sexual orientation (e.g., gay men were more likely to engage in activities such as "cock binding"). Most interestingly, the research team identify four sadomasochistic subgroups based on the type of pain given and received:

- *Typical pain administration:* This involves practices such as spanking, caning, whipping, skin branding and electric shocks.
- *Humiliation:* This involves verbal humiliation, gagging, face slapping and flagellation. Heterosexuals were more likely than gay men to engage in these types of activity.

- *Physical restriction:* This involves bondage, use of handcuffs, use of chains, wrestling, use of ice, wearing straitjackets, hypoxyphilia and mummification.
- *Hypermasculine pain administration:* This involves rimming, dildo use, cock binding, being urinated upon, being given an enema, fisting, being defecated upon and catheter insertion. Gay men were more likely than heterosexuals to engage in these types of activity.

There are many theories as to why people engage in such behaviours from traditional learning theories (based on both operant and classical conditioning) through to psychoanalytic interpretations. Most of these theories place the origins of the behaviour within a developmental framework and argue that the root of the paraphilic behaviour begins in childhood. Somewhere in childhood and adolescence the individual starts to associate pleasure with pain and then becomes sexualized in adulthood.

Freund *et al.* (1995) noted a distinct difference between commonplace consensual and play-oriented sadomasochistic activities, on the one hand, and the more dangerous and potentially fatal practices of a small minority of hardcore sadomasochists, on the other. As with many paraphilias, sexual masochism would only qualify as a mental health disorder if it caused significant psychological and physical impairment, which in very extreme circumstances could be life threatening. Krueger (2010) echoes this and notes in his review of the diagnostic criteria for sexual masochism that the main criticisms and concerns surrounding this behaviour (and paraphilias more generally) are that they "should not be included in the DSM because they are not mental disorders, they are unscientific, they are unnecessary, and to do so pathologizes groups who engage in alternative sexual practices" (p. 348). However, Moser and Kleinplatz (2006) argue there is no evidence that sadomasochists need emergency services more often "than practitioners of other sexual behaviours" (p. 106), although this has been disputed by others in the field. The review by Krueger (2010) concludes:

> "While masochistic and/or sadomasochistic behavior occurs with some frequency in the population and is associated with generally good psychological or social functioning, there are a very small number of cases where masochistic fantasy and behavior result in severe harm or even death. These cases clearly indicate a sexual interest pattern that has become pathological. Since so little is known about this behavior, further research is indicated, and inclusion in the DSM would facilitate this." (p. 353)

Mechanophilia

My partner is a Frank Zappa fan and one of her favourite albums is his 1979 rock opera *Joe's Garage*. On the LP "Joe" is described as an "appliance fetishist" by the "Church of Appliantology" who ends up having a gay relationship with an industrial vacuum cleaner. Although "Joe" is a fictional character, appliance and machine fetishes are not.

According to Aggrawal (2009a) being sexually turned on by machines is a paraphilia called "mechanophilia". Ceilán (2008) describes the same paraphilia as "mechaphilia".

The online Urban Dictionary has a more encompassing definition and defines mechanophilia as:

> "The love or sexual attraction to computers, cars, robots or androids, washing machines and other domestic appliances, lawnmowers and other mechanized gardening equipment. Sexual relations between living organisms and machines."

Mechanophilia not only includes individuals who derive sexual pleasure and arousal from cars (such as Edward Smith, an American man who has had sex with over 1,000 cars), but also from bicycles (such as Robert Stewart, a Briton who ended up in court after being caught having sex with a bicycle). The paraphilia even extends to aeroplanes and helicopters according to Browne (1982). Thompson (2000) argues that motorcycles are often portrayed as sexualized fetish objects by their owners. There would also appear to be some structural and psychological overlap with technosexuality/robot fetishism and objectum sexuality, such as having sexual and/or romantic relationships with inanimate objects (Nelson, 2012).

According to Hickey (2006) in some jurisdictions mechanophilic acts are treated as crimes with perpetrators being placed on the sex offenders' register after prosecution.

I have yet to come across any empirical research specifically on mechanophilia other than case studies. Sex therapist Ian Kerner told *CBS News* that among mechanophiles there is generally "an exhibitionistic element for the person being stimulated by the machine, as well as general submission [and] domination themes," although I am unsure as to whether this is based on anyone Ian Kerner has treated or whether this is just pure speculation. I suspect the latter.

De Silva and Pernet (1992) reported a case study involving an unusual sexual deviation in a young 20-year-old British man ("George") who had little social interaction and was incredibly shy. They reported that his main sexual interest and excitement came from cars, particularly Austin Metro cars. George's family belonged to a strict religious sect who strongly disapproved of any sexual involvement by their son with women. Things changed for George when his parents bought an Austin Metro. George began masturbating inside the car and then outside the car while crouching down next to the car's exhaust pipe. So that he could not be caught masturbating, he would go to great lengths to find deserted places to engage in his sexual activity with the car.

George used to become very sexually excited when the car's exhaust pipe was running and pumping out car fumes. This aspect of "elimination" according to De Silva and Pernet (1992) was an important central element in George's other sexual preferences, particularly his fascination with urination. As a very young child he had an unusual interest in dogs urinating. After the age of 10 years he was more interested in children and adult women urinating. The authors also speculated there may have been an increase in George's arousal due to a "reduction of oxygen intake and related asphyxiation." This was possibly seen as a mild form of hypoxyphilia.

Schlessinger (2003), in a non-academic book, charts his own "personal journey" of coming to terms with his sexual desire for machines and his quest to seek acceptance from his family and friends about his sexual love of machines. The book is detailed in its description of the curves of a reel-to-reel recorder with which he fell in love. Schlessinger ends the book by saying that he has happily come to accept his "quirky sexuality".

Widespread speculation about people ending up in hospital when things go wrong as a result of a paraphilia do not appear to be about mechanophilia at all. Personally, I believe that people who use the vibrations of a washing machine or vacuum cleaner as part of masturbatory sex are not mechanophiles, otherwise anyone using a vibrator would be classed as one. Mechanophiles who have sex with a machine, make love to it and may even develop emotional attachments do so rather than using the appliance simply to heighten sexual pleasure during masturbation. Even though mechanophilia appears to be rare, it is far from fiction. It is certainly an area that would benefit from more empirical and/or clinical research, although there needs to be consensus from those working in the field as to what mechanophilia actually is:

> "There is no one in the world Darius Monty loves more than Goldie. With her perfect curves and flawless body, she's a beauty. And the pub boss's sex life with the hot model less than half his age is better than with any previous girlfriends. But shockingly the object of his full-on passion is a CAR. While many men claim to love their motors, Darius is IN love with his gold-coloured X-Type Jaguar – and makes love to 'her'." (Levy, 2017)

This quote comes from a story in the *Sunday Mirror* for which I was also interviewed. I described Darius as more of an objectophile than a mechanophile, although he does fit both definitions.

Objectum sexuality refers to individuals who develop deep emotional and/or romantic attachments to and have relationships with specific inanimate objects or structures. Such objectophiles express a loving and/or sexual preference and commitment to particular items or structures. This is why I view Darius as more of an objectophile than a mechanophile. It has also been claimed by academics (Marsh, 2010) that such individuals rarely if ever have sex with humans and they develop strong emotional fixations to the object or structure. Unlike sexual fetishism, the object or structure is viewed as an equal partner in the relationship and is not used to enhance or facilitate sexual behaviour. Some objectophiles even believe that their feelings are reciprocated by the object of their desire. According to Levy (2017):

> "Darius fell in love with his Jaguar after buying the executive saloon 2 years ago [in 2015]. His second-hand limo, which was built … in 2004, has startled Darius with the feelings it has aroused. Yet Darius could not fight the urge to live out his sexual fantasies with the car. His passion for Goldie soon became a daily ritual after he returned from his night shift at the pub. And eventually he realised he could no longer hide it from his loved ones. Darius resisted professional help because he thought his liaisons with his motor would become less exciting with time. Despite the negative reaction from his mates, Darius refused to give up on Goldie. Bizarrely, Darius says his relationship with Goldie has gone from strength to strength. He has even retired her from life on the road to keep her in pristine condition. Astonishingly, Darius would still like to find a human girlfriend."

Unlike most objectophiles I have read about, Darius had sexual relationships with women prior to falling in love with Goldie and still wants sex with women in the future. In his interview he was reported as saying:

> "I don't expect people to understand because it's not something I fully understand myself. I didn't choose this but I have fallen for a car, just like other people fall for women. I find her arousing, I love spending time with her and she is very important to me. I don't see her as an object, I look at her and I see my lover. Before I bought Goldie I was in a normal loving relationship with a woman. I didn't see anything strange about myself or my sexuality at all. I've always been a car lover, but if someone told me it was possible to have sexual feelings towards something that's not human I'd have laughed them off just like people laugh at me now. I can't really explain what triggered it, but I went to view Goldie and had always wanted an X-Type Jaguar. Her colour is so unique and after I'd handed over the cash, all I wanted to do was go and polish her. I pulled into the jet wash and was making circular motions on her bonnet with a cleaning cloth when I suddenly felt unexpectedly aroused. It was something about the smooth, shiny paintwork and the perfect curves of the car that got me turned on. I tried to ignore the feeling and just put it down to excitement about having a new car. But when I got home and sat down to watch TV I had a real urge to venture into the garage and visit her in private."

The unexpected sexual arousal that Darius felt when first polishing Goldie appears to be the initial spark of his relationship with the car. Psychologists like myself would claim that this unexpected associative pairing of polishing the car with sexual arousal is something that repeatedly played on Darius's mind and that this formed the basis for a classically conditioned response in which the car itself ended up causing the sexual arousal. As he also explained in his newspaper interview:

> "I had a girlfriend at the time and I didn't dare tell her what was going through my mind so I used the excuse that I'd left my wallet in the car and headed out. I wasn't exactly sure what would happen as the feelings were all new to me. I just knew I felt really turned on by the notion of having sexual intercourse with my new car. Immediately afterwards I felt ashamed and guilty, but I knew right then it wouldn't be the last time. I walked away feeling so confused about what I'd just done. As disturbing as it was, I told myself I couldn't be the only person in the world who had experienced these kinds of feelings."

And Darius was right. There are dozens of objectophiles around the world. While the behaviour is rare, he is certainly not alone. It was when Darius started doing his own research into his behaviour that he began to feel better knowing there were other objectophiles:

> "Knowing others had [sexual and romantic] feelings towards cars, bikes or planes definitely put me at ease, but it was a really difficult thing for me to accept. I was enjoying having sex with my car more than with my girlfriend. I even missed the car when I went up to bed at night and felt bad for leaving her alone in the garage. When I broke the news to my girlfriend she left me right away. I could understand her thinking my behaviour was odd, but deep down there was a sense of relief there for me in knowing that I had got things out in the open and I was free to pursue my relationship with Goldie."

"George" and Darius share few similarities apart from the fact they both have sexual relationships with cars. The fact that two case studies can be so different in terms of aetiology and development of the behaviour suggests that car-loving objectophiles should be an avenue of further research because there are likely to be very different explanations and motivations for the behaviour.

There are a number of different paraphilias that have some association with cars including:

- **Mechanophilia**: Sexual arousal from cars or other machines (a.k.a. "mechasexuality").
- **Symphorophilia**: Sexual arousal from witnessing or staging disasters, such as car accidents. The main characters in Ballard's (1973) novel *Crash* and the subsequent 1996 film adaptation of the same name would therefore be symphorophiles.
- **Amomaxia**: Sexual arousal from having sex in parked cars.

Marsh (2010) describes what she claimed was the first ever research study conducted on a group of 40 objectophiles (i.e., people who experience emotional, romantic, affectionate and/or sexual relationships with objects), 21 of whom shared their experiences. One of those who shared his experiences of mechasexuality had been aware of it for 5 years:

> *"I've been in love with my mom's car and my own car since I got it bought. My car's appearance is what attracts me the most. [I enjoy intimacy with the cars] between twice a week and once every 3 weeks [and] involves cuddling and such affectionate activity, and sometimes masturbation ... However, I'd like to mention that although there can be a little amount of mental role play, I am fully aware that objects are inanimate and that this mostly is a one-sided relation. Although I may consider a human relationship eventually, it has not happened yet."*

There is also the case of a 40-year-old US male airline pilot (married and father of two children) that is worthy of mention (Rupp, 1973). Rupp reported that the man left his home at 6 a.m. and told his wife that he was going shooting in the country. He was found naked except for a large-link 10-foot chain harness secured around his body. The harness was tied around the man's neck in a moderately tight loop and bolted. The chain then went down his chest and was tied into another loop around his waist. This was tied to the bumper of the car. The man's body was found at 7.30 a.m. in a remote area crushed against the left fender of his car. The ignition was on, the engine was running and the driver's door was still open. The steering wheel was tied such that it would go round in anticlockwise circles. His clothes were in the boot of the car. Reconstruction of the events leading to his death showed that he was either being dragged round by the car or running behind it thus producing feelings of asphyxia. When he had finished being sexually turned on he had tried to approach the car door, but had forgotten to undo the chain from the bumper. The chain got tangled up in the car's axle and the man was found strangled to death by the chain. This is obviously a case of a car being used to facilitate another paraphilia (i.e., hypoxyphilia). Clearly, this is a very extreme case. However, much like the other cases outlined in this entry they do at least show that for some people cars are an integral part of their sexuality and sex life.

Medical fetishism

I am sure most of us can remember playing doctors and nurses when we were kids, but there are some people who never seem to grow out of it and engage in what has been termed "medical fetishism". The fetish appears to be quite inclusive and wide ranging because the activity can comprise: (i) individuals who are sexually attracted to people in the medical profession, (ii) individuals (typically heterosexual males) who derive sexual pleasure from their female sexual partners dressing up in a nurse's uniform and (iii) individuals who derive sexual pleasure and arousal from actually being the recipients of a medical or clinical procedure, usually some kind of body examination. Some of these behaviours may be paraphilias or specialized fetishes, such as klismaphilia (i.e., sexual pleasure from receiving an enema). There are also those whose fetish only concerns a very particular branch of medicine, such as dentistry.

The types of activity that have been reported as medical fetishes include genital and urological examinations (e.g., a gynecological examination), genital procedures (e.g., fitting a catheter or menstrual cup), rectal procedures (e.g., inserting suppositories, taking a rectal temperature and prostate massage), the application of medical dressings and accessories (e.g., putting on a bandage or diaper, fitting a dental retainer and putting someone's arm in plaster) and the application and fitting of medical devices (e.g., fitting a splint, orthopedic cast or brace).

Some of these activities, such as having a diaper, catheter or orthopaedic brace fitted, may overlap with other paraphilias. They include infantilism (i.e., deriving sexual pleasure from being an adult baby), catheterophilia (i.e., deriving sexual pleasure from catheters) and apotemnophilia (i.e., deriving sexual pleasure from the thought of being an amputee). In the most extreme cases of medical fetishism even highly invasive medical acts may be performed in an unofficial non-medical setting by untrained individuals for sexual pleasure including giving injections, anaesthesia and actual surgery. The sexual pleasure and arousal may occur in the giver and/or receiver, and much of the activity may be in the form of sexual roleplay. As one online essay on medical fetishism noted:

> "People with an extreme medical fetish use tortuous medical devices, speculums, mouth and anal spreaders, enema kits, probes, etc. They may even consent to false operations where they are surgically opened and, with nothing fixed or removed, sutured closed. An extreme medical fetish can be a dangerous thing ... A medical fetish can include a sexual attraction to medical people. Doctor and nurse porn movies, people receiving medical examinations and so on. Most are simply roleplay."
(Wheelchair Lifestyles website, 2011)

There are also sub-branches of medical fetishism that may have overlaps with BDSM, on the one hand, and sadomasochism, on the other. For instance, a female dominatrix may inflict a medical procedure on her willing submissive subject. Such activity often centres on sexual and/or sensitive body parts including the penis, testicles, nipples and anus. The instruments used may also be heated or cooled to heighten the pain/pleasure. Given the potential danger involved in some of the activities performed and the fact the person administering the procedure (e.g., anaesthesia and surgery) may not have any formal medical training, the risk of permanent body damage or, in extreme cases, death is a possibility. Here, the risk of something going wrong may also be sexually stimulating to the person. Therefore, there appears to be both physical and psychological overlaps with paraphilias such as hypoxyphilia (i.e., deriving sexual pleasure from restricting oxygen supply to heighten sexual arousal).

Medical fetishism within sadomasochistic activity would therefore constitute edgeplay. This is a term used within the BDSM community that refers to sexual activities that push the boundaries of safety (a.k.a. "RACKs" or risk-aware consensual kinks). Those involved in edgeplay are fully cognizant of the fact that their sexual behaviour may result in serious body harm and permanent damage.

Love (2001) noted that some people are sexually aroused by exposing themselves to medical practitioners. This is termed "iatronudia". She claimed that such individuals will pretend to be ill just so that they can undress in front of a doctor. This echoes some online sources who claim that those with medical fetishes may also feign injury and illness, or give themselves self-inflicted wounds just so that they can receive genuine medical help. Such activity would appear to have psychological overlaps with factitious disability disorders, such as Munchausen Syndrome (i.e., feigning illness to draw attention or sympathy from others). This type of behaviour may be considered somewhat safer for the medical fetishist because the procedures would be carried out by someone who is medically trained, but is an abuse of others' time and expertise.

Although there is almost no empirical research on medical fetishism, it would appear that most fetishes, particularly when they are very specific and specialized, are rooted in early childhood experiences and most likely caused by behavioural-conditioning processes. For instance, individuals who can only be sexually turned on by being anaesthetized not only enjoy the act itself but also will usually be sexually aroused by the sight of all the aneasthetic equipment and accessories (e.g., black rubber anaesthetic masks).

As with many other fetishes, the internet has fostered whole online communities of medical fetishists, such as the Gynecology and Medical Examination Fetish Forum or the My Male Medical Fetish. There has been little scientific research into the etiology and psychology of medical fetishism, although Love (2001) speculated that sexual games involving medicine are popular because the anxiety connected with visiting a GP might "lead to a natural increase in energy in a sexual experience." I cannot say I am overly convinced by this explanation. However, in the absence of anything more empirical it is one of the few views a clinician has put forward.

Melissophilia and insect sting fetishes

In this book I have briefly examined formicophilia (i.e., being sexually aroused by insects crawling and/or nibbling on a person's genitals). According to both Aggrawal (2009a) and Love (2001) there is a specific subtype of formicophilia that relates to being sexually aroused by bees (i.e., melissophilia). To date, there has not been a single academic or clinical study examining melissophilia. However, there have been many historical, cultural and/or academic references to the use of bee and wasp stings for sexual purposes including the books by Aggrawal (2009a) and Love (2001) that make passing references to melissophilia.

The most common reference to the use of bee and wasp stings is as a method to bring about penis enlargement. There are many cults that are devoted to the phallus. Furthermore, it is known that many ancient religions, especially those that are polytheistic, such as Hinduism and Greek mythology, have gods with gigantic penises. Similarly, there are also some monotheistic religions (e.g., Judaism) that make reference in the *Tanakh* (i.e., the canon of the Hebrew *Bible*) to promiscuous females who desire males with very large penises. Consequently, men belonging to these religions in various countries have used a variety of methods to bring about penis enlargement including penis gourds, stretching methods and bee stings. Arguably one of the oldest references to insect stings as a way of enlarging the penis was in the *Kama Sutra* (the 4th-century Hindu love manual). Its author Vātsyāyana suggested:

> *"To increase the size and potential of the penis: Take shuka hairs – the shuka is an insect that lives in trees – mix with oil and rub on the penis for 10 nights … When a swelling appears sleep face downwards on a wooden bed, letting one's sex [penis] hang through a hole."*

Twinn (2007) notes that there is an Amazonian wedding ritual that involves covering the penis with a bamboo cane filled with bees as an aid to penis enlargement. The medicinal effects of bee venom and stings have long been known, but there are also inherent dangers. Alqutub *et al.* (2011) sum the situation up concisely when they note:

> *"The use of bee venom as a therapeutic agent for the relief of joint pains dates back to Hippocrates, and references to the treatment can be found in ancient Egyptian and Greek medical writings as well. Also known as apitherapy, the technique is widely used in Eastern Europe, Asia and South America … Unfortunately, certain substances in the bee venom trigger allergic reactions which can be life threatening in a sensitized individual. Multiple stings are known to cause hemolysis, kidney injury, hepatotoxicity and myocardial infarction."*

There are very few reports in the literature about the effects wasp and bee stings have on penises despite the evident dangers. The few that have been reported tend to be on young children stung while playing naked in the summer. I came across a particularly gruesome case with photos of a 3-year-old whose penis had been stung by a bee (Özkan *et al.*, 2011), which you can check out if you have the stomach for it. However, a few academic medical papers make the point that if the act of getting a bee to sting one's penis is self-inflicted and things go wrong such people may be just too embarrassed to seek medical help.

In a book chapter, Love (2005) examined some of the strangest sexual behaviours from around the world. She noted that bee stings have been used by men to extend the duration of orgasm, enhance sensations of the penis and increase penis circumference. She also recounted this anecdote related to a man who got his sexual kicks from bee stings:

> *"Bee stings were once used as a folk remedy for arthritis sufferers. The insects were captured and held on the affected joint until they stung. The poison and the swelling*

it caused alleviated much of the pain in their joints. One male, having observed his grandparents use bees for this purpose and later having a female friend throw a bee on his genitals as a joke, discovered that the sting on his penis extended the duration and intensity of his orgasm. Realizing that the bee sting was almost painless, he developed his own procedure, which consisted of catching two bees in a jar, and shaking it to make the bees dizzy to prevent their flying away. They were then grabbed by both wings so that they were unable to twist around and sting. Each bee was placed each side of the glans and pushed to encourage it to sting. (Stings to the glans do not produce the desired swelling and the venom sac tends to penetrate the skin too deeply, causing difficulty in removing them.) ... Stings on the penis, unlike other areas, resemble the bite of a mosquito ... The circumference of the man's penis increased from 6.5 inches to 9.5 inches. Swelling is greatest on the second day."

This account is by no means an isolated incident as I have come across a number of similar stories online. For instance, in response to a man's online question about whether bee stings have a demonstrable effect on virility and sexual performance, one person responded:

"My boyfriend would [use bee stings] all the time and it would turn me on so much. You squeeze the abdomen of the bee to trigger it into combat mode, so it will sting and get the stinger out. You put the stinger in the urethra and keep on pinching the bee until it releases the venom and stings the penis. The reasons this works is because the venom from the bee makes your penis swell, and well, that just seems to make it harder and larger."

The next account is just an excerpt from the full account and I want to stress that I personally do not advocate trying this. I am merely reporting this account to demonstrate that the practice appears to exist:

"After reading the text for the Kama Sutra [I] have come up with a plan to increase girth using the common paper wasp ... To catch and manipulate the wasps I use a type of lab tweezers ... Once I find the nest I select a worker that is alone and catch it by the wing with the tweezers. Then I place it in a small jar with small holes in the lid ... After I have three wasps then I can rotate them out in a sting session. [With] a partial erection [I] use a pen to mark ½" circles every 1" around the base and a second ring of circles 1" apart. These are your targets. Put the jars in your fridge for a minute or two. NO LONGER! You want to slow them down not kill them. Select your first wasp and grab her wing near the middle with your tweezers ... Manipulate your wasp/tweezer combo to target the circle. Once you have a single sting move on to the next circle target ... When you finish you WILL jump around for a while, but the reward is worth the 5 minutes of discomfort ... You will need to [rub your penis with] olive oil for a few minutes just after the sting treatment ... After 10 nights do another treatment ... Do not use hornets or yellowjackets in place of paper wasps as they hurt a lot more but don't produce any better results. Do not use anything containing caffeine or aspirin during this treatment as they can retard the swelling that you want."

I should also point out there are variations on the theme because some online accounts that I came across involved other types of insect sting being used to increase penis size and girth, such as the stings of fire ants. In fact, I came across some interesting academic papers from South America. Costa-Neto and Marques (2000) in Brazil examined the use of insects and animals for "medicinal purposes". They came across an example of the sting of great ants being used for "strengthening a flaccid penis." There are also other sexual practices that use stinging insects (mainly ants and wasps), but they were used for sexual sadism and sexual masochism purposes, such as practices outlined on websites like the Slave Farm.

The most remarkable sexual bee sting story I have come across is that of Chloe Prince, a transgender woman from Jackson, Ohio, USA who was born male. As a male (called "Ted") "he" married "his" wife, had two children and then claimed in the national press and broadcast media that, as a result of a severe reaction to a bee sting, his testosterone level dropped significantly. Prince claimed that after "she" had been stung, "her" male body developed a more womanly shape. "She" eventually underwent gender reassignment surgery. However, I know of no evidence that bee stings can cause changes in testosterone levels. Prince was diagnosed with Klinefelter's Syndrome, a genetic condition in which human males have an extra X chromosome and that can result in the development of female sexual characteristics, such as increased breast tissue (a.k.a. "gynecomastia").

Menophilia

I apologize in advance if this is "too much information", but back in 1985 I had a brief relationship with a woman who had just come out of a long-term relationship with someone in the Hell's Angels. One of the things she told me was that her ex-boyfriend had earned his "red wings" many times and that he could not wait each month for her to be on her period. For those who are wondering what I am talking about, "red wings" are earned by a Hell's Angels' member when he performs oral sex on a woman while she is menstruating. I later found out other groups of males who spend a lot of time together (such as those in the armed services) also engage in such practices to earn their "red wings".

Many reading this might find my first paragraph on this topic utterly disgusting. For many, blood is associated with injury, trauma and/or violence. The fact that some may associate blood with sexual arousal sets the stage for an uncomfortable psychological and physical dichotomy.

In his book *Hell's Angels: A Strange and Terrible Saga of the Outlaw Motorcycle Gangs*, Hunter S. Thompson (1966) noted that "red wings" meant that "the wearer has committed cunnilingus on a menstruating woman." There were also other types of wings that Hell's Angels' members could earn including "black wings" (engaging in oral sex on a black woman) and "brown wings" (for anal sex with a woman).

Such practices were virtually unknown to anyone outside Hell's Angels' circles until journalists like Thompson started chronicling their activities and interviewing Hell's Angels' members. Although many of the badges, patches and tattoos were worn with pride, they were often earned as part of male initiation rituals, the key components of which are typically pain, sacrifice, disgust and/or a sense of accomplishment. These anecdotes highlight that, for a minority of individuals, performing oral sex on menstruating women is something to be treasured, celebrated and enjoyed sexually. What may have started as a "rites of passage" activity became a regular and – well, at least monthly – highly arousing occurrence. The fact that, for many women, their sexual drives often increase during menstruation may be another reason some men find this so sexually arousing.

In trying to research this topic, I did not come across too much information. In tantric sex the practice is mentioned but not encouraged. However, in *karezza* (a Westernized form of *tantra*) it is viewed as an opportunity for increased intimacy between consenting sexual partners. In voodoo folklore, it is claimed that having oral sex with a woman during her period ties the man to that woman for life.

In this book I have examined paraphilias in relation to other activities that have involved blood including sexual vampirism and vorarephilia (i.e., being sexually aroused by the idea of being eaten, eating another person or observing such a process for sexual gratification). Another blood-related paraphilia of direct interest here is menophilia. Menophilia is a paraphilia in which an individual, almost always male, derives sexual arousal from menstruating females. Such individuals are also aroused by the smell, image, taste and/or feel of the blood expelled during menstruation. As one female menophile reported online:

> *"Blood to me is exciting. Thrilling. A visual delight. It has been that way since I was a young girl. Nosebleeds and the sight of blood was exciting to me. I would sit in the mirror and watch the red rivulets run down my face. I began to menstruate and after a period of self-loathing I began to fear my cycle."*

It has been claimed that some menophiles also enjoy licking used sanitary towels and/or sucking on used tampons. For such individuals there are some clear overlaps between mysophilia (sexual pleasure from filth and unclean items such as soiled knickers) and sexual vampirism. There was also a case of a man (reported on the now-defunct Is It Legal? website) who was both a menophile and a coprophile (i.e., sexually aroused by faeces). He was allegedly caught tampering with public toilets as a way of collecting excreted waste products from female users to fuel his sexual desires. Although anecdotal evidence suggests that most menophiles are male, some lesbians are claimed to enjoy such practices too.

I have yet to come across any psychological theorizing about the roots and causes of menophilia in any academic paper or book. Although I did come across the following online speculation (on the AltExperience.com website), there was seemingly no empirical evidence backing it up:

> *"Some theorize that men lust after menstruating women because they are envious of the woman's body which is in constant preparation for fertilization. Contrary to this, however, is the fact that it is almost impossible for a woman to become pregnant during her menstruation. Either way, a fascination with period blood is a fairly common fetish at [this website]. Luckily for menophiliacs, it is easy to find a female who is willing to have sex during menstruation. Often, women are charmed by men who aren't disgusted by what is a perfectly normal and healthy body process."*

As is the case with many of the paraphilias in this book, there is a complete absence of any academic study on menophilia. Maybe this is one of those paraphilias that is seen as more trivial and/or devoid of academic merit.

Microphilia

Microphilia appears to be an increasingly popular paraphilia in which individuals derive sexual arousal from a fascination with small (miniaturized) people and/or a sexual fantasy involving such people. It is the opposite of macrophilia (i.e., deriving sexual pleasure and arousal from giants or giantesses). Such fantasies appear to include microphiles fantasizing about others shrinking in front of them. Although they may be male or female, shrinking women appear to be more popular based on the content I have looked at on dedicated websites. Alternatively, microphiles may fantasize about their sexual partner shrinking to an abnormal height while they themselves remain unchanged.

As a result of the paraphilia being almost totally fantasy based much of the material from which microphiles gain their sexual gratification is placed and distributed online. There is a wide range of microphile artwork, photographs and videos online. Applications such as Photoshop are widely used to create collages of fake miniaturized people.

The term "microphilia" is rarely used amongst the microphilic community. They prefer to use the abbreviation SW (shrinking women). I presume there is also an abbreviation SM (shrinking men). Although there might be an SM community out there too, they probably do not use the SM abbreviation since in sexual circles that is far more likely to be seen as meaning sadomasochism. Arguably, one of the best online forums that cater to those into all things sexually miniature is The Minimizer website.

There is very little (no pun intended) written about the psychology behind microphilia and no anecdotal evidence. Until some empirical research is undertaken we can only speculate as to the psychological motivations underlying microphilia. Given that microphilia and macrophilia appear to be the psychological and behavioural opposites of one another or at either end of the same continuum, it is easy to speculate that if macrophiles enjoy the behaviour for its dominating aspects, then microphiles do so for its submissive aspects.

Morphophilia

Are you the type of person who finds people very physically different from you physically and sexually attractive? If you do, then you may have engaged in a sexually paraphilic behaviour known as "morphophilia". According to a very simple definition provided by Aggrawal (2009a) morphophilia refers to the gaining of sexual pleasure and "arousal from a person with a different physique." Whereas a definition provided by the less academic Quipper website says it is simply the "love of odd body shapes", Corsini (1999) said that morphophiles are attracted to a partner with bodily characteristics that are different and/or prominent from one's own.

This suggests there are various subtypes of morphophilia because it is the marked discrepancy that is the sexually arousing focus. For instance, anasteemaphilia refers to individuals who derive sexual arousal from people who are much taller or shorter than themselves (i.e., it is the large difference in height that is the primary source of sexual arousal). I would also argue that sthenolagnia (in which individuals are sexually aroused by very muscular people) may also be a subtype of morphophilia. This is lightly expanded upon in the online encyclopedia Encyclo:

> *"[Morphophilia] … in psychiatry, a type of sexual perversion in which sexual arousal and orgasm depend upon some discrepancy between the partner's bodily characteristics and the subject's; that is, the partner must be markedly thinner or taller than the subject."*

The online Gay Slang Dictionary is a little more blunt and describes the condition as a fetish in which the source of sexual arousal is "peculiar body shapes and sizes, such as obese persons, short persons, dwarfism, etc." Milner *et al.* (2008) in their review of paraphilias not otherwise specified (PNOS) noted:

> *"Morphophilia (from the Greek, morphe, "form"; philia, "love" – Money, 1986) involves an erotic focus on one or more of the body characteristics of one's sexual partner. Morphophilia appears to include partialism, which is defined as a focus on a single body part … It is unclear from the literature whether these two categories are unique paraphilias or different names for the same paraphilia. Both morphophilia and partialism are differentiated from fetishism, which involves a focus on 'the use of nonliving objects'."* (American Psychiatric Association, 2000)

Finally, Pranzarone (2000) has an arguably more scientific definition and takes the line that morphophilia is an umbrella term in that it is:

> *"One of a group of paraphilias of the stigmatic/eligibilic type in which sexuoerotic arousal and facilitation or attainment of orgasm are responsive to and contingent on a partner whose body characteristics are selectively particularized, prominent or different from one's own. [Alternative: the bodily characteristics of the partner are selectively particularized, prominent, or essential as a prerequisite to sexuoerotic arousal and the facilitation or attainment of orgasm]."*

As far as I am aware, the only time morphophilia has been mentioned in the academic literature outside a general definition is in relation to feederism where individuals gain sexual arousal, gratification and stimulation through a person's sexual partner being overfed. Elsewhere in this book I mentioned the research of Terry and Vasey (2011) who reported an interesting case study of feederism. The paper claimed that feeders and feedees are individuals who become sexually aroused by eating, being fed and by the idea or act of gaining weight.

Based on various television documentaries on fat fetishes and feederism, I have personally observed that most (male) feeders are substantially thinner than (female) feedees. On this basis, it could be argued that such males may also be morphophiles as they appear to be sexually attracted as much to the fat as they are to the feeding. Obviously, research is needed to support such claims since my own views are speculative and based on slim evidence (no pun intended) to say the least.

Mummification fetishes

One thing that never ceases to amaze me is how specific some of the objects of erotic and sexual focus are when it comes to sexual fetishes and paraphilias. A case in point is mummification (wrapping the entire body in a manner that prevents movement). In the entry on sexual masochism I briefly mentioned the practice of mummification within a sadomasochistic context.

It is probably stating the obvious to say that mummification can be risky for those who engage in the activity. Complications may arise if those encased (in materials such as clingfilm) are unable to signal to their sexual partner that they are having trouble breathing, sweating too much, becoming severely dehydrated or that their blood supply is being severely restricted. Straight after the unwrapping process body temperature may have significantly decreased, so being in a warm environment and/or having warm blankets on hand is an absolute must.

Sexual partners are also advised to have "panic shears" (a.k.a. "trauma shears" by BDSM regulars) readily available at all times so the mummification binding can be cut through quickly and easily should things go wrong. Mummification can also include more "innovatory" techniques. For instance, Meijer (2000), in his paper on *shibari* (Japanese bondage) in the *Secret Magazine*, notes that wet sheets can be a particularly good material for the sexual mummification of submissive sexual partners:

> "A non-rope Japanese mummification is done with wet sheets. Wrap your sub in wet sheets and pull them tight. As the sheets dry they will shrink and the mummification will become even tighter. By using a hair dryer you can not only speed up the process, but also determine what areas you want to shrink first and by doing so will add accents to your bondage."

There would appear to be strong psychological and behavioural overlaps between mummification fetishism and total enclosure fetishism. In fact, I would argue that mummification fetishes are a subtype of total enclosure fetishes.

A few academic studies have noted that mummification exists within the wider gamut of sadomasochistic activities (e.g., Alison *et al.*, 2001). The same authors published a follow-up using the same dataset and reported that, of those who enjoyed physical restriction, 13.4% engaged in mummification activities. Alison *et al.* (2002) combined the results from five previously published studies on sadomasochistic behaviour. They reported that 12.9% of all their sadomasochistic participants had engaged in mummification as a sexual practice.

Similar findings were reported earlier by Weinberg *et al.* (1984). They interviewed sadomasochists over an 8-year period and reported that their behaviour comprised five distinct features: (i) dominance/submission, (ii) roleplaying, (iii) consensuality, (iv) sexual context and (v) mutual definition. Although not directly concerning mummification, it is clear that these features are critical in the extent to which those mummified experience the activity as sexually stimulating.

It would appear from both anecdotal and empirical research that mummification within a BDSM context comprises a significant minority interest and is probably nowhere near as rare as some other sexual behaviours that I have covered in this book.

Muscle worship fetishism

Later in this book I examine sthenolagnia (a paraphilia in which individuals derive sexual pleasure and arousal from people displaying strength or muscles). Another related behaviour is cratolagnia where, according to Aggrawal (2009a), individuals derive sexual arousal and pleasure more generally from displays of strength rather than muscles in and of themselves. Following a blog I wrote on that topic I received a couple of emails from two males who suggested I should explain that although muscle worship has a sexual aspect, it is not the only aspect.

According to a couple of academic authors, muscle worshippers can be of either gender and of any sexual orientation, although many authors appear to suggest it is more prevalent among gay men who view bodybuilders as little more than sex objects and because bodybuilding is common among members of the gay community (Campbell, 2004; Denizet-Lewis, 2009). A quick search online also suggests there is a large gay pornographic market for muscle worship along with numerous webcam muscle worship sites. Muscle worship appears to have crossovers with other sexually paraphilic behaviour, such as sexual masochism.

Richardson (2008) also made some interesting (and important) distinctions between muscle worship and two other erotic practices often associated with bodybuilding termed "hustling" and "sponsorship fantasies". More specifically, Richardson (2008) writes:

> "Alan Klein describes 'hustling' as 'the selling of implicit or explicit sex by a bodybuilder' (1987, p. 132) and this can range from doing stripogram-type work to engaging in full penetrative sex. Likewise muscle worship is not to be confused with 'sponsorship' or 'growth fantasies'. Katie Arnoldi's superb first novel Chemical Pink (a book which will probably become as revered a text for cultural critics of bodybuilding as Sam Fussell's Muscle [1991]) describes, often in lurid detail, the horrors of female bodybuilding sponsorship. In Chemical Pink, Arnoldi depicts the 'sponsorship' agreement between female bodybuilder Aurora and her sponsor Charles. It soon becomes evident that Charles has a Pygmalion fantasy and gains supreme pleasure from his manipulation of Aurora's body, feeding her endless protein-rich meals and hefty cycles of anabolic steroids and growth hormones (Arnoldi, 2001, pp. 100–102, 111). While Henry Higgins delighted in shaping Eliza's social graces, the muscle sponsor wants to build and shape his idealized female body and, as such, muscle sponsorship can be compared to other sexual fantasies, such as 'feederism', in which the manipulation of the sexual partner's weight is the sexual pleasure."

What I found most interesting here is how various aspects of muscle worship are compared with both mainstream (i.e., prostitution) and not-so-mainstream (e.g., feederism) sexual behaviours. Another short article I read on muscle fetishism (outside the gay community as it concerned female muscle growth) on the Sex and the University website (2008) suggested that there were also links with macrophilia (sexual arousal from giants) and breast expansion fetishes:

> "Female muscle growth (FMG) is a fantasy genre involving muscular growth of a woman. Many who enjoy these fantasies are attracted to female bodybuilding or other

muscular women. This interest frequently centers on the biceps. FMG is related to the growth fantasies about giantesses and breast expansion fetishism. This fantasy is sometimes about an equalization or reversal of the stereotypical power relationship (that some people imagine/take for granted) in a heterosexual couple."

As I note later in this book on sthenolagnia, FMG devotees frequent places where female bodybuilders are found, such as gyms, healthclubs and bodybuilding tournaments. However, I also note that some FMG devotion may be based in fantasy rather than actuality, particularly if it is related to aspects of macrophilia and transformation fetishes. For instance, the *Marvel Comics*' character "She-Hulk" is a popular representation of FMG fantasy and can be found on websites, such as the Female Muscle Factory. Although there is little in the way of academic research on the topic, many devotees of muscle worship appear to be sexually aroused by an equalization (or reversal) of the stereotypical power relationship among heterosexual couples.

Narratophilia

Narratophilia is a sexual paraphilia in which an individual derives sexual pleasure from the use of dirty, pornographic and obscene words or sexual story telling with a sexual partner. This can occur face-to-face with a person or via other synchronous media (such as on the telephone including telephonic sex chat line services). This is different from telephone scatophilia as all parties are consenting adults (whereas in telephone scatophilia the person on the receiving end of the obscene and dirty language is a victim who did not give consent to his or her involvement).

According to Money (1986) narratophilia can also be used to describe the reciprocal condition where an individual's sexual focus is on the hearing of someone uttering erotic, obscene or pornographic words or stories. Milner *et al.* (2008) noted:

> "When the criteria for narratophilia are met, the mode of communication can take any form, including telephone sex services, computer-based erotic bulletin boards, and internet emails. Thus, although a new paraphilia, 'chat-scatophilia' has been proposed to describe an erotic focus on sending obscene words over the internet (Abal, Marin, & Sanchez, 2003), we do not believe that a new category for internet transmission of obscene messages is warranted. Furthermore, the degree of overlap between the existing paraphilic categories of narratophilia and telephone scatophilia remains to be determined."

It is thought that many couples use narratophilic elements during their sexual behaviour. Here the use of spoken obscene words or pornographic language heightens the sexual arousal but is not a necessary prerequisite for sexual arousal to occur. As a consequence, narratophilia can be classified into one of three types:

- *Exclusive narratophilia:* The individual is unable to get sexually aroused without the telling of a sexual story or obscene language being used.
- *Preferred narratophilia*: The individual has a preference for narratophilic activities to "normal" and conventional sex. They can still become sexually aroused and have sex without the use of obscene words and/or pornographic stories but would simply prefer to be engaged in narratophilic activity when possible.
- *Optional narratophilia:* Here, the individual may just engage in narratophilic behaviour as a form of sexual experimentation in an attempt to enhance and facilitate conventional sexual behaviour.

Montagu (1986) claimed that narratophilia is more common among men. However, there is no research evidence to empirically confirm the observation. Given that so many couples appear to use narratophilic elements within the context of their conventional sex lives, there has been controversy as to whether narratophilia should even be considered a paraphilia. The American Psychiatric Association (2013) would only consider narratophilia a disorder if the individual was experiencing personal distress or impairment, or was a threat to others.

Nasophilia

Many people are sexually attracted to particular parts of the human body, but they usually relate to those body parts that are traditionally sexualized, such as genitalia, buttocks and breasts. When individuals have a sexual interest and/or are sexually aroused by very specific and exclusive body parts it is known as "partialism". It may additionally be described as a fetish if sexual arousal is only possible when the particular body part is present (e.g., viewed or touched) during sexual behaviour.

One of the more unusual forms of partialism is nose fetishism (a.k.a. "nasophilia" if it is in the form of a paraphilia). Nasophiles can be sexually aroused by the sight, touch and/or the erotic sucking of human noses. Less common (although I have not seen any empirical evidence to back this up) are those who are sexually aroused by having their nose stroked, felt and sucked. Some nasophiles claim they are sexually excited by placing their nose into the closed eyes of their sexual partner. Therefore, nasophilia may have overlaps with oculophilia (i.e., sexual arousal and pleasure from eyes). In very extreme cases, it has even been claimed that some nasophiles are sexually aroused by the picking of noses.

Sigmund Freud famously interpreted the nose as a penis substitute (Freud, 1962). Although I personally have little time for Freud's theories, the nose much like the genitalia has vascular (erectile) tissue that has the capacity to become engorged during sexual arousal. There are certainly explicit links between sex and the nose in the scientific literature. I write about such an association elsewhere in this book where I examine (i) sex and sneezing, (ii) the relationship between sneezing and orgasm and (iii) sneeze fetishism.

Nasophiles typically experience sexual attraction to very specific physical nose variations based on shape, size and nostril form. It is claimed that most nasophiles are extremely opposed to rhinoplasty (i.e., plastic surgery on the nose) because it removes many of the features that they find sexually desirable. Although there is little empirical research, it is believed the behaviour can manifest itself in a desire for actual physical and sexualized contact and interaction with the nose of the person and/or specific fantasies, such as wanting to sexually penetrate the nostrils. In an article published on the (now defunct) Nose Network website, it was noted that:

> "Although most nasophiliacs are men, there are some women out there who do enjoy the sight of big nostrils, well-shaped wings, cute button noses or anything else that tickles their fancy. Most people will not admit to this fetish, however, due to it not

being very acceptable to society. This is really due to a lack of understanding about the whole thing. No one knows exactly where this fetish came from or why it even exists. Some people will admit that they have fantasies about penetrating the nostrils (mostly men), while others have admitted to wanting to suck and lick the nose. As it turns out, the nose is a very erogenous zone, if for no other reason having the knowledge that the partner is very turned on by this act."

Nasophiles may also be sexually aroused by fantasies involving transformation of the nose (i.e., a transformation fetish). These can also be varied, such as the nose changing into that of another species as a form of sexual humiliation (e.g., the snout of a pig) or the nose growing in size very quickly. Such sexual fantasies can be facilitated via role-playing, the use of props, transformational fiction (e.g., Pinocchio-type stories) and/or animated or Photoshop transformation (e.g., modifying and morphing photographs). For instance, check out the Big Nose Appreciation website that is "devoted to women who do not conform to the stereotypical ideal of feminine beauty and whose beauty is enhanced by their larger or uniquely shaped noses." Alternatively, type "nasophilia" into YouTube and see for yourself the kinds of things that nasophiles love (such as nostril flaring).

The study by Scorolli *et al.* (2007), which I have cited a number of times in this book, investigated the relative prevalence of different fetishes using online fetish forum data. The study reported that body part fetishes were most common (33%), followed by objects associated with the body (30%). They also reported that some of the sites featured references to nose fetishes but that this particular fetish accounted for less than 1% of all fetishes.

As with many other fetishes and paraphilias, treatment for nasophilia is generally not sought by individuals unless it becomes problematic in some way and/or they feel compelled to address the condition. It is thought that the vast majority of nasophiles happily accept their fetish.

Nazi fetishism

Academically, there has been little written on Nazi fetishism. Searching online I found dozens of confessions by people claiming to enjoy and be fans of Nazi fetishism. Moreover, there were many websites, such as the uniform fetish site at Live Journal, that feature lots of sexually provocative Nazi fetish clothing. The following shows some of the online accounts that I found. Obviously, I cannot guarantee their veracity, but they all seemed genuine to me:

- Extract 1: "Don't get me wrong. I do not in any way support their murders, torture or anything of the sort. I would never support such heinous actions. That being said … I like Nazis. I like the uniform, the boots (yes, the boots), the fact that they're German/speak German as well as the whole 'Aryan' look. Neatly combed blonde hair and blue eyes. My friends think I'm insane because I'm half black and I like blonde Nazis. Anyway, I love the masculinity they seemed to have. It's very attractive. It's a fetish I have."

- Extract 2: "I am a girl and I am turned on by the Nazi look, blond hair, blue eyes and uniform. I can't help but have thoughts about it. Is there something wrong with me? I think the holocaust was awful and I hate what the Nazis did, but I just can't help it. Am I normal to have such a weird fetish?"
- Extract 3: "Nazi fetishes are actually fairly common in BDSM. There used to be tons of Nazi-themed pornography and general exploitation movies. Although as the years following WW2 pass, it is becoming more uncommon ... The taboo and violence attached to Nazis makes them a popular fetish for people of many races, religions and sexual orientations. Nazi fetishism is currently most popular in Asian and in gay pornography."
- Extract 4: "Lately, I've found myself getting a little too excited thinking about what most would call Nazi fetishism. I already had a bit of a German fetish, what with the accents and appearances. But when SS uniforms started sneaking into my fantasies, when the idea of a little Nazi roleplay started to really appeal, things were different. I even fantasize about my love interest in the uniform (which is ironic because he [her partner] is quite far from being an Aryan)! ... I've uncovered other fetishes I have and now see how this fits in – (i) German accents are extremely sexy to me, (ii) I have always liked uniforms and nice clothes, (iii) taboo appeals to me quite a bit [and] (iv) power and being dominated appeals to me."
- Extract 5: "I have a fetish for uniforms and I don't blame someone for having a Nazi fetish. People who are sharply dressed do look pretty sexy, especially the women's clothing. I don't have a fetish for the accents and everything German ... It could also be how Nazis are frowned upon, so having a fetish for something so controversial and wrong makes it dirty?"
- Extract 6: "[Nazi] fetish is so common in many circles from anime cosplay to gothic culture. They had the most badass uniforms at the time and they still look hot on just about anyone."

Nazi clothing appears to be a fundamental part of the fetish and would appear to be a subtype of uniform fetishism. In 2007 Roxy Music's lead singer Bryan Ferry appeared to praise the Nazi style (both in fashion and architectural terms) when he was quoted in a German newspaper as saying:

> "The way that the Nazis staged themselves and presented themselves, my Lord! ... I'm talking about the films of Leni Riefenstahl ... And the buildings of Albert Speer and the mass marches and the flags – just fantastic. Really beautiful."

However, Ferry's comments caused huge controversy and he then clarified his comments by saying: "I apologise unreservedly for any offence caused by my comments on Nazi iconography, which were solely made from an art history perspective." This type of apology is very similar to the caveats made by Nazi fetishists online in justifying their like of Nazi imagery from a sexual perspective.

One newspaper article quoted [unnamed] "experts" saying: "While the Nazi concept is not unusual in sadomasochistic circles, playing both sides in such a kinky ritual is unusual." Gareth Meade, a senior council officer in London, UK lost his job for gross misconduct after his involvement in Nazi fetishism was exposed by a Sunday newspaper. Photos of Meade posing in Nazi regalia were found on a gay sex website. Meade claimed in the newspaper interview that he was "not a racist" and that his sexual activity was "a private fetish".

Lopez and Godard (2013) studied Nazi fetishism using online forum data. They also view the fetish as a type of uniform fetish. Their paper noted that:

> "Nazi uniform fetishists and roleplayers represent the diversity of BDSM subculture as it is a very unique activity with a specific form of expression. The most salient form of this expression is seen in the style and fashion of these fetishists and roleplayers. Style and fashion expresses autonomy, proclaims messages, establishes boundaries and generates definitions of a subculture (Hebdige, 1979). For uniform fetishists, the uniform creates a context for the BDSM scene. A Nazi uniform is just one type of uniform fetish. We suggest for these participants that they are attracted to Nazism as a movement steeped in violence and evil and the uniform is representative of this movement. BDSM practitioners use the term 'scene' when referring to erotic power exchange."

Lopez and Godard collected data from a BDSM site that had over 900,000 members. They then focused on specific discussion groups within the main site. One of these groups, the Nazi Uniform Fetish and Roleplaying (NUFR) group, had 617 members. The authors also noted that there were at least 12 other similar groups with an interest in Nazi fetishism including Females of the Third Reich (114 members) and SS [*Shutzstaffel* "Protection Squad"] Uniforms and Those Who Love Them (162 members). The NUFR group was chosen as the site to study because it had the largest number of members and the most detailed postings from its members about Nazi fetishism. The data were content-analysed and comprised over 300 threads (approximately 10,000 comments). The authors reported that members discussed the uniforms themselves (including where to acquire them), pointedly disavowed white supremacy and anti-Semitism and emphasized their only interest was in the eroticism associated with the uniforms. The authors also reported that many posts commented on the sex appeal of the uniforms.

As with the posts I found online, Lopez and Godard (2013) noted that their participants were "very careful and went to great lengths to establish that they are not anti-Semitic or supremacists," yet were fully aware that confusion was possible. For instance, some respondents noted:

- *Example 1:* "People tend to automatically assume that someone who finds the uniform or the roleplay sexy is actually a Nazi himself/herself. Which I'm sure can be the case from time to time but couldn't be further from the truth for me. I'm actually the exact opposite."
- *Example 2:* "There are a lot of Jews in this group like me. Except we're clever enough to know the difference between a fetish and actually committing racist acts."
- *Example 3:* "The biggest fan of my ex's SS uniform was a friend of ours who is Jewish."
- *Example 4:* "Jews like to play Nazis and Nazis like to play Jews."
- *Example 5:* "I'm a Jew who likes to keep being a Jew in my Nazi torture roleplaying."

Lopez and Godard also noted that not a single post they examined expressed explicit anti-Semitism. It was the violent nature of Nazism – not anti-Semitism – that motivated the self-presentation of individuals as Nazis among Nazi uniform fetishists. They also added that it was the image of violence that was being portrayed, more than the actual violence. This is because BDSM play is highly controlled (as evidenced by consensual scene negotiation and the use of safewords). Based on the (mainly) qualitative data collected, Lopez and Godard concluded that:

> "Nazi uniform fetish and roleplay is just that, the playing of a role. The fetish serves to enhance the BDSM experience and has little to do with white supremacy or anti-Semitism. The world of BDSM is an erotically charged arena that incorporates a variety of interests, desires and tastes. It is the association with evil that participants in Nazi uniform fetish and roleplay find appealing. The self-presentation of erotic evil serves to contribute to the quality of the BDSM experience and allows participants in this subculture a safe and accepting environment in which to explore and express their fetish. This suggests, as oxymoronic as it sounds, that evil isn't all that bad. The incorporation of evil symbols in a safe, non-harmful, consensual manner to enhance one's pleasure suggests some performances (i.e., roleplaying) serve a purpose in popular culture; it allows us to be bad."

Necrobestiality (zoophilia/necrophilia)

In October 2006 many American papers reported the case of Ronald Kuch, a 44-year-old man from Michigan who was jailed for having sex with a dead dog. The incident was seen by a number of people including staff members of a nearby daycare centre and the police. A summarized account of the incident at the Pet Abuse website (2007) reported:

> "Kuch was arrested after police searched the area of Midland and Carter Roads on October 20 for a man who ran away from a Bay County Animal Control officer. The entire incident was within view of a nearby daycare center ... Kuch was charged with crimes against nature and assaulting a law enforcement officer. Troopers said a woman from the daycare center called Animal Control because there was a dead dog near the property that had been hit by a car several days earlier. Before officers could arrive, the man showed up and began engaging in sexual acts with the dog, police said. The Animal Control officer also reported seeing Kuch involved in the sex act and as he approached him, Kuch shoved him away and ran off ... [Police officers] later learned that the dog, a black labrador retriever, belonged to [Kuch's] girlfriend. The dog had been dead for 4 or 5 days."

Love (2001) defines necrobestialism as referring to "individuals who derive sexual arousal and pleasure from having sex with dead animals." According to Love this may include "bestial sadists" who kill before or during the torture of animals and those who choose to have sex with animals that they already find dead. Aggrawal (2011a) proposed a new classification of zoophilia to include individuals who have sex with dead animals. One of the 10 subtypes (so-called "Class IX zoosexuals") comprises "homicidal bestials" who need to kill animals in order to have sex with them (i.e., necrozoophiles). Aggrawal (2009a) also reported that, despite being capable of having sex with living animals, there is an insatiable desire among Class IX zoosexuals to have sex with dead animals.

The act in which humans have sex with dead animals appears to be incredibly rare. Furthermore, the reason for engaging in such acts may not even be sexually motivated. For instance, Love's (2001) entry on necrobestiality notes that:

> "The Suaheli and Arabian fishermen along the coast of Africa until a hundred years ago believed that unless they had anal sex with the seacows that they netted or that had washed up dead they would be dragged out to sea the next day and drowned by the dead seacow's sister. Many locals would therefore make these fishermen swear by the Koran that they did not have sex with the seacow they were selling at the local market."

There was no reference in Love's book as to where the evidence was for this practice. However, given the thorough job she did on most entries in her encyclopaedia, I have no reason to think this practice was untrue.

There are more recent examples of humans having sex with sea animals. One British tabloid reported that 46-year-old Andrew Dymond was caught with a picture of a man having sex with a dead squid along with pictures of child pornography and other zoophilic pornographic acts including humans having sex with dogs and horses. After Dymond's home computer was seized by police they found a large amount of "grossly offensive" pornography on it including someone "performing an act of intercourse with a dead animal, namely an octopus/squid, which was grossly offensive, disgusting or otherwise of an obscene character."

In a book chapter on paraphilic crime signatures Hickey (2006) reported that the serial killer Jeffrey Dahmer collected animal roadkill, dissected the remains and masturbated over the animals he had cut up because he "found the glistening viscera of animals sexually arousing." Schlesinger's (2004) book on sexual murder reported that: "Dahmer dissected roadkill, butchered small animals, nailed cats and frogs to trees behind his house, and once put a dog's head on a stick." Aggrawal (2009a) also reported the case of 20-year-old Bryan Hathaway from Superior, Wisconsin, USA who in 2006 was arrested for having sex with a dead deer. Hathaway's case is arguably the most notorious case of necrobestiality because the case was reported by the mass media worldwide. The case also raised lots of legal, moral and ethical questions over whether a dead animal was really an animal.

Hathaway was charged with "sexual gratification with an animal", but his legal team argued that the deer carcass was not an animal and that the legal statutes do not prohibit an individual from having sex with a carcass. One of Hathaway's legal team Fredric Anderson said that "If you try to include corpses in the category of 'animals', then 'you really go down a slippery slope with absurd results'." For instance, would the picked-over skeletal remains of a dead animal still meet the definition of an animal? Mr Anderson said that if the carcass was defined as an animal, it would therefore be illegal to have sex with frozen meat or a roast turkey. The state prosecutor James Broughner argued that a deer carcass was still an animal because in Hathaway's own personal statement he had admitted to having sexual relations with a "dead deer" indicating that Hathaway still thought of it as an animal. He also added that pet owners still call their deceased pets animals after death. In March 2007 Hathaway was given probation rather than a prison sentence. However, it was then revealed that Hathaway was later given a 9-month prison sentence for killing a horse so that he could have sex with it.

Necrophilia

One of the rarest of known paraphilias is necrophilia in which a person obtains sexual gratification by viewing or having intercourse with a corpse. It is currently listed in the American Psychiatric Association's (2022) *Diagnostic and Statistical Manual of Mental Disorders* (DSM-5-TR) under "other specified paraphilic disorder" (OSPD). Given the rarity of necrophilia there is a lack of systematically reported empirical data with almost all knowledge emanating from published case studies.

Based on the case study data, necrophilia almost exclusively involves males who are driven to remove freshly buried bodies or seek employment in funeral parlours or morgues. In fact, the biggest study of necrophilic behaviour found that 57% of necrophiliacs were employed in a profession that gave them access to dead bodies (Rosman and Resnick, 1989). However, rare cases of female necrophilia have been documented including the high-profile case of Karen Greenlee.

Arguably, the most comprehensive study in the area is the one by Rosman and Resnick (1989). They reviewed 122 cases comprising 88 from the world literature and 34 unpublished cases of their own. The motivation for engaging in necrophilic behaviour was examined and the results showed that two thirds of necrophiliacs reported the desire to possess an unresisting and unrejecting partner (68%). Other lesser motivations reported included wanting to be reunited with their dead romantic partner (21%), being sexually attracted to corpses (15%), comfort or overcoming feelings of isolation (15%) and/or seeking self-esteem by expressing power over a homicide victim (12%). They classified the behaviour into three subtypes: (i) necrophilic homicide, (ii) "regular" necrophilia and (iii) necrophilic fantasy. British research has also suggested that some necrophiles may opt for a non-living mate because of a consistent failure to create normal romantic attachments with people who are alive.

Rosman and Resnick (1989) also theorized about the situational antecedents leading to necrophilic behaviour. Their theory is that necrophiliacs develop poor self-esteem that may be due to a significant loss. Furthermore, they suggested that necrophiliacs may be fearful of rejection by others and that they desired a sexual partner who is incapable of rejecting them. This suggests necrophiliacs may be socially and/or sexually inept and may hate and/or fear the opposite sex, causing them to seek out non-threatening, subjugated sexual partners (i.e., non-living people). Alternatively, Rosman and Resnick also suggested that necrophiliacs may be fearful of dead people and that they transform their fear into a sexual desire. Perhaps unsurprisingly, necrophiliacs almost always manifest severe emotional disorders.

Kafka (2010a, b) argued that necrophilia could technically be considered a fetish variant because the sexualized object of desire is "non-living", although there are insufficient data to empirically support the argument. Necrophilia can be accompanied by "sadistic acts" and even sexually motivated murder – certainly not behaviours associated with fetishism as currently defined.

The sadistic side of necrophilia has certainly been reported in some of the more extreme case studies. For instance, Skugarevsky *et al.* (2011) presented the case of a young man twice convicted on charges of defiling female corpses and who had undergone a long course of psychiatric treatment. All his necrophilic acts were committed over a 15-year period. In three cases he skinned the trunk of the dead victims, placed the skin on his naked body and then stimulated himself sexually. In several cases he kept mementos from the victims at his home, such as used burial clothes he had removed from the coffins.

Homicidal necrophilia certainly seems to be a distinct subcategory of necrophilia. Stein *et al.* (2010) reviewed 211 sexual homicides. Nearly 8% involved necrophilia (i.e., 16 cases). Their findings suggested that the most common explanation for necrophilia (i.e., the offender's desire to have an unresisting partner) may not always be applicable in cases where necrophilia is connected to sexual murder.

Given the many different types of necrophilic act reported in the scientific and forensic literature, Aggrawal (2009b) outlined a new classification of necrophilia containing 10 different types (Classes I–X):

- *Class I necrophiliacs:* This type comprises roleplayers who according to Aggrawal are only mildly pathological and could be described as engaging in simulated and/or symbolic necrophilia. These individuals never have sex with dead people, but get very sexually aroused when having sex with someone pretending to be dead (i.e., sexual roleplay). Some experts, such as Shaffer and Penn (2006), described such acts as pseudonecrophilia. I would also argue when it comes to somnophilia (i.e., a person obtaining sexual satisfaction with someone who is asleep) that such a paraphilia could be a form of pseudonecrophilia.
- *Class II necrophiliacs:* This type comprises romantic necrophiles who according to Aggrawal display only "very mild necrophilic tendencies". This type of necrophile typically comprises people whose loved ones have just died and who do not seem to fully believe or psychologically appreciate that the person they love is dead. Therefore, the sexual contact may not in the person's view be seen as necrophilic as they still believe the person is alive to them. Aggrawal claims that, in some cases, romantic necrophiles may mummify the body or body parts of their partner. The necrophilic activity is typically short lived and is something that stops once the person fully accepts that their loved one is dead.
- *Class III necrophiliacs:* This type comprises necrophilic fantasizers who according to Aggrawal simply fantasize about having sexual contact with dead people, but never actually engage in the activity for real. Aggrawal claims that such people may become sexually aroused when seeing dead people and may engage in activities that increase their likelihood of seeing the dead (e.g., visiting funeral parlours and cemeteries).
- *Class IV necrophiliacs:* This type comprises tactile necrophiles who according to Aggrawal erotically touch dead bodies to achieve orgasm. They seek out jobs in which they come into regular contact with the dead (e.g., mortuary assistants) and

according to Aggrawal "enjoy touching, stroking parts of the dead body, such as genitalia or breasts or perhaps licking them."
- *Class V necrophiliacs:* This type comprises fetishistic necrophiles ("necrofetishists") who according to Aggrawal do not have sexual intercourse with dead people, but who will if the chance arises "cut up some portion of the body – perhaps a breast – for later fetishistic activities" or may "keep some portion of the dead body – pubic hair or a finger perhaps – in the pocket for continuous erotic stimulation, or sometimes may wear it as an amulet for similar pleasure." Aggrawal says that although necrofetishists may preserve body parts of the dead much as romantic necrophiles do, the motivations are very different as the latter type of necrophile only keeps body parts of someone they love "in order to fill up a psychosexual vacuum that their death has caused."
- *Class VI necrophiliacs:* This type comprises necromutilomaniacs who according to Aggrawal do not engage in sexual intercourse with dead people, but gain sexual pleasure from masturbation while simultaneously mutilating dead bodies. Included within this type of necrophile are those who get sexual pleasure from eating part of the corpse (i.e., necrophagy).
- *Class VII necrophiliacs:* This type comprises opportunistic necrophiles who according to Aggrawal typically engage in "normal" sexual behaviour, but would have sexual intercourse with a dead person "if an opportunity arose".
- *Class VIII necrophiliacs:* This type comprises regular necrophiles who according to Aggrawal are the "classical" necrophiliacs as most people understand them to be. Aggrawal claims that this type of necrophile does not enjoy sexual intercourse with people who are alive and has a distinct preference for sexual activity with the dead. Regular necrophiles will go to extreme lengths to engage in their sexual preference including stealing dead bodies from graveyards or mortuaries.
- *Class IX necrophiliacs:* This type comprises homicidal necrophiles (a.k.a. "homicidophilia" or "lust murder") who according to Aggrawal are the most dangerous type of necrophile (a.k.a. "necrosadists"). Such people will go as far as killing people just so they can have sex with the dead. Aggrawal also says that the behaviour may be described as "warm necrophilia" because sex typically takes place immediately after the killing while the bodies are still warm.
- *Class X necrophiliacs:* This type comprises exclusive necrophiles who according to Aggrawal are arguably the rarest necrophile subtype. Such people are psychologically and physiologically incapable of having sex with the living and therefore are only capable of having sex with the dead. Aggrawal claims that, as a result of dead bodies being the prerequisite for sexual behaviour to occur, the person may go to any lengths to acquire a dead body and, therefore, as is the case with homicidal necrophiles can be extremely dangerous.

Aggrawal's (2009b) typology ranges from minimal to maximal severity, appears to be instinctive or relatively intuitive and is based on clinical case studies, forensic crime data and anecdotal evidence. Ideally, Aggrawal would like his classification to facilitate "uniform statistical compilation of data from around the world, epidemiological surveys, calculation of incidence and prevalence of this phenomena, and treatment."

One of the most bizarre (and arguably disturbing) stories I have come across is the case of a 37-year-old Swedish woman who was arrested in September 2012 by local police for having sex with a human skeleton (Agence France-Presse, 2012). The human remains were found by chance in Kosmosgatan in the Bergsjön district of Gothenburg after someone reported hearing a gunshot coming from the woman's home. Swedish national television SVT reported that she was initially charged with murder, but this was subsequently downgraded to "violating the peace of the dead" by the District Court in Gothenburg. It was alleged that she used the human bones as sex toys. She claimed her sexual activity was a hobby motivated by an interest in history. According to Swedish prosecutor Kristina Ehrenborg-Staffas:

> "I have never heard of a case like this and neither have my colleagues, so I dare to say that this kind of case is quite uncommon ... In the confidential section of the investigation we have material which indicates she used them in sexual situations ... We claim it's her, but she claims it's someone else and that she found the pictures on the Internet ... She has a lot of photos of morgues and chapels, and documents about how to have sex with recently deceased and otherwise dead people ... You have to ask yourself why she would have those pictures ... She admits to having the bones, but says she collected them out of a historical and archaeological interest."

Allegations were also made claiming that the woman boasted to local children and teenagers that she kept many knives, weapons and dead people in her apartment (subsequently confirmed after a police raid found knives and human bones in the woman's living room). One of the teenagers claimed the woman had said to him that she had "killed people and there's blood everywhere." The woman then went to her apartment and a gunshot was heard. Kristina Ehrenborg-Staffas also said:

> "... the woman had used the human bones in an 'unethical' way but [the prosecutor herself] couldn't explain how the accused had managed to assemble almost an entire human skeleton. Thomas Fuxborg, the Västra Götaland police force's press spokesman told SVT at the time of the initial arrest that 'several skeleton parts' were found in the police search. However, there was great speculation as to whether the bones had come from a local graveyard, a hospital, or from a murder. The police could not confirm if the bones came from a male or female, or were from more than one person. Later in court, it was revealed that the woman kept at least six human skulls (one of which was found in her freezer), one human spine, and 'a large number of other [human] bones'."

The prosecuting team presented their evidence, which included two compact discs (one entitled "My necrophilia" and the other "My first experience") containing both written documents and various photographs, such as ones showing the woman hugging and licking a skull. She was also alleged to have sold human skulls to others online. For instance, the court was told that the most recent online transaction was a person in Uppsala (Eastern Sweden) who allegedly bought three human skulls and a human spine. Other evidence shown in court included mortuary photographs, body bags and a drill, all found inside a secret compartment in the woman's apartment. According to the Swedish daily newspaper *Goeteborgsposten* the accused woman, who claimed she was in a relationship, wrote on an online forum:

"My morals set my limits and I'm prepared to take the punishment if something should happen. It's worth it. I want my man like he is, whether he is dead or alive. He allows me to find sexual happiness on the side."

A number of psychological evaluations were carried out, none of which showed she was suffering any mental illness, but did show she was "fascinated" by death. However, there was no evidence that the woman had dug up any graves to access human remains. In agreement with Kristina Ehrenborg-Staffas, Katarina Öberg (Head of Stockholm's Centre of Andrology and Sexual Medicine at Karolinska University Hospital) also claimed that this particular case was the first she had heard of in Sweden:

"During my 10 years I have never had a patient with necrophilia. Although, I guess it is not really something that one confesses to having."

As a result of the prosecutor and the expert witness claiming that the defendant had not done anything illegal, she therefore pleaded "not guilty" to all charges except possession of a firearm. The accused woman was said to have revealed in court:

"I'm not saying I'm the world's nicest or best person. I'm an odd bird. I'm interested in forensics and I'm passionate about osteology. I have photographs of dead people."

Although the charge of necrophilia was dismissed, it was noted by the court that:

"Moving parts of a skeleton is a crime, since she was unauthorised to do so, just as it is a crime to assemble a skeleton and keep it lying on the floor, [and] to keep skeletal parts in plastic bags and use them for trade. [She also knowingly handled the bones] in an undignified manner."

In all the articles and papers that I have ever read on necrophilia, I have never come across a single case, even anecdotally, of someone having sex with a skeleton. The behaviour described here does not fit any of Aggrawal's 10 types of necrophiliac. Therefore, I agree with the Swedish court's decision to dismiss this as a case of necrophilia. Weird and depraved it might be, but using human bones as a "sexual bone" does not fit any definition of necrophilia that I am aware of.

Nun fetishism

A newspaper article in Metro on August 27, 2013 is the closest I have come to any reports on nun fetishism:

"In terrible news for nun fetishists everywhere, the nun beauty contest has been cancelled. The Italian priest who had planned the online 'pageant' for nuns has suspended the project, saying he was misinterpreted and never had any intention of putting sisters on a beauty catwalk. Apparently, he's been feeling some heat from the higher-ups. 'My superiors were not happy. The local bishop was not happy, but they did not understand me either,' Father Antonio Rungi told Reuters by telephone from his convent in southern Italy on Tuesday. 'It was not at all my intention to put nuns on the catwalk,' said Rungi, a priest of the Passionists religious order, speaking from his convent in the town of Mondragone. Rungi's idea appeared in newspapers around the world after he floated the idea of a contest for nuns on his blog, referred to by some as 'Sister Italy 2008'. 'It was interpreted as more of a physical thing. Now, no one is saying that nuns can't be beautiful, but I was thinking about something more complete,' he said."

As far as I am aware, there is no academic literature on nun fetishes. However, in my research I came across an interesting website that focused on 1970s' and 1980s' "nunsploitation" videoclips and "nuns behaving badly in bizarre fetish films", such as three Italian films *The Sinful Nuns of Saint Valentine* (1974), *Images from a Convent* (1979) and *Convent of Sinners* (1986) as well as the 1975 Mexican film *Satánico Pandemonium*. As the anonymous blogger commented, it was particularly the underground cult cinema in Italy, Spain and Mexico where Catholic guilt was most likely transmuted "into sexual fetishism involving naughty nuns, masochism, sadism, whipping and lesbianism." Pierluigi Puccini has a more mainstream selection of films on his Nun's Habits: A Cinematic Fetish webpage including *The Devils* (directed by Ken Russell, 1971), *Killer Nun* (directed by Giulio Berruti, 1978), *Love Letters of a Portuguese Nun* (directed by Jesús Franco, 1977), *The Story of a Cloistered Nun* (directed by Domenico Paolella, 1973) and *To The Devil A Daughter* (directed by Peter Sykes, 1976).

Nun fetishism appears to be a niche market when it comes to genuine sexual fetishes, and there is a complete lack of empirical evidence regarding its existence.

Nyctophilia/Scotophilia

According to Aggrawal (2009a) nyctophilia is a paraphilia in which the individual derives sexual pleasure and arousal by a "love of night". Aggrawal further defines similar if not the same conditions including scotophilia ("turned on by darkness"), lygophilia ("love of darkness") and achluophilia ("arousal from darkness"). Another related condition is arguably amaurophilia ("arousal by a partner who is blind or unable to see due to artificial means, such as being blindfolded or having sex in total darkness"). Love (2001) did not mention any of these paraphilias apart from amaurophilia. Other medical dictionaries conflate darkness and night and define nyctophilia as a preference for the night or darkness (a.k.a. "scotophilia").

As far as I can ascertain, there is no empirical research on this topic at all. Mahony (1989) noted in a paper on voyeurism that the alternative spelling of "scoptophilia, preferred by some of the older German psychoanalysts, must not be confused with scotophilia or love of darkness." This appears to have happened in other academic papers I found directly referring to scotophilia. For instance, one paper dating back over 70 years is that of Caprio (1949), in which the author wrote a paper entitled "Scotophilia–exhibitionism: A case report". However, it turned out to be a paper about voyeurism. More specifically, the paper reported the cases of a mother and son who constantly watched residents for their own sexual arousal through drilled holes in the wall of the house where they lived. Sattler's (1966) theoretical review paper on embarrassment and blushing claimed that "stage-fright and erythrophobia [fear of blushing] are not simply expressions of the warding off of heightened exhibitionism and scotophilia but also develop as a result of previous instinctual conflict." Here again, scotophilia appears to be a synonym for voyeurism rather than a sexual love of darkness.

I was pleasantly surprised to find dozens of references to nyctophilia in the scientific literature, but the overwhelming majority of papers were biological in origin and all referred to non-human species. For instance, Espinasa *et al.* (2016) report that cave amphipods are eyeless troglobitic crustaceans found in caves located in the Northeastern (Allegheny) region of the USA that "exhibit nyctophilia" (literally meaning they love darkness). Therefore, such references have absolutely nothing to do with sexual behaviour whatsoever.

I only managed to find one non-biological academic reference to nyctophilia and this was by Lawson (1994). In actuality, the word "nyctophilia" is only mentioned in passing by Lawson who noted that the term was defined by psychoanalyst Bertram Lewin as "an erotic pleasure in darkness, which enters as a wish-fulfillment element on fantasies of being in the 'womb', or more properly, as the German word *Mutterlieb* ["mother love"] suggests, of being in the mother's body." I was unable to track down the original source so I do not know the context in which Lewin used the word. However, the definition is certainly used in a sexual sense rather than the general "love of darkness" used in biologically based papers.

In all the reading I have done on this topic, there appears to be very little genuine evidence that scotophilia and nyctophilia exist. If they do exist, then few people appear to suffer major problems as a consequence unless their love of the dark leaves individuals feeling so sleep deprived that it interferes with their day-to-day functioning. Maybe these conditions are a subtype of insomnia in which the underlying reasons for not going to sleep are very different from the usual reasons for not being able to sleep.

Objectum sexuality

One of the most interesting documentaries I have ever watched was the British Channel 5 programme "Married to the Eiffel Tower", which first aired on June 4, 2008. The programme featured, via three in-depth case studies, an examination of "object sexuality".

Object sexuality refers to those individuals who develop deep emotional and/or romantic attachments to and have relationships with specific inanimate objects or structures. Such objectophiles express a loving and/or sexual preference and commitment to particular items or structures. They rarely, if ever, have sex with humans and they develop strong emotional fixations to the object or structure. Unlike sexual fetishism, the object or structure is viewed as an equal partner in the relationship and is not used to enhance or facilitate sexual behaviour. Some objectophiles even believe that their feelings are reciprocated by the object of their desire.

Arguably, the most infamous objectophile is Erika LaBrie who "married" the Eiffel Tower in 2007 and now calls herself Erika Eiffel. She first met the Eiffel Tower in 2004 and fell in love with it immediately. She visits her "soul mate" as often as she can afford to and claims her relationship is as real as that between any two consenting adults. Prior to her relationship with the Eiffel Tower, her first object love empowered her to become a two-time world champion in archery. Her first object love was her bow called "Lance". While falling in love with an inanimate object is rare, Erika is not alone.

Erika Eiffel's feelings for the Eiffel Tower are not common, but not entirely unheard of either. Eija-Riitta Berliner-Mauer infamously married the Berlin Wall over 35 years ago and coined the term "objectum sexuality" (OS) to describe her love. Together with the wall, they founded OS Internationale, a support network and educational website for other objectophiles. Unsurprisingly, the formation of the website generated worldwide media attention. Another objectophile who has turned up in the world media is Edward Smith, a 57-year-old man from Washington State in the USA, who admitted to having had sex with over 1,000 cars. He said:

> "I write poetry about cars, I sing to them and talk to them just like a girlfriend. I know what's in my heart and I have no desire to change."

Yet another is Amanda Whittaker from Leeds, UK who gave an interview to the *Daily Mail* regarding her romantic feelings for the Statue of Liberty. She said:

> "She is my long-distance lover and I am blown away by how stunning she is. Other

people might be shocked to think I can have romantic feelings for an object, but I am not the same as them."

Then there is Reighner Deleighnie, a 40-year-old woman from London, UK who claimed that she had fallen in love with a 3-foot statue of the Greek god Adonis that she bought for £395 (Strauss, 2012). Another proud objectophile is Amy Wolfe, a 33-year-old woman from Pennsylvania, USA who declared her romantic feelings for the fairground ride "1001 Nachts" in Knoebels Amusement Park. She fell in love with the ride when she was 13. She said:

"I love him as much as women love their husbands and know we'll be together forever. I was instantly attracted to him sexually and mentally." (Otto, 2009)

She's now marrying the "ride" (ahem!). Finally, Joachim A. from Germany is a 41-year-old man who recognized and accepted his inclination when he was just 12 years old. He said he "fell head over heels into an emotionally and physically very complex and deep relationship, which lasted for years." His partner as a teenager was a Hammond organ. He is now in a steady relationship with a steam locomotive and has been for several years.

It is only relatively recently that academics have started to carry out research into objectum sexuality. Marsh (2010) described what she claimed was the first ever research study conducted on a group of 40 "objectophiles" in which 21 English-speaking participants shared their experiences. On US television Marsh revealed that she supported OS as a legitimate sexual orientation. Her research does not appear to indicate childhood trauma as a factor in the development of OS. She states there would be far more objectophiles were this the case.

German sexologist Volkmar Sigusch (former director of Frankfurt University's Institute for Sexual Science) believes he has unraveled the mysteries of OS – a form of modern "neo-sexuality". He views OS as proof of his hypothesis that society is – increasingly drifting into asexuality. He speculated:

"More and more people either openly declare or can be seen to live without any intimate or trusting relationship with another person. Cities are populated by an entire army of socially isolated individuals. Singles, isolated people, cultural sodomites, many perverts and sex addicts."

However, Sigusch does not want to classify such odd behaviour as pathological. He concludes:

"The objectophiles aren't hurting anyone. They're not abusing or traumatizing other people. Who else can you say that about?"

Earlier in this book I examined whether individuals who have sexual relationships with inanimate objects might also have various subtypes of paraphilia, such as mechanophilia (individuals who derive sexual pleasure from computers, cars, robots or androids and domestic appliances) and robot fetishism (individuals who derive sexual pleasure and arousal from humanoid or non-humanoid robots).

Another individual I was made aware of when I was interviewed about him for the television series *Forbidden* (broadcast on the Discovery Channel). The case involves

Dutchmen Kees van Voorst (KVV) who had "a special love for bikes". He claimed to be in love and to have had sexual relationships with 30 bicycles.

Compared with other objectum sexuals, KVV is not unique – as borne out by the cases of American Edward Smith who has had sex with over 1,000 cars and Briton Robert Stewart who ended up in court after being caught having sex with a bicycle. Thompson (2000) argued that some types of cycle, especially motorcycles, are often portrayed as sexualized fetish objects by their owners.

The television documentary about KVV filmed him in his hometown of Lunteren. The story showed not only how much KVV loves riding bicycles but also how much he was romantically and sexually in love with them. He appeared ecstatic as he rode his favourite bicycles. He introduced the documentary makers to each bicycle by name. The production notes for the television programme highlighted that:

"His favourite [bicycle] is Aunt Ann who he sleeps with at night. He shows us how he dotes on them daily, oiling their chains, pumping up their tyres and polishing their shafts. He reads bike magazines as if they were adult magazines. Kees really does love bikes. In the film we follow Kees as he introduces a new member to his bike family. But his house is so packed full already, he'll have to sell one of his bikes to make room for the new member, an emotional moment. He still doesn't know which bike will go. Once he's decided, he'll say goodbye and then sell his bike to a local person who has answered an ad in the local paper ... We'll see him walk through gigantic bike parking lots with literally thousands of bikes – he'll say hello to them as he walks past. He'll then enter a massive bike store and be weak at the knees with the sexy selection of bike babes hanging from the ceiling. He'll then choose his new love and take her home to meet her new family. After introducing the new bike to her new bike brothers and cycling sisters – the moment of truth, the first ride on the new bike – how will they get on? Will she be as good a ride as she looks? Will he take her off road straight away or build up to it? The film will end with Kees and his feelings about his new bike."

There is little doubt that KVV is one of the world's few genuine objectum sexuals. KVV was not aware that his sexual love of bicycles had a name, but confirmed that the scientific description of the condition matched his own feelings and experiences (i.e., strong feelings of love, commitment and attraction to inanimate items). He was quoted in the documentary as saying:

"I see my love as the same as men and women but with bikes ... I tried to love women but they just don't love me back like a bike can."

Of the 30 bicycles KVV owns 8 have names, but his true love is the bicycle "Aunt Ann". At the time of the interview, he was cycling around 10,000 kilometres a year on his various bicycles. His "special desire" for bicycles began when he was 12 years old:

"His neighbour was visiting with her bike and [KVV] was fixated on it, he pleaded with her to be able to borrow the bike but she wouldn't let him. He was heartbroken. But it wasn't till he was 16 [years old] that he had his first real love. It was then that he really could grasp that his love for bikes went far beyond what could be considered normal – but for [KVV] this is exactly what it was, absolutely normal. He did try

to have relationships with women, he has had two so far in his life but both failed miserably."

To KVV "Aunt Ann" is "his everything". This particular bicycle sleeps in his bedroom, gets kissed goodnight and is the bicycle KVV wants to take with him to his grave. KVV claimed that he cannot imagine a life without his beloved bicycles. The sensation of riding them is unlike anything else he has experienced. He said:

> "When I am on one of my bikes and I'm thinking only about that bike, that is when I feel real love."

KVV's appearance on *Forbidden* was not his first TV appearance. A local Dutch programme profiled KVV and his bicycle love, after which he gained a level of notoriety. His TV appearance did not endear him to the Dutch public. Local residents claimed he brought shame to his hometown of Lunteren. Other than his bicycles, KVV has only one human friend, who did not want to be filmed in the documentary. The only other human that KVV has any kind of regular contact with is a local photographer who takes photos of KVV with his bicycle lovers. KVV's story highlights that, while rare, OS exists and that some human beings can and do have loving sexual relationships with inanimate objects.

Oculophilia

In November 2011 various news reports claimed that Saudi Arabian women with "sexy eyes" were to be outlawed from displaying them in public. This was because Saudi Arabia's Committee for the Promotion of Virtue and Prevention of Vice announced a proposal to pass a law that women with "sexy eyes" must cover them up when out and about in public. This report got me wondering about the interrelationship (if any) between eyes and sex.

There's no doubt that someone's eyes can be a source of sexual attraction. Furthermore, most people are aware that a person's pupils enlarge when someone or something sexually attracts them. In fact, Love (2001) noted that European women used to put chemicals in their eyes so that they would dilate. This was done as a means of making men think that the women in question were attracted to them.

Some people have a fetish for eyes. The condition is called oculophilia and is a paraphilia in which individuals derive sexual arousal and pleasure from eyes. The fetish can manifest itself in a desire for actual physical contact and interaction with the eye. It can also take a number of forms and be very specific. For instance, it has been written that the 17th-century philosopher and mathematician René Descartes had a fetish for women with a squint. He cited his attraction to cross-eyed women as originating from an infatuation with a childhood friend who had a squint. It appears there are modern-day adherents too as borne out by this on an online confessional website:

> "I am attracted to people that have lazy eyes. The more lazy their eye, the more attractive it is to me. It's a huge turn-on, especially eyes that turn outward (e.g., exotropia)."

One specific oculophilic activity involves the licking of eyes for sexual pleasure. According to Love (2001) this activity is called "oculolinctus" (although, personally,

I would call it oculolingus). Oculolinctus appears "to be rare, but there are several cases, including one of a female who in order to orgasm would have to lick the eyeball of her obliging male lover." Love (2001) does add a note of caution that those engaging in the act should be aware that oral herpes (i.e., cold sores) can be transferred to the eye. There may also be other dangers. For instance, a post on the Live Journal website in 2003 claimed that:

"Optometrists are calling for an immediate halt of eye licking by sexual fetishists due to the dangers involved. Particles, debris and plaque collected in the mouth can emerge at the tip of the tongue. During a tongue to eye licking session those particles can easily scrape the cornea causing significant damage to the eyeball. Optometrists are quick to point out that patients do not admit to eye licking as the source of such damage. Most attribute their scratches to sand, pine needles and rusty nails. Optometrists wish to inform the public that they know when their patients are lying about their sexual perversions when they involve the eyeball."

The "Oculolinctus" page on the Everything2 website (2004) claimed in the complete absence of empirical evidence that the oculophilic fetish is:

"A predominantly female one; that is, more women want to do it than men. In the rarest of cases, women have been documented that need to lick the eyeball of their lover in order to achieve orgasm."

Eye socket sex and, more commonly, eye socket rape also appear in Japanese pornographic comics, such as *Hentai Doujinshi* and *Hentai Manga*. There are also occasional reports from the forensic crime literature indicating paraphilic interest in eyes. For instance, White (2007) examined evidence of primary, secondary and collateral paraphilias left at serial murder and sex offender crime scenes. He reported that serial killer Charles Albright may have "raped and killed three prostitutes (collateral paraphilia) for the purpose of carefully extracting their eyes (primary paraphilia of oculophilia)." With regard to sexual eyeball licking, Neustifter (2008) reported that:

"Eyeballs are covered in naturally salty water used to keep them lubricated and clean, which also gives them a distinctively smooth and salty flavour. While the eyeball doesn't feel in the same way that our fingers and tongue do, it can sense pressure and temperature, making eyeball licking an optimal form of stimulation. Pretty much everyone recognizes the eye as a vulnerable area of the body, making it an intimate area for some people. Where there is vulnerability and intimacy, you might just find eroticism! Some folks enjoy doing the licking, both for the sensation and for the ability to enjoy their partner's vulnerability in this way. And for those who like to be licked, they find the situation as well as the physical stimulation to be highly enjoyable. This isn't a universal erogenous zone, so many folks won't get the attraction even if they try it."

This is yet another paraphilic and/or fetishistic behaviour on which there is no empirical research at all. We know next to nothing about the incidence, prevalence and etiology of eyeball licking, let alone why people engage in the behaviour. This is definitely an area that (if you excuse the poor pun) should definitely be looked at in more scientific detail.

Odaxelagnia

In the entry on vampirism as a paraphilia later in this book I examine the related behaviour of odaxelagnia. Both Aggrawal (2009a) and Love (2001) define odaxelagnia as "a paraphilia concerning individuals who derive sexual pleasure and arousal through biting or being bitten." Obviously, odaxelagnia is sometimes associated with sexual vampirism, but it would appear that most forms of sexual biting do not involve bloodletting. Love includes a relatively lengthy entry on sexual biting and reports that "biting is used by some to sexually excite their partner. It is done on the neck, ears, lips, nipples, back, buttocks, genitals, inner thighs, etc. The pressure used depends on their partner's pain tolerance." She also notes that sexual biting is one of the "easiest and most accepted methods" adopted in sexual sadism and sexual masochism. She also claims that sexual biting produces an "increased sensation [and] brings some individuals who are emotionally stressed out of their physical numbness, back into touch with their bodies."

Twinn (2007) reported that on the islands of Trobriand off the east coast of New Guinea, biting off a woman's eyelashes is viewed by the people who live there as a passionate activity! Three books (Aggrawal, 2009a; Love, 2001; Russo, 2008) all make reference to the fact that sexual biting has its own separate section in the *Kama Sutra* (written by Indian philosopher Mallanaga Vātsyāyana in the 4th century). As Aggrawal notes:

> *"The Kama Sutra goes so far as to name all the different kinds of [sexual] bites and scratches, including those focused on the breasts and nipples. Eight kinds of bites are described in the chapter 'On Biting, and the Means to Be Employed with Regard to Women of Different Countries'. These are (i) the hidden bite, (ii) the swollen bite, (iii) the point, (iv) the line of points, (v) the coral and the jewel, (vi) the line of jewels, (vii) the broken cloud, and (viii) the biting of the boar."*

The earliest published empirical research concerning sexual biting was arguably that by Kinsey *et al.* (1948). He and his colleagues report that about half of all the thousands of people they surveyed said they had been sexually aroused from being bitten during sex. However, earlier academic references to sexual biting were made by Ellis (1905). He wrote:

> *"The impulse to bite is also a part of the tactile element which lies at the origin of kissing. As Stanley Hall notes, children are fond of biting, though by no means always as a method of affection. There is, however, in biting a distinctly sexual origin to invoke, for among many animals the teeth (and among birds the bill) are used by the male to grasp the female more firmly during intercourse. This point has been discussed in the previous volume of these Studies in reference to 'Love and Pain' ... The heroine of Kleist's Penthesilea remarks: 'Kissing (Küsse) rhymes with biting (Bisse), and one who loves with the whole heart may easily confound the two'."*

Aggrawal (2009a) makes a number of references to sexual biting in relation to both sadism and necrophilia. In the former, Aggrawal noted that oral sadists manifest "fantasies of chewing, biting, or otherwise using the mouth, lips, or teeth aggressively or destructively." In the latter he noted that one particular type of necrophiliac (a.k.a. "roleplaying necrophiles") sometimes have vampire fantasies where "the lover simulates a killing by biting the neck." Aggrawal (2009a) also reported the case of a woman who imagined she was a vampire. "She would ask her husband to pretend he was dead and then stimulate his organ with her mouth. She would then pretend that the resulting erection was rigor mortis, and this would give her erotic pleasure."

Moser and Levitt (1987) surveyed 225 sadomasochists comprising 178 men and 47 women recruited via an advert in a sadomasochistic magazine about their sexual behaviour. The most common sadomasochistic activities were bondage and flagellation, on the one hand, and bondage only, on the other (50%–80% of the sample). Painful activities, such as biting, use of ice or hot wax and face slapping, were less common (37%–41% of the sample). The most painful activities engaged in, such as piercing, branding, burning, tattooing and inserting pins, were the least common (7%–18% of the sample). These results suggest that biting among the S&M community at least is relatively commonplace.

There has been some clinical research on sexual vampirism (i.e., the rare phenomenon that involves the letting of blood by cutting or biting ultimately leading to sexual arousal). In relation to this sort of sexual biting there has been a lot of psychological theorizing, particularly from a psychodynamic perspective. Jaffe and DiCataldo (1994) in a paper on clinical vampirism made a number of speculations. Basing some of their thinking on Kayton (1972) they wrote:

> "Kayton considers that the vampire myth gives 'a unique phenomenological view of schizophrenia' and indeed overt vampiristic delusions have been associated most notably with this disorder. The connection is particularly salient in the more gruesome cases involving cannibalistic and necrosadistic behavior that resemble the content of schizophrenic delusional material acted out. These cases generally present massive disorganized oral sadistic regressions, depersonalization, confused sexuality, multiple concurrent delusions and thought disorder in content and form. Psychodynamic explanations draw attention to Karl Abraham's biting oral stage during which the infant uses his teeth with a vengeance, to Melanie Klein's description of children's aggressive fantasies and to W.R.D. Fairbairn's notion of intense oral sadistic libidinal needs formed in response to actual maternal deprivation."

I cannot say I am convinced by any of these explanations. However, since there is a paucity of good data, no better theories have been put forward on this behaviour specifically, although there are alternative behavioural theories involving classical and operant conditioning that help in explaining paraphilic behaviour more generally.

Odontophilia

According to Love (2001) odontophilia is a paraphilia that refers to individuals who derive sexual pleasure and arousal from teeth. The online Urban Dictionary goes a little further and describes it as a sexual fetish in which individuals are sexually aroused by (i) licking a sexual partner's teeth, (ii) leaving the imprint of teeth on their lover's skin or vice versa and/or (iii) pulling out a sexual partner's teeth or anything concerning dentistry. The online medical website Right Diagnosis defines odontophilia as referring to "sexual urges, preferences or fantasies involving teeth". Given these definitions, particularly the one in the Urban Dictionary, they suggest an overlap with sexual biting fetishes, such as odaxelagnia.

According to the Right Diagnosis website, treatment is generally not sought for odontophilia unless it becomes problematic for the individual who then feels compelled to address the condition. As is often the case, the majority of sexual fetishists and paraphiliacs simply learn to accept their condition and manage to achieve sexual gratification in an appropriate manner with no problem for the individual or his/her sexual partner.

Olfactophilia

Olfactophilia (a.k.a. "osmolagnia", "osphresiolagnia" and "ozolagnia") is a paraphilia in which an individual derives sexual pleasure from smells and odours. Given the large body of research on olfaction, it is unsurprising that in some cases there should be an association with sexual behaviour. The erotic focus is most likely to relate to body odours of a sexual partner including genital odours. One of my favourite papers examining sex and smell is Hirsch and Gruss (1999). As they noted in the introduction to their study, sex and smell have a long association:

"Historically, certain smells have been considered aphrodisiacs, a subject of much folklore and pseudoscience. In the volcanic remnants of Pompeii, perfume jars were preserved in the chambers designed for sexual relations. Ancient Egyptians bathed with essential oils in preparation for assignations; Sumerians seduced their women with perfumes. A relationship between smell and sexual attraction is emphasized in traditional Chinese rituals, and virtually all cultures have used perfume in their marriage rites. In mythology, rose petals symbolized scent, and the word 'deflowering' describes the initial act of sex ... Dramatic literature abounds with sly references to nasal size as symbolic of phallic size, as in the famous play Cyrano De Bergerac ... Psychoanalysis has made much of these associations. Fliess, in his concept of the phallic nose, formally described an underlying link between the nose and the phallus. Jungian psychology also connects odors and sex."

In contemporary society, perfumes for women and colognes for men are marketed aggressively and are advertised in such a way that suggests sexual success for those who use them. Keep in mind, though, that this is a multibillion pound business and they will say anything to sell their product. Hirsch and Gruss (1999) argue:

"The prominent connection between odors and sex among diverse historical periods and cultures implies a high level of evolutionary importance. Freud suggested that odors are such strong inducers of sexual feelings that repression of smell sensations is necessary to civilization. Anatomy bears out the link between smells and sex: the area of the brain through which we experience smells, the olfactory lobe, is part of the limbic system, the emotional brain, the area through which sexual thoughts

and desires are derived. Brill [1932] suggests that people kiss to get their noses close together, so that they can smell each other (the Eskimo kiss). Or possibly they kiss to get their mouths together so they can taste each other since most of what we call taste is dependent upon olfaction."

I have long been interested in pheromones, and I have published some studies in this area with Dr Mark Sergeant (Sergeant *et al.*, 2005, 2007). Pheromones are chemical substances "produced and released into the environment by an animal, especially a mammal or an insect, affecting the behaviour or physiology of others of its species." They are known to exist across the animal kingdom from insects to primates possibly including humans. However, most robust scientific studies have shown the evidence is relatively weak. If pheromones do exist in humans, then the effects are likely to be very subtle. As Hirsch and Gruss (1999) note:

> "Inside the human brain, near the top of the nose is an anatomical feature that gives us reason to believe that human pheromones exist: the vomeronasal organ. Its function is unknown, but in subhuman primates, this is the area where pheromones act to increase the chance of procreation ... When we exercise, we sweat through endocrine glands. But when we are embarrassed or sexually excited, we sweat through apocrine glands that release high-density steroids under the arms and around the genitalia; their role is unknown. In subhuman primates, the same apocrine glands release pheromones."

Other evidence for the existence of pheromones includes studies showing that women's menstrual cycles tend to synchronize over time when living or working closely together. This is the well-known "McClintock Effect" named after Martha McClintock, the person who first reported it (McClintock, 1971). Other research by Hirsch has shown evidence that links smell with sexual response. For instance, in one of his studies, 17% of patients who had "olfactory deficits" had developed some kind of sexual dysfunction.

Hirsch and Gruss (1999) examined the effects of 30 different smells on male sexual arousal among 31 American participants aged 18 to over 60 years. They underwent various question-based smell tests and their sexual arousal was assessed experimentally by measuring penile blood flow with a penile plethysmograph. The smells comprised 24 different odorants in addition to six combination ones. All 30 odours produced an increase in penile blood flow. More specifically, they reported:

> "The combined odor of lavender and pumpkin pie had the greatest effect, increasing median penile blood flow by 40%. Second in effectiveness was the combination of black licorice and doughnut, which increased the median penile blood flow by 31.5%. The combined odors of pumpkin pie and doughnut was third, with a 20% increase. Least stimulating was cranberry, which increased penile blood flow by 2% ... Men with below normal olfaction did not differ significantly from those with normal olfaction, nor did smokers differ significantly from nonsmokers."

The findings supported Hirsch and Gruss's hypothesis that positive-smelling odours would increase sexual arousal. The authors then went on to speculate a number of reasons as to why this might be the case:

> "The odors could induce a Pavlovian conditioned response reminding subjects of their sexual partners or their favorite foods. Among persons raised in the United States, odors of baked goods are most apt to induce a state called olfactory-evoked recall. Possibly, odors in the current study evoked a nostalgic recall with an associated positive mood state that affected penile blood flow. Or the odors may simply be relaxing. In others studies, lavender, which increased alpha waves posteriorly, [had] an effect associated with a relaxed state. In a condition of reduced anxiety, inhibitions may be removed and thus penile blood flow increased ... Another possibility, odors may act neurophysiologically ... Nor can we rule out a generalized parasympathetic effect, increasing penile blood flow rather than specific sexual excitation ... The specific odors that affected penile blood flow in our experiment were primarily food odors ... Does this support the axiom that the way to a man's heart (and sexual affection) is through his stomach? ... We certainly cannot consider the odors in our experiment to be human pheromones, therefore we believe they acted through other pathways than do pheromones."

Hirsch et al. (1999) repeated the study, but with females assessing their vaginal blood flow, and reported similar effects. In this study they found the largest increases in vaginal blood flow are from candy and cucumber (13%), baby powder (13%), pumpkin pie and lavender (11%) and baby powder and chocolate (4%). Obviously, both these studies suffer from major limitations, such as small sample sizes, all the odours being selected by the researchers and blood flow being the sole measure of arousal.

Odours that are sexually arousing are likely to be very specific and in some cases strange – even bizarre. For instance, I published the world's first case study of eproctophilia (sexual arousal from flatulence and a subtype of olfactophilia; Griffiths, 2013 – discussed earlier in this book). Some paraphilias may have an element of olfaction. For instance, antholagnia refers to individuals who are sexually aroused by flowers. Such arousal may depend on the sight and/or smell of the flowers.

I also came across an article by Bratton (2013) in which the author summarized research examining scents and sexual arousal, although she based most of it on Amen (2007). More specifically, the article noted:

> "Current research also suggests the scent of musk closely resembles that of testosterone, the hormone that enhances healthy libido in both sexes. In scent studies at Toho University in Japan, floral and herbal essential oils were found to impact sexual arousal in the nervous system. But depending on whether you need to stimulate or relax your partner to get them in an amorous mood, you would use different scents. To stimulate the sympathetic nervous system use jasmine, ylang-ylang, rose, patchouli, peppermint, clove and bois de rose. To relax the parasympathetic nervous system use sandalwood, marjoram, lemon, chamomile and bergamot ... Many of these scents are also commonly found in tea such as peppermint and chamomile. Many candles are scented with rose, jasmine, patchouli, sandalwood and bergamot."

There are plenty of websites listing various scents that turn people on, many of which appear to be based upon the research carried out by Hirsch et al. (1999). Research into sex, smell and olfactophilia appears to be a growing area and hopefully my own research has played a small part in stimulating such research.

Omosophilia

While researching sexual piggybacking and "lift and carry" fetishism, I noticed that when I used the words "shoulder" and "fetish" in the same online search, I came across a number of sites where people were discussing their fetishes for shoulders. Although there is little detail in these sources and I have no way of knowing to what extent any are truthful, I have no reason to suspect anyone was lying.

As far as I am aware, not only is there no academic or clinical research on the topic of shoulder fetishes, there is little anecdotal evidence to support it either. Given the complete lack of scientific study relating to shoulder fetishes I have decided to name it a new paraphilia based on traditional nosology using the Greek words for "shoulder" (*omos*) and "love" (*philia*). Thus this "new" paraphilia will be called "omosophilia" – not to be confused with osmophilia in which individuals derive sexual pleasure from specific smells and odours.

Oral partialism

Kafka (2010) defined partialism as "a sexual interest with an exclusive focus on a specific part of the body" that occurs among both heterosexual and homosexual individuals. He further noted in the same paper that partialism is categorized as a paraphilia not otherwise specified in the American Psychiatric Association's *Diagnostic and Statistical Manual of Mental Disorders*. He then went on to say that "individuals with partialism sometimes describe the anatomy of interest to them as having equal or greater erotic attraction for them as do the genitals."

Scientific research has indicated that the most prevalent form of partialism is podophilia (i.e., sexual arousal from feet; Gosselin and Wilson, 1980; Scorolli *et al.*, 2007). Historically, partialism was viewed as synonymous with sexual fetishism. However, Kafka noted there is a "diagnostic separation of partialism (intense, persistent, and 'exclusive' sexual arousal to a non-genital body part) from fetishism (intense and persistent sexual arousal to non-living objects, including some body products)." Although I accept this very subtle difference, I essentially view partialism and fetishism as one and the same. Milner *et al.* (2008) noted that:

> "In 'partialism', the paraphilic focus is on some part of the partner's body, such as the hands, legs, feet, breasts, buttocks or hair. Partialism appears to overlap with morphophilia, which is defined as a focus on one or more body characteristics of one's sexual partner ... it is unclear whether these two categories are unique paraphilias or different names for the same paraphilia. Historically, some authors (e.g., Berest, 1971; Wise, 1985) have included partialism as part of the general definition of fetishism, which once included both parts of bodies and non-living objects (e.g., shoes, underwear, skirts and gloves). Again, however, the [DSM] criteria for fetishism indicate that the focus must involve the 'use of non-living objects', which eliminates body parts from meeting this criterion."

One of the most bizarre cases of partialism in the academic literature is a case study of "oral partialism" by McGuire *et al.* (1998). As far as I can see, the case has only been cited three times in the academic literature, one of which was Persaud (2003). It is from his book that I have taken the case.

The case in question involved a single and severely obese man in his late teens who lived at home with his father and sister (his parents had separated some years before). The man had a borderline intellectual disability. The father described his son as a recluse who spent the majority of the day alone in his room with little or no social interaction with anyone except his family (and even then, the social interactions were minimal). The teenager had very poor personal hygiene, typically wore torn and dirty clothes, rarely washed or bathed and his weight was estimated at around 300 pounds. As a consequence of his very poor hygiene, the teenager "developed ulcerated sores under his arms, above the pubis and in the groin area" (something he had had for most of his teenage years). To treat the sores and skin ulcers he was prescribed a course of antibiotics. However, his overall compliance was low, taking just over half of the tablets initially prescribed, even though he was extensively monitored by the medical staff taking care of him. The teen then claimed that he had lost his antibiotics at home. It was then that the medics discovered what was really going on and why he did not want to take his medication. The unhealed sores and ulcers had taken on sexual significance for the man. As Persaud (2003) summarizes:

> "Upon questioning, the patient reported that he was easily sexually aroused and habitually masturbated at least twice a day, and more often four or five times a day. Ejaculation would always occur. He reported interest in the opposite sex and said that he often fantasized. However, the fantasy content and its accompanying behaviour never involved sexual intercourse, nor indeed any conventional sexual act. The patient's primary sexual fantasy stimulus was that of a woman's mouth, although the fantasy never involved kissing or oral stimulation ... Rather, he imagined the woman licking her fingers or gently biting her own lips. Simultaneously, the patient would put his own fingers into the ulcers/sores in his groin and/or under his arms and then lick the pus from his fingers. It appears that he ingested the pus and found both the smell and taste exciting, although he was unable to pinpoint exactly the sexually stimulating aspect of this act. He reported that the mere sight of a woman with her fingers to her mouth or lips was adequately arousing to initiate masturbation with the accompanying fantasy image and oral behaviour."

As I have noted elsewhere in this book, almost every (seemingly non-sexual) fluid that can come from a human body has a corresponding paraphilia and/or fetish. This includes urine (urophilia), faeces (coprophilia), vomit (emetophilia), blood (menophilia, clinical vampirism and vorarephilia), saliva (spit fetishism), breast milk (lactophilia) and pus (acnephilia). Arguably, this bizarre case shares some similarities with acnephilia as both involve sexual arousal to pus. Nevertheless, they are different in terms of their sexualization.

At the outset the teen was given some psychoeducation about the unhygienic nature of his sexual behaviour. This initially resulted in a behavioural decrease in his strange sexual behavior, although the oral sexual fantasies still persisted. Such psychoeducation has also been successfully used in the treatment of other paraphilias. For instance,

Denson (1982) reported that he used psychoeducation as part of his treatment of a urophile. In his commentary of the case, Persaud (2003) said it was open to debate whether the behaviour should be treated as problematic and/or psychopathological because it had little impact on other people and was not seen by the individual in question as problematic despite its arguably unsavoury nature.

Osmophilia

In 2008 the newspaper *Japan Today* reported the story of 22-year-old gay man Torao Fukuda who was arrested for stealing money and sports kits from eight locker rooms of football clubs in Osaka and Nara, Japan over a 4-month period. It turned out that the money stolen was secondary to the real reason for crime. It transpired that Fukuda liked male athletes' sports uniforms and underwear with the smell of sweat. Based on this brief news report it may have been that Fukuda was an osmophile.

Aggrawal (2009a) defines osmophilia as "a paraphilia in which an individual derives sexual pleasure and arousal from body odours, such as sweat, urine or menses from menstruating females." Campbell (2009) claims that osmophilia is a parosmia (an olfactory dysfunction characterized by the inability of the brain to properly identify an odour's "natural" smell). Based on what I have read on osmophilia, there is no evidence that such people have any kind of "inability" to identify natural smells. Other names for the same condition include osmolagnia, osphresiophilia and ozolagnia.

It should also be noted that Fukuda may have been a salophile too. Salophilia refers to individuals who derive sexual pleasure and arousal from salty things, especially body sweat. As far as I am aware, there is no actual paraphilia concerned with sexual arousal from sweat alone since osmophilia and salophilia are not exclusive to body sweat. There is certainly a market out there for sweat fetishists including online sweat stores and sweat fetish websites, such as Sexy Sweat and Maverick Men.

Research and academic writings on osmophilia are scarce. The first psychological references to the condition were made by Freud at the turn of the 20th century. Friedman (1959) noted that:

"Freud's interest in the vicissitudes of olfaction, both in human evolution and in the psychosexual development of the individual, was documented as early as 1897. In a letter to Wilhelm Fliess he drew a parallel between the two and discussed the organic component of repression: 'To put it crudely, the current memory stinks just as an actual object may stink; and just as we turn away our sense organ (the head and nose) in disgust, so do the preconscious and our conscious apprehension turn away from the memory. This is repression.' This line of thought was developed further by Freud in 1909, when he stated that '... a tendency to osphresiolagnia, which had become extinct since childhood, may play a part in the genesis of neurosis'; and, in a footnote added in 1910 to the Three Essays on the Theory of Sexuality, he said: 'Psychoanalysis ... has shown the importance, as regards the choice of a fetish, of a coprophilic pleasure in smelling'."

Research on osmophilia is sparse and nothing is known about the incidence, prevalence or etiology of such behaviour. For most osmophiles, their sexual attraction to human sweat is something that is simply not problematic to them based on the anecdotal evidence I have collated from online forums. There is, of course, a whole separate research literature on human pheromones.

Pantyhose fetishism

For the benefit of my UK readers, "pantyhose fetishism" is more commonly known in the UK as "tights fetishism" and is very similar to "stocking fetishism". The commonality is the fact they are both clothing items worn on the legs that are often made of nylon and have a silky veneer. The few online articles concerning pantyhose fetishism make similar claims, although empirical evidence for such claims are generally lacking. For instance, the articles claim that pantyhose fetishism is (i) commonplace and (ii) usually first begins in childhood and/or early adolescence after seeing pantyhose being worn by a significant person in the fetishist's life, such as his mother, sister, aunt, grandmother, family friend, neighbour and/or teacher.

As far as I am aware, only one academic paper devoted completely to pantyhose fetishism has ever been published in the psychological literature (i.e., Lothstein, 1997). The paper was written from a psychodynamic perspective. In her paper Lothstein describes this "unique fetish" using clinical vignettes of gender-dysphoric men (i.e., transgender males). The paper claimed pantyhose served a number of different functions, such as the repairing of psychic structure and an expression and defence against underlying aggression. More specifically, she referred to pantyhose as a functional "magic skin" or "second skin" repairing a defective ego and acting as a transitional object to allay annihilation and separation anxiety.

There are a few academic writings that have mentioned this fetishism in passing. For instance, Marshall (1979) reported the treatment by satiation therapy of two male paedophiles, one of whom was also a pantyhose fetishist. No detail was given on this aspect of his sexual behaviour other than he was also a shoe fetishist. Lowenstein (2002) claimed that pantyhose fetishism is "very common", but the only evidence given to support this was a reference to Lothstein's paper, which contained no information on the prevalence of the fetish. Finally, Moser and Kleinplatz (2008), in a book chapter on themes of sadomasochism self-expression, used the example of pantyhose to define and explain what fetishes are:

"A fetish is characterized by sexual arousal to an inanimate object ... Individuals who enjoy SM accessories often describe their interests as fetishes. They find wearing or touching the preferred articles highly arousing. The articles themselves are rarely arousing, but if they are worn by a partner, it heightens the partner's attractiveness and heightens the eroticism of the sex. For example, pantyhose can be a fetish object,

but brand-new pairs, never worn, rarely become a focus of erotic interest. The same pantyhose worn by the participant or a partner can elicit a strong erotic response. Similarly, an article of clothing that reminds the person of a partner or a specific erotic interlude can become a fetish object."

Again, this simply confirms that pantyhose fetishes exist or theoretically exist. However, there is no information on their incidence, prevalence or psychosocial impact. Maybe we will never know how common pantyhose fetishes are, but there appears to be a lot of anecdotal evidence that it exists, that it is male dominated and that there is some crossover with other more empirically established fetishes, such as foot fetishes.

Pecattiphilia

Arguably, one of the rarest paraphilias is pecattiphilia. According to Aggrawal (2009a) pecattiphilia refers to individuals who derive sexual pleasure from sinning or having committed an imaginary crime. Later on the same page, Aggrawal simply defines it as "sexual arousal from sinning or guilt". Love (2001) provides a similar definition and says that pecattiphilia is "the sexual arousal one gets from sinning … this may also display itself as a form of guilt."

Finally, the Right Diagnosis website (2013b) describes the symptoms of pecattiphilia as (i) sexual interest in stealing or sinning, (ii) recurring intense sexual urges involving stealing or sinning and/or (iii) sexual arousal from stealing or sinning. As far as I am aware, there is absolutely no academic or clinical research on pecattiphilia and much of what I have read on the topic is purely speculative. In her encyclopaedia entry Love writes:

"Religious teenagers sometimes suffer from a dilemma when they masturbate because they are taught that God will punish or perhaps kill them for this 'perversion'. A few have grown up with a fascination for sex play that involves life and death risks in order to recapture the same emotional intensity that this fear created. Anther type of 'sinner' may intensify their feelings of guilt by seducing a virgin, a member of the clergy, wearing religious costumes, listening to hymns during sex, or breaking into a church and using the altar to engage in a form of ritual sex. They may also have their partner say things to make them feel shame or guilt."

I have no idea where Love got her information, but it certainly was not from any scholarly texts. I would also argue that some of the types of behaviour listed above overlap with other paraphilias and sexual fetishes including melognia (sexual arousal from music), parthenophilia (sexual attraction to and arousal by virgins), harmatophilia (sexual arousal from incompetence or mistakes), hierophilia (sexual arousal from religious and sacred objects) and uniform fetishism. Love (2001) then went on to say (again in the absence of any empirical evidence) that:

"Those suffering from extreme pecattiphilia may feel an overabundance of guilt and try to reduce these feelings by having their partner chastise or punish them before they orgasm. This seems to relieve their guilt feelings. Some develop a fear of sexually transmitted diseases afterward or salve their conscience by judging their sex partner.

174 Pecattiphilia

In extreme cases, a psychotic person will murder their victim (usually a prostitute) to expiate both their sins."

I am not entirely sure how "extreme pecattiphilia" manifests itself any differently from less extreme pecattiphilia, but the whole paragraph is highly speculative. Nothing that I have read on the origins relating to a fear of sexually transmitted diseases, such as syphilophobia, is linked to pecattiphilia.

Given the arguable overlaps with other sexually paraphilic behaviours, I am really undecided about whether pecattiphilia really exists. As far as I can see there are no published case studies, no online forums for pecattiphiliacs to discuss their sexual preferences and no niche pornographic sites associated with the behaviour. In short, I have found very little evidence even anecdotally that it exists and/or is a genuine paraphilia.

Petticoating

Elsewhere in this book, under transvestic fetishism, I examine transvestism. Note that people who cross-dress typically fall into one of four types of transvestism: (i) transvestic fetishists who cross-dress for sexual pleasure that in some cases may involve sexual arousal from a very specific piece of clothing, (ii) female impersonators who cross-dress to entertain, (iii) effeminate homosexuals who may occasionally cross-dress for fun and (iv) transsexuals who cross-dress because they feel they have been biologically assigned to the wrong sex and typically suffer from a gender identity disorder. However, while researching clothing fetishes I came across a fifth type of cross-dressing called "petticoating" (a.k.a. "pettycoating" and "pinaforing").

Academically, I have only come across a few references to such sexual behaviour, one of which is Aggrawal (2009a). He describes "petticoat punishment" as a variation of transvestism. More specifically, he writes that "a male paraphiliac, afflicted with transvestism and masochism, derives pleasure in getting spanked when he is dressed like a schoolgirl or servant girl." Elsewhere in his book, in a small section on "petticoat discipline", Aggrawal defines the practice as:

> *"... a kind of roleplay or fantasy that revolves around a male being dressed as a girl in front of his mother, sisters or, in some cases, girls of his own age whom he had offended by his boorish behavior. Many mothers who discipline their sons in this fashion have either wanted daughters for long or find it erotic to feminize their sons. This type of punishment is also found in the history of some people who eventually develop transvestic fetishism."*

Love (2001) also has an entry on petticoat discipline in her encyclopaedia. Interestingly, she claims the practice is Scottish in origin and relates to the wearing of kilts. I do not know where her evidence originates as there are no references to back up any of the claims she makes. Nevertheless, Love states:

> *"Petticoat discipline refers to the discipline used on young males whereby they are forced to wear kilts without the sporran (purse) by their mother, sister, governess, or aunt. English and Scottish mothers both used this method for controlling an unruly*

boy. The ploy worked by humiliating or embarrassing the boy so much that he was careful not to engage in any type of activity that would draw attention to himself, thus making him easy to control in public. Older males were sometimes subjected to this type of humiliation due to the power a widowed mother had over their inheritance."

Love then asserts later in the same entry that:

"Sexual literature often relates fiction stories about 14- to 20-year-old boys who are humiliated by a female other than their mother. These females add frills to the boys' shirts, shoes or underpants. The kilt may be cut short so that the lace underwear will show if they bend over. As often is the custom, underpants are not worn with kilts. Most of the storylines include embarrassment suffered from having others look up their skirt, pull their pants down for a spanking, or having females rub against their genitals. Petticoat discipline differs from cross-dressing or transvestism because the intent is to have the masculinity and the identity of the male remain prominent. The male is not trying to pass as female, the change in gender identity would humiliate him nearly as much."

A number of non-academic articles that I have read on petticoating also appear to concur with Aggrawal (2009a) and Love (2001). Such articles refer to the practice being used within sadomasochistic activity as a form of discipline and/or humiliation (a.k.a. "petticoat punishment") that dates back to the mid-1800s. The feminization aspect of petticoating also means that it goes beyond clothing. Individuals may also be forced to have make-up applied, to carry female accessories, such as purses and handbags, and to engage in other activities that are more associated with females, particularly girls, such as playing with dolls.

A 1998 issue of the *International Journal of Transgenderism* included papers that had been presented at the *Third International Congress on Sex and Gender*. In a paper by Gonzalez-Arnal (1998) the author argued that petticoating is a politically incorrect form of sexuality. More specifically, she argued:

"The submissive in a petticoat feels humiliated by having to dress as a woman and by having to behave as a woman. Petticoating has all the ingredients of a straightforward politically incorrect form of sexuality. It considers women's clothing and women's traditional occupations as inferior and humiliating; reinforcing undesirable stereotypes by characterizing females as submissive, passive, helpless and subservient. From a feminist perspective it is a practice that should be avoided … Petticoating is a politically ambiguous form of sexuality."

The same journal issue also featured the work of Peter Farrer who has documented almost all the Victorian literature from 1840 onwards that has referred to the practice of petticoating (Farrer, 2001–2002). He has also edited many books on the topic, although the extracts I found online are from the tradition of literary criticism rather than psychology or sociology.

As with many of the rarer sexual practices, I cannot see there ever being much academic research into petticoating because between consenting adults it is not likely to be perceived as problematic or have any negative psychosocial impact on those practitioners who engage in it.

Piggyback fetishism

Over the last couple of years I have watched a lot of Korean films distributed by Tartan Asia Extreme. One of the things I noticed was that a number of scenes in the films I watched seemed to feature adults giving piggyback rides to other adults. I actually looked up this observation online and was surprised to find quite a few online essays examining this phenomenon. One of the more interesting ones I read was on the Drama Beans website (Girl Friday, 2010). It examined the cultural meaning of piggyback rides in Korean films. One thing that becomes abundantly clear is that piggyback rides in Korea appear to have romantic and arguably sexual undertones. The article I read noted that in Korea there are many references to "skinship", a made-up Korean–English term meaning "levels of physical intimacy or, more simply, touching." The article then went on to say:

"Skinship can range from handholding to kissing, to sex … The most common piggyback scenario is the classic 'I'm-too-drunk-so-will-you-be-my-knight-in-shining-armor-and-carry-me-home'. Every drama has it, and every romantic comedy hero earns his stripes this way … The piggyback is, in essence, an excuse for skinship, seemingly of the most harmless kind. Because it's wrapped in a pretty bow of manly honor and a display of alpha male strength, it earns extra points for making women round the world swoon, thinking why can't my boyfriend do that? … piggybacks are a direct callback to a little girl's relationship with her father. Don't worry, I'm not going to go all Freudian on you. I don't mean it in an icky way. But don't think that fiction in a patriarchal society doesn't reflect the values that are deemed to be right in that culture. Piggyback rides in essence infantilize women to equate them with little girls, and paternalize men to equate them with fathers."

I then through sheer curiosity searched for "piggyback fetishes" online and was surprised to find a number of news articles on the topic. Back in 2009, Kieron Bobbette, a 43-year-old man from Brighton, UK admitted sexually assaulting five teenage girls (aged 13 to 17 years) while he was being given a piggyback by them after pretending he had a bad leg and an ache in his groin. In some cases, he paid the girls to do so. The story was reported at length in the local newspaper *The Argus* (Cridland, 2009). On one occasion, he simply jumped onto a young girl's back without any warning as she walked along the street. The offences took place over a 4-year period (2004–2008). One of Bobbette's victims said she had been forced to give him a piggyback and that, when he was being carried, he asked her to do squat bends with him on her back. Bobbette pleaded guilty, but told the judge: "Can somebody commit sexual assault without knowing they are doing this because I don't feel I have?" According to a later report in *Regency* magazine, Bobbette was given a sexual offences prevention order that banned him from jumping onto the backs of women and demanding a piggyback ride. Bobbette was also added to the Sex Offenders' Register for 5 years.

This does not appear to be an isolated case, because in 2010 Leigh Yeo, an 18-year old teenager from Exeter, UK, sexually assaulted two teenage girls (aged 16 and 18 years) after jumping on their backs for a piggyback ride. It was reported in a news story (*BBC Devon News*, 2010) that one of Yeo's victims was physically sick following the attack and later suffered chronic panic attacks. The second victim was left feeling scared and upset. Yeo was jailed for 15 months and was put on the Sex Offenders' Register for 10 years.

It would also appear that sexual piggyback offences occur in other countries too. In 2009 25-year-old Sherwin Shayegan from Bonney Lake, Washington, USA was arrested for fourth-degree sexual assault following piggyback assaults on male student high-school athletes. According to one newspaper report:

> "The student noticed that Shayegan was behaving strangely, and attempted to leave. At that point, Shayegan is accused of jumping on the student's back and demanding a piggyback ride. It's not the first time that Shayegan has done this, apparently. According to police, he's done this to students in Ellensburg, Bellingham and Centralia. His usual MO is to approach a high-school student athlete, saying he wants to interview them for a school paper. When they agree, Shayegan asks them bizarre questions such as 'Have you crapped your pants?' or 'Looked at other boys in the shower?' When the students, understandably freaked out, try to leave, he will then offer cash, before shouting that it is 'time for a piggyback ride!' and attempting to jump on the student's back."

Shayegan was unable to stop the sexual piggybacks and he was banned from attending sporting events in two US states (Washington and Oregon). In 2012 he was rearrested for the same offence.

Cipriano (2009) briefly examined the "fetishists who just plain get off riding on the shoulders of other people." In his article he interviewed some piggyback fetishists and one of them was quoted as saying:

> "A month ago, when intoxicated, I asked another male friend from Canada to piggyback me. Although the entire session only lasted a minute or two, my sexual drive (not specifically for him) suddenly sparked, more than alcohol can ever do. Halfway through the piggyback, I maneuvered myself to hold on his front, dangling there like a koala."

At first, Cipriano (2009) speculated that piggyback fetishes are based in trust and security. However, after researching the article, he concluded that piggyback fetishists find themselves trapped in a sexually arousing power struggle. Although "the piggybackee can offer suggestions on speed and direction … it's ultimately up to the piggybacker to control the situation." One of his interviewees for the article said that he liked "very much to ride on older men. I can sit on the old man for about 4 minutes and bounce on his shoulders."

In another of the few articles I have come across specifically about piggyback fetishes, the female author and dominatrix Nic Buxom wrote about piggyback fetishes in her 'Featured Fetish' column (Buxom, 2010). Based on her own personal experiences she claimed:

> "Piggybacking! Yes, this is a real fetish. And actually, as I've encountered it, usually the guys want us, the ladies, to give them the piggyback ride. I just thought it'd be cuter to have a chick riding a guy. Unfortunately … this came out creepier than I

expected ... Piggyback fetishists are some of the kindest souls I've had the pleasure of playing with. They're always very sweet and playful. Not all girls do piggyback sessions because they're quite difficult. Being a bigger, stronger lady I love taking them! Piggybackers tend to be smallish. If a huge guy wanted this I don't know that we'd have anyone capable but they tend to be petite or at least slim. Also, they're always very considerate about letting me have short breaks. Piggybackers keep at least their boxers on, they don't get a free chance to rub [themselves] against my back or anything like that. Most of them discovered their fetish sometime in high school or at a young age when a friend of theirs playfully gave them a piggyback ride. You can find piggyback videos all over the net, or so they excitedly tell me."

I went in search of piggyback fetishes online, but was unable to locate a single dedicated online forum and only came across a handful of people who claimed they had (or knew someone) who had a piggyback fetish.

Arguably, the most famous piggyback fetishist in the world is American cartoonist Robert Crumb. The documentary film of his life's work (simply titled *Crumb*) features Crumb getting piggyback rides from several women with powerful legs who were clearly substitutes for sex. In the film one of Crumb's ex-girlfriends claimed the cartoonist liked to receive piggybacks in lieu of sex. Hattenstone (2005) noted in an article in *The Guardian*:

"In the 1990s [Robert Crumb] became famous for a second time when film director Terry Zwigoff made a documentary about his life, Crumb. The film put Crumb's life in context – yes, his foot fetish, his piggyback fixations, and his urge to dominate big, dominant women (in a pretty submissive way)."

Piquerism

Back in June 2007 25-year-old American Frank Ranieri was arrested in New York on charges of assault. He was accused of paying large amounts of money to at least five young females in exchange for poking their buttocks with sharp objects, such as pens, pins and nails while masturbating.

There are numerous examples of such practices. For instance, in the summer of 2011 people in a shopping mall in Fairfax, Virginia, USA were terrorized by someone the press dubbed the "Serial Butt Stabber" and the "Butt Slasher". This was a man who repeatedly stabbed females' bottoms through their clothes. One online article by Dr Judy Kuriansky (2011) noted:

"The so-called Butt Slasher has been pricking women in the rear end with sharp objects in malls in Fairfax, Virginia. Six women have reported being victimized so far shopping at T.J. Maxx, and another 18-year-old at a Forever XXI store, who felt a 'sharp pain' and believed a hanger had struck her, although she noticed a man bending down to pick up clothes supposedly fallen off a rack."

Given the relatively regular incidence of piquerism reported in the popular media, I was quite surprised to find next to nothing academically. There are passing references to piquerism in the clinical and forensic science literature, but nothing (as far as I could find) on the prevalence or etiology of the disorder.

Many authors note the link between piquerism and sexual sadism. Hucker (2011b), in an online article on sexual sadism, reviewed the characteristics and predominate features of what he described as "major sexual sadism". Hucker noted that this type of sexual sadism is typically non-consensual and usually culminates in major injury or death. The article also noted the types of behaviour that accompany major sexual sadism as including (i) severe beatings, (ii) torture, (iii) burning and cutting, (iv) stabbing in the breast or buttocks (piquerism), (v) rape, (vi), murder, (vii) vampirism and (viii) necrophilia. This was also confirmed by Aggrawal (2009a) in his examination of lust murders:

> *"Lust murders are homicides in which the offender stabs, cuts, pierces or mutilates the sexual regions or organs of the victim's body. The sexual mutilation of the victim may include evisceration, piquerism, displacement of the genitalia in both males and females, and the removal of the breasts in a female victim (defeminization). It also includes activities such as 'posing' and 'propping' of the body, the insertion of objects into the body cavities, anthropophagy (consumption of blood and/or flesh) and necrophilia."*

A particularly gruesome case involving piquerism was described by Geberth (1998). Geberth was a former commander of Bronx Homicide, NYPD. He wrote:

> *"The two victims were a mother and her 14-year-old daughter ... Once his victims were unconscious and dead he engaged in hours of sexual deviance with their bodies. His intention was to knock out the 14-year-old and then torture her to death. However, he had hit her with such force that she died. He eviscerated both of his victims. He had sex with their corpses and drank their blood before posing and propping them up with their body parts and inserting a baseball bat into the daughter's vagina. He removed the breasts from the mother and placed them in the bedroom on end tables on either side of the bed where the daughter's body was found. He incised the skin of the pubis from the mother and placed the tissue into her mouth. He incised the skin of the pubis from the daughter's body and placed it upon the right side of her face. He then engaged in post-mortem piquerism by stabbing into the daughter's throat a total of 16 times ... His admitted fantasy was to torture and kill young girls as another male anally sodomized him. All of the cutting, mutilation and overkill-type wound structures were directed towards those parts of the body that the offender found sexually significant to him and these activities served as his sexual stimulus. The piquerism inflicted on the body of the 16-year-old was substitutive for his 'torture' fantasy."*

A number of infamous murderers are known to have carried out major acts of piquerism. Arguably, the most infamous was Jack the Ripper. Keppel *et al.* (2005) concluded that "the injuries sustained by the victims displayed the signature characteristic of piquerism." The Russian mass murderer Andrei Chikatilo (a.k.a. "The Butcher of Rostov") was known to be impotent, but derived sexual satisfaction from stabbing and cutting his many victims. American serial killer Albert Fish (a.k.a. "The Brooklyn Vampire" and "The Moon Maniac" among many other names) was known to have engaged in piquerism with many of his victims. He also had a penchant for self-piquerism, particularly the sticking of pins into himself. The reasons people engage in piquerism have yet to be researched in any depth and most of the theorizing is speculative at best.

Plaster cast fetishism

Back in the early 2000s I remember watching *Plaster Caster*, a documentary film that looked at the life of artist and groupie Cynthia Albritton (a.k.a. "Cynthia Plaster Caster"). Cynthia is infamous for her plaster casting of the penises of rock stars, such as Jimi Hendrix and Noel Redding (both in the Jimi Hendrix Experience), Eric Burdon (The Animals), Wayne Kramer (MC-5), Jello Biafra (The Dead Kennedys) and Pete Shelley (Buzzcocks). She began her career in erotic plaster casting in 1968, but now includes women among her artistic clients, typically making plaster casts of their breasts. Her plaster-casting skills have also been immortalized in song by both Kiss (*Plaster Caster*) and Jim Croce (*Five Short Minutes*).

Sexual plaster casting did not begin with Cynthia Plaster Caster. The practice of mummification within a sadomasochistic context predated it. Such a practice is according to Aggrawal (2009a):

> "An extreme form of bondage in which the person is wrapped from head to toe, much like a mummy, completely immobilizing him. Materials used may be clingfilm, cloth, bandages, rubber strips, duct tape, plaster bandages, bodybags or straitjackets. The immobilized person may then be left bound in a state of effective sensory deprivation for a period of time or sensually stimulated in his state of bondage – before being released from his wrappings."

One type of restrictive mummification not mentioned by Aggrawal is that of plaster cast fetishism. Although there is little academic research on the topic, a quick Google search throws up many dedicated online sites offering hundreds of videoclips for sale and/or sharing. Such websites include Casted Angel (which claims to be the oldest "cast and bandage site"), Cast Fetish, Cast Paradise and Fantacast. Be warned, though, all these sites are sexually explicit.

As well as being a form of extreme mummification, plaster cast fetishism is also a subvariant of "cast fetishism". According to the online Encyclopedia Dramatica plaster cast fetishism entails erotic "concentration on orthopedic casts (plaster, polymer, bandage, etc.). It is usually related to the fetishes of feet, stockings, shoes and amputees." Cast fetishists derive sexual pleasure and arousal from people, typically the opposite sex, wearing casts on their limbs. They may also be aroused by people using crutches or who have a limp. I have come across dozens of people who have posted on online forums claiming they have cast fetishes and/or fixations.

Plushophilia

Aggrawal defines plushophilia as a "sexual attraction to stuffed toys or people in animal costume, such as theme park characters." However, other online sources simply define plushophilia as a paraphilia involving stuffed animals. Sexual and pornographic activities involving animal anthropomorphism including plushophilia are known among the plushophile community as "yiffing".

Plushophiles are often referred to as "plushies", although the term can also refer to stuffed animal enthusiasts (i.e., people who just love cuddly toys) where there is no sexual connotation. Although Gurley (2001) argues plushophilia is often assumed to be a common practice among members of the furry fandom, survey research has shown this not to be the case. For instance, Rust (2001), in an old and unpublished survey of data collected in the late 1990s on 360 members of the furry community (325 respondents from furry conventions and 25 respondents online), suggests fewer than 1% of them were plushophiles (0.3%).

In an attempt to replicate Rust's study, Evans (2008), in a survey of 276 people who self-identified as furries and who were recruited from furry or furry-related online message boards and forums, reported a much higher prevalence rate of plushophilia (7%) than the study by Rust. Nevertheless, this was still a low prevalence rate suggesting that the overlap between plushophilia and the furry fandom is minimal. Evans claimed that because the majority of Rust's survey was conducted in person at conventions, participants were susceptible to social desirability bias when it came to plushophilia. Many plushies do not want any association with furries whatsoever.

Many plushophiles are avid collectors of cuddly toys who began accumulating their collections in childhood, although some are in adulthood before their interest in stuffed toys begins. Some plushies are said to be totally obsessed with their hobby and may share behavioural similarities with pathological hoarders. Among a small minority of plushies, the act of collecting may border on being an obsessive–compulsive disorder. Like many collectors, plushies may focus their collecting behaviour on very specific types of cuddly toy, such as teddy bears. For some plushies, their passion for collecting may lead them to careers that involve making and/or trading plush toy animals. *Wikifur* (2012c) claims:

> "A common practice among plushophiles who are serious collectors is to purchase two of each plushie; one for display and use, and another for safe keeping and preservation. Many plushophiles consider their toys very dear and rarely trade or sell them, even when there are concerns such as limited space and storage."

As mentioned earlier, a small number of furries consider themselves plushophiles. Some furries and/or plushies have specific animistic beliefs (i.e., a set of beliefs concerning the existence of non-human "spiritual beings") that cross over into their love of toy animals. Furthermore, for some furries, toy animals are said to serve as representations of totem animals. *Wikifur* (2012b) defines a totem animal as:

> "An important symbolic object in furry spirituality used by a person to get in touch with specific qualities found within an animal which the person needs, connects with, or feels a deep affinity toward. Some furry lifestylers find they draw spiritual energy from a totem animal which guides their lives and causes them to imitate behaviors of that animal."

182 Plushophilia

Roleplayers among furry fandom members may also create characters based on the idea of living toys and stuffed animal characters. Plushies frequently enjoy interacting with furries whose primary avatar is a toy character. However, as *Wikifur* (2012c) asserts, "not everyone who enjoys playing as or with such an avatar is necessarily a plushophile or collector of stuffed animals in real life."

The sexual element of plushophilia has been overplayed and sensationalized in both the print and broadcast media. Nevertheless, there are plushie sex and dating sites, such as Plushie Love and Plush Yiff. When it comes to plushies where sex is an important part of their activity, such behaviour has been argued by *Wikifur* (2012c) to be a genuine paraphilia:

> *"Depending on the individual, sexual stimulation and plush toys may arise from purely sensual enjoyment, may act as an aid for fantasy gratification and physical or mental stimulation alone or with another person, or may have an animistic and spiritual component. For example, some plushophiles who make use of their toys in intimate ways do so with a partner, while others only experience such feelings toward a plush animal that they view as more than an inanimate object. A common practice among sexual plushophiles is to modify a plush toy in order to make it sexually accessible or to minimize damage to it from such use."*

However, *Wikifur* (2012c) is quick to point out that not all plushies who relate to their toys sexually modify them and not all plushies actually make direct contact with their stuffed toys for intimate stimulation. One infamous plushophile is FoxWolfie Galen who has his own website (FoxWolfie's Plushie Page). In his interview for *Salon* magazine he was first asked how he had sex with a stuffed animal:

> "Well, none of [my toy animals] have an SPA [strategically placed appendage]. It's been thought of a couple of times, but part of the difficulty would be constructing one and not having it fall off the plushie. That's a problem people have dwelled on for a long time. It's usually just cuddling and rubbing with me. There's usually no need for penetration. Most of [my toy animals] don't have an SPH [strategically placed hole], but some do. It's not a requirement for me – if it's there I'll use it, and if not I'm just as happy without it. It all depends on what you allow to happen to them. Some people wear condoms for complete protection."

Galen has more than 1,000 stuffed animals and, when asked how he chooses his "sexual partner", he responded:

> "It's basically the same as with people ... some you're attracted to sexually and some you're not. I'm not interested in just human–human [sex]; it's gotta be human–plushie–human. The person would have to be interested in plush."

Academic research is beginning to be carried out on plushophilia, but only in relation to furry fandom and/or zoophilia. There are some aspects of plushophilia that might have psychological resonance with pathological collecting and hoarding, although most research is likely to examine the more sexual elements of plushophiles' lifestyles.

In 2014 I was the resident psychologist on a 12-episode television series called *Forbidden* made for the Discovery Channel. One of the stories the series reported concerned Peter Banki, a plushophile who appeared in the "Odd Man Out" episode. Before I was interviewed to provide some expert feedback I had to research the story and was also given some production notes as background material.

According to the material provided, Peter has a PhD in German philosophy and is a member of the Philosophy Research Initiative at the University of Western Sydney, Australia, where he lectured and tutored in the School of Humanities and Languages. He was also the founder and host of Schwelle, a not-for-profit organization that offers unusual and experimental workshops promoting a "different intellectual and sexual culture". He is also the curator of Xplore, an annual sex education event. He lives with his girlfriend and is currently living off profits from the festival and taking *shibari* rope classes at home in Bondi (*shibari* is a form of Japanese rope bondage). His hobbies were listed as including cross-dressing, sex education and reading. The production notes also informed me that:

> "Peter Banki has given lectures to hundreds of university students. He's a fully-grown eloquent and intelligent man but he also plays with stuffed toys. In fact Peter sees himself as an advocate for plush play enthusiasts or 'plushies' as they're called. What most would interpret as childish nonsense, Peter sees as a form of self-expression and a creative outlet. With 40-odd animals in his collection, each with their own invented character, profession and history, Peter has created his own fantasy world. His plushies are very important, 'My close friends all know about it, some of them I even involve in playtime with the animals. But generally I only share this world with people I trust.' He's not completely secret about his pastime though. He's given theatrical performances creating voices and characters for stuffed toys to demonstrate to audiences what plush play is all about."

Peter claimed he had been obsessed with plushies ever since he was a child when he would get his parents to talk to his toys. He said "it's something I've always done. I once tried to give it up to keep a girlfriend but I couldn't do it. I got too depressed." Instead of trying to repress his urges Peter embraced them. He regularly slept with the toys. Although Peter is heterosexual, he admits that he is not a "typical" man:

> "Being a man I think implies being an adult and strong and responsible. When I play with the plushy animals I think I'm like a little boy."

The programme presented the case of Peter Banki as what the production notes described a "quirky dichotomy". On the one hand, he is a cultured academic, an adult who lectures and curates festivals. On the other, he is a naughty child who plays with cuddly toys. Peter has created a fantasy world, something that he cultivated from his vivid imagination. Sometimes his behaviour involves erotic roleplaying games. This is the polarity the documentary wanted to capture, something that appealed to Peter too.

On screen Peter was filmed sitting in his lounge watching television and relaxing. He casually mentioned that there was no fun when it is all work and no play and that he enjoyed a little downtime with his "friends". The camera then pulled out to a wider screenshot and revealed his furry plush toy friends sitting either side of him on the couch and on the floor. Peter introduced each and every plush toy friend and described each toy's backstory. He explained that some of his plush toys were in monogamous relationships, some were in naughty adulterous relationships and yet others were polyamorous. The production notes highlighted that:

> "We see how his plush toy relationships manifest into his day-to-day activities. He plays with them on the couch, on the floor of the lounge room, in the laundry, at the dining table, on his balcony/yard and baths them. We see a series of moments where the plush toys are passive participants: he prepares lunch, they're watching; he works at his desk, they're watching; he hangs his washing on the line, they're watching from all the way back on the balcony. Peter even enjoys the odd social outing with his toys. We see him playing hide and seek in the park and pushing them on the swings."

Peter also enjoys playing with other plushie enthusiasts. The documentary filmed other plushies playing with their stuffed animals during Peter's Plush Toy Workshop at the Xplore festival. Peter also showed the programme makers the Plush Toy Animal Collective Facebook page and described their various outings, such as dinners and speed-dating nights. One of his toys "Bunny Junior", described as an old-style Marxist, even had his very own Facebook page featuring photos of his *shibari* rope therapy.

Peter was also filmed on his way to buy a new plush toy to add to his collection. He put three of his animal "friends" into the back of his car and put on their seatbelts. He then went to a restaurant and had dinner with all his plush toys at the table with him. The notes I was given provided a useful case summary:

> "Dr Peter Banki has always played with plush animals. He used to ask his parents to talk to them and they would invent stories. He carried this play on to adulthood. They were always played with in a more intimate environment with people in the bedroom. Now Peter shares his play with the public and with friends. They go to restaurants, they go to parties. The plush animals have names, some speak German, some speak French. Junior the rabbit, for instance, is an old-style Marxist labor leader. As Peter grew older, the animals developed sexual relationships: some are straight, some are homosexual and some like to be spanked. For Peter, it's a way of saying things that can't be expressed otherwise. After simulating sexual play, Peter says he feels really exposed, but in a good way."

Given the lack of research into plushophilia, case studies such as Peter's give us an insight into the life of a plushophile. We do not know how representative Peter is of other plushophiles, but at least his story is out there in a documentary programme and in this book.

Podophilia

Of all the types of sexual fetishes, one of the most common is foot fetishism. Gosselin and Wilson (1980) reported that the three most common body part fetishes are feet, hands and hair. As for me I have never seen the attraction of feet mainly because I taught health psychology to podiatrists and chiropodists for 5 years. I used to sit in on student clinics where I was surrounded by people with the most awful bunions, corns, calluses, blisters and verrucas, enough to put anyone off feet for life. On the plus side

I did manage to turn my podiatry teaching experiences into academic papers, such as one in the *Journal of British Podiatric Medicine* (Griffiths, 1995).

Many names have been applied to the sexual love of feet including foot fetishism, foot worship and foot partialism. Others see the behaviour as a paraphilia. For instance, both Aggrawal (2009a) and Love (2001) describe individuals who have a pronounced interest in and derive sexual pleasure and arousal from feet as having podophilia. It is also worth noting that there are some individuals who have a pronounced interest in feet for aesthetic (attractiveness) reasons, but without any sexual motive. Such people would not be classed as either foot fetishists or podophiles in the definitions provided by Aggrawal and Love.

If you type "foot fetishes" into online search engines, not only do hundreds of webpages come up, but the sheer diversity of what people are into also becomes all too apparent and bewildering to a novice who knows nothing about such fetishes. I also discovered a number of famous people who were allegedly foot fetishists including singer Elvis Presley, pop artist Andy Warhol, author and adventurer Casanova, serial killer Ted Bundy and novelist and poet Thomas Hardy.

Foot fetishes can be very specific as borne out by individual dimensions and features being critical to the podophile. They are usually interested in the size (the foot, the toes, the heel), the shape (flat footed, high arches), the adornments (footwear, jewellery, toe ring, ankle bracelets), embellishments (nail varnish, tattoos, pedicure), non-visual sensory features (touch, smell) and – perhaps most importantly – the type of interaction (massaging, touching, kissing, tickling, licking, sucking). There are also subdimensions of the fetish including those who are really into footwear rather than the feet. This is known as retifism (featured in two earlier entries – altocalciphilia and anthropophagolagnia) after the French novelist Nicolas Edme Rétif who wrote extensively about his own footwear fetish (Kunjukrishnan *et al.*, 1998). Then there are those who like naked feet as opposed to footwear adornments (i.e., aretifism).

Scorolli *et al.* (2007) reported in their prevalence study of fetishes that there were 44,722 members of online fetish forums who have a fetishistic and/or paraphilic sexual interest in feet (47% of all "body part" fetishists that the authors encountered). Among those preferring "objects related to body parts" footwear (shoes, boots, etc.) was the second most preferred (26,739 online fetish forum members; 32% of all "objects related to body parts"), just behind objects worn on the legs and/or buttocks (33%). A report by AOL (2006) ranked all fetish search words and phrases used by their subscribers and found that the most common fetish searched for related to feet.

Most psychological theorizing concerns both fetishes, in general, and foot fetishes relating to early childhood imprinting and conditioning experiences where sexual responses are typically paired with non-sexual objects. Ramachandran (1994) believes that podophilia may arise because the feet and genitals occupy adjacent areas of the brain's somatosensory cortex. He believes that there may be some "neural crosstalk" between the two brain areas. Giannini *et al.* (1998) speculated that the incidence of foot fetishism may increase as a response to epidemics of sexually transmitted diseases (STDs). They noted that there were significant increases of sexual interest in feet during STD epidemics dating back to the 12th century.

Weinberg *et al.* (1995) reported that foot fetishism typically begins around the start of adolescence and that such experiences are viewed as positive. Foot fetishists' sexual behaviour is a product of learning from other males in their environment (fathers, brothers, older peers) – not as a result of social isolation, which is often seen as a precursor and/or risk factor in fetishistic behaviour. Such individuals did not seem to be of one particular personality type either.

Compared with many other types of sexually fetishistic behaviour, foot fetishism has received a fair amount of empirical attention both in the academic and clinical literature, and this may be because foot fetishes are more prevalent than most other types. Most podophiles appear happy and contented with their sexual preference and as a consequence do not generally seek treatment.

Pogonophilia

Pogonophilia is a paraphilia in which individuals derive sexual pleasure and arousal from beards (Aggrawal, 2009a). The source of sexual arousal in pogonophilia may be derived from viewing, touching or in extreme cases eating beard hair. A few online definitions of pogonophilia claim that it is "abnormal affection towards beards". My own research into pogonophilia appears to indicate that sexual arousal from looking at or touching beards seems to be restricted to women and gay men. However, I have yet to come across a single piece of empirical research on the topic and what evidence there is appears to be anecdotal (The Atlantic, 2009).

To my knowledge only one academic has written about beard fetishes at any length (Johnston, 2011). I have to admit I did not read the book because, from the various online summaries I read, I did not think there would be much in the way of psychological insight (since the book focuses on representations of beards in English Renaissance culture).

As with many other paraphilias and fetishes that I have examined, the scientific community knows next to nothing about the incidence, prevalence and etiology of pogonophilia and in all honesty we may never know. Although I am personally interested in the psychology of beards, I doubt pogonophilia will be a topic that ever gets priority in calls for research funding.

Ponyplay

Earlier in this book I examined the furry fandom (FF) and people who like to dress up as animals and have sex dressed as animals. One particular subset of the FF is a group of people who engage in "ponyplay" (PP). PP is overtly more sexualized than FF and is a form of bondage that involves someone dressed as a pony and another as a rider. The human pony (the submissive partner) can be a "ponyboy" or a "ponygirl" who typically wears stylized horse adornments including riding straps, a leather saddle, reins, and a bit in the mouth. The human rider (the dominant) also wears stylized riding accessories, such as a riding crop or a horse whip. The rider may sit on the human pony and/or get the pony to cart him or her around. Mundinger-Klow (2010) noted that "Ponygirl, Ponyboy" was:

"A classic [sadomasochistic] fantasy immortalized in the drawings of John Willie and used in the Sleeping Beauty Trilogy by Anne Rice. Typical pony garb includes a horsehair tail attached to a butt plug, a bit gag and/or bridle head harness, and reins. Often very high heels, a corset and feather plumes in the hair are added. The arms are typically bound behind the back."

However, many people's views of PP if they even have them may have come from the documentary film *Born in a Barn*. This film was:

"An intimate and occasionally humorous look into the extraordinary erotic lives of four seemingly ordinary people. Born in a Barn takes us deep into the world of ponyplay, a fetish in which enthusiasts roleplay as human ponies and handlers. Revealing the complex motives that drive each character to pursue this unusual passion and following them as they each confront the questions that being an erotic equine present, Born in a Barn is a film about finding an identity in the pursuit of an unconventional desire."

Roleplay is nothing new as borne out by the Greek philosopher and polymath Aristotle allegedly loving being ridden like a horse. In fact, PP is in some circles referred to as "The Aristotelian Perversion". Gates (2000) referred to the fact that ponyplay was depicted in Assyrian art dating back to 2000 BC. Gates also noted that in the 19th century human ponyplay existed as an erotic amusement for the upper classes in British colonies.

To date, there has been little empirical research on the topic of ponyplay. Weiss (2006) examined the BDSM community in the San Francisco Bay area in the USA. Her interviewees included people who identified primarily as a pony within a BDSM context. She argued that BDSM sexuality including those who self-identified as a pony should be conceptualized as a form of "working at play" (WAP). WAP recognizes the ways BDSM practitioners move between registers of work (productive labour) and play (creative recombination). Weiss's analysis situated BDSM and other sexualities within "the shifting cultural geography of U.S. late-modernity, drawing attention to the ways sexuality blurs boundaries between individual–social, real–pretend and leisure–labour."

Aggrawal (2011a), in an interesting paper on zoophilia, categorizes those into ponyplay as Class I zoosexuals (i.e., human–animal roleplayers). According to Aggrawal, Class I zoosexuals never have sex with actual animals, but become sexually aroused by wanting to have sex with humans who pretend to be animals and who engage in pseudozoophilic acts (e.g., petplay, ponyplay, ponyism or puppyplay). Personally, I do not class this as a type of zoophilia at all, but I can see Aggrawal's logic in including the furry fandom and PP communities.

Porcinophilia

In this book I have examined various human–animal sexual relationships including zoophiles who have sexual relationships with horses, lizards, dolphins, birds and insects. This entry examines something I am calling "porcinophilia" (i.e., a paraphilia in which humans are sexually attracted to and aroused by pigs). Although there are a number of scientific papers that have made reference to humans having sexual relationships with pigs (both sows and boars), the behaviour has (surprisingly) never been given a name.

Before I researched the material for this entry, my only "evidence" of humans wanting to have sex with a pig was an infamous scene in the 1972 film *Deliverance* starring Burt Reynolds, Jon Voight and Ned Beatty. The scene in the film I am referring to concerns Ned Beatty's character "Bobby" being violently and anally raped by two shotgun-wielding hillbillies and being forced to "squeal like a pig" as it was happening. However, colloquially speaking, this is arguably *nothing* compared with the Belgian film *Vase de Noces*.

Vase de Noces is arguably one of the most disturbing and controversial movies ever made. It was given the title *Wedding Trough* in the UK where it was often referred to as "The Pig Fucking Movie". The film concerns the sexual relationship between a man and his pig. A number of film censors, such as those in Australia, labelled the film an obscenity because of its animal killings (some real, some simulated) and depictions of coprophagia and urophilia (i.e., the eating of faeces and drinking of urine). The film revolves around an autistic man who becomes fixated on a female pig and ends up having a sexual relationship with it, and is psychologically devastated when the pig dies.

Grebowicz (2010) made a passing reference to bestiality involving pigs in a section on "animal rape" based on what she had found online. More specifically, she claimed:

"Numerous sites advertise photo galleries accompanied by narratives of dogs 'raping' innocent girls or other 'first timers'. In all of the sites classified as 'animal rape', the animal, usually a dog, is presented as the perpetrator, not the victim, of a rape. This rape narrative sometimes depends on claims about the animal's intelligence, as in http://www.zooshock.com, which shows photos of a woman having intercourse with a pig. The accompanying narrative states that she was raped by the pig in a shed, a claim which is then supported by the following sentence, which explains that pigs are among the most intelligent animals on the planet, comparable to dogs. The trajectory from intelligence to sexuality is clear: the more intelligent the animal, the more credible the narrative in which the animal is a sexual agent."

Now for something a little more academic. Aggrawal (2009a) reported that the first ever legal reference concerning the punishment for bestiality was in the Hittite compendium of laws. These laws stated that bestial acts carried out by men (but not women) with pigs, sheep, cattle and/or dogs were punishable by death. He also noted that court records available in Europe and the USA between the 14th century and the present day nearly always show males (as opposed to females) as most likely to be charged with bestial offences, and that the most common animals that humans had engaged in sexual activity with in these court cases were horses, pigs and sheep.

In the scientific literature there are a couple of case studies relating to human–porcine sexual relationships. Blondel (1976) reported in a French medical journal that a 46-year-old French farmer had to undergo surgery for peritonitis after anal sex with a boar (i.e., a male pig). Later, Kirov *et al.* (2002) reported that a 62-year-old Bulgarian farmer was treated for a torn rectum after sex with a male pig. The authors noted that: "A transmural tear occurred when pressure exceeded the rectal wall compliance at a fixed point of contact." The farmer had presented at hospital suffering from abdominal pain. Following medical tests it was discovered that the cause of the pain was a small (half a centimetre) ragged tear of the rectal wall. Initially, the farmer was understandably reluctant to tell the medical staff how the injury had been obtained, but eventually he revealed that one of his male pigs had anally penetrated him. Naish (2008), in an article covering this case on his Tetrapod Zoology blog, described the anatomy of a pig's penis. From this description it is easy to see how being anally penetrated by a pig would cause a rectal tear:

> *"The pig penis is somewhat different from the sort of anatomy that we're more familiar with. For one thing, the organ is twisted, with the right corpus cavernosum more strongly developed than the left. The retractor muscle is also attached asymmetrically ... Believe it or don't, by contracting its retractor muscles, a boar makes its penis move in a semi-rotary fashion, and by causing this movement a mating boar can achieve ejaculation even when not thrusting the pelvis in the normal fashion. A glans is absent, and instead the tip of the organ is twisted with a curved and pointed end."*

Twinn (2007) noted that the pig's corkscrew-shaped penis can provide orgasms that last for 30 minutes. Finally, Beetz (2000, 2002) published a study about 32 male zoophiles. She reported that 14% of her participants were most attracted to pigs. However, compared with other forms of animal sexual attraction, pigs were the least sexually attractive animals. That dubious accolade belonged to dogs (87%), horses (81%), cows (32%), goats (28%), sheep (27%) and cats (15%).

Both court reports and scientific medical papers prove that some humans do have sexual relationships with pigs. This is borne out by Beetz's research with self-confessed zoophiles, showing that pigs are among the household pets and farm animals with which humans have had sexual relationships. We know nothing about the prevalence or etiology of such behaviour, but the incidence is likely to be very low.

Pregnancy fetishism

In the entry on lactophilia (i.e., sexual arousal from lactating women), I briefly mentioned maieusiophilia (a.k.a. "cyesolagnia"), a paraphilia and/or fetish in which an individual derives sexual pleasure and sexual arousal from particular aspects of human female pregnancy. Aggrawal (2011a) specifically defines maieusiophilia as "gaining sexual arousal from pregnant women and/or female childbirth". However, other sources define maieusiophilia more broadly to include sexual attraction to women who appear pregnant, attraction to lactation and/or attraction to particular stages of pregnancy from impregnation through to childbirth.

Like lactophilia (a.k.a. "breast milk fetishism") there are other paraphilias that have very specific sexual referents, such as gravidophilia (which simply refers to the fetish of actually being pregnant oneself). There appears to be a widely held belief that the overwhelming majority of gravidophiles are lesbian, but those in the maieusiophile community claim this is simply untrue. As with most types of paraphilia and fetishes, most maieusiophiles are male, typically heterosexual, although there are females of all sexual orientations (heterosexual, bisexual and lesbian).

It has been alleged in various online articles, although I have yet to see the empirical evidence for this, that there are no specific and/or preferred elements within pregnancy fetishism that are common to all maieusiophiles. For instance, it is claimed that some are sexually aroused by pregnant women's mobility and/or how they walk or sleep. Others may be sexually aroused by the body changes that pregnant women experience. As is the case with many paraphilias and fetishes, conventional sex and/or nudity are often not required for the maieusiophile to become sexually aroused.

Other human attributes that remind maieusiophiles of pregnancy may also be a turn-on, such as a woman with a protruding navel or a fat women with a large abdomen. It is not known if there is any fetishistic crossover between maieusiophilia and individuals into fat admiration and fat fetishes. One practice that appears to be liked by both maieusiophiles and fat admirers is the act of belly expansion. This refers to the practice of inflating the belly, typically with air or liquid, until the abdomen is distended. For maieusiophiles this may mean that non-pregnant females can be made to appear pregnant and serve as a visual focus for individual fetishistic episodes to occur.

Despite the increasing awareness of maieusiophilia and an apparent increase in the number of people who are into it, little is known on the etiology and cause behind developing such a fetish. Even among the online maieusiophilia community, there appear to be few commonalities between such people.

Based on what I have read I have no idea how prevalent the activity is. Furthermore, nothing is known empirically about the condition. As with many paraphilic behaviours that I have examined, this appears to be yet another area where academics and/or clinicians need to be doing some research.

Psellismophilia

One Christmas holiday I received a notification from Google Alerts to say that my work on paraphilias had been cited in an article entitled "Forget feet, meet the fetishists turned on by insects, stuttering and stairs" on the Shoofee website. The article was a brief overview of seven paraphilias and fetishes. Many of those listed referred readers to articles on my personal blog. Of the seven listed, I had already written articles on six of them, but I had never done one on the seventh – psellismophilia.

According to Aggrawal (2009a) psellismophilia is a paraphilia that involves becoming sexually aroused by stuttering. Psellismophilia is another paraphilia whose name has been derived from the opposite of a specific phobia (i.e., psellismophobia, an irrational and persistent fear of stuttering). According to the Massive Phobia website, the root word *psellismo* is the Greek word for "stammering".

As with any human behaviour that I know little about, I first did a search on Google Scholar and found that no article had ever been written on the topic. I then did a simple search on Google and again found that no articles had ever been published on the behaviour. However, there were plenty of articles that mentioned it in passing.

Given the complete lack of information on whether there are individuals who are sexually aroused by stuttering, I began trawling various online forums and began to find individuals who confessed online that stuttering was something they found sexually arousing or claimed to know people who were. Obviously, I have no way of knowing the veracity of the claims made, but most appeared to be genuine to me.

Whether psellismophilia ever becomes the focus of serious academic study remains to be seen, but I doubt it will unless any negative consequences arise from the behaviour. I have come across nothing suggesting that the condition (if it genuinely exists) is any way detrimental.

Psychrocism

Pagophagia is a condition in which people obsessively and/or compulsively chew on ice. It is often viewed as a form of pica and considered by many psychologists as an obsessive–compulsive disorder. Pagophagia is not the only human behaviour that can be done excessively and requires ice. Psychrocism refers to individuals who derive sexual pleasure and sexual arousal from either being cold themselves or by watching someone else who is cold.

The only case that I have come across in the academic literature is in Hirschfeld (1948). Hirschfeld reported the account of a male who had a sexual cold fetish. The quote below is a self-confessed admission from the man himself:

> *"The thought and sight of chilly dress or pictorial representations of it, induce in me considerable erotic pleasure. My wife naturally has no idea of my abnormal sensations in this respect, and when I make a drawing of the type with which you are familiar, say, a drawing representing a girl with bare arms and shoulders, and dressed only in the flimsiest of undies, on the ice in the skating rink, she always regards it as a joke, for she naturally does not take seriously the exaggerations in which my imagination revels. Such fantasies, accompanied by masturbation, have frequently come to me at times when sexual intercourse with my wife has been impossible for physiological reasons. These fantasies were confined to a single subject – immature girls wearing the lightest clothes in winter."*

A later brief overview of psychrocism by Love (2001) makes reference to the fact that some people's masturbatory practices involve putting a towel in the freezer and then laying it out on their genitals. Others, she claims, use icicles as part of sexplay. She also reports a personal communication from a man in California, USA who told her that on several occasions after winter-swimming in the ocean for over half an hour he obtained an erection that lasted 2 to 3 hours on average. So the sexual attraction is a long-lasting erection, but what are the consequences? Love notes that:

> *"Exposure to intense cold creates a sharp sensation that is similar to other physical stimuli that produce tension. The mind changes its focus from intellectual pursuits to physical awareness. Many [sadomasochistic] players use cold contact to heighten awareness of skin sensations. They often alternate cold with heat, such as ice cubes and candle wax."*

This description is an example of what is known as "temperature play" (a subtype of "sensation play"), which is a form of BDSM sensual play in which various substances and/or objects are used to stimulate neuroreceptors in the human body for the sensual effects caused by hot and/or cold. Substances used by BDSM practitioners may include water/ice, various oils, hot wax, chocolate syrup, whipped cream, melted butter, chilled fresh fruit and steamed vegetables. Objects are often chilled in ice-cold water or warmed in preheated water to enhance the sensation. Such objects may include cutlery, ball chains and jewellery (e.g., necklaces). To intensify or amplify the effect in temperature play, bondage and/or blindfolds may sometimes be used. Iceplay, a form of temperature play (and sexual foreplay), typically involves moving ice cubes and the like across a person's naked body, as was seen in the 1980s' Hollywood film 9½ Weeks.

Other practices known to occur during iceplay include ice-water enemas, which for some may be more to do with klismaphilia (i.e., sexual arousal from enemas, more generally, and the use of ice dildos where water is frozen inside a condom and then used as a masturbatory tool). BDSM practitioners are warned that ice on, and especially inside, the body can lead to a dramatic reduction in blood flow and in worst case scenarios can result in comas. Ice can cause excessive tissue damage due to the formation of ice crystals in cells and blood vessels. Freeze damage (e.g., frostbite) and other cold injuries (e.g., chilblains) happen at much slower speeds than is the case with "temperature play" burn and/or heat injuries.

In self-styled "Doctor of Perversity" Beth Brown's article on "temperature play" (Brown, 1996) she reported:

> *"Temperature play with cold can be particularly wicked, because it is easy for a bottom to confuse hot and cold sensations. John Varley's Titan series contains a scene in which a man is interrogated by being shown a hot poker, and then tortured blindfolded. He thinks his testicles are being burned with the hot poker, but when the blindfold is removed, he finds himself sitting in a pool of melted ice ... When heat and cold are used together in a scene the feelings are much more intense, because alternating hot and cold sensations can confuse the nerves. Hot and cold nerve endings respond to differences from body temperature, but when rapidly repeated changes in temperature are administered to an area, these calculations can become wildly inaccurate."*

Brown (1996) also made the point that a person's psychological state has an impact on how the sensations are experienced as well. Much of the way in which temperature (hot and/or cold) is experienced is affected by the person's expectations. She says this is nowhere more true than the anaesthetist's slogan "pain is in the brain".

Pyrophilia

Pyrophilia (a.k.a. "pyrolagnia" and "sexual arson") is a paraphilia in which a person derives sexual arousal from fire and/or fire-starting activity. It is sometimes confused with pyromania, but pyromaniacs do not get any sexual pleasure when they start fires. Most of what is known academically comes from case studies published in the academic and clinical literature. Writings dating back to the 19th century have suggested that psychosexual factors may sometimes play a role in pyromaniac activities. Pyrophilia is thought to be very rare and there are no incidence or prevalence studies on the condition. Even in major texts on paraphilias, such as that by Laws and O'Donohue (2008), it is not mentioned. In Aggrawal's (2009a) book it is only given 10 lines and much of that is taken up with speculation about the Roman Emperor Nero being a possible pyrophiliac.

Quinsey et al. (1989) examined arsonists and sexual arousal to fire setting. They wanted to further explore the extent to which pyromania was sexually related. They measured and compared the penile responses of 26 arsonists and 15 non-arsonists to audiotaped narratives. The narratives were categorized as (i) neutral, (ii) heterosexual activity and (iii) fire setting motivated by (a) sexual excitement, (b) general (unspecified) excitement, (c) insurance, (d) revenge, (e) heroism and (f) power. They found penile responses to all categories were negligible, although both the heterosexual activity and the sexual excitement fire-setting categories produced more erectile activity than the neutral category. However, Quinsey et al. (1989) reported there were no significant differences between arsonists and non-arsonists from any of the story categories. They argued that their data demonstrated no support for the idea that sexual motivation is commonly involved in arson.

Cox (1979) stated that, having set a fire, the fire fetishist "will claim that he has had his best ever orgasm as he watched the flames leap up," although such a claim was unsubstantiated by anything else in the book chapter. Lande (1980), arguably, described the first case study of a pyrophiliac. Lande reported the case of a 20-year-old male with a history of arson associated with masturbation as his sole means of obtaining sexual arousal and gratification. Physiological and subjective measures of sexual arousal were taken while he looked at various photographs. The man was most sexually aroused by those involving fire with lesser sexual arousal when looking at photographs of naked females. He was treated using orgasmic reconditioning to increase heterosexual arousal, and covert sensitization to decrease arousal related to fire. At the end of treatment, arousal was greater for heterosexual sex than for fire stimuli.

Bourget and Bradford (1987) reported two cases of pyrophilia. Their two cases were both adult male arsonists whose intense interest in fire was sexually fetishistic. However, these cases concentrated more on their treatment than the psychological motivations underlying the activity.

Litman (1999) reported the case of a married 25-year-old male pyrophiliac. He voluntarily referred himself for psychological assessment at the request of his wife as a consequence of psychopathology and sexually motivated fire-setting activities. However, he himself did not see his sexually motivated fire setting as a problem. He would set fire to anything at hand when the urge struck him, such as paper or clothing. He told Litman that for as long as he could remember he had been sexually aroused by fire and had a frequent irresistible compulsive urge to set fires.

He recalled that his fascination with fire may have started when helping his mother to shovel coal and touching it to see how hot it was. He had also burned himself by accident on a number of occasions. He told Litman that he was "used to pain" because his father had regularly physically abused him when he was a child. Litman (1999) reported the man had actually engaged in behaviours designed to induce pain with fire for sexual stimulation including sitting on a hot stove or wrapping a pair of trousers around his arm and setting fire to them. His antidepressant medicine helped reduce his thoughts about fire setting, but he stopped taking it as a result of side-effects. His wife subsequently left him because of his sexual fascination with fire.

Balachandra and Swaminath (2002) described what they believed was the only case in the literature of a female arsonist, a 29-year-old heterosexual woman with a fire fetishism. The case history revealed she had been sexually abused at the age of 8 years, and that during adolescence she had been cruel to animals and began setting small fires. She used to scout for places to set fires and focused on setting fire to bins and recycling containers. No-one was ever hurt or burned as a result of her activities. She would hide, watch the fire and then go home and masturbate while thinking about the fire she had just started. She also kept a detailed diary of every fire she had started. The behaviour escalated and she had started over 175 fires by the time she received psychiatric help. The authors reported:

"The motives were described as an outlet for anger, sexual motivation and satisfaction, and an intense preoccupation with fire, together with tension and affective arousal that was relieved by setting fires. There was no correlation between the fires and her menstrual cycle or substance abuse."

These case studies when taken together suggest that pyrophilia does not appear to include behaviours commonly associated with pyromania, such as watching neighbourhood fires, setting off fire alarms deliberately, getting non-sexual satisfaction from being around those who work in the fire services, starting fires to garner attention from fire service personnel and showing indifference to human life or property after setting fire to something. It also appears that sexual arousal may not always depend on an actual fire as it may also be facilitated by photographs and verbal stories about fire and/or arson. While seemingly rare, case studies show that pyrophilia is a real clinical entity.

Persaud's (2003) book *From the Edge of the Couch* included an interesting case study by Shiwach and Prosser (1998). The paper concerned the treatment of an "unusual case of masochism" in which the individual in question gained sexual arousal and pleasure from being burnt (i.e., pyrophilia) and crushed (i.e., crush fetishism), which often meant he was in dangerous and potentially life-threatening situations. As the authors summarized:

"Masochistic sexual activity is potentially dangerous, rarely reported voluntarily, and hard to treat. [Our paper] describes a masochist patient who received sexual gratification from being burnt or crushed. Anti-androgen medication [leuprolide acetate], serotonin uptake inhibitor [fluoxetine], and psychodynamic psychotherapy along with sexual education and social skills training and aversive behavior therapy [covert sensitization and olfactory aversion] were all tried over a period of 9 months. The response was measured by effects of treatments on the frequency of erotic fantasies and masturbation."

The male masochist was a single 38-year-old man who turned up at a hospital burns unit for treatment to extensive burns on his lower body (around 20% of his total body area) before being referred to the psychiatric unit. His pyrophilic urges and interest in being crushed were longstanding and dated back to mid-adolescence. The incident that led to the hospital admission had involved one of the man's regular ways of gaining sexual arousal which was to set fire to refuse-collecting trucks (a.k.a. "dumpsters") while he was inside them and simultaneously masturbating. Persaud (2003) noted that:

> '[The man] would then masturbate before getting out [of the dumpster]. His burns had occurred when a plastic dumpster melted and turned over. His first sexual experience at age 15 [years] had occurred when he curled himself up in an oven and ejaculated – an adventure that had been prompted by having been threatened as a child with being roasted 'like a pig' as a punishment. A social isolate, he enjoyed watching videos and reading about people being burned at the stake or crushed. He had also attempted autoerotic asphyxia, but relinquished this as 'too dangerous'."

The recollection of ejaculating while inside an oven appears to be a critical event in the acquisition and development of the man's unusual sexual preferences. As Persaud also noted:

> "[The man remembered] entering a big unlit oven out of curiosity and liking the warmth and sense of suffocation but did not realize he had ejaculated until the third such instance. He remained a socially isolated virgin and gave a history of sexual disinterest in males or females and of ignorance of sexuality in general ... Twice he came close to self-immolation after pouring gasoline on himself ... he denied getting any pleasure out of seeing other people suffer ... he worked in places where he could have easy access to large waste disposers, ovens and box compactors."

Consequently, Persaud thought (as I do) that learning theory best explained this man's etiology and that psychoanalytic factors like guilt and punishment may have also been important. This particular case was also reported by Williams (2006). Williams noted the man had been arrested on a number of occasions for climbing into refuse-collecting dumpsters and had also broken his pelvis as a consequence of being crushed by a box compactor. Williams further noted that "clearly, most experts would agree that acting out fantasies in these dangerous situations posed a significant risk of severe physical harm and death, not to mention being illegal." More specifically, Persaud (2003) reported that:

> "[The man] would climb into refuse collecting trucks and ejaculate at the sensation of being crushed, only escaping at the last possible minute. He admitted masturbating almost daily to deviant sexual fantasies or to pictures of fire, people being burned or crushed, and even just the sight of chimneys. Recently he had been climbing into a large dumpster, pouring alcohol on the refuse and setting it on fire. He managed to masturbate and get out of the refuse bin with minor burns twice, but the plastic dumpster eventually melted and overturned, causing the injuries he now had."

Queefing fetishism

I have a feeling I may have broken at this juncture one of the few taboos that remain in today's world by examining vaginal flatulence (a.k.a. "varting", an amalgam of the words "vaginal" and "farting"). The term "queefing" is based on the onomatopoeic sound made by vaginal flatulence (a.k.a. "fanny farting", at least in the UK). A short entry on queefing as part of the Fetish University series of articles at the Masturbation Fascination website noted that:

> "A queef is a vaginal fart. A queef is the expulsion of wind from the vulva – normally during sexual intercourse or other sexual activities … Truth is, it's highly, highly embarrassing. I think most women have experienced it at least once in their lifetime and [there] is really no sexy way to brush it off. Unless, of course, your partner has a queef fetish."

All my research leads me to conclude that fetishized vaginal flatulence appears to be relatively rare, although there are certainly pornographic films where queefing has been eroticized. The most notable of such films is *Amber the Lesbian Queefer* starring Amber Rose and directed by Mimi Miyagi from the Philippines. Critics argue this is one of the "worst porn movie titles of all time".

Queening fetishism

While researching the entry on squashing fetishes, I came across an online account from a dominatrix talking about queening fetishes. According to Aggrawal (2009a) queening is a BDSM practice in which one sexual partner sits on or over another person's face "typically to allow oral–genital or oral–anal contact, or to practice ass worship or body worship." In the book's glossary of sexual terms, Aggrawal (2009a) simply defines queening as "sitting on the side of a person's face as a form of bondage." In a book chapter, Love (2005) included a short section on queening. She wrote:

> "The term queening refers to the European practice of a dominant female using a man's head as her throne. The woman sits in one of several positions, either on the side of the man's head or so that his nose is near her anus with his eyes covered by her genitals. The object of queening is bondage or breath control, not cunnilingus. The man

may wear supplemental restraints on the wrists and ankles. A slightly comparable American sex scene is where a stripper completely disrobes and stands over a sitting male with his head tilted back so that her genitals are only a couple of inches above his face. She stays in this position, moving her pelvis to the music for about five minutes. The male is not permitted to touch her in any manner during this exhibition."

In my own research I came across the Informed Consent website (a UK BDSM website) which highlighted queening as its "fetish of the week" back in September 2010. As a consequence, it featured people writing about their queening experiences. I collated a few extracts here to provide a flavour of what people enjoy about queening from a personal standpoint:

- Extract 1: 'I practice [queening] and regard it more in [an orally erotic] way than as a means of breath play. Although I know for some the oral element doesn't feature at all. For me, the breath play aspect is a fairly insignificant part of it.'
- Extract 2: 'I love all aspects of it. The sheer enjoyment of someone dominating me by pushing their body down on my face; the oral sex; the worshipping of an anus; the smells and tastes; the inability to control my breathing; being pushed right to the edge, gasping for the slightest bit of air. I love it when Mistress loses herself in the moment so much so that she forgets about me, and I literally have to protect my own breathing/life.'
- Extract 3: 'It's one of my favourites, yet very rarely practiced ... it encompasses so much ... from total control to total intimacy.'
- Extract 4: 'Personally, I love [queening] and just can't get enough of it. I seem to never get bored of it. The ultimate for me is for Mistress to sit on my face and conduct some nipple torture or put candle wax on my chest. I think this is proper pain and pleasure mixed up perfectly.'

The bottom line (no pun intended) about queening fetishes is that almost all the information we have appears to have been written by those who actually engage in the practice. There is nothing written academically except passing references in academic books on unusual sexual practices. There is also the question of whether those who engage in the behaviour view it as fetishistic and whether academics would class the behaviour as a genuine fetish. Based on what I have read, queening appears to be an adjunct to other types of sexually paraphilic behaviour, such as sexual masochism, rather than a standalone fetish, although for some people it may well be a genuine fetishistic sexual activity.

Quicksand fetishism

Quicksand fetishism appears to be a subtype of taphephilia. Aggrawal (2009a) defines taphephilia as "deriving sexual pleasure and arousal from being buried alive." Ntumy (2013) in an article entitled "Girls stuck in quicksand" claimed it to be one of the six most bizarre "safe for work" fetishes they list. Ntumy noted:

"There's no official name for this weird fetish – yet – but that doesn't mean the internet isn't full of videos and photos depicting it. For some people, the idea of a person, *especially a woman, nearly drowning in quicksand is quite the turn-on. Perhaps these viewers imagine themselves as a hero who can swoop in and save the day. Or maybe these people are aroused by the woman's fear. Either way, this is a fetish we hope you won't experience any time soon. This is a perfect example of a nearly 'safe for work' fetish – it requires no nudity or sex, and it in fact involves a situation in which sex would be utterly impossible. It's people who get aroused at the sight of fully clothed women sinking in quicksand."*

Ntumy then went on to say things that I have confirmed for myself when visiting such websites as Quicksand Visuals and Quicksand Fans:

"A cursory search online would reveal tons of sites dedicated to compiling clips from various sources of girls drowning in quicksand, and then there are the niche video sites dedicated to providing original content (there probably is a booming industry in quicksand pit installation these days). On those sites, elaborate storylines are created to justify how these lovely ladies came to be trapped in the unforgiving, bottomless pit of certain-yet-sexy death. So ... maybe the quicksand thing triggers some 'damsel in distress' response in the [brain's cortex]? If there's anything lonely internet tough guys love, it's sitting behind their keyboards visualizing all the many ways they would totally jump in and save the unfortunate lady fake drowning in a boggy marsh."

Unsurprisingly, there are no academic papers on quicksand fetishes and very few articles of any description on the topic. I have no idea how common quicksand fetishes are, but I would suspect such fetishes to be very niche. I doubt whether the fetish is the only type of fetishistic behaviour among such people as there is so much crossover with many other different niche fetishes, such as stuck fetishism, buried fetishism and damsel-in-distress fetishism. As with many other extreme sexual behaviours I have examined, I cannot see this becoming an area of serious academic study any time soon, but that does not mean it is not an interesting topic.

Rectal foreign bodies

Elsewere in this book I looked at the practice of urethral manipulation in which men insert objects into their urethra for sexual stimulation. Another similar sexual practice is the insertion of foreign bodies into the rectal passage. Most of what is known academically and clinically about this comes from people (almost always male) who turn up at a hospital emergency department requiring treatment, such as the removal of a foreign body that has become trapped inside their rectums. Goldberg and Steele (2010) noted that "retained rectal foreign bodies have been reported in patients of all ages, genders and ethnicities, and more than two-thirds of patients with rectal foreign bodies are men in their thirties and forties."

There are dozens and dozens of papers on the topic of rectal foreign bodies and the list of objects and items that have been removed by doctors is almost as long as the number of papers that have been written. This list includes vegetables (e.g., potatoes, cucumbers, carrots, turnips and onions), fruit (e.g., bananas and apples), other foodstuffs (e.g., salami and hard-boiled eggs), food and drink containers (e.g., glass bottles, plastic bottles, peanut butter jars and glass tumblers), sporting items (e.g., baseballs, ping-pong balls and tennis balls), household and kitchen objects (e.g., candles, lightbulbs, broomstick handles, spatulas and mortar pestles), sex toys (e.g., vibrators and dildos) and improvised objects (e.g., a sand-filled bicycle inner tube, a plastic fist and forearm, shoehorn, axe handles, an aluminium money tube, whip handles, soldering irons, glass tubes and a frozen pig's tail). Some of these can be very dangerous such as lightbulbs that break with broken glass bits perforating the rectum and/or colon and in one case leading to peritonitis (Schaupp, 1981). Despite the many published case studies, there are no estimates of the incidence of rectal foreign body insertion among the population as almost all that is known is only based on people who end up seeking medical intervention.

Many of the people seeking treatment are gay men, although some of the literature features females who have been rectally assaulted. Object removal by a medical team can sometimes be difficult. For instance, Benjamin *et al.* (1969) described an instance where a lightbulb was lodged in a patient's rectal cavity and the medical team had to improvise to remove it. They had to attach a lightbulb socket to the end of a stick, insert the homemade device into the patient's rectum, screw the socket onto the lodged lightbulb and then pull it out the same way it went in. In the same paper the authors described how a medical team removed a glass tumbler from one man. In this case the team managed to pour molten plaster into the tumbler along with some rope placed in the molten plaster. When the plaster had set and stuck to the inside of the glass they pulled the tumbler out using the rope that had set in the hardened plaster.

There are cases in the literature where a foreign body has remained inside the rectal cavity for long periods. For instance, one case reported that a man had a vibrator removed after 6 months of it being inside him, by which time it is presumed the batteries had stopped working (Buzzard and Waxman, 1981). Papers have also reported the many alleged non-sexual reasons as to how such objects came to be lodged in the rectum in the first place. Common ones include accidentally falling on the specified object or item after showers or baths and deliberate insertion of the object or item to dislodge constipated fecal mass. Some stories are a little more elaborate such as one reported by Graves *et al.* (1983) where a man said he had slipped on a glass jar while washing his dog in the shower. In the same paper another man who was found to have a vibrator stuck in his rectum claimed to have been abducted and sexually assaulted by a group of men rather than admit that the incident was self-inflicted.

One of the most bizarre cases ever reported was in a paper by Lo *et al.* (2004). The authors described what they believed was the very first case of something living lodged in the rectal passage. After reporting abdominal pain and being diagnosed with peritonitis, an X-ray revealed that the patient, a 50-year-old man, had a 50-cm-long eel stuck inside his abdomen. He claimed he had inserted it to relieve his constipation. The authors provided all the photographic evidence in their paper. A paper on anorectal trauma by Eckert and Katchis (1989) is worth mentioning at this point. They commented on what has now come to be called "felching". More specifically, they said:

> *"A sexual practice has been mentioned where living rodents, including gerbils and mice, have been inserted into the rectum; the animal's futile efforts to claw its way to safety result in mucosal tears in the rectum."*

However, no actual cases of felching have ever been reported in the medical literature.

Robot fetishism

Earlier in this book I examined agalmatophilia in which individuals derive sexual arousal from an attraction to (usually nude) statues, dolls, mannequins and/or other similar body-shaped objects. Some scholars have claimed that robot fetishism is another type or at least an extension of agalmatophilia. Robot fetishism (a.k.a. "ASFR" – named after alt.sex.fetish.robots, the name of a now-defunct newsgroup – or "technosexuality"). It refers more specifically to individuals who derive sexual pleasure and arousal from humanoid or non-humanoid robots. The original ASFR manifesto stated:

> *"The alt.sex.fetish.robots (ASFR) newsgroup is dedicated to the discussion of the concept of sex with or sexual attraction to robots and robot-like beings. This can range from metallic, non-humanoid machines to humanoid androids. Discussions can deal with specific fantasies, fiction relating to the topic and connected ideas like people behaving like [or being] turned into human mannequins, dolls, toys and other*

hypnosis and mesmerism fantasies that involve the mechanical/monotone response that appeals to the members."

Technosexuality can be fantasy-based arousal in which the robot fetishist merely thinks about sexual scenarios involving robots and/or can involve sexual activity with people dressed in robot costumes. Sexual arousal may be greater the more the person imagines or dresses as a robot or sounds and acts in a robot-like manner. Those into this fetish call themselves "ASFRians" and/or "technosexuals". Some of them like to imagine removing skin or bits of the body to reveal electronic circuitry. You can imagine that they get turned on by everything from the *Six Million Dollar Man* through to *The Terminator*.

Robot fetishism can sometimes include other fetish variants, most notably transformation fetishes in which individuals get sexually excited by imagining themselves turning into a robot. They are conceptually similar to furries who get sexually excited by imagining themselves transformed into an animal or animal hybrid. Similar to furries, robot fetishism could be viewed as another form of erotic anthropomorphism. It is also claimed that, when transformation and/or roleplaying are involved, the activity may be viewed as a form of erotic objectification. There are also similarities to mechanophilia (i.e., sexual arousal from cars or other machines).

According to the ASFR websites that I have visited, technofetishists comprise two distinct but not necessarily mutually exclusive types of technosexual fantasy. As one 2011 online essay on the now-defunct Stupid My Cupid website claimed:

"The first group is simply based on a desire to have a ready-made android or gynoid [female robot] partner that is desired for sex, companionship or any combination of the two. The main distinguishing feature of this type is that the android is completely artificial 'built' and manufactured solely to fulfill the desires of its owner. The second type of fantasy is referred to as transformation. This involves a human who is either willingly or unwillingly turned into an android. That person can be either oneself or one's partner, or sometimes both. It is usually the process of transformation that is the focus of this fantasy. Many people in the ASFR community prefer either one or the other. In some cases, this preference is very strong and divisive within the community. People may even be repulsed by the behaviors of the opposite group. In other cases, there is equal appreciation for built robots and transformation."

A survey carried out on the Fembot Central website of 318 technosexual members reported that 66% of ASFRians had a preference for built robots while the others preferred transformation (18%) or some combination of both (16%). Gates (2000) reported that some technofetishists do not like synthetic partners at all and prefer their fantasies to involve humans dressed as robots as part of fantasy sexplay.

The expression of technosexuality is somewhat limited in that it can only be acted upon in a few ways, such as a masturbatory fantasy or as sexual roleplay. Nevertheless, a large market for technosexual art has developed that caters for and helps to enable robot fetishism (i.e., it can help sexually stimulate ASFRians).

As far as I am aware, there is no academic research on robot fetishism beyond theoretical essays. While of interest, it would be really useful to know how big the technosexual community is and what the motivations are for engaging in such behaviour. Although submission/dominance is an obvious theme, there is no literature to confirm or disconfirm such speculation. I will leave you with a quote by Shaw-Garlock (2011), who probably did not have robot fetishists in mind when she wrote it, but which has great resonance with this topic:

> "Today, human and sociable-technology interaction is a contested site of inquiry. Some regard social robots as an innovative medium of communication that offer new avenues for expression, communication and interaction. Others question the moral veracity of human–robot relationships, suggesting that such associations risk psychological impoverishment. What seems clear is that the emergence of social robots in everyday life will alter the nature of social interaction, bringing with it a need for new theories to understand the shifting terrain between humans and machines."

Rubberdolling

Earlier in this book I look at doll fetishism in which individuals derive sexual pleasure and arousal from dolls and doll-like objects. When it comes to rubberdolling (the practice of individuals dressing up head to toe as a rubber doll), as far as I am aware there is no academic research on it, although there are clearly psychological and behavioural overlaps with other more academically researched areas including transvestic fetishism, rubber/latex fetishism and sadomasochism. In fact, many people might view such activity as extreme cross-dressing where men (but occasionally women) transform themselves into walking talking dolls, completely concealing their real identities.

Rubberdolling is a relatively new phenomenon that has come to the fetishistic fore over the last two decades. Most rubberdollers attribute the rise of rubberdolling to the work of German fetish photographer Peter Czernich who started the fetish magazines *Marquis* and *Heavy Rubber*. Rubberdollers are typically encased in latex rubber with exaggerated and accentuated Barbie-type female features, such as huge breasts, incredibly small waists, exaggerated thighs and hips, elongated fingernails, extra-long eyelashes and bright and excessive make-up. Typically, the only areas of human flesh that remain uncovered are holes for the eyes, nose and mouth. According to an article on rubberdolling at the Rubber World Rendezvous website (2013) there are four basic categories to which rubberdolling can apply:

- *Submissive dolls:* This is where individuals dress up as a rubber doll as part of a submissive role within a sadomasochistic relationship. Here the doll acts as a service submissive/slave and is utilized by others (usually the dominant partner) for their own sexual entertainment purposes. The dominant partner controls everything that the doll does and the costume often restricts the doll's movements. The doll essentially becomes totally objectified and is at the total mercy of their dommes [female dominant dominatrix] or mistresses. Here, rubberdolls may also be engaging in the behaviour as part of an encasement and/or rubber bondage fetish.
- *Sissy dolls:* This is where individuals dress up as a fetishistic "sissy" rubber doll

within the transgender and transvestite community. The activity may also be part of "cosplay" (i.e., costume play). The Rubber World Rendezvous website claims these people use *"the rubber doll theme as a vehicle for play, disguise, sissification, cross dressing … This generally follows a common theme of Forced Femme or being turned into a female doll animate or inanimate. Again shape-altering garments and female masks figure in this identity change. Many equate this to being turned into a Barbie doll. Many [transvestites] who like shiny materials are now dressing in latex and rubber as part of their look and while not wearing masks they are considered a rubber doll."*

- *Show dolls:* This is where individuals dress up as a rubber doll for exhibition purposes and may be part of either the BDSM and/or transvestite and transgender communities. In sadomasochistic relationships show dolls are made to look as pretty as possible by their dommes or mistresses to show off to others in the rubber-dolling scene, such as at fetish balls. Here, the dominant partner may actually play with the submissive as if it was a real doll. Show dolls are typically female in appearance, and the female form is accentuated and exaggerated.
- *Art dolls:* This is where individuals dress up as a rubber doll as an art form or art statement (i.e., a piece of "living art" or "street theatre") and may have nothing to do with sex or fetishistic sex (i.e., it is purely about seeing the doll from an aesthetic perspective). Such dolls may also be used to feature in fetish photography magazines.

Although there seems to be a growing array of fetish photography magazines, there is little in the way of an established literature on rubberdolling. Nevertheless, there are quite a few rubberdollers who have their own webpages. One of the more interesting and in depth is the Swedish Rubber Puppett website (2012). The site's owner is very open and reflective about his rubberdolling. I reproduce here what he has to say in his own words:

> *"I am a [rubberdoller] from the very south part of Sweden with a deep love for latex. I created this site to be able to reach out to other latex lovers and to make new friends all over the world. The rubber scene in Sweden is quite limited, especially if you are into dolling. I have been into latex and anything tight and shiny for as long as I can remember and some time ago I dressed up as a doll and I instantly felt this was my 'thing' … Many people think of a rubberdoll as something passive and submissive, which is often the case. However, I am neither passive nor submissive and do this for entirely different reasons. For me it is all about dressing up and [transforming] myself into a different character. Perhaps this is similar to people who are into cosplay … Like an exhibitionist I love the way people turn their heads and look at me, some with fascination and some with fear in their eyes."*

Arguably, the most interesting part of Rubber Puppett's account is when he talks about where his love of dressing in rubber came from. He reports that:

> *"I have been into rubber, latex and all shiny and tight things for as long as I can remember. As a young child I loved to dress up in rain clothes. I can remember the nice*

feeling I got the first time I tried a couple of waders. Now I am more focused towards latex, but I am still quite fond of those things, especially rubber boots. It wasn't until I left home to study that I came into contact with latex … I did like the look of it and I decided to buy some simple garments for me and my girlfriend. I instantly fell in love with the tight feeling of the rubber clothes, the smell and the look of them. I soon ordered some more latex clothes such as hoods, stockings and dresses. When I first saw myself in the mirror wearing a hood I was instantly hooked. Since that day I have worked on my rubberdoll persona to create my fantasy woman."

Based on what I have read, I would not describe this account of rubberdolling as typical (and neither does he). Whether any academic research ever gets carried out on the topic remains to be seen, but it is certainly an area of psychological interest.

Sadism

Sadism (the act of obtaining sexual arousal through the giving of physical or psychological pain) and masochism (the act of obtaining sexual arousal through the receiving of physical or psychological pain) are paraphilias that are often viewed as two variations of the same phenomenon. However, in this entry I examine sexual sadism in isolation.

von Krafft-Ebing (1886) is often credited with introducing the term "sadism" deriving the name from the Marquis de Sade whose French novels often feature such behaviour. Despite the increase in knowledge of and theorizing about sexual sadism, the psychopathology of the behaviour is still uncertain and an all-encompassing theory of the etiology of sexual sadism has yet to be developed and empirically tested. Furthermore, the labelling and defining of sexually sadistic behaviour is further complicated by the fact that many people enjoy some form of aggressive behaviour during sex, such as spanking, the gentle biting of nipples and giving love bites. This makes the label "sadomasochism" seem somewhat inappropriate.

According to the American Psychiatric Association's *Diagnostic and Statistical Manual of Mental Disorders* (2022) sexual sadists require the "psychological or physical suffering of another person, as manifested by fantasies, urges or behaviors" to induce sexual excitement. However, researchers in the field claim that such definitions are difficult to apply in practice, resulting in experienced clinicians interpreting screening criteria inconsistently in the diagnosis of sexual sadism.

The situation was complex even when von Krafft-Ebing (1886) first wrote on the topic. For instance, he described what he believed were distinct subtypes of sexual sadism including (i) lust murder (where sexual arousal is integral to the act of killing), (ii) necrophilia, (iii) injury to women through flagellation or stabbing, (iv) defilement of women, (iv) other types of assaults on women such as cutting off their hair, (v) whipping of boys, (vi) sadism toward animals and (vii) sadistic fantasies without the occurrence of any actual sadistic acts. Another sadistic act that has been reported in more recent times is piquerism (discussed in an earlier entry) in which the assailant stabs a female victim, typically in the breasts or buttocks, and then runs away.

The true prevalence of sexual sadism among the general population is unknown (American Psychiatric Association, 2022). Kinsey *et al.*'s (1948, 1953) seminal studies of human sexual behaviour reported that 22% of the males and 12% of the females responded erotically to stories with sadistic themes. Other research studies estimate that 10%–20% of couples have engaged in sadomasochistic activities during sex, but that much of this was symbolic. However, most of the little research that has been published on sexual sadism tends to be based on sex offenders and sexual killers.

Among sex offenders the prevalence of sexual sadism is estimated to be less than 10%, and around one third of sexually motivated homicides involve sexually sadistic behavior (American Psychiatric Association, 2022). However, these estimates have been reported to be much higher (as much as 50%) depending upon the criteria used to define and diagnose sexual sadism in the first place. Prevalence estimates are further complicated because some in the area note that sadism and masochism are complementary disorders or separate poles of the same disorder. There is certainly a lot of empirical support that sadism and masochism often co-occur, such as Spengler's (1977) study of 245 German sadomasochists (see the entry on masochism).

The American Psychiatric Association (2022) also reported that (i) 2.2% of males and 1.3% of females reported BDSM behaviour in the previous year (using data from a representative Australian population) and (ii) 2.7% of males and 2.3% of females reported engaging in sexually sadistic behaviour (among the national Finnish population).

Abel et al. (1988) reported that 18% of sadists were also masochistic, 46% had raped, 21% had exposed themselves, 25% had engaged in voyeurism and frottage and 33% had molested children. Similarly, Gosselin and Wilson (1980) reported an overlap among various paraphilias. Their sample comprised 87 rubberites, 38 leatherites, 133 sadomasochists, 205 transvestites (including transsexuals) and 25 dominant females. They found that 4% of sadomasochists were also transvestites, 29% of sadomasochists were also fetishists and 35% of sadomasochists were also fetishists and transvestites. They also reported that the most common objects used by sadists to inflict pain on their sexual partners were belts, whips, canes, shoes and paddles.

There is a wide variety of psychological explanations relating to the etiology of sexual sadism, although most reviews claim there has been little new contemporary theorizing. Most branches of psychology (psychophysiological, psychodynamic, cognitive and behavioural) have developed their own theories, but little research has confirmed them. Psychobiological explanations for sexual sadism and the motivation behind serial sex murderers by the examination of chromosomal, endocrine, hormonal and/or neurological abnormalities have typically been based on single case studies or very small samples. Therefore, the results remain tentative and inconclusive.

Early behaviourist theories argued that sexual sadism begins during childhood. Through both operant and classical conditioning, sexual urges, excitation and/or arousal are consistently paired with aggressive stimuli. Sexual fantasy and masturbation then reinforce and maintain the sadistic behaviour. Other psychologists claim that personality may play a role in the conditioning process along with social modelling and disinhibition.

Malcolm MacCulloch (probably best known as Moors Murderer Ian Brady's psychiatrist) and his colleagues claimed that behavioral explanations for the development of sadistic sexual fantasy do not adequately explain the initial development of sadistic sexual fantasy (MacCulloch et al., 1983, 2000). They attempted to explain the initial development of sexual sadism using research on early childhood abuse and animal models of conditioning. They claimed that sadistic fantasies resulted from a combination of early childhood abuse, classical conditioning and operant conditioning.

Salirophilia

Salirophilia is a paraphilic sexual fetish in which individuals experience sexual arousal from soiling or dishevelling the object of their desire, typically an attractive person. Salirophilic behaviour may include a range of activities, such as tearing or damaging the desired person's clothing, covering them in mud or filth or messing up their hair or make-up. The fetish never involves harming or injuring the person at all, only messing up how they look in some way, shape or form. The fetish was thought to be mainly heterosexual in origin, although McCary and McCary (1982) say it was known to occur within same-sex relationships.

Salirophilia is sometimes related to other fetishes and paraphilias including urophilia (deriving sexual pleasure from urine), coprophilia (deriving sexual pleasure from faeces), mysophilia (deriving sexual pleasure from filth), sploshing (a.k.a. "wet and messy fetishism", deriving sexual pleasure from wet substances – but not body fluids – deliberately and generously applied to either naked or scantily clad individuals), *bukkake* (a.k.a. "face painting", the act of many men ejaculating over a man or woman simultaneously or over photographs) and *omorashi* (deriving sexual pleasure from having a full bladder and/or feeling sexually attracted to someone else who has a full bladder). Salirophilia may also extend to other areas, such as forcing a sexual partner to wear torn or poorly fitting clothing that make the person look more unattractive.

Other variations of the fetish may also include people becoming sexually aroused by acts of vandalism and defacement of statues and photos of attractive people including celebrities. Videos of individuals ejaculating over celebrity photographs are known as "tributes" within the fetish community.

As far as I am aware, the only academic paper on salirophilia is one of my own case studies (Griffiths, 2019). It concerned "Jeff" who was a 58-year-old Australian heterosexual. He was well educated with a long career in forensic medicine. Jeff claimed his first salirophilic act was when he was young. He remembered he wanted to masturbate in strange places outdoors and used to masturbate in a dirty garage lying under a cabinet in dirt. As an educated man with obvious knowledge of psychological theory, he told me that his behaviour was most likely explained by behavioural conditioning and that the behaviour could be generalized to other similar activities. More specifically, he reported:

> "I believe it is hard to define what aspects of salirophilia I personally like. I have a view that it is a simple psychological classical conditioning which has paired an act, or environment with sexual stimulation and eroticism and ultimately an orgasm. I just find the defilement of an attractive woman's body erotic."

Jeff said that he engaged in solitary salirophilic practices regularly but very infrequently with female partners. He also admitted that he twice paid a woman to participate in salirophiliac activities *"defiling her with dirt in a factory rape scenario."* He said it was extremely difficult to find other like-minded female partners who share his interests.

Jeff admitted that he found it *"extremely erotic"* to watch others engage in salirophilic acts in the form of pornography and online videos. However, he had not witnessed an actual salirophiliac act watching someone else in a real situation. He admitted that he watched pornography involving *"forced bukkake, spit play, and rape in forests".* He also mentioned a particular porn star who specialized in pornography associated with rotten food play, with her allegedly appearing visibly distressed by having rotting decomposing food rubbed over her body and being forced to eat it.

He was also a big fan of the television show *Fear Factor* in Britain and Australia which often has beautiful women performing tasks for prize money involving acts that are a turn-on due to the defilement nature of the quest, such as being forced to eat revolting combinations of rotting food and being submerged in foul-smelling fluids. These were sources of sexual arousal for Jeff.

Jeff was asked if there was any connection between his salirophilic fetish and any other fetishistic behaviors that he engaged in. In response to this, Jeff said there was a connection between salirophilia and *"watching scat movies, participating in urolagnia with the female, licking feet, food play (rotten), entomophilia, aspects of bestiality (not actual sex with animals but seeing a woman being licked by the animal and her body having animal body fluids on it)."*

He also said he had no intention of seeking psychological treatment for his paraphilia because it did not cause any issues in his working life (although he illegally used other people's properties to engage in salirohilic activity). He lived in a semirural environment and had had *"access to over 25 properties for isolated sexual activities picked purely for the filthy environment."* Jeff also provided great detail about how he selected derelict and decrepit houses in which to engage in salirophilic sexual practices. Jeff would check to see if the property was unfurnished and vacant, and would examine pictures of the backyard and garages to see if they would be suitable for salirophilic sex.

The prevalence and incidence of salirophilia appears to be negligible given the fact that no case studies apart from my own have ever been published in the peer-reviewed literature. Treatment for salirophilia is rarely sought unless the condition becomes problematic for the individual in some way. Although the individual may feel compelled to engage in the paraphilic behaviour, anecdotal evidence suggests that the great majority manage to integrate their fetishistic behaviour within their day-to-day lives without harming anyone including themselves.

Scrotal infusion

One of the more unusual male sexual acts that I have come across while researching paraphilias is scrotal infusion (a.k.a. "ballooning" – not to be confused with "balloon fetishism"). This is a sexual practice in which fluid (usually saline solution) is injected into the scrotal sac as a way of making it balloon in size. A very similar practice is scrotal inflation in which air or other gases are injected into the scrotal sac. Both scrotal infusion and inflation are potentially dangerous, and individuals engaging in such acts are at risk of scrotal cellulitis, subcutaneous emphysema, Fournier's gangrene (a type of necrotizing infection or gangrene usually affecting the perineum) and/or an air embolism. The latter two complications can be potentially fatal, particularly among those with HIV. Local nerve damage can also be caused by improper placement of the injecting needle. If there are no complications, then the saline injected into the scrotal sac eventually absorbs into the body over a 3-day period.

To date, there have only been a few case studies published in the medical literature. Summers (2003) reported a case study of a 37-year-old man who presented for medical attention with a very swollen and painful scrotum:

> "[The man] reported that he had always had the impression that his genitalia were smaller than desired, and as a result he had searched the internet for a solution. He found a website that supplied him with a 'scrotal inflation kit' ... Unfortunately, the patient still had enlargement of the scrotum 4 days after the infusion, and it was quite painful ... He was initially pleased with the results, but then he developed erythema and pain during the next 2 days ... The swelling of the scrotum completely consumed his penis. At 2-week follow-up [following treatment], the patient's erythema had nearly resolved, and his scrotum was reduced to approximately 20% of its size at presentation."

In his discussion of the case Summers (2003) noted that "the term scrotal inflation seems to be common in the lay literature." However, he could only locate two previous studies relating to gaseous inflation of the scrotum (i.e., Bush and Nixon, 1969; Sharma, 1980). The issue most stressed by Summers was that "remarkably, the equipment required for scrotal inflation can be obtained over the internet without a prescription." Yoganathan and Blackwell (2006) reported the case of a 52-year-old man (white, gay and HIV positive) who turned up at their hospital wanting medical attention for a painful scrotum:

> "He had obtained information and a disposable scrotal infusion toolkit from a website and had infused 2 litres of normal saline into his scrotum over 2 hours, 3 days previously. He had done this many times before without complications and the swelling had previously resolved over 2 days. On this occasion he sought medical advice because the pain and swelling had lasted for more than 3 days ... Examination revealed a grossly swollen, erythematous, tender scrotum suggestive of severe cellulitis ... A Prince Albert ring and scars from previous infusions were also noted ... Despite the severity of his illness, the patient declined to stop this practice and he was therefore advised on how to reduce the risk of complications."

The authors recommend patients be educated about the dangers of scrotal inflation procedures and strongly discouraged from doing so. They also say that clinicians should be aware of unusual sex practices and associated possible rare causes of scrotal cellulitis, such as scrotal infusion and inflation.

Scuba fetishism

In this book I have looked at aquaphilia (a.k.a. "hydrophilia" – a paraphilia in which individuals derive sexual pleasure and arousal from water and/or watery environments including bathtubs or swimming pools). However, I came across a subtype of aquaphilia (i.e., scuba fetishism) in which, according to Gamotin (2009), individuals are sexually aroused by scuba diving, snorkelling or the wearing of diving equipment. Scuba fetishism may also have some psychosexual crossover with athyphilia (a paraphilia in which individuals get sexually aroused by depths or deep water).

There are many scuba fetish websites including some that feature "drowning fetishes", such as the Aqua Entertainment site. Be warned, though, this and most other sites mentioned are sexually explicit. As far as I can ascertain no academic research on scuba fetishism has been done, so everything is (at best) anecdotal.

As with other rare sexual behaviours that I have examined, I cannot see scuba fetishism ever becoming an area of scientific research. Nevertheless, the occasional case may make its way into the forensic literature if things go tragically wrong, such as accidental death from asphyxiation. However, as already noted, there have been auto-erotic water-related deaths published in the medical forensic literature (i.e., Sauvageau and Racette, 2006a, b; Sivaloganathan, 1984), neither of which involved the use of scuba gear.

Semen fetishism

I was once sent an email by one of my regular blog readers saying I should write an article on "semen fetish", something that had never crossed my mind. The email I was sent pointed out that articles I had written covered paraphilias and fetishes concerning almost every other body fluid, such as urine, faeces, blood, menstrual blood, saliva, tears, breast milk, snot, phlegm, vomit, pus and earwax, but not the most obvious (namely, semen).

There is a lot of talk online about the almost mythical status that semen has been afforded. This is typified by a story I came across while researching this topic. In April 2010 a news programme (*BBC News*, 2010) reported the case of Nissim Aharon, an Israeli, who was jailed for 10 years after tricking five gullible women of various ages into various sexual acts including rape and sodomy by claiming that his semen was "holy and had healing powers". Aharon pretended to be a rabbi and a spy working for Mossad, the Israeli intelligence agency. He claimed that his "holiness" would be passed on to those who touched him physically and that his semen would cleanse their bodies. He was eventually arrested in August 2009.

Another seemingly relevant topic that I found online in relation to semen fetish was talk on various sexual forums about the love of *bukkake* and *gokkun* in pornographic films. Be warned, though, my descriptions are sexually explicit.

Bukkake is a sexual act most commonly seen in hardcore pornographic films, in which a group of men simultaneously ejaculate over a woman or man. Original *bukkake* videos are Japanese and date back to the advent of videos in the 1980s. However, *bukkake* videos, while still arguably a minority market, have been made for both European and American audiences with an increasing number of such films made for the gay market. *Gokkun* is also a sexual act that is Japanese in origin and is where a man or woman consumes the semen of one or more men from a drinking receptacle (e.g., cups, glasses, beakers, etc.).

As I noted above there is almost no empirical research on semen fetish, and the

Semen fetishism   211

"evidence" I have collated here is at best anecdotal. The fetish may well exist. However, compared with other body fluid fetishes, semen fetish appears to be either much rarer or just much less reported online and in academic journals.

I have covered some pretty weird sexual fetishes since I started writing on the subject. Nothing really surprises me when it comes to what humans find sexually arousing, but I did once come across a paper that took me by surprise (Tremayne, 2009). His article is the only academically written publication that I have ever read exploring the topic of "used condom fetishes". I did some other searches of academic databases, but failed to locate a single other paper on the topic. He notes:

> "For someone with a condom fetish, this might mean gaining pleasure from looking at pictures or videos portraying people ingesting or masturbating with used condoms. Others might search for discarded condoms to masturbate into or ingest the contents. Some men 'condom hunt' in areas where people have public sex, such as car parks or wooded areas."

Tremayne's own research indicated that used condoms can be purchased online. He made reference to a particular fetish website Condom Swappers, which allows men to swap used condoms by mail for (presumably) sexual purposes. In the name of research I checked out the site and can report that at the time I accessed it there were 3,984 members, nearly 11,000 posts on 182 different topics, over 15,000 photographs and 358 videos. There were also 45 specialist subgroups within this particular used condom community. Most of the members appeared to be gay or bisexual, although that is my impression rather than anything empirically based. Tremayne reports that most of the membership (at the time of his paper) were men from the UK and the USA.

Tremayne's interest in the topic of used condom fetishes stemmed from his concerns about whether men who engaged in this particular sexual practice were at risk of contracting a sexually transmitted infection (STI). Tremayne reported:

> "Some might consider this practice to be risk free as it is accepted that organisms causing STIs cannot live outside the human body. However, a few reports suggest that some microorganisms survive under the right conditions. [A 1986 study by Dr. L. Reznick and colleagues] experimented with a highly concentrated preparation of HIV to see how long it would live in differing environments. The virus recovered after a week in an aqueous environment at room temperature and for more than 3 days following drying. This study used a falsely concentrated viral preparation, but it is not known how long HIV could survive in a knotted condom, sent in a sealed envelope and received within a day or two."

There are also other studies indicating microorganisms that cause STIs can survive on public toilets. For instance, Potasman *et al.* (1999) reported testing for the presence of three specific STI microorganisms *Ureaplasma urealyticum* (UU), *Mycoplasma hominis* (MH) and *Chlamydia trachomatis* (CT) in 50 public toilet bowls. They reported that five of the 50 bowls (10%) were contaminated with at least one of these microorganisms. More specifically, UU was detected in four toilet bowls, MH in three and CT in one. UU survived on the rim of the toilet for up to 2 hours. Tremayne (2009) also reported that there was one case in the medical literature of a man contracting gonorrhoea following the use of an inflatable doll. I tracked down the original case study (Kleist and Moi, 1993):

> "The skipper of a trawler, who had been 3 months at sea, sought advice for urethral discharge. His symptoms had lasted for 2 weeks. A urethral smear showed typical intracellular gram-negative diplococci, and a culture was positive for [gonorrhea]. There had been no woman on board the trawler; he denied homosexual contacts; and there was no doubt that the onset of the symptoms was more than 2 months after leaving the port. A few days before onset of his symptoms, [the skipper] had roused the engineer in his cabin during the night because of engine trouble. After the engineer had left his cabin the skipper found an inflatable doll with an artificial vagina in his bed, and he was tempted to have 'intercourse' with the doll … The engineer was examined, and was found to have gonorrhea. He had observed a mild urethral discharge since they left port … He admitted to having ejaculated into the 'vagina' of the doll just before the skipper called him, without washing the doll afterwards."

Other researchers have noted that gonorrhoeal cells can survive on various materials stored at room temperature. Srivastava (1980) reported that live gonorrhoea cells can survive up to 3 days on both hard and soft materials. As a result of this and other evidence, Tremayne (2009) speculated:

> "It is possible that those who satisfy their used condom fetish are placing themselves at risk. It is conceivable that STIs could be transmitted by the act of masturbating, ingesting or inserting the contents into the anus. At some point, this could mean that sexual health professionals could be meeting men presenting with STIs without the implied sexual contact."

As far as I can ascertain, no research has been conducted on used condom fetishes and there are no statistics on how prevalent such practices are, but I would expect them to be relatively rare. There are certainly online accounts suggesting that there are people who engage in imbibing the contents of used condoms. Feel free to check out such online accounts, but once again – be warned, you may find the content distasteful (no pun intended). Other anecdotal cases I came across online suggest that heterosexual females may sometimes have an attraction for such behaviour. Although Tremayne's paper raises interesting (theoretical) possibilities as to whether used condom fetishes could result in the spread of an STI, it would appear that, to date, there are no recorded instances of an STI being contracted via a used condom.

Taktak *et al.* (2015a) reported a case study of a 39-year-old man with an "ejaculate fetish". Following a crime in which he molested a 16-year-old male adolescent the man had been arrested by Turkish police. In fact, it turned out the man had already spent 10 years in prison for armed robbery when he was in his twenties and was released from jail when he was 31 years old.

The judicial authorities demanded that the man undergo psychiatric assessment because one of his behaviours was the buying of ejaculate from young men, which he would then smear on his genitals for sexual satisfaction. The act of smearing semen on his body had begun in prison when he would smear semen on body wounds incurred accidentally in prison, which provided (presumably) therapeutic relief (as the prison did not provide medicine or cream for such injuries). Taktak *et al.* also claimed that the act of taking semen from other prisoners and applying it to wounds and sores was commonplace in the prison in which he was incarcerated. Following his release from prison, he continued the habit and "became obsessed with it and he bought semen from different people on a monthly basis and spread it on the genital area." Fifteen days prior to psychiatric assessment, he was accused of molesting a 16-year-old adolescent while trying to buy semen from him. The adolescent was reported as saying:

> "A man held my arm and said that he had a job for me and he would give money if I do that job. I told him if I can do, I would do. He said he would be there [an hour and a half] later, and told me to find him. After he came, he told me that he buys human sperm, and asked me if I give him sperm, which surprised me a lot. Then he took three or four plastic bags out of the pocket of his jacket full of white things. He said these bags are the sperms that he bought from three or four kids. In exchange of sperm, he gave things like money, stereos and televisions."

The adolescent's father found out what had happened to his son and caught the man who wanted his son's semen. The man told the adolescent's father that he wanted the semen to alleviate itchiness. After psychiatric examination by the authors, the man was described as having mildly depressive emotions, natural psychomotor activity, sufficient cognitive function and no delusions and/or hallucinations. He also had a history of alcohol and marijuana abuse, but since leaving prison had stopped abusing these substances. Using the Minnesota Multiphasic Personality Inventory (MMPI), the authors said he had inconsistent behaviour, difficulty in controlling his impulses, was angry and short tempered, displayed antisocial behaviour, was sexually deviant, had obsessive sexual thoughts, was socially isolated and had a negative self-perception. They also claimed that his psychological profile suggested an antisocial or schizoid personality disorder.

Taktak *et al.* noted that the father of the man with the ejaculate fetish had also been in prison on a number of occasions, that his mother and her relatives looked after him and his younger brother and that they had had "a hard life" while growing up. Between the ages of 11 and 12 years he started masturbating regularly (sometimes a few times a day). During early adolescence he began engaging in frotteurism (rubbing his genitals up against other people), particularly on bus journeys. Now, as a man, he claimed he could not masturbate without the use of other people's semen. He began buying other men's semen when he got out of prison ("from 30 young men in exchanges for money") and always carried semen with him wherever he went.

Taktak *et al.* (2015a) also noted that, unlike most other fetishes, the sexualization of semen as a fetish did not occur until he was in prison (i.e., adulthood rather than childhood or adolescence). I am not sure why (based on the evidence in the paper), but they also speculated that the man's semen fetish was used to "overcome low self-esteem and a sense of failure" and that the fetish behaviour "occurred from a trauma caused by the bad attitude of [his] parents at an early age, and [that] such negative experiences contributed to the emergence of fetish behavior." The authors further claimed that:

"He discovered the fetish object to deal with the anger for the negative events he faced when he was in prison for 10 years for armed robbery. Impulse control is likely to be impaired because of the adverse conditions created by the prison."

They also describe the man's semen fetish as a "mental illness". In fact, the paper seems to imply that all fetishes are mental illnesses, which is clearly not the case as most non-normative sex is non-problematic for those engaging in such behaviour. However, by diagnosing the man as having a mental illness it meant that he was not mentally competent enough to stand trial. The authors concluded:

"In our case the number of [victims] is few, but [our patient is] respectively harmless to the victims and not dangerous. He cannot control his urges and behaviors. For [these] kinds of cases, generally, diminished criminal responsibility is decided, but for this case it was decided that he has no criminal responsibility."

Sexsomnia

Over the last 15 years there have been an increasing number of papers published on sexsomnia (a.k.a. "sleep sex"). There have also been a lot of high-profile media cases in which women have claimed that their sexsomnia had ruined their lives or men had been arrested for committing sexual assaults while asleep. Sexsomnia is a condition that is highly prevalent among sleepwalkers. It is where people engage in sexual acts while still asleep, such as masturbating, fondling either themselves or others and oral sex or sexual intercourse with another person.

Sexsomniacs claim they do not recall or remember anything they did while asleep, which raises interesting questions if criminal sexual acts are committed without individuals being aware that they have even done anything wrong. Some in the field have claimed the disorder is relatively common, but often goes unreported because of the shame and embarrassment the condition brings. In addition to sleepwalking, there are other sleep-related disorders that sexsomniacs may suffer from including nightmares, bedwetting and sleep apnoea (abnormal breathing while asleep). Many of these behaviours are known as parasomnias (i.e., sleep disorders that involve abnormal and unnatural movements, behaviours, emotions, perceptions and dreams). They are events that occur intermittently or episodically during the night.

In the first academic paper on sex during sleep Shapiro *et al*. (1996) claimed that having sex during sleep could be conceptualized as a new type of parasomnia. Then, Rosenfeld and Elhajjar (1998) wrote the first paper using the term "sleepsex". They described two case studies of individuals having sex while asleep. The more interesting second case concerned a sleepwalker who committed a sexual assault and used somnambulism as his legal defence. Following this Shapiro *et al*. (2003) published the first paper using the term "sexsomnia".

Unsurprisingly, sexsomniacs are often told by others that they are engaging in sex while asleep. However, for many the disorder may not be problematic, particularly within the confines of a stable romantic relationship. According to Mangan and Reips (2007) some couples embrace sexsomnia describing it as an exciting addition to their normal sex lives. The behaviour may have been going on a long time – sometimes years – before the individual seeks medical help. Despite many people not believing that sexsomnia is a genuine medical condition, the condition has been confirmed by various sleep disorder specialists by video-recording sufferers while they are asleep.

Schenk et al. (2007) reported that bouts of sexsomnia can be triggered by such factors as physical contact with another person in bed (64%), stress (52%), fatigue (41%), alcohol use (14.6%) and drug abuse (4.3%). Sleep deprivation was also identified as a risk factor.

Shapiro et al. (2003) asserted that sexsomnia should be considered a distinct entity in the family of parasomnias since there was evidence of the involvement of specific motor and autonomic activation systems. However, they also made the point that it can be difficult to distinguish between typical sleepwalking and sexsomnia. They claimed that what was unique about the condition was the involvement of a partner who was usually more than just a witness. Anubhav and Bhatia (2011) pointed out the main differences between sleepwalking and sexsomnia:

- Sexsomnia originates in most cases from non-rapid eye movement sleep (whereas sleepwalking usually originates from slow-wave sleep).
- Sexsomnia can occur any time during sleep (whereas sleepwalking usually occurs in the first one third of the night).
- Sexsomnia involves widespread autonomic activation (whereas in sleepwalking autonomic activation is largely limited to cardiorespiratory functions).
- Sexsomnia involves frequent sexual arousal (whereas in sleepwalking sexual arousal is not present).
- Sexsomnia bouts possibly exceed 30 minutes (whereas sleepwalking bouts are usually under 30 minutes).
- Sexsomnia can involve exceptional violence or injurious behaviour (whereas sleepwalking involves occasional violence, injury and self-injury).
- Sexsomnia occurs predominantly in adults (whereas sleepwalking occurs predominantly in children).

These differences do at least suggest that sexsomnia and sleepwalking may be distinct clinical entities. Shapiro et al. (1996) stated that the main features of sexsomnia often include sexual arousal with autonomic activation, such as nocturnal erection, vaginal lubrication, nocturnal emission, wet dreams, sweating and cardiorespiratory response. However, there are some case studies in the literature that do not appear to have shown signs of sexual arousal. Despite these differences, most sleep experts consider sexsomnia to be a variant of sleepwalking as most sexsomniacs also sleepwalk.

Based on a review of all published case studies at the time, Andersen et al. (2007) asserted that sleepsex somnambulism is a predominantly male disorder, but that the basis for male predominance in sexsomnia is not known. They further reported that females almost exclusively engage in masturbation and sexual vocalizations, whereas males commonly engage in sexual fondling and sexual intercourse with females.

Mangan and Reips (2007) conducted an online survey of visitors to the Sleepsex.org website run by the principal author. Data were collected over a 3-month period and generated 226 responses. Up until their 2007 study only seven academic papers had been published and only 30 sexsomniacs had been surveyed (the largest sample size being 11 people, 6 of whom were reported in a previous paper by the same authors). Unfortunately, the focus of the paper was on how the internet can be used to collect data on little-studied groups and as such presented very few findings. They noted that adult sexsomniacs sometimes come into contact with minors (in this survey 6%) and that the legal implications of reporting this are serious.

Trajanovic *et al.* (2007) used the same dataset from the Sleepsex.org website to show that females accounted for almost one third of the sample (31%) and that the mean age of the total sample was just over 30 years. The participants typically reported multiple sexsomnia episodes that were usually triggered by body contact, stress and fatigue. A small number of participants reported that their sexsomniac behaviour had led to police and legal intervention (8.6% males and 3% females), some of which had involved minors (6% of the total sample). The authors claimed the study confirmed previous anecdotal evidence about the gender and age distribution, the trigger factors and medicolegal aspects of sexsomnia.

Mangan (2004) examined first-person reports of individuals' experiences of sexsomnia. Qualitative analysis of 121 sexsomniacs resulted in six distinct themes: (i) fear and a lack of emotional intimacy; (ii) guilt and confusion; (iii) a sense of repulsion and feelings of sexual abandonment; (iv) shame, disappointment and frustration; (v) annoyance and suspicion; and (vi) embarrassment and a sense of self-incrimination. Mangan claimed his results suggested that sexsomnia could elicit negative emotions and cognitions that may become a source of personal and relational distress.

Klein and Houlihan (2010) examined relationship and sexual satisfaction, sexual functioning and sexual desire among 32 sexsomniacs who were recruited online. Compared with controls, sexsomniacs reported lower levels of sexual satisfaction, lower levels of relationship satisfaction and similar levels of sexual desire. They also reported that more frequent incidence of sexsomnia resulted in lower sexual satisfaction. However, frequency was not found to impact on the level of sexual desire or relationship satisfaction. Four fifths of the sexsomniacs (81%) also reported at least one sexual problem.

Sexual calligraphy fetishes (*oshouji*)

I have more than a passing professional interest in Japanese sexual culture. For instance, throughout this book I make reference to various Japanese sexual practices and sex-related topics including *tamakeri* (i.e., the masochistic practice of getting sexual pleasure and arousal from being kicked in the testicles), *hentai* (i.e., Japanese hardcore *Manga* cartoon pornography), *shokushu goukan* (i.e., tentacle rape), *nyotaimori* (i.e., eating a variety of foods or a whole meal off somebody's naked body), *omorashi* (i.e., deriving sexual pleasure from having a full bladder or a sexual attraction to someone else experiencing the discomfort of a full bladder) and *burusera* (i.e., Japanese shops that sell amongst other things soiled female undergarments and fetishist school uniforms). There are also some sexually paraphilic behaviours that have their own names within Japanese sexual culture, such as *chikan* ("frotteurism").

While reading an online article on "[Ten] sex fetishes you won't believe exist", I spotted one on the list that I had not written about before: *oshouji*. In fact, not only had I not written about *oshouji*, I had never even heard of it before. *Oshouji* is a calligraphy fetish (calligraphy being the art of producing decorative handwriting or lettering with a pen or brush). *Oshouji* specifically involves calligraphy where the decorative writing is done on a person's (usually naked) body. According to many online websites, all of which basically use the same definition, *oshouji* is "an ancient tradition and refers to the writing of degrading words in calligraphy on your partner [and is] one of the more artistic fetishes Japan has to offer." As sex blog writer Coco La More noted:

> "I am intrigued. Such rich beauty and absolute pleasure. The artistic passion the calligrapher must be feeling. I can just imagine the intense emotion felt by both. I will be adding this one to my list."

According to the Exapamicron website *oshouji* dates back to the Edo Period of feudal Japan (a.k.a. "the Tokugawa Period"). The Edo Period was the period between 1603 and 1868 in the history of Japan. Like other Edo forms of eroticism, such as *shunga* (a Japanese term for erotic art), *oshouji* is considered traditional, rich and decadent. The website also claimed *oshouji* is "not a fetish in the sense that the painted person becomes aroused by the paint, it's more about the thrill of degrading someone."

As far as I am aware, no academic writing has been done or research undertaken on the topic. *Oshouji* (if it really exists) appears to be a much less prevalent activity than some of the other Japanese sexual practices I have written about, although in the absence of any research papers on most forms of Japanese sexual subculture, no-one can be really sure how widespread any of these activities are.

Sexual cannibalism

In this entry I examine cannibalism among humans. I say "among humans" because sexual cannibalism is quite common among some arachnid and insect species. As Love (2001) noted, sexual cannibalism is known to occur in some types of spider, praying mantis, scorpion, cricket, grasshopper and fly. Among humans, sexual cannibalism is extremely rare and most of those who engage in cannibalistic acts for sexual purposes are generally considered sociopaths.

Of course, cannibalism for non-sexual purposes (a.k.a. "anthropophagy") has long been known among certain tribes and cultures. Throughout history, cannibalism has been practised in many forms across Asia, Australia, Europe and the Americas. Though rare today, it is still believed to be practised on a few remote islands of Asia and Australasia. Cannibalism can be classed as either endocannibalism (i.e., consumption of another human being from within the same group or community) or exocannibalism (i.e., consumption of another human being from outside the group or community). Some acts of endocannibalism are actually acts of necro-cannibalism (a.k.a. "necrophagy"; i.e., the eating of flesh from dead humans) in which dead people's body parts are eaten either as part of the grieving process as a way of guiding the souls of the dead into the bodies of the living and/or as a way of imbibing the dead person's "life force" or more specific individual characteristics. Such endocannibalistic practices were common among specific tribes in New Guinea, which led to the prion disease kuru. However, it is known that many males among such tribes would not consume females for fear of emasculation. Exocannibalistic acts were most often carried out as part of a celebration victory after battles with rival tribes.

Something I would call "sexual autophagy" refers to the eating of one's own flesh for sexual pleasure. I am basing this subtype on an entry I came across in Love (2001) relating to a case study reported by von Krafft-Ebing (1886):

> "Krafft-Ebing recorded the case of a man who at 13 [years of age] became infatuated with a young white-skinned girl. However, instead of desiring intercourse, he was overwhelmed by the urge to bite off a piece of her flesh and eat it. He began stalking women, and for years he carried a pair of scissors with him. He was never successful in accosting a woman, but when he came close he would cut off and eat a piece of his own skin instead. This act produced an immediate orgasm for him."

This account seems to be confirmed by some online articles on sexual cannibalism claiming that cannibals feel a sense of euphoria and/or intense sexual stimulation when consuming human flesh. All of these online accounts cite the same article by Clara Bruce ("Chew on This: You're What's for Dinner"). However, the article is actually fake news. Those citing Bruce's article claimed cannibals compare eating human flesh with having an orgasm and that eating human flesh causes an out-of-body experience with effects comparable with taking the drug mescaline. In another publication that I have failed to track down (and which again may be a fake story), the following snippet appears on at least 20 websites with articles on sexual cannibalism:

> "Lesley Hensel, author of 'Cannibalism as a Sexual Disorder' [says] eating human flesh can cause an increase in levels of vitamin A and amino acids, which can cause a chemical effect on the blood and in the brain. This chemical reaction could possibly lead to the altered states that some cannibals have claimed to have experienced. However, this theory has not been substantiated by scientific evidence."

There is almost nothing written from an academic or clinical perspective about gynophagia. In fact, when I typed in "gynophagia" only one reference turned up. That was Herrick (1892), which only mentioned gynophagia in passing. If you really want to find out what gynophagia disciples are into, I suggest you check out the Carnal Consummations fetish website. I have already warned you about the explicit nature of such websites.

Sexual urtication (masochism)

Earlier in this book I looked at the use of bee stings as a means for men to increase the size of their penises. It was while researching that issue that I came across another sting-related sexual practice called "urtication". Although there are numerous scientific papers on urtication, particularly relating to the physiology of nettle stings, the treatment of nettle stings and medical uses, such as the treatment of joint and back pain (Randall *et al.*, 1999), I was unable to locate a single academic paper on the sexual use of stinging nettles. If you really are interested in learning more about the use of stinging nettles in BDSM practices from a practical rather than an academic point of view, then check out the FAQ page of the Sado-Botany website.

Siderodromophilia

> "[On] February 27th [2012], a man surnamed Cai was taken to court after being arrested by railway police for renting a train lounge car to hold a sex party, with the police preliminarily charging him with violating public decency. [On] February 23rd, Taiwanese [Director of Public Prosecutions] Ye Yijin revealed that someone had booked a [railway] lounge car to hold a '1 woman 18 men' group sex orgy." (Fauna, 2012)

This news item got me wondering what academic and/or clinical research has been done relating to sexual arousal from trains and/or sexual activity in trains. I examined the relationship between sex and cars in entries on objectum sexuality, mechanophilia and symphorophilia, as well as that between sex and aeroplanes in the entry on acrophilia, but train sex had not been on my fetishistic radar until I read the Taiwan train orgy story. I then found out that there is a paraphilia solely relating to trains.

There are certainly objectophiles who claim to have emotional and sexual relationships with trains. The most infamous case was that of Joachim A. from Germany who claimed to have had a longstanding "steady relationship" with a steam locomotive outlined in an article in *Der Spiegel* (Thadeusz, 2007). The article claimed Joachim A. had "been pretty faithful to his steam locomotive recently" and that he had recognized and accepted his objectum sexuality inclination just prior to his teenage years. He once fell "head over heels" in love with a Hammond organ and had "an emotionally and physically very complex and deep relationship which lasted for years." The article went on to say that:

> "Since he is particularly aroused by the inner workings of technical objects, repair jobs have often led to infidelity in the past. 'A love affair could very well begin with a broken radiator,' the now-monogamous lover says, remembering how his earlier affairs began. Joachim gradually realized that 'you can reveal yourself to an object partner in an intimate way, in a way that you would never reveal yourself to any other person.' That includes the desire to 'experience sexuality together'."

Any Freudians reading this will no doubt be aware that, according to Sigmund Freud, the train would be analogous to the male penis. I do not believe any of this myself, but it would be remiss of me not to mention it. In a short online article about railways Christian Hubert also makes reference to Freud and noted that:

> "Both Freud and Karl Abraham indicated the connection between mechanical agitation and sexual arousal in the train. This joy found its repressed counterpart in the fear experienced by neurotics in the face of accelerating or uncontrolled motion as the fear of their own sexuality going out of control."

After reading this I decided to try and track down (no pun intended) the original source and appear to have found it. Freud (1962) devoted a whole section to what he termed "mechanical excitation". However, after searching all the usual academic databases I did not manage to locate a single paper that has examined siderodromophilia. Maybe this is because the definition is so ill-defined and/or has little academic or clinical relevance.

Sitophilia

There has long been an association between eating and sexual behaviour on many different levels. Eating and sex are both basic human needs and sometimes interact more directly. Many would also agree that eating in and of itself can be a sensual activity. There are also some foods that are considered to be aphrodisiacs, such as oysters and chocolate. They are considered to have aphrodisiac properties, even though there is a lack of empirical evidence. The important factor is that if people believe the food in question has such arousing properties, then there is likely to be some kind of placebo effect.

In this book I have already looked at feederism in which sexual arousal and gratification is stimulated through a person gaining body fat. Later in this book I examine vorarephilia in which people are sexually aroused by the idea of being eaten, eating another person or observing such a process for sexual gratification. Another eating-related sexual behaviour is sitophilia in which the individual has an erotic attraction to and derives sexual arousal from food. Sitophilia can also include sexual arousal caused by erotic situations involving food that may comprise many different types of activity and involve those who:

- Eat a particular foodstuff off the body of another (e.g., licking chocolate mousse off the breasts of a naked partner).
- Eat a variety of foods or a whole meal off somebody's naked body (such as the Japanese practice of *nyotaimori*).
- Use a foodstuff to enhance a particular sexual act (e.g., sucking on a lime before engaging in oral sex to swell the taste buds and create more sensitivity when licking genital tissue). This could also technically involve the use of a foodstuff to enhance genital lubrication, such as olive oil.
- Use food as a method of control and/or flagellation in sadomasochistic activity (e.g., throwing oranges at a partner's buttocks as a form of sexual humiliation or punishment). A dominant partner can also choose to control a submissive partner's eating habits and food intake as a regular part of their sex play. Some dominant individuals will restrain their submissive partners' hands and order them to eat from a dish on the floor. This can be a highly sexually charged situation for those into erotic humiliation.

- Use food as a masturbatory aid. This may include males hollowing out foodstuffs, such as a pumpkin into which they ejaculate, and females using phallus-shaped foods as a penis substitute, such as cucumbers.
- Drink a body fluid, such as semen, after it has been blended into other foods (e.g., mashed potato) following masturbation.
- Drink body fluids as part of another drink (e.g., adding ice cubes made of semen to a piña colada where the saltiness of the semen counteracts the sweetness of the pineapple).
- Use food to enhance sexual intercourse for both partners, such as inserting strawberries into the vagina before intercourse or placing a slit plum over an erect penis. Such activities add volume and pressure to the sexual act.
- Use food to aid sexual stimulation and erotic pleasure, such as inserting grapes into the rectum. Variations of such activities include inserting particular foodstuffs, such as ginger into the rectum (a.k.a. "figging"). Ginger has also been documented as being inserted into the vagina and urethral opening.

There are also various subtypes of sitophilia, such as botulinonia in which sausages are used sexually. Similarly, those who use foods as proxies for dildos, such as cucumbers, aubergines, carved-out melons and butternut squash, may also qualify as sitophiles. I have yet to read a single academic or clinical paper that has been published on the topic, although there is a lot of online activity surrounding those who get sexually aroused by food.

One of the strangest sitophile stories I have read concerns the case of the "Swiss Cheese Pervert". In the run-up to Christmas 2013 a chubby man estimated to be in his forties was driving around the Mayfair district of Philadelphia, USA and exposing his genitals to a number of women while seated in his sedan. However, this was no ordinary case of exhibitionism. As the *Fortean Times* (2014) reported:

> "He would then dangle a large slice of Swiss cheese over his penis and offer to pay the women to perform sexual acts on him using the snack. At least two other women received messages on [the] OKCupid [online dating website] they believed were from the same man, describing how being unpopular with women drove him to have sex with cheese. He offered to pay $50 for a woman to pleasure him with a slice. The city's police suspect[ed] 41-year-old Chris Pagano since he was arrested in 2006 and 2009 for allegedly propositioning women with Swiss cheese on the streets of Norristown, Philadelphia. Pagano claimed that the latest incidents had nothing to do with him – but the picture he used on Facebook was the same as the one on the OKCupid profile message sent to a woman asking her to indulge his cheese craving."

Pagano's previous arrests were well documented in the local Philadelphia press and one journalist (Fiorello, 2014a, b) wrote a number of stories about Pagano's sexual exploits. In one of his stories he obtained the court documents relating to arrests in 2006 and 2009, and one extract, with the woman's name removed to protect her identity, read that:

> "[The woman] told police that at approximately 0030 hours she was walking home from a store, the male approached her from behind and asked her a question. The male removed a large block of cheese from his pocket and told [the woman] that he would pay her $20 to rub the Swiss cheese on his penis. [The woman] became alarmed and fled on foot toward her residence. The male offered [the woman] more money as she fled the area. [The woman] described the male as white, balding, and weighing over 300 pounds."

Following reports in the local press, in late 2013 a woman Gabby Chest telephoned the police saying that she had got an email on the OKCupid website from a "really strange guy" fitting the description of Pagano, who in his message wrote that he was "looking for someone to perform masturbation on him with cheese." In the online message to Ms Chest the man admitted that he had great difficulty in initiating relationships with women because of his weight problem. This, he claimed, led to his cheese fetish, which helped him deal with his sexual urges.

One arguable subtype of sitophilia relates to individuals who have fruit fetishes and/or specifically use fruit as part of their day-to-day sexual activity. Fruit fetishism also has overlapping behavioural and psychological characteristics with other fetishes that I have written about previously including "wet and messy" fetishism and *nyotaimori* (i.e., eating a variety of foods or a whole meal off somebody's naked body). Almost every article about fruit fetishes on the internet mentions the fact that some types of fruit, most notably bananas, can be used as a dildo substitute for men and women, used anally and vaginally, respectively.

As you can probably guess, there is almost nothing in the academic literature on fruit fetishism. However, there are well over 100 papers on the topic of foreign bodies that have been removed from rectums by doctors (as noted in an earlier entry, no pun intended). Many papers have reported the removal of fruit stuck in rectums, such as bananas and apples. Other papers report cucumbers as rectal foreign bodies and report them as vegetables, but cucumbers are actually fruits.

Fruit fetishism and/or engaging in sexual practices with fruit are probably more widespread than might be initially imagined, but on the positive side there appear to be few problems from a psychological perspective. However, as the medical literature has frequently reported, help is only sought when fruit used in sexual practices, most commonly masturbation, gets stuck inside a sitophile's rectal passage.

Sneezing fetishes

There are reports in the medical and psychological literature dating back to the 1890s of sexually induced sneezing in both men and women. The phenomenon is characterized by sneezing during sexual arousal and/or orgasm. Individuals in such cases sneeze as a direct result of sexual thoughts, arousal, intercourse and/or orgasm. Furthermore, sneezing may occur at any point during sex and, most significantly, occurs independently of any external nasal stimuli or allergens.

The first verified report of the phenomenon is thought to be Mackenzie (1898). A few years later Gould and Pyle (1901) also referred to the condition. I managed to track down the original quote about a man:

"… who, when prompted to indulge in sexual intercourse, was immediately prior to the act seized with a fit of sneezing. Even the thought of sexual pleasure with a female was sufficient to provoke this peculiar idiosyncrasy."

Based on a paper submitted to the American Medical Association, Jeffrey Wald, a specialist in asthma and allergies, reported in the US newspaper *Pittsburgh Post-Gazette* (1988) the case of an American middle-aged man who continuously sneezed following sex. He attributed the sneezing to "vasomotor rhinitis", a condition in which the nasal passages are chronically inflamed and characterized by hyperactive or imbalanced control of central nervous system responses. Similarly, Bhutta and Maxwell (2008) cited a case from 1972 involving a 69-year-old man who suffered severe bouts of sneezing after orgasm or whenever he thought of sex.

Bhutta and Maxwell (2008) further noted that both the men and women in their study used online forums to seek out help or explanations for the phenomenon they experienced. Such people often feel embarrassed about bringing up the matter with the medical profession and prefer to seek help and advice anonymously. The authors further reported that these online data showed: (i) 3 people who claimed they always sneezed after orgasm and (ii) 17 people who said they sneezed immediately when they thought about sex. Bhutta and Maxwell speculated that the link between sex, orgasm and sneezing is most likely caused by a fault in the autonomic nervous system (i.e., the part of the nervous system that is involved with heart rate, blood flow and digestion). They argued that the nerves that control breathing, blood pressure, pupil construction, sneezing and digestion run close to each other in the brain stem. They further speculated that light-sensitive sneezing and sex-related sneezing occur when these signals become "muddled". One of the authors (Bhutta) told the BBC in an interview:

> "[The relationship between orgasm and sneezing] certainly seems odd, but I think this reflex demonstrates evolutionary relics in the wiring of a part of the nervous system called the autonomic nervous system. This is the part beyond our control, and which controls things like our heart rate and the amount of light let in by our pupils. Sometimes the signals in this system get crossed, and I think this may be why some people sneeze when they think about sex."

Dr Bhutta also told the BBC that embarrassment or social inhibition may have prevented others from admitting the problem to the medical or psychological community. Another potential explanation may relate to the fact that, like the genitalia, the nose also has vascular (erectile) tissue that has the capacity to become engorged during sexual arousal and trigger a sneeze. Others have noted the ejaculatory-like qualities of the sneeze, such as 1980s' television "sexpert" Dr Ruth (Westheimer) who observed that "an orgasm is just a reflex, like a sneeze."

On a related issue, there is also a condition coined "honeymoon rhinitis" in which men and women experience nasal irritation and inflammation of the mucous membrane inside the nose during sex. Monteseirin *et al.* (2001) reported a study of 23 allergy sufferers (9 women and 14 men) all of whom had experienced sneezing, rhinorrhoea and nasal obstruction immediately after (but never before or during) sexual intercourse lasting for approximately 5–15 minutes. The research team also got all 23 participants to climb two flights of stairs on three separate occasions to equate the energy expenditure used during sex, but none of them suffered any rhinitis following the task. The exact mechanism by which sex initiates and/or facilitates honeymoon rhinitis is not known. However, the authors speculated that emotional excitement and anxiety may be the trigger factors for post-sex rhinitis rather than exertion.

For most people sneezing is just a common everyday biological act. However, for some a sneeze appears to be much more and something sexual. If you think sneezing fetishism is rare, then just type in "sneeze fetish" to an online search engine and see what you get. There are loads of dedicated websites on the sexual and sensual aspects of sneezing (e.g., Sneeze Fetish, Sneezing Fetish Online).

Somnophilia

Somnophilia is a paraphilia in which sexual arousal is derived from intruding on, caressing and/or fondling someone, typically a stranger, while they are asleep without force or violence. However, some definitions of somnophilia, while all connected with sleep, sometimes slightly differ. For instance, some definitions of somnophilia say that it refers to actually having sexual intercourse with a sleeping partner (rather than just touching someone sexually while she is asleep). Another definition I came across says that somnophilia also includes having sex (raping) with someone while she is unconscious. This latter variation may have come about as a consequence of the increased use of drugs, such as rohypnol (a.k.a. "roofies") that have been implicated in sexual offences like date rape.

Some signs or symptoms that may point to somnophilia include recurring thoughts regarding unconscious or sleeping individuals and feeling sexual urges when in contact with or in the proximity of such people. While there is speculation about the treatment (e.g., hypnosis, behavioural therapy and 12-step programmes), it is not valid unless the behaviour becomes destructive, problematic, involves sexually criminal activity and becomes a legal issue.

Empirically, very little is known about somnophilia and, as far as I am aware, there are no data concerning its prevalence, etiology or treatment – not even a single case study. Various sexologists and authors have made reference to it including Money (1990a, b), Butcher (2003) and Flora (2001). Burg (1982) suggested the possibility of a continuum of erotic focus from somnophilia fantasy through to acts involving necrophilia. In fact, sometimes somnophilia has been described as "pseudo-necrophilia" in that both paraphilias involve having sex with a human who is not aware and/or conscious and has not given consent.

Spanking

According to Aggrawal (2009a) "erotic spanking" (a.k.a. "spankophilia") is the practice of spanking another person for the sexual gratification of either or both parties. He also reports that notable "spankophiles" include poet Algernon Swinburne (as repeatedly implied in his poetry) and the philosopher Jean-Jacques Rousseau (as detailed in his autobiography *Confessions*).

Aggrawal reported that many spankophiles make use of a "spanking bench" (a.k.a. "a spanking horse"), a piece of furniture that is used to position the person receiving the spanking (a.k.a. "the spankee"), which may or may not have restraints. Aggrawal also made reference to the 19th-century British dominatrix Mrs Theresa Berkley, someone who Aggrawal claimed became famous for her invention of the Berkley Horse, a multi-functional device that combined a spanking bench with several other sadomasochistic functions.

Most academic research papers, such as Wiederman (2003), report that spanking is part of a much wider range of sadomasochistic activities including binding, gagging, blindfolding, whipping, choking, cutting and piercing. Breslow *et al.* (1985) examined the sexual activities of 182 sadomasochists (130 men, 52 women) and reported that the most preferred sexual activities for both sexes were spanking and involvement in master–slave relationships. A similar finding was reported by Moser and Levitt (1987) who surveyed 225 sadomasochists recruited from a specialist sadomasochism (SM) magazine (178 men and 47 women). They reported the most common SM behaviours were flagellation (spanking and whipping) and bondage (rope, chains, handcuffs, gags) in which 50% to 80% of the participants engaged.

Kahr (2007) reported the results of a survey on adult sexual fantasies of 13,500 British men and women of all sexual orientations. Of these, 18% of the men and 7% of the women had specific spanking fantasies. Spanking may also be associated with other paraphilias. For instance, Arndt (1991) studied a small sample of 21 klismaphiliacs (20 of whom were male). Klismaphilacs are individuals who derive sexual pleasure and arousal from enemas. Of this small sample, 40% reported accompanying paraphilic interests that included mild spanking and other punishments suggestive of sexually masochistic behaviour.

Although empirical evidence suggests that erotic spanking is not particularly prevalent among the general population (at least in terms of engaging in such behaviour regularly), most academic research appears to indicate that erotic spanking is towards the "softer" end of sadomasochistic activities, and that almost all instances of erotic spanking are consensual, enjoyable and non-problematic. Consequently, treatment for the behaviour is rarely sought.

Spectrophilia

Whereas exophilia is a paraphilia in which individuals derive sexual pleasure and arousal from extraterrestrial, robotic, supernatural or other non-human lifeforms, in this entry one of its subtypes is examined in more detail – more specifically, the one in which people derive sexual pleasure and arousal from ghosts and spirits (a.k.a. "spectrophilia"). The only academic reference to spectrophilia I have ever come across is Aggrawal (2009a) who defines it more widely as sexual arousal "from looking at oneself in a mirror; arousal from images in mirrors; coitus with spirits; and sexual attraction to ghosts." However, most online sources note that the paraphilia concerning sexual arousal from mirrors is termed "katoptronophilia". Therefore, this entry only focuses on being sexually aroused by ghosts and spirits.

As is the case with exophilia, online sources claim, unsurprisingly, that the overwhelming majority of spectrophiles never claim to have had sex with a ghost or spirit, but are sexually excited and aroused by the thought of doing so. Therefore, the main sexual outlet for spectrophilia would appear to be masturbation. One website featuring a short synopsis on spectrophilia claimed (without any supporting evidence) that those afflicted with the condition:

> "… leave their windows open so hopefully a ghost just might be floating on by, and suddenly get in the mood to ravage them … For those seeking sexual union with a ghost, however, the only solution is to seek out haunted mansions and hope for the best, or try to coerce the ghost into experiencing the pleasures of the flesh again."

As far as I am aware – and here I agree totally with Stollznow (2011) – there is no scientific (i.e., empirical) evidence of spectrophilia. There have been various interviews with people claiming to have had spectrophilic experiences. However, all such interviews were either undertaken by television documentaries and/or people claiming to be psychics, ghost hunters and/or paranormal investigators. For instance, the *Ghostly Lovers* television programme that first aired on the Travel Channel in February 2011 has featured a number of women who claim to have had sex with ghosts, usually their dead husbands, and talked about all the physical consequences of making love with ghosts including orgasm. Others are totally convinced that ghostly sex is a reality, but, unsurprisingly, these claims come from those who have a vested interest in the topic and who make their living from paranormal phenomena. The people who have claimed to have had sex with ghosts and/or spirits may well totally believe they have experienced supernatural sex. However, just because the person says they experienced something does not mean that they have. They may just think that they have.

Spit fetishes

In this book I have examined many different body substances that have formed the basis of paraphilic and/or fetishistic behaviour. One body fluid that has not really been the subject of scientific research is saliva and how it relates to saliva fetishes and spit fetishes (*New Zealand Herald*, 2007). In fact, the only purely academic reference I could find was Zerubavel (1991) who reported that many Americans seem to find sex "morally repugnant" because the body fluids associated with sex (i.e., saliva and semen) are sticky, a liminal category between solid and liquid.

From my reading on this topic, there appears to be a difference between saliva fetishes and spit fetishes. Saliva fetishes do not really appear to share much in common with spit fetishes since the latter appear to be more a part of sadomasochistic sexual activity. For instance, at the All Experts website (2012) one of the female "experts" Hollie wrote speculatively about spit fetishes in response to one man's question as to what spit fetishes actually involve. Her perspective was clearly from those with an interest in sexual sadism and sexual masochism. She wrote:

"A spit fetish could manifest itself in a number of ways ... either partner could have a fetish to be spat on, usually this is always closely linked to that individual seeking domination from the spitter, making the person being spat on submissive. It may also be part of sexual humiliation and other aspects of BDSM. Or an individual could have the need to spit on someone that would probably make them dominant and to want to control and/or humiliate their partner sexually. Or ... both people could either enjoy to be spat on or to be the spitter ... this could work both ways and simultaneously."

In fact, much of the online literature on spitting fetishes as opposed to saliva fetishes appears to be rooted in BDSM and is usually referred to as "spitting domination". The dominant partner may spit into his submissive partner's face and/or mouth. The submissive partner may also be forced to swallow the liquid spit if her mouth is spat into. Compared with all other paraphilic and fetishistic behaviours concerning sexual arousal to human body fluids, there is significantly less written about saliva and spitting fetishes. Whether academic and/or clinical research is needed is at present debatable.

Squashing fetishism

While researching fat fetishes I came across the practice of "gut flopping". According to the online Urban Dictionary gut flopping is "where a large-bellied individual raises his or her stomach and allows it to drop upon his or her sexual partner in a way that creates a smack sound [and] is an act performed for sexual pleasure." There is little written about it academically (or non-academically for that matter). However, one variant of this that appears to be very popular among a minority of men is "BBW squashing" in which men are squashed by one or more big beautiful women (BBW) for sexual pleasure (a.k.a. "crushing" or "smashing"). One such BBW by the name of Massive Mocha appeared on *Dr. Drew*, a US television show, in October 2011 talking about her experiences as someone who catered for men's fetishes to be sat on and squashed by very large women. Massive Mocha revealed that men ask her to sit on them until they feel they are going to pass out from loss of breath.

According to the Squashing Fetish website there are many variations of the fetish. Heterosexual squashing comprises very obese women squashing smaller, typically thin, men. Homosexual squashing comprises very obese men squashing much smaller men. For some, fantasizing about being squashed may satisfy their sexual fetish. This may include someone weighing anything from 200 pounds to 600 pounds sitting, standing or jumping on the submissive and/or crushing his face, belly and/or chest resulting in the person being squashed squirming. The relationship is all about control and is psychologically similar to the dominant and submissive in sexual sadism and sexual masochism. Being unable to breathe or breathe properly appears to be critical in the fetish and in that sense shares similarities with hypoxyphilia (i.e., autoerotic asphyxiation in which individuals derive sexual arousal and pleasure from restricting their oxygen supply).

Earlier in this book I examined macrophilia (i.e., sexual pleasure and arousal from giants) and crush fetishism (i.e., sexual pleasure and arousal from crushing or being crushed). There seems to be some psychological similarities between BBW squashing and these other paraphilias and fetishes. For instance, some macrophiles date extraordinarily tall women (a.k.a. "Amazons") even if they have to pay for the privilege to do so, such as women like Mikayla Miles who is nearly 7 feet tall in her fetish boots, and 6 feet 4 inches without the boots. She provides private sessions for macrophiles to engage in behaviours, such as trampling, which has a lot of resonance with BBW squashing. Although research has been carried out into both sadomasochistic sexual activity and fat fetishes, there is little on where they intersect. This would certainly be a fruitful area for further empirical investigation.

Sthenolagnia

"We've all gasped with disbelief at the mega-bronzed muscle-bound ladies in those weird bodybuilding competitions, but sthenolagnia is a condition where men find that hugely sexually attractive. These men like to be wrestled, lifted up and even carried around by their big iron-pumping dreamgirls." (Burt, 2007)

Reports of sthenolagnia among both males and females of all sexual orientations date back to the 1800s. The term "sthenolagnia" is thought to have been first coined by Hirschfeld (1948). The term is not in popular usage and most contemporary sthenolagniacs define themselves as "muscle worshippers" (itself a sub-branch of the more general "body worshippers"). Love (2001) referred to sthenolagnia and cratolagnia, but only in an entry on wrestling for erotic purposes.

There appear to be different subcategories of sthenolagnia one of which involves men deriving sexual arousal from female muscle growth (FMG), particularly bicep growth. They frequent places where female bodybuilders are found, such as gyms, healthclubs and bodybuilding tournaments. However, some of this may be based in fantasy rather than actuality, particularly when it relates to aspects of macrophilia and transformation fetishes. For instance, *Marvel Comics* character "She-Hulk" is a popular representation of FMG fantasy and can be found on websites, such as the Female Muscle Factory. FMG can also be related to other specific fetishes, such as those surrounding breast expansion fetishism. Although there is little in the way of academic research on the topic, many muscle worshippers appear to be sexually aroused by equalization or reversal of the stereotypical power relationship among heterosexual couples.

Muscle worshippers can derive sexual arousal from simply touching someone with highly visible muscles (a.k.a. "a dominator"), typically a fitness instructor, a bodybuilder or a wrestler. The various tactile activities that can facilitate sexual pleasure include rubbing, massaging, kissing, licking and/or all manner of activities, such as lifting, carrying and engaging in wrestling moves. Muscle worshippers themselves are typically (but not always) much smaller and skinnier than the dominator. According to Davis and Lubovich (2008) individuals conforming to this stereotype are called "schmoos" or men who worship women's muscles.

This is another in the long list of paraphilic and fetishistic behaviours that we know little about empirically. Given the lack of references in the clinical literature it would appear that treatment is not generally sought and that such people live happily with their fetish.

Stigmatophilia

Another little-researched paraphilia is stigmatophilia. This refers to individuals who derive sexual pleasure and arousal from a partner who is marked in some way. Traditional definitions of stigmatophilia referred to such individuals being sexually aroused by scarring, but more recent formulations of stigmatophilia include those who are sexually aroused by tattoos and piercings (i.e., body modifications, especially relating to the genitals and/or nipples). According to Money (1984) stigmatophilia can also refer to the reciprocal condition where the sexual focus is the person who has the scars, tattoos and/or piercings. Other later definitions claim "a person with this fetish [a stigmatophile] is sexually aroused by body piercing and tattooing but not ear piercing" (Gay Slang Dictionary).

Caliendo *et al.* (2005), in their research on intimate body piercings, surveyed a convenience sample of intimately pierced individuals (63 women and 83 men) across 29 US states in which participants reported having nipple piercings (43%), genital piercings (25%) or both (32%). Compared with the general US population, those with sexual piercings were significantly younger, less ethnically diverse, better educated, less likely to be married, more often homosexual or bisexual and initiated sexual activity at a younger age. Among this sample the average age for first nipple piercing was 25 years and for genital piercing it was 27 years. Their reasons for getting the piercings were uniqueness, self-expression and sexual expression.

Arguably, one of the best papers on motivations underlying tattooing and body piercing is Wohlrab *et al.* (2007). They established 10 broad motivational categories of the motivations for getting tattooed and body pierced. These were: (i) beauty, art and fashion, (ii) individuality, (iii) personal narratives, (iv) physical endurance, (v) group affiliations and commitment, (vi) resistance, (vii) spirituality and cultural tradition, (viii) addiction, (ix) sexual motivations and (x) no specific reasons, such as doing it on impulse or doing it while intoxicated. In relation to sexual motivations, the authors noted:

> "Nipple and genital piercings are quite common and serve as decoration, but also for direct sexual stimulation. Expressing sexual affections or emphasizing their own sexuality through tattooing and body piercing are also common motivations."

Although research has been undertaken in recent years, it does not really make specific reference to stigmatophilia because it tends to concentrate on specific types of self-inflicted body modification, particularly tattooing and body piercing, rather than on those who have been left with wounds inflicted by third parties (e.g., facial scarring).

Strabismusophilia

The website Divine Caroline (2012) provided a list of 18 fetishes, 17 of which I knew about. The one that I had little awareness of was "cross-eyed fetishism", although I was aware of "oculophilia" in which individuals are sexually aroused by eyes. If such a fetish exists, then I would name it "strabismusophilia" after the medical condition in which a patient's eyes are not aligned.

Having already written on eye fetishes more generally earlier in this book, I would argue that strabismusophilia is a subtype of oculophilia because the condition manifests itself in a desire for actual physical contact and interaction with the eye, albeit a very particular type of eye. The website Page Pulp (2014), in an article about the sexual fetishes of famous authors, alleged that F. Scott Fitzgerald had a foot fetish, James Joyce (Joyce, 1975) had a fart fetish, Lord Byron was a sex addict, the Marquis de Sade had a fetish for "anything and everything" (the most notable being sadomasochism) and the philosopher René Descartes had a cross-eye fetish. Descartes' sexual fetish for cross-eyed women is well documented (von Krafft-Ebing, 1886). Descartes himself wrote that:

"As a child I was in love with a girl of my own age, who was slightly cross-eyed. The imprint made on my brain by the wayward eyes became so mingled with whatever else had aroused in me the feeling of love that for years afterwards, when I saw a cross-eyed woman, I was more prone to love her than any other, simply for that flaw ... The impression made in my brain when I looked at her wandering eyes was joined so much to that which also occurred when the passion of love moved me, that for a long time afterward, in seeing cross-eyed women, I felt more inclined to love them than others, simply because they had that defect; and I did not know that was the reason."

Voorhoeve *et al.* (2011) also discussed Descartes' passion for cross-eyed women. The authors reported the story of Queen Christina of Sweden asking Descartes what causes us to "love one person rather than another before we know their merit." According to Voorhoeve *et al.*:

"Descartes replied that when we experience a strong sensation, this causes the brain to crease like a piece of paper. And when the stimulus stops, the brain uncreases, but it stays ready to be creased again in the same way. And when a similar stimulus is presented, then we get the same response, because the brain is ready to crease again. And what did he mean by all this? Well, he gave an example. He said that all his life he had had a fetish for cross-eyed women. Whenever he came across a cross-eyed woman, desire would enflame him. And he figured out ... after introspection, that this was because his brain had been strongly creased by his first childhood love, who was cross-eyed."

This classical conditioning-type explanation was also alluded to by Ben-Zeév (2011). The article seeks an answer to the question "Why did Descartes love cross-eyed women?" Ben-Zeév responded:

"It would appear that when Descartes fell in love with the young girl, he loved her whole Gestalt [configuration], which included other characteristics, but her crossed eyes were the most unique. This feature of the girl distinguished her from most other girls. It is as if he subconsciously thought that every woman who shared that distinctive feature would have the other positive characteristics of the girl with whom he had originally fallen in love and would therefore generate the same profound love. This attitude makes him perceive these women as beautiful ... However, the fact that the girl he fell in love with had the distinctive feature of crossed eyes did not mean that her

other characteristics would be shared by other women who have the same feature. In fact, however, this mistaken association set off a feeling of love when he encountered this characteristic in other women ... It is a kind of Pavlovian response which makes us more likely to love this person."

From my own research I have come to the conclusion that cross-eyed fetishism (a.k.a. "strabismusophilia", to give it my term) probably exists, but is very rare with an incredibly low prevalence rate among the general population. It may be a subtype of both oculophilia and teratophilia (sexual arousal towards ugly people), but further research is needed to confirm such a speculation.

Stuck fetishism

Another one of the strangest fetishes that I have come across is "stuck fetishism" in which individuals derive sexual pleasure and arousal from other individuals and/or themselves being immobilized in some way in a "sticky situation" (either literally or metaphorically). It was while I was researching three other paraphilias – claustrophilia (deriving sexual arousal from being confined in small places), taphephilia (deriving arousal from being buried alive) and wamming/sploshing (deriving sexual arousal from wet and/or messy [WAM] situations) – that I first encountered online references to stuck fetishes. According to Nation Master (2013d) not only does "stuck fetishism" involve immobilization, but sexual arousal is also gained from the individual struggling to escape from the situation. There may be elements of both sexual sadism (and domination) and sexual masochism (bondage and submission) in these scenarios, but the primary focus of the arousal is actually being stuck and/or trapped.

Unsurprisingly, there is no scientific research on the topic of stuck fetishism, so the claims made online cannot be verified. Nevertheless, both assertions have good face validity and could be argued to be common sense based on what we know about other similar fetishes. Therefore, the fetish does appear to exist as evidenced by there being dedicated sites, such as the Stuck Head First website, the Stuck and Struggle website and the Sticky Review website. There are also online discussion groups on topics like "glue bondage" at websites, such as the Alt Bondage Narkive and The Bound Forum. Given the medical dangers inherent in some of the scenarios, such as playing with superglue or cement, the most likely way for case studies to enter the academic literature will be in the form of medical papers reporting on cases where something untoward and/or life threatening has happened.

Tamakeri (masochism)

> "My boyfriend keeps asking me to kick him in his balls as hard as I can, and he says he's 'into it'. I love my boyfriend and I will do anything that makes him happy. He would do the same for me too, but is this normal?"

I came across this opening quote while doing some research on sexual masochism. I thought nothing of it at the time, except thinking it was a fairly painful way to get your sexual kicks – no pun intended. However, I have since come across a few online articles all noting that this specific type of masochistic practice is known as *tamakeri* in Japanese culture. The first time I came across it was in an online article called "Ten fetishes and paraphilias" (A-Proper-Blog, 2010) The unnamed author of the article wrote that:

> "The name [tamakeri] translates from the Japanese as 'ball kicking', and that tells you all you need to know, really. It's a paraphilia, and also a genre of pornography involving women abusing men by their testicles, marketed to masochistic men excited by the prospect."

A number of online sites, such as the Kicked in the Groin website, confirm that *tamakeri* is a practice in which men receive kicks in the testicles for sexual pleasure. It also appears in Japanese films, such as the horror film *Horny House of Horror*. The practice was also referred to in two books I have read, one of which (Twinn, 2007) describes *tamakeri* as "another Japanese contribution to sexual culture: the desire to watch a woman kick a man in the testicles, which has a healthy porn industry to cater to it." The other was Aggrawal (2009a) who described *tamakeri* as "arousal when a female kicks a man in the testicles; a variant of masochism, prevalent in Japan." As you can guess from this very brief overview, I did not manage to locate a single academic paper on the topic of *tamakeri* – not even a passing reference. I can only conclude that if the practice exists, then it would appear to be relatively rare.

Telephone scatologia

Telephone scatophilia (a.k.a. "scatologia" and "telephonicophilia") is a paraphilia that comprises overt or covert repetitive telephone calls with sexual and/or obscene content to an unsuspecting victim (Kaur and Pankaj, 2009). The behaviour is also known to have a high association with other paraphilic disorders, such as voyeurism and exhibitionism. Money (1986) defines it as "deception and ruse in luring or threatening a telephone respondent, known or unknown, into listening to, and making personally explicit conversation of a sexual nature." It is also worth noting, as with some other paraphilias, such as exhibitionism and voyeurism, it is not the act itself that is deviant, but the very fact it involves a non-consenting victim makes it an interpersonal transgression.

Telephone scatophilia (scatolagnia) was listed as "other specified paraphilic disorder" (OSPD) in the American Psychiatric Association's (2022) *Diagnostic and Statistical Manual* (DSM-5-TR). Paraphilias listed in the OSPD category are said to occur much less frequently than paraphilias that are individually listed, but it has been noted that telephone scatophilia occurs on a much wider scale and magnitude than other paraphilias, such as necrophilia, zoophilia and klismaphilia in this category. There are certainly surveys suggesting that relatively large numbers of women have received obscene telephone calls, although it is theoretically possible for just one telephone scatophiliac to make hundreds (if not thousands) of telephone calls to different women. Almost all telephone scatophiliacs are male.

The prevalence rate of telephone scatophilia is unknown. One Canadian study reported that 6% of male students and 14% of paid male volunteers admitted to having made obscene phone calls. However, most research relies on case studies or surveys of paraphiliacs. For instance, in a study of 561 non-incarcerated paraphiliacs, Abel *et al.* (1988) reported that 19 men in their sample (3.3%) said they had engaged in telephone scatologia. In another study of 443 non-incarcerated paraphiliacs, Bradford *et al.* (1992) reported that 37 men in their sample (8.3%) had engaged in telephone scatologia. Price *et al.* (2002) examined an outpatient sample of 206 men with paraphilias and paraphilia-related disorders and reported that 20 men in their sample (9.7%) had a lifetime diagnosis of telephone scatolophilia. They further reported that there was a significant comorbidity between telephone scatologia and compulsive masturbation, voyeurism, telephone sex dependence and exhibitionism. Compared with other paraphiliacs, telephone scatophiliacs had a greater number of lifetime paraphilias. Similar findings have also been reported in other studies. Matek (1988) suggested that the methods associated with both telephone scatophilia and paraphilias, such as exhibitionism, demonstrate the person's attempts to express aggression, to exhibit power and control and to gain recognition. However, unlike exhibitionists, telephone scatophiliacs usually want complete anonymity.

Matek (1988) further claimed there was another type of obscene telephone caller: men who ring telephone crisis lines in order to request help from female volunteers, talk about sexual material and masturbate while talking to the female. Matek also reported the most common characterstics of obscene telephone callers were low self-esteem and anger toward women. Other associations reported were brain damage, mental retardation, intoxication and psychosis. According to Hocken and Thorn (2017) those who engage in the activity:

> "… are more commonly heterosexual males, discovered in young adulthood, possess an average or elevated sex drive, have limited social interactions, secondary level

education, have menial jobs and have tried and failed to maintain long-term marital-type relationships ... Perpetrators of obscene phone calls are frequently acquainted with the victim, although the victim may not recognise them at the time of the call or even subsequently."

There are a number of theories as to how telephone scatophilia develops. Freund (1990a, b) claimed that behaviours like telephone scatophilia are caused by "courtship disorders". He proposed normal courtship comprises four phases: (i) location of a partner, (ii) pre-tactile interactions, (iii) tactile interactions and (iv) genital union. Freund also proposed that obscene telephone calling is a disturbance of the second phase of the courtship disorder. Similarly, Money (1986) proposed the "lovemap" theory suggesting that paraphiliac behaviour occurs when an abnormal lovemap develops and interferes with the ability to participate in loving sexual intercourse. In such a model, telephone scatologia is classified as an allurement paraphilia involving the preparatory or courtship phase prior to genital intercourse. Despite these models describing many cases of telephone scatophilia, there is empirical evidence that some obscene telephone callers display normal courtship behaviour.

Tentacle erotica fetishism

Later in this book I examine toonophilia, a paraphilia in which individuals are sexually and/or emotionally attracted to cartoon characters. I should also mention that some toonophiles are very specific in regard to what they find erotic and that one particular subtype of toonophilia involves individuals who find Japanese anime characters particularly erotic. While researching that topic I came across the lecture notes of an unnamed academic (posted by one of his/her students) that I found interesting, although I do not know what the primary sources for the notes were. I am aware that Japanese comics are known as *manga* and that cartoon pornography is highly prevalent inside and outside Japan and is known as *hentai*.

One aspect of *hentai* that I kept coming across was tentacle porn (a.k.a. "tentacle rape"). A number of articles I have read say that *shokushu goukan*, as it is known in Japan, dates back to the 18th century, although the more recent tentacle rape genre is generally attributed to *urotsukidoji*, a type of *manga* created by controversial erotic cartoonist Toshio Maeda who emphasizes the elements of sexual assault. Maeda claimed to have introduced tentacle porn as a way to circumvent Japan's very strict censorship laws. These laws did not allow the depiction of penises, but at the time (i.e., 1986) did not forbid sexual penetration by anything else, such as tentacles or robotic appendages. In an online article on "depraved fetishes that are older than you think," Reed (2010) reported that:

"Whether animated pornography is less 'harmful' than non-animated pornography is something I will leave to others more knowledgeable than me to debate. However, there is clearly a market for hentai more generally, and tentacle porn more specifically as evidenced by those who sell it commercially. The whole area raises interesting moral questions."

Teratophilia

I am sure I will receive some criticism for examining the issue of sex and ugliness, so I apologize in advance if you feel I should not be writing about such things and feel it to be politically incorrect. However, there is a long history of psychological research on attractiveness, which by implication usually means that any findings reported as relating to attractive people would mean the opposite applies to ugly people. I am the first to admit that sexual attractiveness is highly subjective and can depend on many factors including the physiological state of the viewer (therefore the apt pun that "beauty is in the eye of the beer holder").

A number of years ago newspapers in the UK, such as the *Daily Mail* (e.g., Kendall, 2010), reported a story that argued being ugly might actually help in attracting the opposite sex. The story was based on the work of Australian Robert Brooks (a Professor of Evolution at the University of New South Wales) who claimed that having an "unusual appearance" can prove a useful asset in attracting a mate. Brooks was quoted as saying that "ugly individuals can sometimes do better than good-looking ones," although I ought to point out that his research was carried out on animals and not humans. Paul Rainey, a biologist at Oxford University, supported Brooks' view in the *Daily Mail* article, and said that "beauty is in the eye of the beholder. If everyone is going after the most common characteristics, then someone who targets the rare ones, would have an advantage."

This short introduction brings me to what I really wanted to focus on – the paraphilia "teratophilia". There are various subdivisions of teratophilia of which the most researched is arguably acrotomophilia, which refers to people who derive sexual pleasure and arousal from amputees. I would also argue that paraphilias, such as stigmatophilia in which individuals derive sexual pleasure and arousal from a person who is marked (i.e., scarred), in some way would also qualify as a subtype of teratophilia.

Although there is empirical research on both acrotomophilia and stigmatophilia, there is nothing as far as I can tell on teratophilia. There are certainly online forums where individuals have discussed their attraction to ugly people and a quick online search shows there is a fair amount of pornographic material that features physically unusual people suggesting there are people out there who find such things sexually arousing.

If the number of female accounts is to be believed, then it may be an indicator that females are less concerned with sexual attractiveness in a man (i.e., men value attractiveness in women more than women value attractiveness in men). Given the general lack of research in the area this is a topic that is certainly worthy of scientific investigation.

Thigh fetishism

Thigh fetishism might appear a somewhat obvious topic to write on given all the previous body part fetishes I have looked at, such as foot fetishism and shoulder fetishism. However, there is no academic research on the topic and most non-academic articles that I have read tend to concentrate on thigh-boot fetishism rather than thigh fetishism in and of itself. According to the Kinkly website (2015):

> "Thigh fetish refers to a sexual arousal by or sexual interest in thighs. Typically, it is a male interest in female thighs. However, it can apply to a woman's interest in female thighs, a woman's interest in male thighs, or a male's interest in male thighs. Usually the fetishist is attracted to the naked thighs. The thighs don't even need to be extremely sexualized for the fetishist. Often it is the gap between a high boot and edge of skirt, or knee high socks and edge of skirt that arouse the fetishist more than sexualized images of thighs."

The Self-Help Sexuality website adds that "some men have a thigh fetish where they are turned on by the glimpse of a woman's inner thigh or when a woman opens her thighs. Some men enjoy kissing and licking a woman's inner thigh." Both of these descriptions are fairly commonsense and, arguably, do not need empirical research to back up the claims made.

A study by Turnbull *et al.* (2014) is the only piece of empirical research I found referring to thigh sexuality. The authors conducted a survey of 800 participants (mainly British and Sub-Saharan Africans) in an attempt to ascertain which erogenous zones were the most sensitive in males and females. The participants were asked to rate 41 body parts for erogenous intensity on a 10-point scale. Unsurprisingly, the highest rated body parts for sensitivity were the clitoris among women (mean rating 9.17 out of 10) and the penis among men (mean rating 9.0 out of 10). Inner thighs were rated the fourth most erogenous zone by men (mean rating 5.84 out of 10; back of thigh 2.48 out of 10; outer thigh 1.91 out of 10) and the seventh most erogenous zone by women (mean rating 6.7 out of 10; back of thigh 2.6 out of 10; outer thigh 1.96 out of 10).

As with many fetishes I have examined I cannot see thigh fetishism being the topic of any in-depth empirical research simply because it suffers from the "so what?" factor. Who would be interested in such research and why?

Thumb/Thumbsucking fetishism

In this book I examine a number of sexual behaviours involving hands. These include handwear fetishism, fingernail fetishism, and hands on hips fetishism. However, it was while I was researching belly inflation fetishes that I came across a man on the Yahoo! Answers website claiming he had a belly inflation fetish and a thumb fetish. There was also another person who responded saying he too shared the same fetish.

I had never read anything on standalone thumb fetishes. I would also point out that thumbsucking is just one of many baby-like behaviours that paraphilic infantilists enjoy, but do not necessarily see as a source of arousal in and of itself. As far as I am aware, there has never been any empirical research on thumb fetishism. However, there are various online websites and forums that feature individuals who claim to have very specific types of thumb fetishes.

While researching this topic I also came across the remarkable story of American Rafe Biggs (from Oakland, California; Tungol, 2013). In 2004 Biggs fell off a roof and broke his neck leaving him paralyzed from the chest down. He obviously thought he would never experience any kind of sexual pleasure again, but he was wrong:

> "Turns out he can. Biggs, 43, says that his thumb is his 'surrogate penis', and that he gets 'orgasmic sensations' whenever it's stimulated. 'I never thought it would be possible, but massaging and sucking on my thumb, feels a lot like my penis used to feel – it's really hot,' said Biggs, whose girlfriend helped him discover this phenomenon a year after the accident. Sex therapists like Lisa Skye Carle, who works with Biggs, call it a 'transfer orgasm' – where another place on the body gives the same sensation. Biggs has made it his mission to help quadriplegics lead sexually fulfilling lives, working with the group 'Sexability', an 'organization committed to empowering people with disabilities to explore sexuality and creating intimate loving relationships. Since our beginning in 2006, we have been working with individuals, groups and organizations to transform sexuality and disability'."

Toonophilia

While researching the furry fandom (i.e., individuals who derive sexual pleasure from dressing up as an animal and/or derive sexual pleasure from having sex with someone dressed as an animal) and objectum sexuality (i.e., individuals who develop deep emotional and/or romantic attachments to specific inanimate objects or structures), I kept coming across various online references to toonophilia.

Toonophilia is a paraphilia in which individuals are sexually and/or emotionally attracted to cartoon characters including Japanese anime characters. A number of slightly different definitions can be found online, some of which claim that toonophilia only applies to individuals whose primary or exclusive sexual interest is in cartoon characters. There also appear to be other similar paraphilias, such as fictophilia, in which individuals are romantically and/or sexually attracted to fictional characters in books and gameophilia in which individuals are romantically and/or sexually attracted to fictional videogame characters, such as *Tomb Raider*'s Lara Croft. One (now defunct) website claimed that toonophilia is seen as a lifestyle and that "due to the absence of physical contacts between humans and cartoon characters" most toonophiles' sexual activity, unsurprisingly, consists of masturbation. I have only ever come across one academic reference to toonophilia and that was in Aggrawal's (2009a) book. However, there is nothing more than a one-line definition of toonophilia (a.k.a. "schediaphilia").

One of the most infamous toonophiles is cartoonist and comic book artist Robert Crumb who has gone on record saying that as a youngster he was sexually attracted to Bugs Bunny when he was dressed in drag. More specifically, he said:

> "When I – what was it? – about five or six … I was sexually attracted to Bugs Bunny. And I … I cut out this Bugs Bunny off the cover of a comic book and carried it around with me. Carried it around in my pocket and took it out and looked at it periodically, and … and it got all wrinkled up from handling it so much that I asked my mother

to iron it on the ironing board to flatten it out, and ... and she did, and I was deeply disappointed 'cause it got all brown when she ironed it, and brittle, and crumbled apart."

In one of the regular polls carried out on the Deviant Art website, 58 "deviants" responded to the question "Do you have toonophilia?" Of these, 60% responded that they did ($n = 35$), 14% responded "not really" ($n = 14$) and 16% responded "sort of". Yes, I know it is not scientific and it is a very small number of respondents, but that was the only numerical data of any description I could find. McCombs (2008) reported that some toonophiles want to make their relationships with cartoon characters official. According to them the Toonophile Planet website was offering marriage certificates as long as the cartoon character was not already married to another toonophile. At the Go Petition website there was a genuine petition asking for relationships and marriages between humans and cartoon characters to be made legal. The petition said:

> "Toonophilia is a growing belief. Not only do our kind love cartoon/videogame characters, we feel their presence and our love for them is as real as you and me. Toonophiles are registering marriages to their virtual lovers on the internet and the number of virtual marriage certificates are growing. Examples of toonophile-oriented websites are www.sonic-passion.com, www.toonophilia.net. These marriage certificates sadly are only virtual. We desire to have 'legal' marriage certificates with our name and loved one's name written on it. I have never been interested in relationships with real people and am only interested in virtuality. This petition will be sent to the BBC as soon as enough signatures have been signed. We the undersigned request that you allow the marriage between humans and virtual cartoon/videogame characters be permitted in the UK."

McCombs (2008) further noted that other sites, such as the ToonsPortal website, feature obscene and/or pornographic images and videos of many different cartoon characters like *The Flintstones* having sex. In Monroe's (2012c) online essay about toonophilia she claimed, despite there being nothing to back it up, that:

> "Sexy for the toonophile need not be a blatantly erotic character like Jessica Rabbit or Betty Boop, rather the subject of affection and desire can be any animated or sketched figure from Bugs Bunny to Ms Pacman. Toonophiles are known to carry pictures of their adored character and even collect the plush toy and figurine versions of them. Some toonophile-friendly sites even allow members to wed their preferred character, provided that character is unspoken for. There is an abundance of sites on the web that cater to this fetishist's fantasies. A range of characters can be watched performing pretty well every – and any – kind of sexual act imaginable. By far the most popular form of cartoon pornography on the Internet is served up courtesy of the Japanese anime market. The pornographic cartoons in the anime style are casually called hentai. The word's etymology gives insight into what the original artists of this style thought of their work, as the word can be translated as 'perversion'."

From my research into videogame playing I can certainly see echoes of toonophilia among younger players when looking at videogame characters, such as Lara Croft. In previous articles I have asked myself what explains Lara's immense popularity (Griffiths, 1998b). At one level this may seem fairly obvious – she's a big-breasted digital icon. However, most *Tomb Raider* players are not lusting adolescents. I questioned a group of players and asked them why *Tomb Raider* was such a good game. The single most important factor appeared to be the problem-solving component as part of the treasure hunt genre. Her physical attributes did not seem to be important for most players apart from the youngest teenagers. Maybe it is among this group of teenage videogame players that toonophile tendencies might begin to develop.

Trampling fetishism

While researching crush fetishes, I came across Semple's (2009) article about trampling fetishism (a.k.a. "trampling" among those who engage in the activity). Most online sources that discuss trampling note that since the act of being trampled upon can be very painful, it must have close links or associations with sexual sadism and sexual masochism.

As far as I am aware, no empirical research has ever been carried out on trampling fetishism, so I have no idea how prevalent or widespread the activity is. There are certainly a number of online discussion groups. Furthermore, be wary of searching for "trampling fetish" on YouTube, especially if you are easily shocked.

Semple (2009) highlighted the case of Georgio T., a 48-year-old Maltese immigrant who called himself "The Human Carpet" because he got his sexual kicks from people walking and trampling all over his body. Typically, he would walk into a public meeting place, such as a bar or nightclub, carrying a carpet under his arm. He would then proceed to wrap the carpet around himself, lie down on the ground and place a sign next to himself with the simple instruction for people to "step on carpet" (the more the better he claimed in the article with a particular preference for women in stiletto heels). The edges of his customized carpet were sewn together in the shape of a cylinder. This allowed Georgio to slip in and out of the carpeted tube easily.

He then stayed wrapped up inside the carpet for up to 4 hours at a time (the longest stint being 11 hours). He was a regular "performer" at sex fetish parties and charged around $200 a session, but insisted he did it for pleasure – not profit. He knew of only one other person in the New York area called "Kevin Carpet" who also made a living from being trampled upon. His largest "customer" was a 390-pound man. He claims he was "motivated by a desire to push his own boundaries and those of others [and] likes intense parties where the flow of body-stompers is constant." Georgio told Semple that his fascination for being trampled on began in early childhood and became a central part of roleplaying games he engaged in as a child:

> "I loved to have weights on me … I liked having my cats walk over me. [If] somebody wanted to be the carpeter, then I would want to be the carpet … It's my fun [and] people are [now] paying me to have fun. The more people who pile [clearly Georgio has a sense of humour] on [me], the better. The higher they jump, the better. There's hardly any middle ground. [People] are either shocked and don't want to do it or they're thrilled to do it."

240   Trampling fetishism

Georgio claimed the behaviour was only a sexual fetish when beautiful women stepped on him. When men or plain-looking women stomped on him he still found it enjoyable, but not sexually stimulating. Semple (2009) said:

> "[Georgio] spoke rhapsodically about one woman who spent nearly 2 hours standing on him at Lotus, a club in the meatpacking district, and toying with his face using the heels of her shoes. After she was done, the woman leaned down and thanked him, and said that she never thought she would be able to do something like that … These sorts of personal connections are what make it all worth it, he said."

Georgio's experience is in no way unique as I have come across countless online stories and admissions about the sexual desire to be trampled upon including an interesting interview with a foot trampler at the Sexy Tofu website (2012).

I once filmed an interview about a trampling fetishist as part of the television programme *Forbidden* on which I was the resident psychologist. The television programme followed the story of a man called Frank O'Brien. Frank recalled his fetish developing during early to mid-adolescence. As a 15-year-old teenager, he would trick the girls he knew into stepping on him by inventing games that resulted in him being trampled upon. As the show's production notes reported:

> "[Frank would] invent games to race girls to the door of his cubby house and have them wrestle or sit on him in the process. In the backyard pool he'd encourage them to step on him underwater. Ever since he can remember Frank has wanted to get under a girl's foot … You could say Frank gets a 'kick' out of it. And among friends Frank is known simply as 'Step on Me'. For Frank, there's nothing finer than having a woman walk all over him."

By his early thirties Frank's trampling fetish began to take up more and more of his time. In his social life he started attending as many sadomasochistic shows as he could and he longed for dominant mistresses who would help cater to his trampling fetish. The backstory I received about Frank noted that:

> "The mistresses he saw early in life largely turned Frank away from the idea of trampling. They were more prostitutes than professional mistresses with an idea of what he really wanted. Back in those days there was no training for mistresses in trampling and this really has only taken off in Australia since the early 2000s. Now there are mistresses who train specifically in trampling."

According to Frank, Melbourne is the centre of Australia's BDSM culture and he introduced the *Forbidden* film crew to the niche trampling community that existed there. Frank's favourite club was Provocation, which hosted a monthly fetish social event. Frank's backstory notes also reported:

> "But his idea of getting down on the dance floor is a little different from most. When Frank gets down, he literally gets down. He has a special mat that he lies on to make the experience slightly more bearable but comfort is not exactly what Frank is looking for. He'll bring with him a platform that he'll set up beside his mat; written across it are the words 'step up here – girls only'. And that's exactly what Frank wants. He'll lie

there for hours in the club, enjoying the feeling of women trampling him. Some wear stilettos, some are in platform shoes and others go barefooted – he doesn't discriminate about what kind of footwear is permitted, but generally sharper and more pointy shoes offer greater satisfaction for [him]."

Frank described himself as naturally submissive. Moreover, he had weekly trampling sessions with "Mistress Spanklet", who was Frank's long-term friend and a dom–sub "play partner". Frank described these weekly sessions as his "drug fix" and something he "couldn't live without". Despite having had some of his bowel removed and it being dangerous for him to have someone trample on his stomach, he cannot stop it. He now tries to avoid tummy trampling, but noted that:

"Trampling can be on any part of the body, including the more sensitive regions of the face, throat and genitalia. [He] enjoys cock and ball trampling on a weekly basis with Spanklet. His face, arms and legs are also prime trampling ground in private and in public."

In fact, Frank claimed that he was responsible for the first ever online penis-trampling photograph. In 1999 Frank claimed he took the full weight of a woman in sharp red stilettos twisting as hard as she could on his penis. Frank claimed the photograph taken by the woman's sexual partner kick-started "the worldwide cock-trampling trend".

There appears to be little academic research on the topic. Nevertheless, anecdotal evidence suggests there is, unsurprisingly, an overlap between trampling fetishes and foot fetishes (podophilia) on which there is quite a lot of academic research, given it appears to be the most prevalent type of fetishism. Obviously, Frank's case is extreme and was heavily interwoven into his life. While there appear to be addictive elements to his behaviour, I do not believe that Frank's trampling fetish is an addiction: bizarre and extreme – yes; addictive – no. However, I am happy to be proved wrong.

Transformation fetishes

While researching a number of topics including furries (sexual pleasure from dressing up as an animal or having sex with others dressed up as an animal), technofetishism (sexual pleasure and arousal arising from humanoid or non-humanoid robots), macrophilia (sexual arousal from a fascination with giants and/or a sexual fantasy involving giants) and agalmatophilia (sexual arousal from an attraction to statues, dolls, mannequins and/or other similar body-shaped objects), I constantly came across references to "transformation fetish" (TF). Basically, a transformation fetish is a form of sexual fetishism in which an individual derives sexual arousal from descriptions about or depictions of people being transformed into other beings or objects.

There is a very active online TF community, although some "TF fans" (as they seem to like being called) have no sexual interest as such but take an active interest in "transformation art" and "transformation fiction". After looking at the posts on such sites there does not seem to be any distinction between fetish and non-fetish fiction, but some members of the online TF community are far more sexually orientated in their postings. For instance, one website I checked out was set up to house fetish-inspired work comprising "stories, drawings, renderings and photo-manipulations depicting many transformation fetishes. These fetishes include, but are not limited to, transformation into toys, latex/rubber, spandex, balloon, zentai, clowns, toons, mannequins, robots and statues."

The posts I have read on various TF websites indicate that the transformations typically involve a human of either gender, but more often female, being transformed into some other form. For instance, check out the stories at the Experience Project website or the Fetish Transformation website.

I also read that the transformations are typically non-consensual with "the transformer often becoming confused, scared or angry as the changes take place, although some transformations are gladly accepted and even chosen by their victims." TF websites contain many examples of "conversion" across both animal-type and developmental stages. Common conversions include felines (kittens, cats, lions, tigers), canines (puppies, dogs, foxes, wolves) and equines (foals, ponies, horses). However, many are depicted as half-human, half-animal hybrids with the appealing characteristics of both highlighted. As one TF fan site asserted:

> "Furries are usually bipedal and have the ability to speak, walk, talk, and think like a normal human. Many in the TF community, even those with an interest in TFs other than animal, adopt a made-up identity as a furry, known as a fursona. It should be noted that like the TF community not all furries are involved with the fetish aspects of anthropomorphic media. There are some large differences between the communities."

Another type of TF is common among technosexuals (a.k.a. "robot fetishists"). A common fantasy among such people involves transformation into a robot. Some have argued this is very similar to agalmatophilia (i.e., attraction to or transformation into statues or mannequins) and in this sense could be viewed as a form of erotic anthropomorphism.

Looking at TF across the whole sexual fetish spectrum, some would argue that there are many different core types of transformation including transforming into inanimate everyday objects, transforming into other humanoid-looking forms (e.g., statues, dolls and robots), transforming into other living things (e.g., animals, animal hybrids and alien lifeforms), transforming into different and/or extended versions of the self in either fantasy (e.g., becoming a giant or the body aging years in just a few seconds) or reality (e.g., via body modification and/or gender reassignment sex changes).

Blanchard (1989) introduced the concept of autogynephilia, which refers to "a male's propensity to be sexually aroused by the thought of himself as a female." This formed the basis of Blanchard's hypothesis that there are two distinct manifestations of male-to-female transsexualism (i.e., homosexual and autogynephilic). It could also be argued that such thinking may be akin to transformation fetishes.

Transvestic fetishism

There is much debate about whether transvestism can be classed as a disorder and/or is more sexually deviant than any other paraphilia. Transvestism has traditionally been defined as the cross-dressing in clothes worn by the opposite sex for sexual pleasure.

However, there are a number of groups of people who may dress themselves in the clothes of the opposite sex, but may experience absolutely no sexual arousal whatsoever. Therefore, those who study paraphilic behaviour are more likely to use the term "transvestic fetishism" to describe the small group of people, typically male but there are some documented female cases in the literature, who derive their sexual pleasure from cross-dressing. Therefore, transvestite groups (where the word simply refers to cross-dressing) may comprise:

- Transvestic fetishists who cross-dress for sexual pleasure and who in some cases may be sexually aroused by a very specific piece of clothing.
- Female impersonators who cross-dress to entertain.
- Effeminate homosexuals who may occasionally cross-dress for fun.
- Transsexuals who cross-dress because they feel they have been biologically assigned to the wrong sex and typically suffer from a gender identity disorder.

These different groups show that, unlike all other paraphilias (e.g., necrophilia, zoophilia and hypoxyphilia), the motivations for cross-dressing may not necessarily be sexually motivated and therefore are unlikely to be viewed as either deviant or disordered.

The latest version of the American Psychiatric Association's DSM-5-TR (2022) defines transvestic disorder as "recurrent and intense sexual arousal from cross dressing, as manifested by fantasies, urges, or behaviors … [that] cause clinically significant distress or impairment in social, occupational, or other important areas of functioning" (p. 798). Interestingly, Newring *et al.* (2008) think it is possible that future books on sexual deviance will not include transvestic fetishism as a sexual deviance, but rather as a sexual variance. The DSM-5-TR notes that the prevalence of transvestic disorder is unknown but appears to be more prevalent among males than females. It also cited Swedish research that 3% of males report having been sexually aroused by cross-dressing.

There have been a number of relatively large-scale studies of transvestism. Docter and Prince (1997) surveyed 1,032 transvestites, and Långström and Zucker (2005) examined tranvestism in a Swedish community survey of 2,540 adults. This and other research has suggested there appear to be at least two distinct subgroups of transvestic fetishists dubbed "periodic transvestites" and "marginal transvestites":

- *Periodic transvestites:* These transvestites experience psychological satisfaction with their male gender, their sexual identity and their cross-dressing activity. Furthermore, they have no desire to pursue any other form of feminization.
- *Marginal transvestites:* By contrast these transvestites experience psychological dissatisfaction with their male gender and sexual identity. The sexual arousal experienced from cross-dressing is typically lower than that of periodic transvestites. They may also engage in other feminization activities including hormone treatment, body hair removal and, in extreme cases, surgical reconstruction. Some marginal transvestites may therefore include transsexuals who cross-dress not only for sexual pleasure but also for gender synchrony.

As with many other paraphilic behaviours, there is a relative lack of data, most of which come from clinical case studies. Based on what has been published, the data suggest that the majority of transvestic fetishists report cross-dressing in secret before the onset of adolescence. Although the act of cross-dressing as children may provide excitement and fun, the activity is unlikely to be particularly sexualized. For instance, clothes that belong to females in the house may trigger and/or facilitate pleasant sensory experiences brought about by perfumes and by feelings of familiarity and comfort. Case study evidence suggests the act of cross-dressing during adolescence becomes increasingly paired with sexual urges and arousal (e.g., erections and ejaculation) and in some cases may lead to thoughts of being female in public or in private.

However, some sexologists have speculated that transvestic behaviour develops via classical conditioning after accidental exposure to female clothing or to a female undressing. Similarly, it has also been suggested transvestic behaviour may be negatively reinforced when it is used as a means of coping during times of emotional distress. A number of studies have reported high rates of parental separation during transvestic men's childhoods. The etiology of transvestism appears to be similar to other paraphilic behaviours (i.e., early conditioning experiences), although there are case studies of parental punishment in which boys were humiliated by being forced to wear girls' clothes leading to transvestism. According to Zucker *et al.* (1997) such parental separation may explain the need for transitional objects that many children eventually develop.

Most transvestites do not seek professional help as they do not experience any distress associated with their behaviour. Moreover, even with therapy, it is unlikely the behaviour will change, especially when such individuals want to carry on cross-dressing.

Trash bag fetishism

Sex and bin liners (a.k.a. "plastic trash bags" for my North American readers) are probably two things that rarely occur in the same sentence let alone an individual's sexual behaviour. However, I was surprised to find that fetishistic behaviour concerning trashcans and bin liners is more common than I ever thought. I will start with a true story from here in the UK.

Back in February 1993 a 20-year-old man, Karl Watkins, appeared at Hereford Crown Court charged with five counts of outraging public decency. The first set of charges related to making love to pavements. Although his defence claimed it was a case of mistaken identity, Watkins had been found many times by passers-by face down on the pavement with his underpants and trousers around his ankles thrusting up and down into the ground. He was found guilty and sentenced to prison where he served 18 months.

However, in April 1995 Watkins was back in court, this time charged with simulating sex with black plastic bin bags in front of adolescent girls. In court he revealed that he had had a 9-year fetish with plastic sacks and that he loved the "feel and touch of the bin liners". The court heard how he went out nights and spent his time in rubbish dumps. He was also found having simulated sex inside wheelie bins and the back of dustbin lorries (a.k.a. "trash trucks"). He admitted that his "ultimate sexual fantasy" was to be in a dustbin lorry as the bin bags were being crushed. Once again he was convicted of outraging public decency, but this time was put on probation for 3 years and ordered by the judge to seek psychiatric help for his sexual proclivities.

Although this may be an extreme case of someone caught engaging in his preferred sexual behaviour, this may be just the tip of the iceberg. Evidence for such a claim is borne out by a few self-confessions that I found online from people who have presumably never been caught in public having sex with a bin bag:

Extract 1: "I am a 22-year-old male from the UK and I was wondering if it is normal to have a fetish for bin bags or what you Americans call 'hefty bags'? I have had this fetish since I was a little boy and have often wondered if this is normal?"

Extract 2: "For some reason I have always liked the look of black trash bags – of course, not ones that actually have trash in them (trash is disgusting). I have always liked how the bags themselves are shiny, soft and I love the sound of the plastic. Is this normal?"

Extract 3: "I'm a 24-year-old guy. I just wondered is my fetish OK? I love the feel of plastic, it feels so nice (plastic sheets + wearing plastic bin bags, etc.) and I like to see girls wearing bin bags as well. Also I like girls having paint poured over them too whether it ruins their clothes or not, and one girl I know says she will get wrapped in a plastic sheet and have paint poured over her. Am I a freak?"

Extract 4: "I have a sexual fetish that seems quite unique (I would be pleased if anyone else told me otherwise). I like to put my penis through a bin bag and thrust until I climax. I have no idea where this came from or how it developed. I think it may be the mystery of what my penis is rubbing against. (Oh! What's that, broken glass or some ash?) ... I have a healthy relationship with my girlfriend who has no idea (an ex-girlfriend caught me once but I pretended I was sleepwalking). Sometimes I don't wash my penis after bin bag sex and then enjoy the thought of my dirty penis entering my girlfriend during sex. I even think of bin bags while having sex with her (she is very pretty). What's wrong with me?"

Extract 5: "I'm a single straight 20-something-year-old guy who loves wearing clean unused plastic garbage/trash/bin bags as shirts in private. I'm even wearing one right now as I write this. I wear them because I like the feel of them on my skin. They're more comfortable to wear than others think. I also think they turn me on if worn by the opposite gender. I'm totally serious about all of this."

When I first started looking into this sexual practice, I thought confessions like the ones above would be a rarity, but I was surprised to find quite a number of online sites and discussion forums dedicated to the practice of "trashbagging". For instance, one site that appears to get a lot of traffic is the Trash Can Stories website (2012). There is a helpful FAQ page that includes some operational definitions of such practices as "trashbagging", "bagging" and "trash fetish":

- *Trashbagging:* "This is where people love to enclose themselves, be enclosed or enclose someone else in a plastic garbage bag or several. They love the feel of the

smooth slippery plastic; sometimes involving breathplay, others more into messy situations with food or garbage thrown in with them. The fantasy may also involve being placed in a trashcan, garbage bin or dumpster to await their fate at the hands of the garbage truck."
- *Bagging*: "Enclosing either yourself (solo) or being enclosed inside one or more plastic garbage or trash bags. Possibly bound, gagged or made immobile, or just left inside naked and left as trash. This may also involve breathplay or the moving of the bagged person to another location or even to a dumpster for disposal as trash."
- *Trash fetish*: "The appeal of being enclosed inside a trash bag or several, dumped with rubbish or have rubbish dumped in with them, and/or just left sometimes inside the bags themselves or disposed of inside a dumpster."

The descriptions of trashbagging suggest overlaps with other fetishistic and/or paraphilic behaviour, such as salirophilia in which individuals experience sexual arousal from soiling or dishevelling the object of their desire. Another obvious overlap is with hypoxyphilia in which individuals experience sexual pleasure from having their oxygen supply restricted, thus heightening their sexual arousal. The high-profile autoerotic asphyxiation deaths in the UK of both journalist and Tory politician Stephen Milligan in 1994 and television presenter Kristian Digby in 2010 involved plastic bin liners being found over their heads at the scene of death. Whether trash bag fetishism ever becomes the topic of serious scientific investigation remains to be seen. There are certainly no academic studies on the topic of which I am aware.

Trichophilia

Allen (2011) related in a newspaper article the story of Danilo Restivo, a man with a fetish for cutting off women's hair, who was sentenced to 30 years in prison following his killing of 16-year-old Elisa Claps in 1993 in Potenza, Italy. He was also convicted of killing 48-year-old Heather Barnett in 2002 in Bournemouth, UK. The murders were described as ritualistic and both involved the victims' breasts being cut off and strands of their hair being placed in the victims' hands. Another link between the two cases involved 15 women reporting their hair had been involuntarily cut on buses in both Bournemouth and Potenza around the time of the murders. Clearly, Restivo is not a typical trichophile (a.k.a. "hair fetishist") and is not representative of those who enjoy this paraphilia. However, it is one of the few times that hair fetishism has been highlighted by the mass media.

The fetish has been observed in both males and females, although as with most fetishes and paraphilias it appears to be predominantly male. Individuals with hair fetishes may also have very specific attributes as to what is most sexually arousing, such as the hair being from a stranger rather than someone they know, hair length, hair colour, hair style and whether the hair is wet or dry. They may also prefer hair to have been washed with a particular shampoo or hairspray suggesting an overlap with olfactophilia (i.e., the deriving of sexual pleasure and arousal from particular smells).

Other variants may include deriving sexual pleasure from having hair cut, shaved and/or washed. In fact, there is a fetish for manipulating and/or shampooing hair known as "tripsoplagnia". Freud believed that men cutting long female hair may represent a man's fear of castration. In such a case the woman's hair represents a symbolic penis and by cutting it off the male restores his dominance. There is absolutely no empirical evidence for such claims, but Freud is one of the few people to put forward a psychological explanation.

I have not come across a single empirical study. However, given the absence of any academic research literature, the assertions made can at the very least provide a pathway for confirmatory studies to be carried out. Volk and Sagan (2009) claimed the roots (no pun intended) of trichophilia may lie in the physiological feelings that the body experiences when hair is played with in some way. More specifically, they claimed:

> "Being groomed, having one's hair cut, like a massage, caresses, or laughter can produce endogenous endorphins, the body's own pleasure drugs."

I have yet to track down any study (or studies) demonstrating this. Nevertheless, based on other pleasurable activities that have been shown to produce endorphins, there is no reason to think this is not the case with hair grooming. In their study on fetishes Scorolli *et al.* (2007) reported that body part fetishes are the most common (33%). They further found that trichophilic fetish sites accounted for 7% of all websites studied comprising 6,707 fetishists in total. A further 864 fetishists visited other types of body hair websites, such as depilation, beards and pubic hair sites.

To date, there are no detailed accounts of trichophilia in the clinical literature. von Krafft-Ebing (1886) noted the case of a man married to a bearded lady. After her death, he was so distraught that he constantly searched for another. Note here that trichophilia is implied. Like many other fetishes and paraphilias that I have examined, this is yet another one where there is a need for further research.

Unbirthing fetishism

In vorarephilia (a.k.a. "vore", "phagophilia"), in which individuals are sexually aroused by the thought of being eaten, eating another person or observing such a process for sexual gratification, I noted that one of the subcategories of this sexually paraphilic behaviour was "vaginal vore" in which an individual is sexually aroused by the thought of being consumed by a vagina and taken into the womb. This is commonly referred to as "unbirthing" (a.k.a. "reverse birth") if the participants are human. Among the furry fandom, who dress up and fantasize about being animals, the process is known as being "re-whelped"). A short article on unbirthing at the Oh Internet website (2012) claimed that "unbirthing fetishes are most commonly found in the furry community," although there is no empirical evidence to support this claim.

The simplest definition of unbirthing is that it is a paraphilia that involves being "swallowed" alive by female genitalia. As with most forms of vorarephilia, the paraphilia is fantasy based as it is not humanly possible to be unborn. Most unbirthing sites feature masses of fan art and fan fiction, such as the Mindless Consumption website. However, there are also some very specialist types of unbirthing sites, such as the Pony Inside Story website that (predictably) only features unbirthing pony stories and art. According to a *Wikifur* (2009) article on unbirthing:

> "A less common but still significant minority also practice UB-vore wherein the female unbirther's body ultimately consumes the unbirthed. Another variant on this is males absorbing others (generally other males) as a form of male pregnancy. This is known as cock vore and often involves hypertrophilia and/or macrophilia."

Macrophilia, which I covered earlier in this book, refers to individuals who are sexually aroused by giants. Hypertrophilia describes individuals – usually macrophiles – who are sexually and/or emotionally attracted to "hyper-endowed" characters. Hypertrophic individuals typically feature overexaggerated and impractically large sexual and erogenous characteristics. The entry on unbirthing in the online Encyclopedia Dramatica (2011a) claimed that US grunge group Nirvana may have unwittingly started the fetish in their 1993 hit single *Heart-Shaped Box* from their final studio album In Utero when they sang:

> *Broken hymen of Your Highness/I'm left black*
> *Throw down your umbilical noose/So I can climb right back.*

However, I know of no academic research on unbirthing, although there are a number of online articles that examine the phenomenon and its underlying motivation and meaning. For instance, the *Wikifur* (2009) article made a number of interesting observations:

> "For many, unbirthing is attractive in its symbolic meaning. The opportunity to trust someone quite literally with one's entire life, to be nurtured and protected, is what attracts the unbirthed. On the other side, the unbirther can demonstrate her care for another in a deep, trusting way, and enjoy something living inside her, a sensation often attractive in and of itself."

For others unbirthing has dominant, controlling and almost sadistic elements in which the person being unbirthed becomes dependent upon the vaginal enveloper for oxygen and sustenance. Individuals undergoing unbirthing become restricted in what they can do because movement is almost totally inhibited and the senses are all but redundant having been enveloped and swallowed. For some, the age regression aspect and returning to the womb is said to be sexually arousing. As the *Wikifur* (2009) article noted:

> "Returned to the womb, an unbirthed creature grows younger; the unbirther may choose to rebirth their guest at any point or simply regress the unbirthed past the point of conception, effectively erasing their existence. There are many variations on this theme, some overlapping with the oviposition [paraphilia]. [For others the] overlap between fans of unbirth and those of vore lies in the endosomatophilia paraphilia, or attraction to fantasies involving complete encapsulation of a living thing within the body of another living thing. A second overlap between the two lies in absorbing or digesting an unbirthed creature: a form of genital vore."

Compared with other paraphilias that have not been researched empirically, the number of online forums that cater for vorarephilia in all its subvarieties including unbirthing appear relatively large with fairly large numbers of members. It is certainly an area in which I would personally like to carry out some research.

While researching unbirthing I came across quite a few references to "partial unbirthing". I had my doubts as to whether partial unbirthing (a.k.a. "adult heading") could be anything but a fantasy-based paraphilia until I came across what appear to be actual photographs and videos of the practice online, such as those on the partial unbirthing page of the Encyclopedia Dramatica (ED) website (be warned, the page that opens shows photographs of men with their heads inside vaginas). In part of an online article on vorarephilia, the Serial Killer Calendar website (2012) is surprisingly knowledgeable about paraphilic behaviours and notes it sometimes goes by the name "adult heading". Looking at the same online photographs as I had looked at, the article claimed "there is controversy about whether it has ever truly happened and disagreements about whether photos of the practice are Photoshop fakes". The same article also questioned the feasibility of the practice in relation to restricting the oxygen supply of someone inserting his head, although this would arguably be an added turn-on for a hypoxyphiliac. The ED article also notes:

> "Partial unbirthing (adult head insertion into the vagina) [is a] real practice as opposed to fantasy, it is not a category of 'vore'. It is only done by sex partners who

> both find it safe and extremely enjoyable. It is a fetishism that is extremely rare and probably one of the rarest of all human sexual activities. The reason for this is that to be mutually enjoyable and erotic it requires that the vagina must stretch to an enormous size."

I have no evidence to dispute such claims, but given the sheer pragmatics involved, the claims do not seem unreasonable. *Wikibin* (2012) featured one of the more in-depth articles on partial unbirthing (but given that Wikibin features articles deleted from Wikipedia, such information should be treated with caution). It claimed that the activity is, unsurprisingly, "extremely uncommon" and "much more common as a pure fantasy than in actuality". The article also claimed that there have been attempts, but it does not say by whom or what, to subclassify partial unbirthing under a new category called "endosomatophilia". The article estimated that fewer than one in a million sexual partners had actually engaged in partial unbirthing, although personally I think this figure is still too high. The article also claimed that it is mutually enjoyable and erotic for couples who engage in the practice:

> "It requires that the vagina must stretch to enormous size. This requires a consenting, cooperative and extended effort between the sexual partners with both partners considering the same fetish to be erotic … This of course is only possible where the woman has an extremely huge opening of her pelvis. Such a huge or Justo Major Pelvis is also called a 'giant pelvis'. This condition is where the minimum pelvis size is enlarged uniformly in every direction by a linear factor of 1.5, or more than the average 11-inch wide pelvis. This 16.5-inch 'or more' Justo Major pelvic width is a condition that is only present in less than one in a thousand adult women."

The article also claimed that some normal-sized women sometimes stretched their vaginas to facilitate orgasmic stimulation. This is sometimes as a consequence of the woman having a "fullness fetish" (a.k.a. "a bulk intromission fetish", at least according to the article). I have tried to look for further information on this fetish, but have yet to find anything. Although this would appear to be exceedingly rare, the *Wikibin* (2012) article says that with "gradual repeated stretching they occasionally stretch almost to the walls of their pelvic bone opening" to the size of a newborn baby's head.

There remains the fundamental issue of whether partial unbirthing is humanly possible. There is no academic or clinical research on partial unbirthing fetishes. However, after reviewing what scant anecdotal evidence there is, I am convinced that partial unbirthing fetishes exist at the very least in fantasy form. There are certainly examples of online fictional fantasy stories involving partial unbirthing. However, I remain ambivalent as to whether the practice can be achieved in actuality. The evidence such that it is suggests it is theoretically possible, but whether there are genuinely recorded cases is suspect at best.

Urethral manipulation

While I was researching urophilia (see next entry), I came across a number of articles and papers on urethral manipulation fetishes in which individuals get sexually aroused by the insertion of "foreign bodies" into their urethras. Almost all the work published in this area is in the form of clinical and/or medical case reports. Moreover, almost all the cases are men who insert various objects into their penis as a form of sexual stimulation. Having said that, various authors have noted women may also engage in urethral stimulation.

Most case reports are about men who have ended up having to seek medical help because the foreign body that has been inserted has become stuck inside their penises. Therefore, most of what we know is only based on urethral manipulation and stimulation that has gone wrong. Based on case reports, it is estimated that almost all men and about 85% of women who engage in urethral manipulation do so for sexual stimulation. Individuals who engage in urethral manipulation are often suffering psychiatric disorders, are high on drugs, are mentally confused, are sexually curious and/or do it to get relief from urinary symptoms.

There is also a relatively developed glossary of terms used among the gay community, in particular, for such urethra-stimulating behaviours including:

- Sounding: The insertion of an object into the urethra.
- Meatotomy: The dilation of the urethra using a medical dilating device such that the urethra is stretched to eventually facilitate a finger or a penis.
- Meatotome: A scalpel used to enlarge the urethral opening.
- Meatorrhaphy: The procedure of enlarging the urethral opening.
- Meatometer: An instrument for measuring the urethral opening.

The range of objects that have been used include straws, cylindrical batteries, pens, pencils, candles, lipstick containers, small wooden sticks, swizzle sticks, glass beads, wires, Allen keys, buckshot, cuticle knives and razors. Such practices can lead to a wide array of medical problems including urinary tract damage and blockages, urinary tract infections and bladder infections. For instance, Goldstone (1999) reported the case of a man who inserted a piano wire into his penis that resulted in it getting knotted in his bladder and his bladder having to be cut open to get it removed.

Wise (1982) reported urethral stimulation may occur actively during sexual activity, such as masturbation, or passively via medical procedures requested by the person. He also observed that the behaviour shared features with both fetishism and masochism, although very few who engage in such practices report pain. Therefore, the association with masochism does not seem justified based on the clinical evidence reported. Kenney (1998) believes that what initiates the acquisition of such behaviour is an accidentally discovered pleasurable stimulation of the urethra, which is then repeated using objects of unknown danger and driven by a psychological predisposition to sexual gratification.

Even though most reports are medical in origin, some psychoanalysts claim that individuals with a fetish or preference for urethral stimulation have underlying problems of fixation, regression or castration. Reviews of data from case reports suggest that the focus of arousal for the individual is not on the objects that are inserted into the urethra.

van Ophoven and de Kernion (2000) published a paper which is arguably the most comprehensive review on "penile foreign body insertion". The authors reviewed 800 cases in the published literature between 1755 and 1999. They categorized the range of objects inserted as:

- Animals or parts of animals (e.g., coyote's rib, dog's penis, leech, snails and animal bones).
- Plants and vegetables (e.g., slippery elm, grass, cucumbers and pistachio shells).
- Sharp and lacerating objects (e.g., pencils, pins and needles).
- Wire-like objects (e.g., cables, catheters and rubber tubes).
- Fluids and powders (e.g., nasal mucus ['snot'], glue and cocaine).

However, individual case reports have included some really bizarre and unusual objects. Jaiswal (1992) reported the case of a 28-year-old Indian man who ended up getting a penicillin bottle containing iodine stuck in his foreskin. The man had inserted the bottle during masturbation to tickle his penile glans. It was so firmly impacted that the bottle could only be removed under general anaesthetic.

Kim et al. (2002) reported what they believed to be a unique case of a 41-year-old man who presented himself for medical attention as a result of a urethral blockage. It turned out that the lower urinary tract obstruction was because the man had self-injected foam sealant into his urethra.

Lamberth (1997) reported the case of a 36-year-old man who inserted a safety pin into his urethra for sexual pleasure. After 10 hours of failing to remove the safety pin he sought medical attention. Lamberth claimed this was only the second case of using safety pins reported in the medical literature.

The insertion of foreign bodies into the penis is rarely fatal. However, Byard et al. (1982) reported the case of a 40-year-old man who inserted a pencil into his penis, but was unable to remove it. Unfortunately, he failed to seek medical help, developed sepsis and died as a consequence. Given that almost all reports of urethral sexual stimulation are case study reports, there are no estimates as to how prevalent this sexual practice is among the general population.

Chattopadhyay et al. (2011) asserted that the insertion of foreign bodies into the urethra as a part of paraphilic behaviour is "fraught with complications". They reported the case of a 25-year-old male goldsmith who inserted a 60-cm electrical wire with a 5-mm diameter into his urethra. The wire got stuck and caused heamaturia (i.e., blood in his urine) and incontinence along with a lot of pain and discomfort. It was removed by open cystoscopy (opening up the bladder in an endoscopic procedure). The authors associated the behaviour with depression and an anxiety condition. The man was subsequently prescribed antidepressants to prevent any future occurrences. Similar cases have also been reported in various other papers. For instance, Stravodimos et al. (2009) reported the case of a 53-year-old Greek man who presented with a bloody urethral discharge after having inserted an electrical wire in his urethra for masturbatory purposes.

Bedi et al. (2010) reported the case of a 62-year-old man who inserted two household AAA batteries into his urethra that had got stuck and then presented at hospital in pain. This was not an isolated incident as the year before the same patient had an endoscopic procedure to remove a pen lid from his urethra. Moon et al. (2010)

reported the case of a 50-year-old man who sought medical treatment after a week-long period of pain. It turned out that 3 years previously he had inserted a plastic chopstick into his urethra for sexual pleasure, although this had not caused any pain despite the fact that it remained inside him. Another patient inserted a round magnet into his urethra in an attempt to remove the chopstick. However, this failed to remove the chopstick and then the magnet got stuck. Matters got worse when he inserted a second magnet in an attempt to remove the first one resulting in the second magnet getting lodged in his urethra. The authors noted that what made their case so interesting is the fact a foreign body had remained in the bladder for such a long time without causing severe irritation and pain (see also Aliabadi *et al.*, 1985).

Urophilia

In this book I have already covered coprophilia, a paraphilia in which people are sexually aroused by faeces. Another related paraphilia is urophilia (a.k.a. "urophagia", "urolagnia", "renifleurism", "undinism", "ondinisme") in which people are sexually aroused by urine (i.e., the sight or thought of either the act of urination or the urine itself). In non-scientific circles it is more popularly called "water sports", "golden showers" and more crudely "piss play". Furthermore, there are dedicated websites where "pee lovers" can meet up.

Press reports reveal there are a number of celebrities who engage in the activity. For instance, in an interview with the music magazine *Blender* the Puerto Rican popstar Ricky Martin stated that he enjoyed "golden showers". The actor Andy Milonakis and host of MTV's *The Andy Milonakis Show* said in an interview with *People Magazine* that he liked the feeling of "warm urine" on his chest during sexual intercourse. Interestingly, Grosskurth (1980) reported that Havelock Ellis – one the founding fathers of sexology – was aroused by the sight of a woman urinating.

In the American Psychiatric Association's (2022) *Diagnostic and Statistical Manual of Mental Disorders* (DSM-5-TR), urophilia (like coprophilia) is currently listed under "other specified paraphilic disorder" (OSPD). As with all paraphilias in the OSPD category, diagnosis is only made if:

> "… *recurrent and intense sexual arousal involving urine … has been present for at least 6 months and causes marked distress or impairment in social, occupational, or other important areas of functioning.*" (p. 802)

Urophiliacs typically derive sexual pleasure from urinating on and/or being urinated upon by another person. Some urophiliacs also bathe in urine, enjoy smelling people in urine-soaked clothes and/or engage in urophagia (i.e., drinking urine). For urophiliacs the drinking of urine typically takes place while someone urinates directly into their mouths. Urophagia in and of itself is not necessarily a sexually arousing activity as there are many urine drinkers who do it for ritualistic or ceremonial purposes – not for sexual pleasure. Some even think there are health or cosmetic benefits as borne out by individuals who engage in "urine therapy".

However, the act of urophagia may be sexually stimulating for urophiliacs. They may also engage in the activity as part of other paraphilic activity, such as sadism, masochism, voyeurism and infantilism (i.e., being sexually excited from dressing as an adult baby). Some urophiliacs may also experience sexual arousal from having a full bladder and/or feel sexually attracted to someone else who has a full bladder ("bladder desperation") or wets themselves (i.e., "panty wetting" or wetting the bed). In Japan this latter paraphilic behaviour occurs as part of a fetish subculture known as *omorashi* and is seen as different from urophilia.

Mundiger-Klow (2009) wrote a whole book on urophilia comprising 15 urophiliac case studies but, despite the academic credentials of the author and the lengthy accounts, the book was little more than a collection of erotic stories based around urophiliacs with little analysis provided by the author.

To date, there has been very little scientific research and almost all of what is known is based on either case studies or co-occurring behaviour with other paraphilias. For instance, in a survey of 561 non-incarcerated individuals seeking treatment for paraphilias, Abel et al. (1988) reported that many paraphiliacs engage in more than one paraphilic behaviour. For instance, all the zoophiles in the sample reported more than one paraphilia and for a small number this included urophilia. However, it appears that urophilia is most likely associated with sadomasocism. For instance, in a study of 245 male sadomasochists Spengler (1977) reported that 10% of those surveyed had an interest in urophilia. This finding is similar to that of Buhrich (1983) who reported that 8% of his sample of sadomasichists had an interest in urophilia.

Denson (1982) noted that urine fulfills many different functions for urophiles. Such functions include (i) serving as a fetishistic object, (ii) being used to humiliate or be humiliated (i.e., through urinating on another person or being urinated upon) and/or (iii) capturing the spirit of a sexual partner. Based on the case studies examined, Denson argued that urination may serve masochistic and/or sadistic purposes and that therefore urophilia should be labelled "uromasochism" or "urosadism".

While most explanations for paraphilic urophilia focus on early behavioural conditioning in childhood and adolescence, Money (1980) wrote that:

"Some years ago, when I visited the Yerkes Primate Laboratory in Atlanta ... How, I asked, did a wild chimpanzee mother keep its baby clean from soiling? The answer was that, as in many other species, she licks it clean ... Among the people of Bali, in Indonesia, small dogs lick the babies clean ... The dog's assigned duty is to provide diaper service by licking clean the baby, and the mother, whenever the baby soils. Subsequently I have learned that Eskimo mothers once had a custom of licking their babies clean. Even though human primates have graduated from using the mother's snout end to keep the baby's tail end clean, it is safe to assume that as a species we still possess in the brain the same phyletic circuitry for infant hygiene as do the subhuman primates. Just as males and females have nipples, so also do both sexes have these brain pathways that relate to drinking urine and eating faeces. These are the pathways that, when they become associated with neighboring erotic/sexual pathways, produce urophilia and coprophilia as paraphilias."

Additionally, in an online essay examining the "forced retention of bodily waste" among children, Couture (2000) made the following observations in relation to the origin of urine-related paraphilias:

> "Some sufferers of forced waste retention develop sexual fetishes involving waste and waste retention ... adult respondents reported using masturbation as a way to dissociate from the pain of a full bladder. Websites that cater to the sadomasochistic desires of urolagnia ("water sports") enthusiasts are prevalent on the internet ... Adults who engage in urolagnia are often re-enacting scenes from childhood, some of which involved denial of toilet use by schoolteachers or caretakers for purposes of punishment or containment ... Due to the close proximity of the urethra and bladder to the sex organs, some adults who chronically suffered this form of bodily control as children developed a conditioned response in which wetting themselves or bladder tension was association with sexual arousal."

Although there is still much to learn in this area, there are certainly some interesting speculations as to the origins and initiation of urophilic behaviour.

Ursusagalmatophilia

Teddy bears and sex are two things that rarely appear in the same sentence. Having said that, the film *Ted* was described in one film review as "rude, crude and lewd. We don't expect our teddy bears to be like that, but foul language, weed smoking and promiscuous sex are all in a day's work/play for the title creature in *Ted*." However, early in 2011 there were many news reports of 28-year-old American Charles Marshall being arrested for the fourth time since 2010 when he was seen by a number of eyewitnesses masturbating in front of a teddy bear in Ohio. On this latest occasion, he was caught in an alleyway masturbating in front of a teddy bear and close to where he could be seen by children. His first arrest was back in February 2010 when he was caught masturbating in front of a stuffed animal in a public library toilet. In late 2010 he was caught with a teddy bear for a second time. Marshall admitted in court that having sex with stuffed teddy bears had been "an ongoing problem". This appeared to be true because in August 2011 he was caught in public yet again having sex with a teddy bear.

This type of sexual behaviour is known as "plushophilia" and is something I looked at briefly in that entry earlier in this book. Aggrawal (2009a) defines plushophilia as a "sexual attraction to stuffed toys or people in animal costume such as theme park characters." However, as I mentioned in that entry, other online sources simply define plushophilia as a paraphilia involving stuffed animals. The reason I am focusing on sex with teddy bears is because there actually is a paraphilia that solely relates to deriving sexual pleasure and arousal from teddy bears known as "ursusagalmatophilia".

The online Urban Dictionary simply defines ursusagalmatophilia as "the fetish for teddy bears". This is not only a subtype of plushophilia but also, given the name of the paraphilia, appears to be a subtype of agalmatophilia in which individuals derive sexual arousal from an attraction to statues, dolls, mannequins and/or other similar body-shaped objects (a paraphilia already examined in this book in the entry on agalmatophilia). Interestingly, there are now press reports surfacing that the titular hero of the film *Ted* is becoming a sex symbol for plushophiles.

Most lovers of teddy bears have no sexual inclinations towards them at all and their hobby is known as "arctophily". However, in some circles arctophilia is viewed as a subtype of zoophilia and includes humans having sex with real bears. As far as I am aware, there is no academic or clinical research on ursusagalmatophilia, although as the newspaper story on Charles Marshall highlights it does appear to exist even though it is rare. It is also featured in most online lists of the Top 10 or Top 20 weirdest fetishes and paraphilias compiled by such websites as Coed Magazine, Pop Crunch, Dating Dish, Paraphilia Dramatica and Plucky Charms.

I have searched every database I can think of to get some information about teddy bear fetishes, but there really is not a lot out there. You can certainly buy teddy bear fetish fiction, such as Jade Scott's short story *Taming My Teddy Bear: An Erotic Story*, on legitimate sites like Amazon. However, it is hard to know if such fiction is based on anything other than one person's fantasy or whether it is written from the position of personal experience. In one of the few online articles about ursusagalmatophilia, Toddy English wrote about her relationship with Adam, an ursusagalmatophile:

> "He started showing me pictures of all these teddy bears. The photos of the teddy bears were really cute. I just found it bizarre that all of his wallet photos were of teddy bears. One of them was of him sitting on his bed surrounded by teddy bears. Adam also had a picture of a really big bear (life-sized) that he named Robbie. I thought nothing about it, initially. It seemed innocent enough … That was until he told me what he liked to do with those damn bears. [Adam] got aroused having oral and anal copulation with Robbie … He further elaborated that he had been in actual threesomes with Robbie … At first I thought he was playing. But as he continued his expression never changed. Adam was being for real. Hell, the way he discussed it he LOOKED like he was getting turned on … I asked Adam had he ever had sex without a bear around. He answered honestly and said no."

Again, this is a second-hand account based on one person's perception of another person's behaviour. The first-hand account presented by English again suggests teddy bear fetishes exist, but there is no third-party verification. Unless a person's fetish becomes a criminal behaviour like that of Charles Marshall, the behaviour is unlikely to be the topic of scientific investigation.

Vacuum cleaner sex/fetishism

While researching an article on bizarre sexual injuries, I came across a paper on penile skin loss by a group of plastic surgeons (Tolba *et al.*, 2014). The authors noted that penile skin loss "can result from traction by mechanical devices, such as farm or industrial machinery, or by suction devices, such as vacuum cleaners." This got me wondering to what extent sexual injuries caused by vacuum cleaners had been reported in the medical literature. The earliest paper that I could find on the topic was Fox and Barrett (1960) who reported three cases of similar-looking penile injuries caused by three British men seeking sexual stimulation from a vacuum cleaner.

In a letter to the editor, Zufall (1973) described a penile laceration caused by a vacuum cleaner, although he does not mention any sexual motive for the injury. However, in a follow-up letter to the editor, Mannion (1973) responded that:

> "[Dr. Zufall] appears to regard these injuries as possibly accidental. We in urology tend to believe that they occur as a form of masturbation. I have had a patient with this injury who admits to this practice, and a number of urologists also have had similar cases as we discovered at a meeting of the New England Section of the American Urologists Association in October 1972. Many of the urologists present knew of this injury."

Citron and Wade (1980) reported another four case studies of penile sexual injuries caused by vacuum cleaners. Wenderoth and Jonas (1979) examined 48 masturbation injuries and reported that 12 comprised foreign bodies introduced into the urethra and urinary bladder, while the other 36 comprised "vacuum cleaner injuries" to the penis. McAninch *et al.* (1984) examined major injuries to the testicles, penis and genital skin from trauma in 62 of their patients over a 6-year period (1977–1983). They reported seven suction-end vacuum cleaner injuries in their sample. Benson (1985) investigated whether vacuum cleaner injuries to the penis were a common urologic problem. He presented five case studies of such penile injuries including one of a man who had lost the glans of his penis. Benson concluded that "contrary to apparent public appreciation, injury due to this form of autostimulation may not be unusual."

Rossi *et al.* (1991) reported the case of penile injury caused by masturbating using a vacuum cleaner. The vacuum cleaner caused skin lesions and urethral lacerations that were successfully treated. The authors stressed "the extreme rarity of the case". Since then academic papers on the topic appear to have dried up somewhat.

In 1998 a news story made worldwide headlines when a 51-year-old man from Long Branch, New Jersey, USA cut off half an inch of his penis and nearly bled to death after masturbating with a vacuum cleaner. He first told legal and medical authorities that he had been stabbed in his penis by someone as he slept. However, it later became apparent that he was trying to gain sexual pleasure from the vacuum cleaner's suction, but did not realize there was a blade that pushed dust into the vacuum cleaner's bag. Fortunately, medics at Monmouth Medical Center stopped the bleeding saving the man's life, but were unable to reattach the severed part of his penis. As far as I am aware, this case was never reported in the medical literature – just the popular press.

Notwithstanding the lack of academic papers, Falk *et al.* (2005) reported the case of a 61-year-old man who was admitted to hospital with a partially severed penis. The authors reported:

> *"The head of the penis (glans) had been completely severed, and the skin of the shaft and the corpora cavernosa had been ripped open. In the hospital the patient reported that his penis got caught in the hose attachment of an old Kobold vacuum cleaner that he was using to inflate an air mattress. He later made contradictory statements in his report to the insurance company, so we were asked to reconstruct the circumstances of the accident. The literature available to us only makes clinical observations about similar accidents, always with the assumption that the vacuum cleaner was used during masturbation or in order to achieve an erection. According to our reconstruction of the accident and an investigation of the vacuum cleaner attachment, however, we could not rule out the possibility of a household accident as described by the patient."*

The lack of modern definitive reports in the medical literature about masturbatory penile injuries caused by vacuum cleaners suggests they are either less commonplace than they used to be and/or there are as many as there have ever been over the last few decades, but are not as journal worthy since they are no longer novel.

There are a couple of case studies in the forensic literature that have featured vacuum cleaners in autoerotic deaths. Imami and Kemal (1988) reported the case of a 57-year-old white American male with a history of heart disease and chronic pancreatitis. The man was found naked slumped over his vacuum cleaner after a neighbour wondered why the vacuum cleaner had been on continuously for a long time. The man was found leaning against the dining table with his testicles, buttocks and thighs tightly bound with women's tights. Near the table was a jar of urine, jars of lubricant and a wooden table leg covered in faecal excrement. The man was covered in burns from the vacuum cleaner. No defect was found in the vacuum cleaner. The autopsy revealed that the man suffered a heart attack while engaged in the autoerotic activity. The wooden table leg had been used in an attempt to stimulate orgasm via anal penetration. His wife had caught him masturbating with the vacuum cleaner before and let it be known they had not had sex for 5 years. The death was classed as natural rather than accidental.

Vampirism

Although vampirism as a paraphilia has been noted in the academic literature for many years going right back to von Krafft-Ebing (1886), there has been very little empirical research and most of what is known comes from clinical case studies. To complicate things further, many experts believe vampirism (i) is rarely a single clinical condition, (ii) may or may not be associated with other psychiatric and/or psychological disorders (such as severe psychopathy, schizophrenia, hysteria and mental retardation) and (iii) may or may not necessarily include sexual arousal. Other related conditions have been documented, such as odaxelagnia (deriving sexual pleasure from biting), haematolagnia (deriving sexual satisfaction from the drinking of blood), haematophilia (deriving sexual satisfaction from blood in general) and auto-haemofetishism (deriving sexual pleasure from the sight of blood drawn into a syringe during intravenous drug practice).

Vandenbergh and Kelly (1964) defined vampirism as "the act of drawing blood from an object (usually a love object) and receiving resultant sexual excitement and pleasure." Bourguignon (1977) described vampirism as a clinical phenomenon in which myth, fantasy and reality converge. He noted that other paraphilic behaviour may be involved including necrophagia, necrophilia and sadism. He further noted that "vampirism is a rare compulsive disorder with an irresistible urge for blood ingestion, a ritual necessary to bring mental relief; like other compulsions, its meaning is not understood by the participant."

Prins (1985), arguably the most cited paper in the field, proposed there to be four types of vampirism, although confusingly one of these subtypes is not actually vampiric as no blood ingestion takes place and some of the satisfaction gained may not necessarily be sexual. According to Prins' typology these four types are:

- *Necrosadistic vampirism* (i.e., deriving satisfaction from the ingestion of blood from a dead person).
- *Necrophilia* (i.e., deriving satisfaction from sexual activity with a dead person without the ingestion of blood).
- *Vampirism* (i.e., deriving satisfaction from the ingestion of blood from a living person).
- *Autovampirism* (deriving satisfaction from the ingestion of one's own blood).

According to Prins' typology vampirism evidently overlaps with necrophilia. However, earlier papers such as Vandenbergh and Kelly (1964) clearly differentiated between necrophilia and vampirism arguing that vampirism should not be confused with necrophilia given that it is often focused on the living. Vandenbergh and Kelly also differentiated it from sexual sadism because vampirism does not always include pain and suffering.

In fact, Yates *et al.* (2008) included the "rare phenomenon" of vampirism in their review of the literature on sexual sadism. Drawing on the work of Jaffe and DiCataldo (1994), they described individuals who get sexual arousal from bloodletting either through cutting or biting, as well as a small minority who also enjoy sucking and/or drinking blood. Vandenbergh and Kelly (1964) further noted that the sucking or drinking of blood from a wound is often an important part of the act, but not necessarily essential.

Using the American Psychiatric Association's *Diagnostic and Statistical Manual of Mental Disorders* (DSM), Milner et al. (2008) argued that if someone's vampirism caused pain and suffering to the victims, then it should be classed as a sexually sadistic paraphilia. However, if victims do not suffer in any way, then the vampirism should be classed as a paraphilia not otherwise specified (PNOS). Milner et al. argued this approach is consistent with other PNOS classifications involving body fluids/substances other than blood, such as urophilia (urine) and coprophilia (faeces).

Any discussion of vampirism would not be complete without at least a mention of Renfield's Syndrome (RS), although it has yet to be included in the *Diagnostic and Statistical Manual of Mental Disorders*. Renfield was a fictional mental patient in Bram Stoker's novel *Dracula* (1887) who ate living things (flies, spiders, birds) believing that this would bring him greater "life force" powers. RS was first so called in a paper by Noll (1992). It is a rare psychiatric compulsion, not necessarily sexual and often linked with schizophrenia, in which sufferers feel compelled to drink blood. As with some of the papers written on vampirism as a paraphilia, this has also been called "clinical vampirism". Like the character Renfield himself, RS sufferers believe that they can obtain increased power or strength (i.e., "life force") through imbibing the blood of others (Occult and Violent Crime Research Centre, 2012).

RS sufferers are predominantly male, although there are known female vampirists. Moreover, as is the case with many paraphilias, the disorder often originates from a childhood event in which the affected individual associates the sight or taste of blood with psychological and/or physical excitement. It is during adolescence that the attraction to blood can become sexual in nature. Clinical evidence suggests female RS sufferers are unlikely to assault others for blood, but male RS sufferers are potentially more dangerous. It has been noted that RS usually comprises three stages:

- *Stage 1.* Autovampirism (a.k.a. "autohemophagia") is the first stage in which RS sufferers drink their own blood and often bite or cut themselves to do so, although some may just pick at their own scabs.
- *Stage 2.* Zoophagia is the second stage in which RS sufferers eat live animals and/or drink their blood. The sources of animal blood may come from butchers and abbatoirs if they have no direct access.
- *Stage 3.* True vampirism is the final stage in which RS sufferers drink blood from other human beings. The sources of blood may be stolen from blood banks or hospitals or may be direct from other people. In the most extreme cases RS sufferers may commit violent crimes including murder to feed their craving.

Benezech et al. (1981) reported a case study of cannibalism and vampirism in a French paranoid and psychotic schizophrenic. After trying to kill a number of people mainly neighbours between 1969, when he was 29 years old, and 1978, he attempted a vampiric rape of a child in 1979. Although he was stopped, he went on later that day to murder an elderly man and successfully ate large pieces of the victim's thigh and attempted to suck his blood. In this instance vampirism was seen as secondary to his schizophrenia. Kelly et al. (1999) reported a similar case involving a 21-year-old Eastern European schizophrenic vampirist. However, the patient made no attempt to suck blood from himself or others, but instead frequented a hospital accident and emergency department in search for a supply of blood for transfusion.

Halevy *et al.* (1989) reported the case of a 21-year-old man who had been in prison since he was 16 years old. The man suffered from anaemia and gastrointestinal bleeding as a result of self-inflicted injuries and blood ingestion on multiple occasions. One incident involved him cutting his arm with a razor blade, draining the blood into a glass and then drinking it. He was classed as an "autovampirist" according to Prins' (1985) typology, although Halevy *et al.* were unable to determine whether any sexual motivation was involved.

Hemphill and Zabow (1983) examined four vampirists in depth, one of whom was John Haigh, the English "acid-bath murderer" who killed six people during the 1940s and drank their blood. Hemphill and Zabow further noted that Haigh and the three other vampirists in their study had a history since childhood of cutting themselves and had drunk their own blood and that of others whether human or animal to relieve their cravings. All four vampirists were said to be intelligent with no evidence of mental instability or psychopathology in any of their family histories.

Gubb *et al.* (2006) reported a case study of a 25-year-old African man suffering from "psychic vampirism". They argued that this particular type of clinical vampirism had never been reported in the literature before. The man was brought in for psychiatric treatment by his mother after he had become withdrawn, stopped socializing, was undressing in public and started talking to himself. He claimed to hear the voice of "Sasha", a "flame vampire from the scriptures of Geeta". The man himself believed he was "Vasever – lord of the vampires". He claimed to have survived by hunting as a vampire by "hurting" more than 1,000 humans "zooming in and out of them" rather than biting them. Schizophrenia was diagnosed. The authors claimed that vampirism was only of academic interest "because of its relative scarcity", but did not influence the diagnosis or treatment in any particular way.

Gubb *et al.* concluded that vampirism may be representative of some pathology other than schizophrenia or simply represent an alternative belief system. Unlike other vampirism cases in the clinical literature, there was an absence of a fully developed psychopathic personality or of sexual and gender identity disorders. This, they speculated, "may have protected the man from developing the homicidal, cannibalistic, libidinal and sexual features of vampirism seen in other cases."

Veil fetishism

In this book I examined various subtypes of clothes fetishism, such as garment fetishism and handwear fetishism, although they do not have entries of their own. However, while doing that research, I soon realized that some people's fetishistic desires are very specific when it comes to clothing (e.g., particular types of uniform or particular types of footwear). One of the more unusual clothing fetishes is veil fetishism.

From the online articles that I have come across, veil fetishism appears to be an almost exclusively male fetish in which individuals have a fetishistic sexual desire for women wearing veils over their faces, although paradoxically most women who wear veils for religious reasons are obliged to do so by their menfolk to stop others lusting after them. A few online articles claim this has led to tension among online communities where Muslims and veil fetishists share the same virtual space, although I have not come across this myself despite looking for it.

A number of online articles claim one of the main reasons veils have permeated into Western consciousness is the increase in the number of media images of veiled women in the news following the 9/11 attacks in 2001 and the West's war on terror. However, as far as I am aware, there is no academic research on veil fetishism, although there is much speculation as to its motivational roots.

Despite much pop psychology insight online, I could not find a single piece of evidence, empirical or otherwise, to support any of the speculations made by academics or non-academics. Although veil fetishism has been little studied scientifically and maybe never will justify being studied, the phenomenon clearly exists. Despite the prevalence of such behaviour being very rare, its incidence may well be on the increase given the growing number of websites dedicated to such practices.

Venatophilia

In an online article about cartoon quicksand fetishes (discussed a little later in this entry), there was mention of a fetish group Giant Video Game Girls who appear to have coined the term "venatophilia" from the Latin word for "game" (*venatus*). Venatophilia is supposedly a sexual attraction to or a fascination with videogame characters. Venatophilia also gets a mention on the Wiktionary protologism page, a page that lists prototype neologisms (a.k.a. "newly coined words or expressions"), where it is listed alongside venatology ("the study of games, the act of playing them and the players and cultures surrounding them"), venatomania (an obsession with games) and venatophobia (a fear of games). Personally, I find this somewhat strange as most paraphilias derive from Greek rather than Latin names. If this paraphilia exists, then I would argue it is a subtype of toonophilia (sexual attraction to cartoon characters).

Cartoon quicksand fetishes are an integration of quicksand fetishism (a form of stuck fetishism) and cartoon fetishism (a.k.a. "toonophilia"). Gravning (2015) featured an interview with "quicksand artist" A-020 who draws fictional damsels stuck in quicksand, typically wearing a "tight miniskirt, pantyhose, heels and boots". Should you be interested there is a lot of art featuring women stuck in quicksand on the Deviant Art webpage. In the interview A-020 said:

> "I'm open with [my quicksand cartoon fetish] online because I'm comfortable under a screenname … Though when it comes to knowing me in person, it's pretty much a secret! I haven't been in a situation where I had to reveal this fetish … I was pretty young, maybe 7 or 8, when I started seeing quicksand scenes in a movie or a TV show. Some of those films I recall seeing were Beastmaster, The NeverEnding Story, A Nightmare on Elm Street 4 and Ursus in the Valley of the Lions … Once in a while, I'd fantasize about it."

Gravning (2015) made the point that there are other fetishes that cartoonists incorporate into their videogame graphics. Some of these are strange behaviors like unbirthing (a.k.a. "returning to the womb"), such as those featuring Princess Peach and Pokemon characters and vore (a.k.a. "vorarephilia", see entry later in this book). In fact, Tipado (2015) wrote about the "vore fetish of game characters swallowing each other whole."

In the wake of the makers of World of Warcraft launching the videogame Overwatch, which according to Yenisey (2016) was "an over-sexualized first-person shooter featuring tons of big-breasted anime chicks," there was an 817% increase on Pornhub for Overwatch-related searches, particularly for the buxom character Tracer.

So, what is the underlying psychology behind fetishes and sexual attraction to videogame characters? Gravning (2015) interviewed the evolutionary psychologist Catherine Salmon, who responded:

> "If somebody gets attached to a character because they play a game a lot and fantasize about that character, it wouldn't be surprising that they take that character and stick it somewhere else. It's not surprising that some of the female characters in videogames who are heroines and are portrayed as very sexual characters in terms of the way that they're drawn might end up as the stars of gamers' sexual fantasies. The social aspect of using familiar characters is another reason for using them in quicksand imagery and other fetishes. If you use a known character for a fetish, it gives your work some degree of a built-in audience, a device often used for fanfiction … There is a community of men who are creating and sharing these stories or these images. If they share an interest in the original material as well, then using that original material creates an additional commonality of interest. It's one thing to have your sexual fantasies and it's another thing to share your sexual fantasies. If you're creating art or fiction and you're putting it on the web, you're not just doing it for yourself, it's not just your fantasy that you're jerking off to, you're giving that to other people as well. To do that, you find a built-in community if you're using a shared character."

Gravning (2015) noted some "shared characters" find themselves in "exactly the same situations that these artists fetishize" and asked evolutionary psychologist Catherine Salmon whether witnessing individuals repeatedly stuck in quicksand when a child could possibly lead to such unusual fetishes:

> "It could be something like that. Whether its quicksand or tar pits, there's things like that in children's cartoons. It could be something as simple as that. Part of it is the damsel in distress kind of image. Watching 'Wonder Woman' caught in that kind of circumstance when people are younger – [it's] an image that's eroticized, a very sexually drawn, very feminine image. And they might enjoy watching that sort of thing or the struggle, as she's trying to get out of whatever that circumstance is. There are a lot of unusual circumstances in cartoons and fantasy and you may get aroused while you're watching it and then carry some of that too."

Gravning (2015) also interviewed sex therapist Elizabeth Lars who shares my own view on this by alluding to classical conditioning. Elizabeth Lars calls such associations "accidents of learning" in which the associations "don't have to be exactly like the fantasy that comes, it just has to resemble it." Furthermore, she went on to speculate:

> "[Quicksand fetishists] probably fantasized and got into the feeling that goes with that, not just watching. It could [also] be identifying with it. The kid imagining himself stuck in quicksand in the victim's place, for example, could be part of its erotic appeal. You could either be observing it or experiencing it. You could be doing both at the same time in a fantasy. Some evidence certainly suggests that sexual patterns are already there, for sure in males, by the age of eight. They may or may not have begun masturbating to fantasies until adolescence, but something is going on internally at a very young age. This highly influential period of age eight through adolescence is also probably for many a prime time for the ingestion of the bizarre imagery and situations contained in videogames and cartoons, which often also incorporate sexualized heroines. It looks like what we call fetishes are remarkably easy to install in the early learning experiences. Same thing about fears too."

Back in the late 1990s I had a regular column with the now-defunct magazine *Arcade*. My very first column (Griffiths, 1998b) was on the psychology of *Tomb Raider*, the sexualization of lead character Lara Croft and the influence it might have on young boys and emerging adolescents. This was echoed by neuroscientist Ogi Ogas who in another interview by Gravning (2015) said that when pubertal males spend a lot of time with sexualized videogame characters like Lara Croft:

> "They are seeing these characters during their formative time. They are kind of perfect and ideal – and you don't have to actually interact with them. Psychologically, it's truly like a stripped-down, pure erotic stimulus. So it's much easier to imprint on that, to fetishize that. Part of the fascination is simply being culturally exposed to characters like Lara Croft ... [In relation to quicksand fetishes] the notion of being smothered or trapped is universal in the sense that it exists to greater and lesser degrees all over. It's not just one or two people that have it. It is found in a lot of places. Clearly our normal brain design is not that far removed from [wanting to be] enveloped. It's probably something to do with our tactile system, our touch system of the brain, that's quite naturally wired to our sexual arousal system. The tactile system is also interconnected with sensations like being smothered and being interred, being dowsed with water. Probably, somehow – and I'm speculating here – that's what got crossed up for whatever reasons. How someone's brain entangles sexual arousal with the notion of being trapped or smothered might simply be a perturbation of the neural system. A quirk in the brain, essentially. It could be some randomness in the seemingly infinite complexity of your DNA. So, from a perspective rooted in computational neuroscience, niche sexual desires needn't be wholly, or at all, explained as the result of social construction or evolutionary adaptation. As we're learning more about the genetics of brain construction, we're coming to understand the genetic expression that leads to different neural wiring is highly variable and dependent on so many things [that] could happen in the womb, things that happen in early life, different environmental things. There's just myriad, myriad factors that can cause unusual neural wiring to arise."

Based on what I have seen and read online, venatophilia appears to exist, although it could be argued that videogame fetishes are just subclasses of other types of fetishes and paraphilias, such as toonophilia, vorarephilia, unbirthing and stuck fetishism.

Vermiphilia

In this book I have looked at a number of sexually zoophilic behaviours relating to creepy crawlies of one description or another including ants, bees and wasps, such as formicophilia in which individuals derive sexual pleasure and arousal from insects crawling and/or nibbling on their genitals. Turning now to "worm sex" (pun intended), I think I should start by trying to explain why worm sex has been given so many different names including vermophilia, helminthophilia and scoleciphilia (abnormal affection towards worms and/or being infested with worms) – not to mention subvariants, such as taeniophilia/teniophilia (i.e., abnormal affection for tapeworms).

Although the words for these alleged sexual practices can be found in many online A–Z lists of paraphilias, they appear to have been derived from opposite phobic behaviours (i.e., helminthophobia, scoleciphobia and vermiphobia, all of which are defined as the fear of worms and/or the fear of infestation with worms). For the remainder of this entry I will use the term "vermiphilia" as I have come across a lot of people in the academic biological worm world using the word "vermiphilic" to describe an intense liking for worms. However, this appears to be used in the context of having an academic research-like interest in them rather than anything sexual.

It will probably come as no surprise that there is no academic literature on vermiphilia and that all the material I have collated can be best described as anecdotal. The only article of any length I have come across on the topic of vermiphilia is that of Amano (no date). The article is basically a case study about the owner of a Japanese company called *Genki*. Check out their website, but be warned it is very sexually explicit. I also mentioned *Genki* in the entry on formicophilia and described it as a style of erotic art and pornography that features women covered with various creatures, typically insects or small sea creatures. The article actually spent more time talking about *Genki*'s owner's haemorrhoids and his quest for anal orgasm, but he did manage to write the following:

> "I direct films that involve women in sexual congress with all kinds of living sea creatures and reptiles including dojo loaches, earthworms, frogs, sea cucumbers, octopi and even an anaconda. I didn't really have any kind of grand concept behind making these films, except I want to make people amazed. And also make something I wanted to watch; at the end of the day, I'm just a very selfish person. This month, I shot a new film featuring mealworms and earthworms. I bought 30 kg of them and used them all. I felt bad for the actress but they weren't cheap, and I'd spent more of the budget on the worms than the actress. Did you know mealworms bite? Apparently, they do and, according to the actress, it's really painful!"

Looking at this written confession along with some of the films at his *Genki* website, it is obvious that as a film director he clearly made these films for his own (presumably sexual) pleasure and that the actresses who participated appear to get nothing from the act apart from being paid (at least I hope they got paid). Whether others watching derive any sexual pleasure and arousal is highly debatable. I would also argue that there are sexually sadistic undertones to the whole process and practice of naked females having worms placed into their genital orifices. However, this practice is not restricted to women as I have also found guides to "worm torture" being used within gay sadomasochistic practices in online "dehumanization" sex games, such as those at the Berlin Queer website.

Vorarephilia

Vorarephilia (a.k.a. "vore") is a paraphilia in which people are sexually aroused by the idea of being eaten, eating another person or observing this process for sexual gratification. Since such behaviour is unlikely to actually be carried out by a vorarephiliac, the behaviour is more likely to be fantasy based via different media (e.g., fictional stories, fantasy art, fantasy videos and bespoke videogames). The behaviour does not necessarily involve digestion and/or pain. Probably as a result of it being both rare and fantasy based, it does not appear in any psychiatric manuals such as the American Psychiatric Association's *Diagnostic and Statistical Manual of Mental Disorders*.

Vorarephilia can sometimes co-exist with other fetishistic behaviour, such as masochism (sexual arousal from receiving pain), hypoxyphilia (sexual arousal from suffocation and oxygen restriction) and "snuff" fetishes (sexual arousal from seeing someone die). In some cases vorarephilia has been argued to be a variant of macrophilia (i.e., sexual fascination and/or fantasy relating to giants). Most of the fantasies of vorarephiliacs involve being the ones being eaten (i.e., the "prey"), although a few like to be the "pred" (taken from the word "predator"). Some vorarephiliacs are known to derive pleasure, sometimes sexual, from watching some animals (e.g., snakes) eating other animals whole.

Many types of vorarephilia have been documented (Lykins and Cantor, 2014) including hard vore and soft vore. Being primarily fantasy based, almost any orifice or body part can be capable of vore (e.g., vaginal vore, anal vore and cock vore). They can be summarized very briefly as:

- Hard vore (a.k.a. "gore") is where someone is subjected to horrific injuries and involves lots of blood because of the ripping, cutting, biting, tearing and/or chewing of flesh. It is not typically thought of as either sensually or sexually motivated.
- Soft vore is where someone who may not necessarily be a willing victim is consumed alive and whole and is typically unharmed before reaching the stomach, but then may be asphyxiated and/or digested. Compared with hard vore, soft vore is usually seen as more sensual and sexually oriented.
- Female genital vore (a.k.a. "vaginal vore") is where someone is consumed by the vagina and taken into the womb, something that is often referred to as unbirthing or a reverse birth.
- Male genital vore (a.k.a. "cock vore") is where someone is consumed by the urethral opening of the penis and taken into the scrotum, prostate or bladder.
- Anal vore is where someone is consumed by the anus and taken into the rectum, colon or stomach.
- Breast vore is where someone is consumed by the nipples and taken into the breast.

The motivational driving force underlying vorarephilia in some ways appears to resemble that of sadomasochism from a dominance and submission perspective. Devouring someone could be viewed as the ultimate act of dominance by a predator and the ultimate act of submission by the prey. Paradoxically, most vorarephiliacs have no real interest in cannibalism, although a few do. Possible vorarephiliacs include Issei Sagawa from Japan who in 1981 killed and then ate a Dutch woman Renée Hartevelt and the serial killer Jeffrey Dahmer who killed 17 men and boys. He engaged in cannibalistic and necrophilic acts with his many victims between 1978 and 1991.

However, the most infamous vorarephiliac is arguably Armin Meiwes from Germany. Pfafflin (2008) referred at length to this case. Computer technician Meiwes gained worldwide media attention as the "Rotenburg Cannibal" for killing and eating a fellow German who was also a computer technician. Meiwes had allegedly been fantasizing about cannibalism since his childhood and frequented cannibal fetish websites. He even posted around 60 advertisements asking if anyone would like to be eaten by him. Meiwes claimed around 200 men responded to his request, but only one finally met him face to face.

In March 2002 Bernd Jürgen Brandes responded to Meiwes' advertisement on the internet. Meiwes claimed that at their one and only meeting at Meiwes' house their first cannabilistic act involved Meiwes biting off Brandes' penis and then the two of them jointly cooking and eating it. Brandes then drank lots of alcohol, was given some cough syrup, took sleeping pills and was videotaped being stabbed to death by Meiwes in his bath. The body was then stored and over time Meiwes ate large amounts of it (about 20 kg). The one aspect that shocked most people was not the fact that Meiwes ate a lot of Brandes' body, but that Brandes appeared to consent to being eaten.

Little is known about how prevalent this type of behaviour is, although Meiwes claimed that, based on his internet activity on cannibal fetish websites, there were at least 800 Germans who shared his passion for wanting to eat another person. The number of people who have a desire to be eaten and actually go through with it is likely to be incredibly small, but the internet helped Meiwes locate a willing victim.

Voyeurism (Upskirting)

Voyeurism basically refers to sexual arousal from viewing others naked or in a state of undress and/or watching others engaged in sexual activity. However, whether this is genuinely a paraphilia is debatable given the large number of individuals who will have engaged in some form of voyeurism in their lives. For example, in a Canadian survey cited by the American Psychiatric Association (2022) the lifetime prevalence of voyeuristic behaviours was reported in over one third of the sample (50.3% among males, 21.2% among females). However, voyeuristic disorder is defined by the American Psychiatric Association (2022) in the DSM-5-TR as:

"Recurrent and intense sexual arousal from observing an unsuspecting person who is naked, in the process of disrobing, or engaging in sexual activity, as manifested by fantasies, urges, or behaviors. The individual has acted on these sexual urges with a

nonconsenting person, or the sexual urges or fantasies cause clinically significant distress or impairment in social, occupational, or other important areas of functioning." (pp. 780–781)

The ratio of voyeuristic behaviour tends to be higher among males than among females (approximately 2:1 to 3:1), although the number of women with voyeuristic disorder is thought to be very low. In one Austrian study of 1,346 incarcerated sex offenders the prevalence of voyeuristic disorder was 3.7% (American Psychiatric Association, 2022).

Voyeuristic acts are arguably the most common of potentially law-breaking sexual behaviours, and these types of behaviour have evolved. Upskirting is one of many newer sexual acts that are present among those individuals who have a voyeuristic disorder. This refers to taking a photograph (typically with a smartphone) up someone's skirt without their permission. There are now campaigns in many countries to get upskirting criminalized (it is now a criminal offence in the UK). In an article for the *Law Gazette* in July 2017 forensic psychologist Julia Lam made countless references to upskirting in an overview of voyeuristic disorder. She noted that:

"Voyeuristic Disorder is a paraphilic/psychosexual disorder in which an individual derives sexual pleasure and gratification from looking at naked bodies and genital organs, observing the disrobing or sexual acts of others ... Instead of peeping in situ using high-powered binoculars, with advances in technology such as camera phones and pin-hole cameras, voyeurs can now record the private moments with their devices: taking upskirt photos of unsuspecting individuals on escalators, or filming women in various states of undress in toilets and changing rooms. Voyeuristic behaviour is on the rise ... Learning theory suggests that an initially random or accidental observation of an unsuspecting person who is naked, in the process of disrobing, or engaging in sexual activity, may lead to sexual interest and arousal; with each successive repetition of the peeping act reinforcing and perpetuating the voyeuristic behaviour."

She reported that voyeurism is the most common type of sexual offence and that voyeurs can be men or women but that *"men are commonly the perpetrators in the peeping acts/upskirt, with women being the victims."* She noted that the lifetime prevalence of voyeuristic disorder is around 12% among men and 4% in women, and that the causes of voyeurism are unknown. She then went on to say:

"The new vocabulary [word] 'upskirt' is both a verb (the practise of capturing an image/video of an unsuspecting and non-consenting person in a private moment) and a noun (i.e., the actual voyeuristic photos or videos made; referred as 'voyeur photography') ... While most voyeurs film for self-gratification (i.e., using upskirt materials for fantasy and masturbation), there are offenders who make upskirt photos and videos specifically for uploading onto the internet (e.g., fetish and pornographic websites and video-sharing sites like YouTube) for monetary profit."

Lam also talked about her treating upskirting voyeurs and recounted one case which she claimed was a compulsion. The case involved a male university student who was very sport active but who masturbated excessively whenever major sporting events or important exams were imminent as a coping strategy to relieve stress. Upskirting was another one of his coping strategies and he was eventually arrested for his behaviour. Lam then went on to report:

> "Every morning after he woke up, he would feel the urge to go out to find his 'targets'. Although he knew it was very risky to take upskirt [photos] on MRT [mass rapid transit] escalators, he felt compelled to satiate his urges and gratification, and was oblivious to his surroundings (e.g., passers-by, security staff and CCTV) and the risk of being arrested. He could still feel the thrill and excitement, but he no longer enjoyed the act. It had become more like a compulsion … He was prescribed medication to manage his mood and urges to act out, and attended psychotherapy to work on his voyeuristic behaviour and learn more effective coping skills. He has since graduated from university, and has not breached the law with [upskirting] behaviour again."

Another source suggesting that upskirting may be a compulsive behaviour comes from the details of those arrested and prosecuted. For instance, one infamous example in the UK (in 2015) was the case of Paul Appleby who managed to take 9,000 upskirting photos in the space of just 5 weeks (suggesting that he was doing it all day every day to have taken so many photos). Appleby was finally apprehended when he was caught bending over to take a photo up a woman's skirt in a shop. In the court case a mitigating factor for Appleby's behaviour was that he was "addicted" to upskirting. The fact that Appleby did not receive a custodial sentence suggests the excuse of being "addicted" to the behaviour led to the judge being more lenient.

Another British case highlighted the ingenious methods used to aid upskirting. Stafford Cant used spy cameras hidden inside one of his trainers, his key fob and his wrist watch to engage in upskirting women (as well as filming the backs of their legs) who were shopping in a Cheshire village. Acting on a tip-off his house was raided and the police found 222,000 videos and pictures dating back 7 years. "Addiction" was again used as a mitigating factor in the crimes, but this time it was not addiction to voyeurism but an addiction to collecting things. Despite his "addiction", Cant was jailed for 3 years after pleading guilty to outraging public decency, voyeurism and possessing and distributing indecent images. Finally, it is worth mentioning that men can also be the victims of upskirting and that men wearing kilts are protected by the UK ban on upskirting too (BBC, 2018).

Waxplay fetishism

A few academic studies into sadomasochism have examined various niche practices including waxplay. In the entry on psychrocism (individuals who derive sexual pleasure and sexual arousal from being cold or by watching someone else who is cold), I quoted from Love (2001):

> "Exposure to intense cold creates a sharp sensation that is similar to other physical stimuli that produce tension. The mind changes its focus from intellectual pursuits to physical awareness. Many [sadomasochistic] players use cold contact to heighten awareness of skin sensations. They often alternate cold with heat, such as ice cubes and candle wax."

Alison *et al.* (2001) reported that the most popular sadomasochistic (SM) activities were flagellation and bondage. However, less reported SM activities such as piercing, asphyxiation, electric shocks, use of blades/knives and fisting are the most harmful. The researchers further explored variations in SM activities. Waxplay fell into the "typical pain administration" group. Such variations are:

- Typical pain administration involves such practices as spanking, caning, whipping, skin branding, use of hot wax and electric shocks.
- Humiliation involves verbal humiliation, gagging, face slapping and flagellation. Heterosexuals were more likely than gay men to engage in these types of activities.
- Physical restriction includes bondage, use of handcuffs, use of chains, wrestling, use of ice, wearing straitjackets, hypoxyphilia and mummifying.
- Hypermasculine pain administration involves rimming, dildo use, cock binding, being urinated upon, being given an enema, fisting, being defecated upon and catheter insertion. Gay men were more likely than heterosexuals to engage in these types of activities.

Sandnaba *et al.* (2002a, b, c), in follow-up studies by the same team on the same sample of sadomasochists, reported that 35% of their participants had engaged in hot waxplay. From these few studies it would appear that waxplay among SM practitioners is relatively prevalent, although there appear to be few data about how regularly waxplay is engaged in.

Weather fetishism

Weather can affect mood and for some people can lead to extreme depression in the form of seasonal affective disorder (SAD). There also seems to be some evidence that weather can affect people's sex lives. Being too hot or too cold is likely to lessen the desire to engage in sexual behaviour. Most academic research appears to indicate that sex drives are higher in spring and summer. One of the reasons given for this is that during spring and summer there is more sun and that melanocyte-stimulating hormone (MSH) stimulates sex, particularly among women.

A number of studies have indicated that during the spring and summer months the body produces more serotonin (a.k.a. "the feelgood neurotransmitter") because of the increased luminosity of sunlight. During the winter months, as the amount of sunlight decreases, the body produces more melatonin, which appears to inhibit sex drives. However, there is wide individual variation and the weather and subsequent hormone stimulation differ highly from one person to the next. Joshi (2010) reported that:

> "Sunlight has a direct effect on the brain's serotonin production, according to researchers at the Human Neurotransmitter Laboratory and the Alfred and Baker Medical Unit, Baker Heart Research Institute, Australia. Our serotonin levels increase with increase in luminosity. And how does that matter? Among other things, serotonin also regulates arousal, says Ray Sahelian, MD, author of Mind Boosters ... Not just serotonin, but sunlight affects many other hormones in our body as well, some of which are associated with mood and pleasure feelings, according to professor Carmen Fusco, an instructor in pharmacology. It decreases melatonin, norepinephrine and acetylcholine and increases cortisol, serotonin, GABA and dopamine. The summer heat is good for your sex life too. It works on your muscles by relaxing them and intensifies sensations of the skin. Further, the heat slows us down. This helps us get in touch with our more subdued sensual side, according to psychologist Stella Resnick, PhD, author of The Pleasure Zone."

Herbert (2009) noted that the spring and summer months may reduce sex drives among some people. This is particularly true of those who suffer reverse SAD and get the summer blues as opposed to the stereotypical winter blues. She noted that:

> "Though rare, reverse seasonal affective disorder is when warmer temperatures make a person feel cooped up instead of carefree. Characterized by anxiety, decreased appetite, insomnia and irritability, the condition is triggered by longer days and too much heat and/or light. Those who experience reverse SAD report feeling attacked by the sun and tend to go into twilight mode – avoiding sunlight at all costs, taking frequent cold showers and scampering from one air-conditioned environment to the next."

However, there may be some genuine weather-related paraphilias. This entry came about as a result of the following online admission by someone with a sexual attraction to rain on the Is It Normal? website:

> "I wouldn't really know if this is considered a fetish or not, but rain really turns me on. The cloudy weather or late night rain makes me really horny. I can be in my room

all alone and bored and just the fact that it's raining really excites me. It's not to go outside and have sex while rain is pouring on you. It's to have sex while it rains. This thought is really sexy to me, and I really want to try it. I've been told this is a fetish, but I don't see it that way."

This snippet reminded me of the dark side of rain fetishism. It brought to mind the case of Lam Kor-wan, the so-called "Hong Kong Butcher" (a.k.a. "Rainy Night Butcher"). The case was reported by Aggrawal (2011a). Kor-wan was brought to trial in 1983, convicted and sentenced to death by hanging, which was commuted to life imprisonment without parole. In addition to being Hong Kong's most notorious necrophile, he also became infamous for always attacking his victims during inclement weather. Aggrawal (2009a) reported:

"In 1982, at the age of 27, while working as a taxi driver, [Kor-wan] is known to have abducted and killed at least four women. After killing, he would have sex with their dead bodies, often taking videos of his necrophilic acts. He would then mutilate their bodies and keep their sexual organs in Tupperware containers in his bedroom. For this idiosyncrasy, he was also known as The Jars Murderer. The rest of the bodies were disposed of via his taxi in the New Territories and on Hong Kong Island. As he would often attack his victims during inclement weather, he was also known as The Rainy Night Butcher."

Whether (or should that be "weather"?) such paraphilias genuinely exist is debatable. I have not been able to locate a single academic or clinical case study relating to those listed by Aggrawal (2009a). However, weather conditions have been shown to affect mood and "normal" sexual behaviour, so there is no reason to think that on occasions they may lead to non-normative sexual behaviour.

Wedding ring fetishes

In January 1995 a UK Channel 4 television documentary programme *Equinox* examined paraphilias in a programme called "Beyond Love". Sexologist Dr Gene Abel was one of the many experts interviewed for the programme and related a story about a man with an unusual fetish. His sexual turn-on was gold wedding rings. In recounting the individual's story, Abel said that the fetish was very specific and that the ring had to be of a particular width (6 mm to 10 mm if I recall correctly) for it to be sexually stimulating to the man in question. The roots of the fetish were established in childhood and first arose when he used to sit on his babysitter's knee and play with her ring (twirling it around on her finger). Playing with the ring while sitting on the knee of an attractive woman led to sexual arousal. However, over time the ring itself became the source of sexual arousal via continued associative pairing (i.e., sexual arousal from the sight of the female babysitter's ring became a classically conditioned response).

The man told the sexologist he had now married, but his wife was unaware of his fetish. However, he could not get sexually aroused and make love to her unless she was wearing her wedding ring and he was twirling it on her finger during sexual intercourse. The man got into the habit of walking up to female strangers, commenting how lovely their wedding rings were and asking if he could take a photograph of them. He would then use the photographs as source material for masturbatory purposes. This anecdotal case story might sound a little bizarre, especially as there is no paraphilia that refers to being sexually attracted to gold wedding rings, although Aggrawal (2009a) did mention timophilia, a paraphilia in which individuals gain sexual pleasure and arousal from gold or wealth.

However, Abel *et al.* (2008) provided a written account of this case as one of six unusual case studies. The man in question was given the pseudonym "Mr. Rings" whereas the protagonists in the other five case studies were "Mr. Cartoons", "Mr. Feet", "Mr. Balloons", "Mr. Cigarettes" and "Mr. Spanking". In all of these cases including that of "Mr. Rings" the authors noted:

> "The fetish objects in these case histories were unique enough, and the attraction to the objects strong enough, that the individuals could clearly track their interest from early childhood through adulthood. It is much easier to retrieve remote, explicit memories, such as events (e.g., a party where balloons popped) or playing with objects, than to recall the process of sexual development with no distinct markers in the individual's history. Because these distinct experiences pre-dated identified sexuality, became a focus of attention for the individual and then were incorporated into the individual's sexual interests and masturbatory fantasies, it was possible to accurately track the patterns of sexual arousal. We were also able to clearly identify how these men attempted to blend their deviant interests into sexual relationships with partners and the consequences of their efforts."

As far as I am aware, this is the only academic paper to have examined ring fetishism, but my own research on the topic has led me to the conclusion that the case of "Mr. Rings" is not unique. I found a few accounts in various online forums. In all honesty, and despite finding this interesting, I cannot see wedding ring fetishism ever being the topic of in-depth psychological research, particularly as the behaviour appears to be non-problematic in the main.

Wet and messy (WAM) fetishism

In the entry on salirophilia (a.k.a. "saliromania"), a paraphilia in which individuals experience sexual arousal from soiling or dishevelling the object of their desire, typically an attractive person, I noted that salirophilia was related to other fetishes and paraphilias such as "sploshing" (deriving sexual pleasure from wet substances, but not body fluids, being deliberately and generously applied to either naked or scantily clad individuals). The word "sploshing" (a.k.a. "wet and messy" fetish, "WAM" fetish or "wamplay") is thought to have been derived from the UK-based fetish magazine *Splosh!* that began publishing in 1989, ran for 40 issues and featured stories and photographs of women in messy situations.

In 2005 "wamplay" made the news in the UK when Bernard Bertola, a teacher from Halifax in West Yorkshire, was given a 2-year conditional registration order for searching for WAM-related terms on one of the school's computers. As Coates (2005) noted:

> "A school's former head of IT has been disciplined for watching bizarre Internet porn where women were covered in beans, spaghetti, pies and trifles. Bernard Bertola, who taught for nearly 20 years at Hipperholme and Lightcliffe High School, was found guilty of unacceptable professional conduct by the General Teaching Council. He was given a 2-year conditional registration order, which means he can remain on the register of teachers but must adhere to conditions. Bertola used a school computer to view internet sites such as 'Messy and Wet', 'Gunge Tank' and 'Messy Mania' … The Council said he had knowingly accessed sites inappropriate for a school environment. 'If he hadn't expected sexual images you would not expect to see words such as "sexy blonde actress gets pie after pie",' said presenting officer Bradley Albuery. An IT manager had spotted Bertola viewing food fetish websites in June 2003 from a monitoring computer in another room."

Interestingly, this news story also mentioned Bertola viewing food fetish sites. Food fetishes and paraphilias, such as sitophilia (see earlier entry in this book), are different from "wamplay". However, there are clearly behavioural and possibly psychological overlaps between the two fetishistic behaviours.

As far as I am aware, no empirical or clinical research has been published concerning WAM fetishes. Gates (2000) noted that individuals who are into WAM fetishes derive sexual arousal from substances that are deliberately and generously applied onto their or others' naked skin, predominantly the face, or onto people's clothes while they are still wearing them.

An important thing to note in relation to WAM fetishes is that they do not involve body fluids as such, although body substances are part of other paraphilias such as coprophilia (faeces), urophilia (urine), lactophilia (breast milk), menophilia (menstruated blood) and emetophilia (vomit).

Whether WAM fetishes ever become the subject of serious academic research is debatable. I think probably not, but that does not mean they are not of psychological interest. As with most fetishistic behaviours, my guess is that most wammers' behaviour will have been reinforced via classical and/or operant conditioning experienced in childhood or adolescence. I would also be interested to know what other fetishistic behaviours co-occur with sploshing, principal among which would be sitophilia or salirophilia.

Wiccaphilia

> "For years I have had a real fetish for witches – I believe it's called wiccaphillia [sic] – or something like that! My wife indulges my interest and she has 16 sexy witch outfits!" (Sexy Witch website)

Various websites list hundreds of types of paraphilias many of which are simply the names of specific phobias with the suffix "-phobia" replaced by the suffix "-philia". One paraphilia that often appears in these lists such as the one at the Sensual Swingers website is wiccaphilia (sexual arousal from witches and witchcraft). I initially assumed it was just based on the opposite phobia (i.e., wiccaphobia – fear of witches) and did not really exist. Furthermore, there is not a single reference to wiccaphilia in any academic article or book that I am aware of.

However, in the course of my research on this topic, I came across lots of references to the sexuality of witches, but they were light-hearted and non-academic. Such references included: photographic sites of the 25 sexiest witches; artistic sites of the sexiest witch pin-ups (i.e., drawings and paintings rather than photographs); the sexiest witches seen in the movies; articles on having sex with witches and "wiccan sex"; and articles on the application of make-up for sexy witches. Furthermore, there is the Sex, Fetish, Witch, Art photographic website run by a woman who claims: "I'm a 50+ year old average everyday woman who still likes 'sex', is a 'fetishist', identifies strongly with my natural 'witch' instincts and gets off on 'art'. I see myself as a type of carnal muse."

Given the lack of empirical data, there is nothing known about wiccaphilia, about whether such a paraphilia really exists or about its incidence, prevalence and etiology. In the unlikely event it does exist there could perhaps be some psychological crossover with individuals who have specific uniform fetishes.

Woolies fetishism

In an online article Morgan (2009) noted that:

> "There are some people who love wool so much that they make bodysuits out of them, to wear them constantly. There is even a French wool fetishist forum to discuss their love for wool clothing. Some of these advanced knitters take their clothing experience to the next level."

Human beings appear to have the capacity to fetishize about almost anything. Woolies are individuals who derive sexual pleasure and arousal from wearing wool, typically in the form of full-body "wool suits". I should mention that the term "woolies" appears to be the collective name used in Europe whereas in America such people are often referred to as "sweaterers". In this entry I use the term "woolies" irrespective of where such people are located. Given that there is absolutely no scientific research on woolies suggests either that the fetish does not really exist or that it is a relatively newly realized fetish.

There is certainly a lot of anecdotal evidence that woolies exist. On a personal level, I was interviewed for a television documentary *Forbidden* on the Discovery Channel about the practice and asked to comment on the case studies that appeared in the programme. For instance, one of the woolies featured was an American, Scott from Florida, who perhaps unsurprisingly ran a small company selling sweaters and said he had a "lifelong obsession" with wool. As a boy he claimed he would steal sweaters to hide in his school locker or in the woods near his house. At the time of recording, he had a collection of about 3,000 sweaters and claimed to be sexually attracted to anyone wearing a sweater including men (even though he is heterosexual). The programme's research team told me that:

> "Scott wears a sweater outside as much as possible, he's also got a special two-piece with knitted pants that he wears around the house. Scott describes it as a secret fetish

because no one knows that he's actually getting turned on just by walking the streets in his sweater. Scott regularly holds sweater photoshoots. Here he'll introduce us to other like-minded 'sweaterers' who travel to meet up with him and have some sweater fun and model the gear."

The programme also featured a German female "Lady Mohair" who sold full-body knitted outfits to people worldwide. In the programme she introduced the audience to a few of her more "eccentric" woolies such as "Knuti" who assumed the persona of a woolly polar bear. However, there are also various online discussion forums for those who engage in the behaviour such as the Woolfreaks website. Perhaps the largest collection of sexualized (as opposed to sexy) costumes worn by woolies can be found on the French online fetish forum Doctissimo. Be warned, though, some of the photographs are very sexually explicit and take the form of crotchless costumes. In an online article on woolies Sangbleu (2012) claimed that:

"The wool fetish is possibly one of the most mundane but simultaneously bizarre fetishes in existence. 'Woolies' as they have become to be known partake in the enjoyment of feeling the warm and fibrous softness of wool in its many different textures and knitted techniques upon their own or others' skin. This could be from the subtleness of a woman wearing a turtleneck sweater or to the other extreme of being partially mummified in countless layers of blankets."

I realize that in the absence of any academic research, this entry leans more towards anecdotal journalism than something more considered and empirical. However, my own view is that wool fetishists do exist but, as with many other niche fetishes I have covered, the incidence and prevalence is likely to be very small.

Xenophilia

One of the least researched paraphilias is xenophilia, perhaps because there does not appear to be common agreement on what it actually is. A number of sources including Twinn (2007) and the Right Diagnosis website (2012f) define xenophilia as "a sexual attraction to strangers". The Psychologist Anywhere Anytime website defines xenophilia as "sexual attraction to foreigners". However, it further adds that "in science fiction, [xenophilia] can also mean sexual attraction to aliens." I examined sexual attraction to aliens in the entry on exophilia (a paraphilia that relates only to sex with extraterrestrials). Franklin (2010) also defines xenophilia as "erotic attraction to … foreigners or extraterrestrials". Finally, Aggrawal (2009a) defines xenophilia as individuals who gain sexual pleasure and arousal "from strangers … foreign customs, traditions, and foreigners".

One of the reasons there are so many different definitions is that xenophilia was probably first deemed the opposite of xenophobia. The literal translation of xenophilia is the love of anything foreign. From this perspective "foreign" can mean different things to different people, which is why there is such a difference in the definitions of xenophilia.

To date, academic and clinical work into xenophilia has been extremely limited. Smith (2012), in an online essay about xenophilia, describes it as "an affection for unknown objects or people … [and] could be used to describe those who enjoy swinging or cruising." Personally, I think this stretches the definition of xenophilia beyond what it was originally envisaged as, but both swinging and cruising can include having sex with complete strangers, especially cruising.

Sex Obsessed (2009) is an online article and one of the few I have read that has speculated about the motivations of xenophiles. It says that xenophiles might be a "group of people who are allergic to commitment." I very much doubt such motives would be universal to xenophiles. Such a speculation could only apply to a very loose definition of what xenophilia means in paraphilic terms. Obviously, this is an area that would benefit from some academic research. However, any researchers with a desire to examine the area would have to be very clear about the operational definition of xenophilia they use to examine such people.

Zelophilia

According to Aggrawal (2009a) zelophilia is a paraphilia in which individuals derive sexual pleasure and arousal from jealousy. This is the only academic definition I have ever come across. However, as academic definitions go, it is not the most helpful because it does not say what kind of jealousy sexual arousal is linked to. Anecdotally, I am assuming that at the heart of zelophilia is a person being turned on by his or her sexual partner having a sexual and/or romantic relationship with another person.

If zelophilia genuinely exists and online posts are accurate, then some people may have indicative signs of what I would expect zelophiles to experience, such as a psychological and behavioural overlap with cuckold fetishes. The Kinky Kelley website (2011) has a short online article on zelophilia and is in agreement with Aggrawal (2009a) that the primary source of the sexual arousal is jealousy. Although it makes other unsubstantiated claims, it notes more specifically that:

> *"Zelophilia is a condition in which a person becomes sexually aroused by feelings of jealousy. This is a diagnosed medical condition that can be managed if the sufferer is able to learn to deal with and accommodate the fetish in some way. However, if zelophilia becomes an issue, it can be treated with psychoanalysis, hypnosis and therapy ... While jealousy most often leads to harsh words, angry feelings, tears and sometimes break-ups, those with the zelophilia fetish get sexually aroused by jealous feelings. Managing this fetish within a healthy sexual relationship can be a real challenge."*

The information by Kinky Kelley (2011) may have been based on the zelophilia entry at the Right Diagnosis online medical website as the wording and claims are very similar. The Right Diagnosis website claims that:

> *"Treatment [for zelophilia] is generally not sought unless the condition becomes problematic for the person in some way, or they come under scrutiny of the legal system, and become compelled to address their condition. Many people simply learn to accept their fetish and manage to achieve gratification in an appropriate manner."*

My own observation that zelophilia shares similarities with cuckold fetish has also been made by others. For instance, the article on zelophilia by the admittedly non-academic Fetish University run by female dominatrix "Empress Ivy" on her Masturbation Fascination website noted:

"I see this particular fetish most frequently with cuckold and coerced [fellatio] or bisexual fantasies. Most start out with the admission of their wife's infidelity and they go into great detail about how jealous they felt that their wife was with another man. A man that is stronger, more masculine, has a bigger [penis], and can sexually satisfy her in ways the husband could not. Obviously the initial admission of this would spark jealousy, or perhaps resentment, but at the same time – when these events are recalled the callers clearly become aroused by it."

Zelophilia appears to be yet another paraphilia about which we know next to nothing. Although there appears to be some anecdotal evidence that it exists, the evidence is far from conclusive.

Zoophilia

Zoophilia (a.k.a. "bestiality") is typically defined as relating to recurrent intense sexual fantasies, urges and sexual activities with non-human animals. In the American Psychiatric Association's (2022) *Diagnostic and Statistical Manual of Mental Disorders* (DSM-5-TR), zoophilia (like necrophilia) is currently listed under "other specified paraphilic disorder" (OSPD). Kinsey *et al.* (1948, 1953) reported that 8% of males and 4% of females claimed to have had at least one sexual experience with an animal. Their seminal reports came as a shock to anyone reading them. As with necrophiliacs who are often employed in jobs that provide regular contact with dead people, Kinsey *et al.* claimed a much higher prevalence for zoophilic acts among those who worked on farms and reported that 17% of such males had experienced an orgasmic episode involving farm animals.

The most frequent sexual acts engaged in with animals involved calves, sheep, donkeys, large fowl (ducks, geese), dogs and cats. Males were most likely to engage in penile–vaginal intercourse or to have their genitals orally stimulated by the animals. Female zoophilia was most likely to involve household pets licking their genitals. Less commonly, women had trained dogs to mount them and engage in intercourse. Money (1984) asserted that zoophilic behaviours are usually transitory and only occur when no other sexual outlet is available. However, this does not concur with more recent research.

Studies of zoophilia since 2000 have typically collected their data online from non-clinical samples. Such studies include interviews carried out by Beetz (2000) with 32 zoophiles, Williams and Weinberg (2003) with 114 zoophiles and Miletski (2002) with 93 zoophiles. For instance, Miletski (2002) recruited zoophiles using advertisements in a zoophile magazine. These studies all reported that male and female self-identified zoophiles were attracted to animals out of a desire for affection and a sexual attraction toward and/or a love for animals. Many of the zoophiles in these three studies preferred sex with animals over sex with humans.

Miletski's study comprised 82 male and 11 female zoophiles. The most reported sexual fantasies of the sample were having sex with animals (76% males and 45% females) and watching other humans have sex with animals (35% males and 40% females). The reasons men said they engaged in sex with animals were sexual attraction to the animal (91%), love and affection for the animal (74%) and the animals being accepting and easy to please (67%). Only 12% said it was because no human partners were available, and only 7% said it was because they were too shy to have sex with humans. The main reasons women said they engaged in sex with animals were sexual attraction to the animal (100%), love and affection for the animal (67%) and because (in their view) the animal wanted it (67%). Most of the sample preferred sex with dogs (87% males; 100% females) and/or horses (81% males; 73% females). Only 8% of males wanted to stop having sex with animals and none of the females.

Miletski (2017) has gone as far as to claim that zoophilia could perhaps be considered an alternative sexual orientation. Although Miletski's study has never been published in a peer-reviewed academic journal, it is available as an ebook (Miletski, 2002). Miletski also noted that her participants differentiated themselves from bestialists who use animals as sex objects without emotional attachment.

Beetz's study comprised 32 male zoophiles who reported that they had sex with dogs (78%), horses (53%), cats (13%) and farm animals (19%). Over half (56%) had never sought therapy because many of them believed they had a very close emotional attachment to their animals that was mutual. They reported they loved their animal partner in much the same way as others love their human partners. They were devastated when their animal partner died. They also claimed they cared about the sexual pleasure of their animal partner as well as their own. Beetz (2000) also examined how their interest in zoophilia began. She reported:

> *"Some have always been interested in their preferred animal and only later developed sexual fantasies about them. Some read books/magazines about zoophilia (e.g., the Sex Atlas). Some found it very exciting to watch animals mating on TV (especially on the Discovery Channel in the US) and fantasized about that. Others started to touch the genitals of their pet dogs out of curiosity, in some cases the dog came up and licked the person's genitals. Others did not remember when their fantasies started, but the behavior often started with nonsexual cuddling with the animal and then became sexual. So we see that there are a lot of ways that can lead up to the first sexual experience with an animal."*

In all three studies the most commonly preferred animals with which to engage in sex were dogs or horses. However, it must be noted that these three studies, while extensive compared with the case reports published since Kinsey (1948, 1953), collected data from non-clinical samples. Therefore, unlike case study reports, the participants did not appear to be suffering any significant clinical distress or impairment as a consequence of their behaviour.

There may of course be other more idiosyncratic explanations for zoophilic behaviour. There are a number of medical conditions that may account for zoophilic behaviour such as cerebral tumours located in the frontal lobe, the lymbic system or hypothalamus. Ene and Sasaran (2011) described the late onset of zoophilia in a 42-year-old man who suddenly started engaging in zoophilic behaviour following an aneurysm in the posterior cerebral artery. More specifically, he developed a sexual interest in the hens in his garden. He was caught having sex with the hens by his wife on a number of occasions. Unfortunately, the man died a few weeks later following another aneurysm. Jimenez-Jimenez *et al.* (2002) highlighted the case of a 74-year-old man who developed zoophilic tendencies 5 days after the start of his dopaminergic therapy for Parkinson's disease.

Aggrawal (2011a) outlined a new typology for zoophilia. Aggrawal's rationale for developing this was rooted in his belief that terminologies describing zoophilic acts "are at best vague and are not used universally in the same sense" by researchers working in the field of zoophilia. For instance, Aggrawal noted that there was a multiplicity of different terms that often describe slightly different aspects when a person has a sexual relationship with an animal such as zoophilia, zoophilism, zooerasty, zooerastia, bestiality and bestiosexuality. Aggrawal's new typology described 10 different types of zoophile (Class I zoosexuals to Class X zoosexuals, presented below) and was based on both the empirical/clinical literature and informed theoretical speculation:

- *Class I zoosexuals:* This type comprises *human–animal roleplayers*. These individuals never have sex with actual animals but become sexually aroused through wanting to have sex with humans who pretend to be animals. This appears to include members of the furry fandom and subsumes those individuals who engage in these pseudo-zoophilic acts (e.g., petplay, ponyplay, ponyism or puppyplay). According to Aggrawal those individuals who participate in human–animal roleplay involve one person taking on the role of a real or imaginary animal in character including appropriate mannerisms and behaviour. Outside the world of furries, Aggrawal claims that human–animal roleplay is sometimes used in sadomasochistic contexts (involving bondage and domination) where the partner is reduced to the status of an animal.
- *Class II zoosexuals:* This type comprises *romantic zoophiles*. Aggrawal claimed this type of zoophile keeps animals as pets as a way to get psychosexually stimulated without actually having any kind of sexual contact with them. This appears to be a theoretical type of zoophile as I have never come across any cases in the clinical literature that would be classed as this particular type.
- *Class III zoosexuals:* This type comprises those individuals whom Aggrawal describes as *zoophilic fantasizers*. Aggrawal claims these people fantasize about having sexual intercourse with animals but – like Classes I and II – do not actually have sex with animals. It is claimed that this type of zoophile may masturbate in the presence of animals, although Aggrawal provides no evidence of such people actually existing. Aggrawal claims that zoophilic voyeurs and zoophilic exhibitionists are subsumed within this particular zoophilic type.
- *Class IV zoosexuals*: This type comprises *tactile zoophiles* who get sexual excitement from touching, stroking or fondling an animal or their genitals but do not actually have sex with the animal. Aggrawal claimed that some tactile zoophiles engage in zoophilic frotteurism and that for sexual pleasure rub their genitals against animals. Again, Aggrawal presents no empirical evidence for the existence of such people.
- *Class V zoosexuals*: This type comprises what Aggrawal calls *fetishistic zoophiles*. These individuals keep various animal parts (especially fur) that they then use as an erotic stimulus and a crucial part of their sexual activity. Such individuals have been reported in the clinical literature including the case of a woman (Randall *et al.,* 1990) who used the tongue of a deer as her primary masturbatory aid.

- *Class VI zoosexuals*: This type comprises *sadistic bestials* where the source of sexual arousal comes from the torturing of animals (i.e., zoosadism), but does not involve sexual intercourse with the animal. There has been quite a lot of evidence in the empirical literature that such zoophilic activity exists (see the final entry in this book).
- *Class VII zoosexuals:* This type comprises *opportunistic zoosexuals* who have normal sexual encounters, but as Aggrawal argues would not refrain from having sexual intercourse with animals if the opportunity arose. Aggrawal claimed that such behaviour occurs most often in incarcerated or stranded persons, or when the person sees an opportunity to have sex with an animal and they are sure no-one else is present (e.g., farmhands). Aggraval claimed that opportunistic zoosexuals have no emotional attachment to animals despite having sex with them.
- *Class VIII zoosexuals*: This type comprises *regular zoosexuals* ("classic" zoophiles as Aggrawal calls them). These individuals prefer sex with animals than sex with humans, but are capable of having sex with both. Such zoophiles will engage in a wide range of sexual activities with animals (e.g., masturbation, oral sex, vaginal sex, anal sex). These people love animals at an emotional level and have sex as part of a loving relationship. Aggrawal also included a subclass within this category called "regular zoophilia by proxy". Here, Aggrawal described cases of men who forced their wives to be vaginally penetrated by dogs for their own sexual satisfaction.
- *Class IX zoosexuals:* This type comprises homicidal bestials who need to kill animals in order to have sex with them (i.e., necrozoophiles). Although capable of having sex with living animals, there is an insatiable desire to have sex with dead animals. Reports of such behaviour have been noted in the literature (such as the serial killer Jeffrey Dahmer on whom I commented in my blog on zoosadism).
- *Class X zoosexuals:* This type comprises what Aggrawal refers to as *exclusive zoosexuals*. These are individuals who only have sex with animals to the exclusion of human sexual partners (i.e., those identified in the clinical literature as zooerasts).

Aggrawal claimed that his new classification may help in treating such people. He says that the zoosexuals in Classes I to V may be treated by simple behaviour modification techniques whereas zoosexuals in Classes VI and above need more rigorous treatment (e.g., pharmacological interventions). Only time will tell whether this new taxonomy is adopted by the field, but the classification does seem to have overall face validity even if a few of the classes are theoretical rather than actual.

Finally, it is worth noting that papers and editorials have been published in the *Veterinary Journal (VJ)* about the violent sexual abuse of female calves (Hvozdik *et al.*, 2006). Vets often have to deal with animals that have been sexually abused by humans and do not like the term "zoophilia" as it tends to focus on the human perpetrator – not on the harm that might result for the animal. A 2006 editorial in the *VJ* claimed that the sexual abuse of animals is almost a last taboo – even to the veterinary profession. Beirne (1997) argued the sexual abuse of an animal should be understood as sexual assault because (i) human–animal sexual relations almost always involve coercion, (ii) such practices often cause pain and even death to the animal and (iii) animals are unable either to communicate consent to us in a form that we can readily understand or to speak out about their cause.

Zoosadism

Zoosadism refers to the pleasure – often sexual – that individuals attain by causing sadistic cruelty to animals. In many people's minds, violence towards the animal is often automatically implied when they think of bestial acts. However, I would point out that academic research indicates that sex with animals by zoophiles is often considered by them as "sensual and loving" and does not necessarily include force, violence and/or sadism. In fact, Beetz (2002) said that: "zoophilia itself does not represent a clinically significant problem and is not necessarily combined with other clinically significant problems and disorders, even if it may be difficult for some professionals to accept this."

Notwithstanding such research, links between sadistic sexual acts with animals and subsequent behaviour, such as human sexual sadism and sexual murder have been much researched. Those who inflict pain and suffering on animals are more likely than those who do not to be violent towards humans. It has been well documented that some rapists and murderers have sadistically hurt and/or killed animals in their childhood and that some have engaged in bestial acts. Furthermore, some studies have shown that around a third to a half of all sexual murderers have abused animals during childhood and/or adolescence, although the sample sizes of such studies are usually relatively small. However, most research has reported that one of the most important warning signs or risk factors specifically relating to the propensity for sex offending is animal cruelty when accompanied by a sexual interest in animals. In a study of psychiatric patients who tortured cats and dogs Felthous (1980) reported that all of them had high levels of aggression towards people including one patient who had murdered a boy.

Schlesinger (2004) provided in great detail some particularly gruesome stories of compulsive homicide killers. One such case was Peter Kürten who terrified Düsseldorf in Germany. Schlesinger reported:

"At age 9, Kürten committed his first murder by throwing a boy off a raft and preventing another youngster from rescuing the child. Kürten was also a thief and a burglar, and he spent a number of years in prison for assorted offenses. While there, he poisoned several inmates in the prison hospital. After his release the offender attacked 29 people and killed several others including a 5-year-old girl. He also broke into the home of a 13-year-old girl, attempted to strangle her and killed her by cutting her throat with a knife ... Up until he was apprehended the compulsion to kill became overwhelming. Kürten attacked men, women and children, killing them by knifing, choking or cutting their throats."

Kürten's background was also disturbing. As Schlesinger (2004a, b) further reported:

"Kürten had sex with his sisters; however, his preferred form of sexual activity in his developing years was bestiality. He became friendly with a dog catcher who taught him how to torture and masturbate animals. From ages 13 through 15 he engaged in numerous sexual acts with pigs, sheep and goats, sometimes stabbing the animals to death while having intercourse with them."

In Germany there have been an increasing number of violent crimes against horses. The deliberate cutting, slashing and/or stabbing of horses (a.k.a. "horse ripping") has been accepted as a criminal offence in Germany and has led to a number of studies on the topic. Horse ripping has been defined as a destructive act "with the aim to harm a horse or the acceptance of a possible injury of a horse, especially killing, maltreatment, mutilation and sexual abuse in a sadomasochistic context." Bartmann and Wohlsein (2002) examined 193 traumatic horse injuries over a 4-year period. They reported that at least 10 of the injuries including wounds from knives and guns were acts of zoosadism. Furthermore, Schedel-Stupperich (2002) examined all the incidents of horse injuries from 1993 to 2000, of which there were 1,035. One quarter of all the injuries were cuts and stabs to the genitalia of horses and another quarter involved injuries to the necks and/or heads of horses. Since most of the horses injured were female, Schedel-Stupperich (2002) concluded such acts should be described as rape.

Wochner and Klosinski (1998) examined 1,502 aggressive children and adolescents requiring treatment at their Child and Adolescent Psychiatry Unit. They reported that 25 of them, all boys, had engaged in zoosadistic activities. Perhaps unsurprisingly, the incidence of zoosadistic acts increased with age. The authors speculated that the zoosadistic acts may have been connected to problems of puberty and proving their manhood.

Aggrawal (2011a) proposed a new classification of zoophilia to include what he termed "sadistic bestials" and "homicidal bestials". Unsurprisingly, sadistic bestials derive sexual pleasure from the torturing of animals. He argued sadistic bestials use animals for sexual excitement, but do not engage in sexual intercourse with them. He defines homicidal bestials as zoophiles who kill animals in order to have sexual intercourse with them. He terms this latter act as "necrozoophilia". According to Aggrawal (2011a) homicidal bestials are capable of having sexual intercourse with live animals, but their need for sexual intercourse with dead animals is greater.

Hickey (2006) reported that serial killer Jeffrey Dahmer collected animal roadkill, dissected the remains and masturbated over the animals he had cut up because he "found the glistening viscera of animals sexually arousing." Schlesinger (2004a, b) reported that "Dahmer dissected roadkill, butchered small animals, nailed cats and frogs to trees behind his house, and once put a dog's head on a stick." Aggrawal (2011a) further reported the case of 20-year-old Bryan Hathaway from Minnesota, USA who was arrested for having sex with a deer carcass. He had been out cycling and by chance came across the dead deer. He was later charged with violating a law prohibiting "sexual gratification with an animal" and fitted Aggrawal's classification as a necrozoophile, although Hathaway did not actually kill the animal himself.

References and Further Reading

Abal, Y.N., Marin, J.A.L. & Sanchez, S.R. (2003). Nueva parafilia del siglo XXI: Chat-escatofilia. *Archivos Hispanoamericanos de Sexología,* **9**, 81–104.

Abel, G.G. & Osborn, C. (1992). The paraphilias: The extent and nature of sexually deviant and criminal behavior. *Psychiatric Clinics of North America,* **15**, 675–689.

Abel, G.G. & Rouleau, J.-L. (1990). The nature and extent of sexual assault. In: W.L. Marshall, D.R. Laws & H.E. Barbaree (Eds), *Handbook of Sexual Assault: Issues, Theories, and Treatment of the Offender* (pp. 9–21). New York: Plenum Press.

Abel, G.G., Becker, J.V., Mittelman, M., Cunningham-Rathner, J., Rouleau, J.L. & Murphy, W.D. (1987). Self-reported sex crimes of nonincarcerated paraphiliacs. *Journal of Interpersonal Violence,* **2**, 3–25.

Abel, G.G., Becker, J.V., Cunningham-Rathner, J., Mittelman, M. & Rouleau, J.-L. (1988). Multiple paraphilic diagnoses among sex offenders. *Bulletin of the American Academy of Psychiatry and the Law,* **16**, 153–168.

Abel, G.G., Coffey, L. & Osborn, C.A. (2008). Sexual arousal patterns: Normal and deviant. *Psychiatric Clinics of North America,* **31**, 643–655.

Adams, C. (2002). *Were there really vomitoriums in ancient Rome?* Straight Dope. Retrieved November 1, 2002 from http://www.straightdope.com/columns/read/2421/were-there-really-vomitoriums-in-ancient-rome

Adams, K.A. (1981). Arachnophobia: Love American style. *Journal of Psychoanalytic Anthropology,* **4**, 157–197.

Agence France-Presse (2012). *Swedish woman arrested for using human skeleton for sex.* Raw Story. Retrieved November 20, 2012 from http://www.rawstory.com/rs/2012/11/20/swedish-woman-arrested-for-using-human-skeleton-for-sex/

Aggrawal A. (2009a). *Forensic and Medico-legal Aspects of Sexual Crimes and Unusual Sexual Practices.* Boca Raton, FL: CRC Press.

Aggrawal, A. (2009b). A new classification of necrophilia. *Journal of Forensic and Legal Medicine,* **16**, 316–320.

Aggrawal, A. (2011a). A new classification of zoophilia. *Journal of Forensic and Legal Medicine,* **18**, 73–78.

Aggrawal, A. (2011b). *Necrophilia: Forensic and Medico-legal Aspects.* Boca Raton, FL: CRC Press.

Agnew, J. (1982). Klismaphilia: A physiological perspective. *American Journal of Psychotherapy,* **36**, 554–566.

References and Further Reading

Agnew, J. (2000). Klismaphilia. *Venereology*, **13**(2), 75–79.

Allen, C. (1969). *A Textbook of Psychosexual Disorders* (Second Edition). London: Oxford University Press.

Allen, E. (2011). Ritualistic hair-fetish killer serving life in British prison is convicted in Italy of 1993 teen murder. *Daily Mail*, November 12.

Aliabadi, H., Cass, A.S., Gleich, P. & Johnson, C.F. (1985). Self-inflicted foreign bodies involving lower urinary tract and male genitals. *Urology*, **26**, 12–16.

Alison, L., Santtila, P., Sandnabba, N.K. & Nordling, N. (2001). Sadomasochistically oriented behavior: Diversity in practice and meaning. *Archives of Sexual Behavior*, **30**, 1–12.

All Experts (2004). *Fetishism/Spit fetish*. Retrieved January 14, 2004 from *http://en.allexperts.com/q/Fetishism-2835/spit-fetish.htm*

All Experts (2012). *Fetishism/Amaurophilia*. Retrieved February 22, 2012 from *http://en.allexperts.com/q/Fetishism-2835/2012/2/amaurophilia.htm*

Alqutub, A.N., Masoodi, I., Alsayari, K. & Alomair, A. (2011). Bee sting therapy-induced hepatotoxicity: A case report. *World Journal of Hepatology*, **27**, 268–270.

Amano, D. (n.d.). *Worm sex*. Bizarre. *http://www.bizarremag.com/fetish/interviews/6055/worm_sex.html?xc=1*

American Psychiatric Association (1987). *Diagnostic and Statistical Manual of Mental Disorders* (Third Edition, Revised). Washington, DC: American Psychiatric Association.

American Psychiatric Association (2000). *Diagnostic and Statistical Manual of Mental Disorders* (Fourth Edition, Revised). Washington, DC: American Psychiatric Association.

American Psychiatric Association (2013). *Diagnostic and Statistical Manual of Mental Disorders* (Fifth Edition). Arlington, VA: American Psychiatric Publishing.

American Psychiatric Association (2022). *Diagnostic and Statistical Manual of Mental Disorders* (Fifth Edition, Revised). Arlington, VA: American Psychiatric Publishing.

American Psychological Association (2007). *APA Dictionary of Psychology*. Washington, DC: American Psychiatric Association.

Andersen, M.L., Poyares, D, Alves, R.S.C., Skomro, R. & Tufik, S. (2007). Sexsomnia: Abnormal sexual behavior during sleep. *Brain Research Reviews*, **56**, 271–282.

Angelowicz, A. (2012). *TLC's "Strange sex": Sex furniture and sleep orgasms*. The Frisky. Retrieved August 28, 2012 from *http://www.thefrisky.com/2012-08-28/tlcs-strange-sex-sex-furniture-sleep-orgasms/*

Anubhav, R. & Bhatia, M.S. (2011). Is sexsomnia a new parasomnia? *Delhi Psychiatry Journal*, **14**, 378–380.

Anxiety Zone (2013). *Frotteurism*. *http://www.anxietyzone.com/conditions/frotteurism.html*

AOL (2006). *The AOL search data: Self identified fetishers*. https://web.archive.org/web/20070221135508/http://www.aphrodisiology.com/aol-fetisheshttps://web.archive.org/web/20070221135508/http://www.aphrodisiology.com/aol-fetishes

A-Proper-Blog (2010). *Ten fetishes and paraphilias*. Retrieved November 19, 2010 from *http://a-proper-blog.blogspot.co.uk/2010/11/ten-fetishes-and-paraphilias.html*

Archwired (n.d.). *Braces in the bedroom: Will braces affect your sex life?* http://www.archwired.com/BracesandSex.htm

Area Orion (2011). *Lift and carry.* Retrieved October 19, 2011 from *http://areaorion.blogspot.co.uk/2011/10/lift-and-carry.html*

Arndt, W.B. (1991). *Gender disorders and the paraphilias.* Madison, CT: International Universities Press.

Arnone, J.M., Conti, R.P. & Preckajlo, J.H. (2024). Coprophilia and coprophagia: A literature review. *Journal of the American Psychiatric Nurses Association,* **30,** 8–16.

Art-Sheep (2015). *"Doorknob girl": Japan and the trend of girls licking doorknobs.* Retrieved August 17, 2015 from *http://art-sheep.com/doorknob-girl-japan-and-the-trend-of-girls-licking-doorknobs/*

Ashcroft, B. (2011a). *The art of girls licking doorknobs.* Kotaku. Retrieved August 9, 2011 from *http://kotaku.com/5838276/the-art-of-girls-licking-doorknobs/*

Ashcroft, B. (2011b). *What is Japan's fetish this week? Glasses.* Kotaku. Retrieved April 21, 2011 from *http://kotaku.com/5792396/whats-japan-fetishizing-this-week-glasses*

Asia One News (2012, January 4). Man has "acupuncture" fetish.

Backwashzine (n.d.). *Acnephilia: More commonly known as zit fetish.* http://www.backwashzine.com/acnephilia.html

Baguley. S. (2006). *Pediculosis pubis* (crab lice). In: S. Baguley, S. Kumar & R. Persaud (Eds), *Key Topics in Sexual Health* (pp. 150–162). London: Taylor & Francis.

Balachandra, K. & Swaminath, S. (2002). Fire fetishism in a female arsonist? *Canadian Journal of Psychiatry,* **47,** 487–488.

Baring, J. (2013). *Perv: The Sexual Deviant in All of Us.* New York: Scientific American/Farrar, Strauss & Giroux.

Barone, J.E., Sohn, N. & Nealon Jr, T.F. (1976). Perforations and foreign bodies of the rectum: Report of 28 cases. *Annals of Surgery,* **184**(5), 601–604.

Bartmann, C.P. & Wohlsein, P. (2002). Injuries caused by outside violence with forensic importance in horses. *Dtsch Tierarztl Wochenschr,* **109,** 112–115.

BBC Devon News (2010, July 1). Drunk Exeter "piggy back" sex attacker, 18, jailed.

BBC News (2005, January 20). Surgical mask fetishist jailed.

BBC News (2010, April 26). Israel jails man for "holy semen" sex abuse.

BBC News (2018, June 19). Upskirting ban also protects men in kilts.

Bedi, N., El-Husseiny, T., Buchholz, N. & Masood, J. (2010). "Putting lead in your pencil": Self-insertion of an unusual urethral foreign body for sexual gratification. *Journal of the Royal Society of Medicine, Short Reports,* **1**(2), 18.

Beetz, A.M. (2000, June). Human sexual contact with animals: New insights from current research. Paper presented at the *Fifth Congress of the European Federation of Sexology, Berlin.*

Beetz, A. (2002). *Love, Violence, and Sexuality in Relationships between Humans and Animals.* Germany: Shaker Verlag.

Beetz, A. (2004). Bestiality/zoophilia: A scarcely investigated phenomenon between crime, paraphilia, and love. *Journal of Forensic Psychology Practice,* **4**(2), 1–36.

Beier, K. (2008). Comment on Pfafflin's (2008) "Good enough to eat". *Archives of Sexual Behavior,* **38,** 164–165

Beirne, P. (1997). Rethinking bestiality: Towards a concept of interspecies sexual assault. *Theoretical Criminology*, **1**, 317–340.

Belk, R.W. (2003). Shoes and self. *Advances in Consumer Research*, **30**, 27–33.

Beneke M. (1999). First report of nonpsychotic self-cannibalism (autophagy), tongue splitting, and scar patterns (scarification) as an extreme form of cultural body modification in a western civilization. *American Journal of Forensic Medicine and Pathology*, **20**, 281–285.

Benezech, M., Bourgeois, M., Boukhabza, D. & Yesavage, J. (1981). Cannibalism and vampirism in paranoid schizophrenia. *Journal of Clinical Psychiatry*, **42**(7), 290.

Benjamin, H.B., Klamecki, B. and Haft, J.S. (1969). Removal of exotic foreign objects from the abdominal orifices. *American Journal of Proctology*, **20**, 413–417.

Benson, R. (1985). Vacuum cleaner injury to penis: A common urologic problem? *Urology*, **25**(1), 41–44.

Ben-Zeév, A. (2011). Why did Descartes love cross-eyed women? The lure of imperfection. *Psychology Today*, November 29.

Berest, J.J. (1971). Fetishism: Three case histories. *Journal of Sex Research*, **7**, 237–239.

Berger, B.D., Lehrmann, J.A., Larson, G., Alverno, L. & Tsao, C.I. (2005). Nonpsychotic, nonparaphilic self-amputation and the Internet. *Comprehensive Psychiatry*, **46**, 380–383.

Bezeau, S.C., Bogod, N.M. & Mateer, C.A. (2004). Sexually intrusive behaviour following brain injury: Approaches to assessment and rehabilitation. *Brain Injury*, **18**, 299–313.

Bhugra, D. & De Silva, P. (1996). Uniforms – fact, fashion, fantasy and fetish. *Sexual and Marital Therapy*, **11**, 393-406.

Bhutta, M.F. & Maxwell, H. (2008). Sneezing induced by sexual ideation or orgasm: An under-reported phenomenon. *Journal of the Royal Society of Medicine*, **101**, 587–591.

Biles, J. (2004). I, insect, or Georges Bataille and the crush freaks. *Janus Head: Journal of Interdisciplinary Studies in Literature, Continental Philosophy, Phenomenological Psychology and the Arts*, **7**(1), 115–131.

Bilyeu, A.S. (1998). Trokosi – The practice of sexual slavery in Ghana: Religious and cultural freedom vs. human rights. *Indiana International and Comparative Law Review*, **9**, 457.

Binet, A. (1887). Le fétichisme dans l'amour. *Revue Philosophique*, **24**, 143–167, 252–274.

Blanchard, R. (1989). The concept of autogynephilia and the typology of male gender dysphoria. *Journal of Nervous and Mental Disease*, **177**, 616–623.

Blanchard, R. & Collins, P.I. (1993). Men with sexual interest in transvestites, transsexuals, and she-males. *Journal of Nervous and Mental Disease*, **181**, 570–575.

Blanchard, R. & Hucker, S.J. (1991). Age, transvestism, bondage, and concurrent paraphilic activities in 117 fatal cases of autoerotic asphyxia. *British Journal of Psychiatry*, **159**, 371–377.

Blanchard, R., Lykins, A.D., Wherrett, D., Kuban, M.E., Cantor, J.M., Blak, T., Dickey, R. & Klassen, P.E. (2008). Paedophilia, hebephilia, and the DSM–V. *Archives of Sexual Behavior*, **38**, 335–350.

Blondel, P.H. (1976). Perforations digestives d'étiologie insolite: Deux cas. *Nouv Presse Med*, **5**, 915.

Boiteau, M. (2011). "I know just what she wants": Constructing gender, sexuality, and relationships on The Doll Forum. Master of Arts Thesis, Department of Sociology, University of Manitoba, Canada.

Bourget, D. & Bradford, J.M.W (1987). Fire fetishism, diagnostic and clinical implications: A review of two cases. *Canadian Journal of Psychiatry*, **32**, 459–462.

Bourguignon, A. (1977). Status of vampirism and autovampirism. *Annales Médico-Psychologiques*, **1**(2), 181–196.

Bradford, J.M.W., Boulet, J. & Pawlak, A. (1992). The paraphilias: A multiplicity of deviant behaviors. *Canadian Journal of Psychiatry*, **37**, 104–108.

Bratton, S. (2013). Scents that trigger arousal. *Personal Life Media*, October 10.

Brenner, M. (2009). *Wet Goddess*. London: Eyes Wide Open.

Breslow, N., Evans, L. & Langley, J. (1985). On the prevalence of roles of females in the sadomasochistic subculture: Report of an empirical study. *Archives of Sexual Behavior*, **14**, 303–317.

Brill, A.A. (1932). Sense of smell in the neuroses and psychoses. *Psychoanalytic Quarterly*, **1**, 7–42

Brittain, R. (1970). The sadistic murderer. *Medicine, Science, and the Law*, **10**, 198–207.

Brown, B. (1996). *Temperature play*. Black-Rose, Issue 2.4. Retrieved February 4, 1996 from *http://www.black-rose.com/cuiru/archive/2-4/dr2-4.html*

Brown, D. (2008). *The completely pointless Google experiment*. Danny Brown. Retrieved November 17, 2008 from *http://dannybrown.me/2008/11/17/the-completely-pointless-google-experiment/*

Brown, M.L. & Rounsley, C.A. (1996). *True Selves: Understanding Transsexualism: For Families, Friends, Co-workers, and Helping Professionals*. Hoboken, NJ: Jossey-Bass.

Brown, N. (2011). *You can't make love without wearing a mask*. Howtoaskoutagirl. Retrieved December 11, 2011 from *http://www.howtoaskoutagirl.info/tag/mask-fetish*

Brown, S. (1995). *The Fortean Times Book of Weird Sex*. London: John Brown Publishing.

Browne, R.B. (1982). *Objects of Special Devotion: Fetishism in Popular Culture*. Nampa, ID: Popular Press.

Brundage, S. (2002). Fetish confessions: Telling loved ones about your fetish is as easy as solving fractured quadratic equations. *The Wave Magazine*, July 31.

Bruno, R.L. (1997). Devotees, pretenders and wannabes: Two cases of factitious disability disorder. *Journal of Sexuality and Disability*, **15**, 243–260.

Brunvand, J.B. (2001). The colorectal mouse. *Encyclopedia of Urban Legends*. London: W.W. Norton & Company.

Buhrich, N. (1978). Motivation for cross-dressing in heterosexual transvestism. *Acta Psychiatrica Scandinavica*, **57**, 145–152.

Buhrich, N. (1983). The association of erotic piercing with homosexuality, sadomasochism, bondage, fetishism, and tattoos. *Archives of Sexual Behavior*, **12**, 167–171.

Buhrich, N. & Beaumont, T. (1981). Comparison of transvestism in Australia and America. *Archives of Sexual Behavior*, **26**, 589–605.

Burg, B.R. (1982). The sick and the dead: The development of psychological theory on necrophilia from Krafft-Ebing to the present. *Journal of the History of the Behavioral Sciences*, **18**, 242–254.

Burgess, A.W. & Hazelwood, R.R. (1983). Autoerotic deaths and social network response. *American Journal of Orthopsychiatry*, **53**, 166–170.

Burt, J. (2007). Top five freaky fetishes. *The Sun*, September 7.

Busch, K.A. & Cavanagh, J.R. (1986). The study of multiple murder: Preliminary examination of the interface between epistemology and methodology. *Journal of Interpersonal Violence*, **1**, 5–23.

Bush, G. & Nixon, R. (1969). Scrotal inflation: A new cause for subcutaneous, mediastinal and retroperitoneal emphysema. *Henry Ford Hospital Medical Journal*, **17**, 225–226.

Butcher, N. (2003). *The Strange Case of the Walking Corpse: A Chronicle of Medical Mysteries, Curious Remedies, and Bizarre but True Healing Folklore*. New York: Avery.

Butler, B. (2015). *Newest sexual fetish: Getting alien eggs laid inside you*. PhillyMag. Retrieved August 17, 2015 from http://www.phillymag.com/g-philly/2015/08/17/newest-sexual-fetish-getting-alien-eggs-laid-inside-you/

Butler, C. (2011). *The "B" Spot: An examination of erotic fixations on bald men*. Hairloss. Retrieved September 27, 2011 from http://www.hairloss.com/home/hes-hot-and-has-hair-loss.html

Buxom, N. (2010). *Featured fetish: Piggy-backing*. Nic Buxom. Retrieved February 7, 2010 from http://nicbuxom.blogspot.co.uk/2010/02/featured-fetish-piggy-backing.html

Buzzard, A.J. & Waxman, B.P. (1979). A long standing, much travelled rectal foreign body. *Medical Journal of Australia*, **1**, 600.

Byard, R. (1994). Autoerotic death: Characteristic features and diagnostic difficulties. *Journal of Clinical Forensic Medicine*, **1**, 71–78.

Byard, R.W., Eitzen, D.A. & James, R. (2000a). Unusual fatal mechanisms in non-asphyxial autoerotic death. *American Journal of Forensic and Medical Pathology*, **21**, 65–68.

Byard, R.W., Kostakis, C., Pigou, P.E. & Gilbert, J.D. (2000b). Volatile substance use in sexual asphyxia. *Journal of Clinical Forensic Medicine*, **7**, 26–28.

Calef, V. & Weinshel, E.M. (1972). On certain neurotic equivalents of necrophilia. *International Journal of Psychoanalysis*, **53**, 67–75.

Caliendo, C., Armstrong, M.L. & Roberts, A.E. (2005). Self-reported characteristics of women and men with intimate body piercings. *Journal of Advanced Nursing*, **49**, 474–484.

Campbell, E. (2004). *Getting It On Online: Cyberspace, Gay Male Sexuality, and Embodied Identity*. London: Routledge.

Campbell, R.J. (2004). *Campbell's Psychiatric Dictionary* (Eighth Edition). Oxford: Oxford University Press.

Campbell, R.J. (2009). *Campbell's Psychiatric Dictionary* (Ninth Edition). Oxford: Oxford University Press.

Caprio, F.S. (1949). Scoptophilia, exhibitionism: A case report. *Journal of Clinical and Experimental Psychopathology*, **10**(1), 50–72.

Cargan, L. (1986). Stereotypes of singles: A cross-cultural comparison. *Archives of Sexual Behavior*, **27**, 200–208.
Ceilán, C. (2008). *Weirdly Beloved: Tales of Strange Bedfellows, Odd Couplings, and Love Gone Bad*. Guilford, CT: Lyons Press.
Chattopadhyay, S.D., Das, R., Panda, N., Mahapatra, R.S., Biswas, R. & Jha, A. (2011). Long electric wire in urethra: An unusual paraphilia. *Jurnalul de Chirurgie, Iaşi*, **7**, 437–440.
Cipriano, A. (2009). *Five ridiculous [safe for work] fetishes*. Cracked. Retrieved March 17, 2009 from *http://www.cracked.com/article_17149_5-ridiculous-safe-work-fetishes.html*
Citron, N.D. & Wade, P.J. (1980). Penile injuries from vacuum cleaners. *British Medical Journal*, **281**(6232), 26.
Coates, B. (2005). Teachers, naked women and beans. *Halifax Evening Courier*, February 4.
Collar 'n' Cuffs (2010). *Smoking fetishism (capnolagnia)*. Retrieved February 19, 2010 from *http://collarncuffs.com/resources/doku.php?id=capnolagnia*
Connelly, M. (2009). *The Scarecrow*. London: Orion.
Cooper, A.J. (1996). Autoerotic asphyxiation: Three case reports. *Journal of Sex and Marital Therapy*, **22**, 47–53.
Cordner, S.M. (1983). An unusual case of sudden death associated with masturbation. *Medicine, Science and Law*, **23**, 54–56.
Corsini, R.J. (1999). *The Dictionary of Psychology*. London: Psychology Press.
Couture, L.A. (2000). *Forced retention of bodily waste: The most overlooked form of child maltreatment*. http://www.nospank.net/couture2.htm
Cox, M. (1979). Dynamic psychotherapy with sex-offenders. In: I. Rosen (Ed.), *Sexual Deviation* (pp. 306–350). Oxford, UK: Oxford University Press.
Crawford, C. & Krebs, D, (1998). How mate choice shaped human nature. *Handbook of Evolutionary Psychology: Ideas, Issues, and Applications*. London: Lawrence Erlbaum Associates.
Crazy News (2011). *The pervert who got sexual thrills in cow manure*. Retrieved March 24, 2011 from *http://weirdcrazynews.blogspot.co.uk/2011/03/pervert-who-got-sexual-thrills-in-cow.html*
Crépault, C. & Couture, M. (1980). Men's erotic fantasies. *Archives of Sexual Behavior*, **9**, 565–576.
Cridland, A. (2009). Piggy-back sex pest admits Brighton and Hove offences. *The Argus*, August 22.
Croarkin, P., Nam, T. & Waldrep, D. (2004). Comment on adult baby syndrome. *American Journal of Psychiatry*, **161**, 21–41.
Curren, D. (1954). Sexual perversion. *Practitioner*, **172**, 440–445.
Daily Mail (2010, December 29). Millionaire BBC TV presenter Kristian Digby suffocated to death accidentally "when sex game went wrong".
Daily Mail (2011, March 12). S&M can be "criminal even if it's consensual" says judge in Craigslist sex-slave case.
Daily Mail (2014, January 13). "Swiss Cheese Pervert" terrorizes Philadelphia asking women to perform sexual acts on him using a slice of fromage.

Daily Mirror (2010, June 17). Fowl play: Man kills himself after being caught by wife having sex with chicken.
Daily Mirror (2011, March 24). Pervert who got sexual thrills in cow manure sent to prison
Daily Star (2015, December 9). Weirdest sex toy ever? Fake alien penis designed to lay eggs in people.
Daily Telegraph (2008a, May 21). Man admits having sex with 1,000 cars.
Daily Telegraph (2008b, July 18). Octopus sex man gets off.
Daily Telegraph (2010, January 21). Tree sex man ordered to leave park.
Darcangelo, S. (2008). Fetishism: Psychopathology and theory. In: D.R. Laws & W.T. O'Donohue (Eds), *Sexual Deviance: Theory, Assessment and Treatment* (Second Edition) (pp. 108–118). New York: Guilford Press.
Davis, S.L. & Lubovich, M. (2008). *Hunks, Hotties, and Pretty Boys*. Newcastle-upon-Tyne, UK: Cambridge Scholars.
De River, J.P. (1958). *Crime and the Sexual Psychopath*. Springfield, IL: Charles C. Thomas.
De Silva, P. and Pernet, A. (1992). Pollution in "Metroland": An unusual paraphilia in a shy young man. *Sexual and Marital Therapy*, 7, 301–306.
Dekkers, M. (1994). *Dearest Pet: On Bestiality*. New York: Verso.
Denizet-Lewis, B. (2009). *America Anonymous: Eight Addicts in Search of a Life*. New York: Simon & Schuster.
Denko, J.D. (1973). Klismaphilia: Enema as a sexual preference. *American Journal of Psychotherapy*, 27, 232–250.
Denko, J.D. (1976). Klismaphilia: Amplification of the erotic enema deviance. *American Journal of Psychotherapy*, 30, 236–255.
Denson, R. (1982). Undinism: The fetishizaton of urine. *Canadian Journal of Psychiatry*, 27, 336–338.
Descartes, R. (1978). *Moral Philosophy and Psychology* (translated by John J. Blom). New York: New York University Press.
Dewaraja, R. (1987). Formicophilia, an unusual paraphilia, treated with counseling and behavior therapy. *American Journal of Psychotherapy*, 41, 593–597.
Dewaraja, R. & Money, J. (1986). Transcultural sexology: Formicophilia, a newly named paraphilia in a young Buddhist male. *Journal of Sex and Marital Therapy*, 12, 139–145.
Dietz, P.E., Hazelwood, R.R. & Warren, J. (1990). The sexually sadistic criminal and his offenses. *Bulletin of the American Academy of Psychiatry and the Law*, 18, 163–178.
Dinello, F.A. (1967). Stages of treatment in the case of a diaper-wearing 17-year-old male. *American Journal of Psychiatry*, 124, 94–96.
Dirty Mag (2011). *Fetish fix: Liquidophilia*. Retrieved September 12, 2011 from http://dirtymag.com/fetish-fix-liquidophilia
Divine Caroline (2012). *Eighteen sexual fetishes that sound made up (but they're not)*. The Date Report. Retrieved September 20, 2012 from http://www.thedatereport.com/dating/sex/sexual-fetishes-emetophilia-tree-sex/
Dixon, D. (1983). An erotic attraction to amputees. *Sexuality and Disability*, 6, 3–19.

Docter, R.F. & Prince, V. (1997). Transvestism: A survey of 1032 cross-dressers. *Archives of Sexual Behavior*, **26**, 589–605.

Douglas, J.E., Burgess, A.W., Burgess, A.G. & Ressler, R.K. (1992). *Crime Classification Manual*. San Francisco: Jossey-Bass.

Downing, L. (2004). On the limits of sexual ethics: The phenomenology of autassassinophilia. *Sexuality and Culture*, **8**, 3–17.

Eckert, W.G. & Katchis, S. (1989). Anorectal trauma: Medicolegal and forensic aspects. *American Journal of Forensic Medicine and Pathology*, **10**, 3–9.

Ellis, H. (1905). *Studies in the Psychology of Sex* (Vol. 4). Philadelphia, PA: F.A. Davis Company.

Encyclopedia Dramatica (2011a). *Unbirthing*. Retrieved August 14, 2011 from https://encyclopediadramatica.se/Unbirthing

Encyclopedia Dramatica (2011b). *Partial unbirthing*. Retrieved May 25, 2011 from https://encyclopediadramatica.se/Partial_Unbirthing

Encyclopedia Dramatica (2012). *Frottage*. https://encyclopediadramatica.es/Frottage

Encyclopedia Dramatica (2016). *Quicksand fetish*. Retrieved May 4, 2016 from https://encyclopediadramatica.se/Quicksand_Fetish

Ene, S. & Sasaran, A. (2011). Zoophilic behavior in a patient with posterior cerebral arterial aneurysm. *Romanian Neurosurgery*, **18**, 349–355.

Enquist, M., Aronsson, H., Ghirlanda, S., Jansson, L. & Jannini, E.A. (2011). Exposure to mother's pregnancy and lactation in infancy is associated with sexual attraction to pregnancy and lactation in adulthood. *Journal of Sexual Medicine,* **8**, 140–147.

Escoffier, J. (2011). Imagining the she/male: Pornography and the transsexualization of the heterosexual male. *Studies in Gender and Sexuality*, **12**, 268–281.

Espinasa, L., Collins, E., Finocchiaro, A., Kopp, J., Robinson, J. & Rutkowski, J. (2016). Incipient regressive evolution of the circadian rhythms of a cave amphipod. *Subterranean Biology*, **20**, 1–13.

Evans, K. (2008). *The furry sociological survey.* http://www.furrysociology.net/report.htm

Evcimen, H. & Gratz, S. (2006). Adult baby syndrome. *Archives of Sexual Behavior*, **35**, 115–116.

Everything2 (2004). *Oculolinctus*. Retrieved December 24, 2004 from https://everything2.com/title/Oculolinctus

Falk, J., Riepert, T. & Rothschild, M.A. (2005). [Traumatic partial amputation of a penis: A reconstruction of the circumstances of the accident] [in German]. *Versicherungsmedizin/herausgegeben von Verband der Lebensversicherungs-Unternehmen eV und Verband der Privaten Krankenversicherung eV*, **57**(1), 17–19.

Farrer, P. (2001–2002). *Petticoat punishment in erotic literature* (Parts 1–7). http://www.petticoated.com/0603/petpunessay7SU03.html

Fauna (2012). *Sex party on Taiwan train involved 17-year-old girl and 18 men.* China Smack. Retrieved March 31, 2012 from http://www.chinasmack.com/2012/stories/sex-orgy-on-taiwan-train-involved-17-year-old-girl-and-18-men.html

Felthous, A.R. (1980). Aggression against cats, dogs, and people. *Child Psychiatry and Human Development*, **10**, 169–177.

Fetipedia (2012). *Choreophilia*. Fetbook. Retrieved December 10, 2012 from http://www.fetbook.it/wiki/index.php?title=Choreophilia

Fetish Freedom (2012). *Acousticophilia: Sound fetish.* http://www.fetishfreedom.co.uk/articles/acousticophilia_sound_fetish_150.htm

Figging and Anal Discipline (2005). *Why figging enhances sex.* Figging. Retrieved November 19, 2005 from http://www.figging.com/2005/11/19/why-figging-enhances-sex/

Fiorello, V. (2014a). *Is this guy the Swiss Cheese Pervert?* PhillyMag. Retrieved January 11, 2014 from http://www.phillymag.com/news/2014/01/11/norristowns-swiss-cheese-pervert/

Fiorello, V. (2014b). *Here are mugshots of alleged Swiss Cheese Pervert Chris Pagano.* PhillyMag. Retrieved January 11, 2014 from http://www.phillymag.com/news/2014/01/13/mugshots-swiss-cheese-pervert-chris-pagano/

Fir & Main (2008). Siderodromophilia and other loves. *Wordpress,* April 24. Located at: http://vcredit.wordpress.com/2008/04/24/siderodromophilia-and-other-loves/

First, M.B. (2005). Desire for amputation of a limb: Paraphilia, psychosis, or a new type of identity disorder. *Psychological Medicine,* **35**, 919–928.

Fleischl, M.F. (1960). A man's fantasy of a crippled girl. *American Journal of Psychotherapy,* **14**, 741–748.

Forbidden Light (2007). *Katoptronophilia: Love for mirrors. Journals of an Intelsexual.* Retrieved December 4, 2007 from http://intelsexualism.blogspot.co.uk/2009/12/katoptronophilia-love-for-mirrors.html?zx=ac769a5283ebf462

Fortean Times (2014, March 1). Please cheese me ..., p. 10.

Fox, M. & Barrett, E.L. (1960). "Vacuum cleaner injury" of the penis. *British Medical Journal,* **1**(5190),19–42.

FoxWolfie's Plushie Page (2012). *Definitions.* http://www.velocity.net/~galen/furrydef.html

Franklin, A. (2011, November). Imagined big cats in the English countryside. *Proceedings of 2011 TASA Conference.* Newcastle, Australia: Local Lives/Global Networks.

Franklin, K. (2010). Hebephilia: Quintessence of diagnostic pretextuality. *Behavioral Sciences and the Law,* **28**, 751–768.

Freeman, B. & Chapman, S. (2007). Is "YouTube" telling or selling you something? Tobacco content on the YouTube video-sharing website. *Tobacco Control,* **16**, 207–210.

Freud, S. (1930). *Civilization and Its Discontents.* London: Hogarth Press.

Freud, S. (1953). *Studies on Hysteria* (Standard Edition). London: Hogarth Press.

Freud, S. (1962). *Three Essays on the Theory of Sexuality* (translated by James Strachey). New York: Basic Books.

Freund, K. (1990a). Courtship disorders: Toward a biosocial understanding of voyeurism, exhibitionism, toucherism, and the preferential rape pattern. In: L. Ellis & H. Hoffman (Eds), *Crime in Biological, Social, and Moral Contexts* (pp. 100–114). New York: Praeger.

Freund, K. (1990b). Courtship disorder. In: W.L. Marshall, D.R. Laws & H.E. Barbaree (Eds), *Handbook of Sexual Assault: Issues, Theories, and Treatment of the Offender* (pp. 331–342). New York: Plenum Press.

Freund, K., Watson, R. & Rienzo, D. (1988). The value of self-reports in the study of voyeurism and exhibitionism. *Annals of Sex Research,* **2**, 243–262.

Freund, K., Seto, M.C. & Kuban, M. (1995). Masochism: A multiple case study. *Sexuologie*, **4**, 313–324.

Freund, K., Seto, M.C. & Kuban, M. (1997). Frotteurism and the theory of courtship disorder. In: D.R. Laws & W.T. O'Donohue (Eds), *Sexual Deviance: Theory, Assessment, and Treatment* (pp. 111–130). New York: Guilford Press.

Friday, N. (1973). *My Secret Garden*. New York: Simon & Schuster.

Friedman, P. (1959). Some observations on the sense of smell. *Psychoanalytic Quarterly*, **28**, 307–329.

Full Wiki (2013). Bellypunching. *http://www.thefullwiki.org/Bellypunching*

Fuller, B. (2012). Dentist disqualified over "needle fetish". *Sydney Morning Herald*, August 21.

Gallagher, P. (2015). *The inflatable rubber fetish of Mr. Blow Up*. Dangerous Minds. Retrieved February 11, 2015 from *http://dangerousminds.net/comments/the_inflatable_rubber_fetish_of_mr._blow_up*

Gamotin, D. (2009). World's freakiest fetishes. *The Gazette*, February 14. *http://www.gazette.uwo.ca/article.cfm?section=Campus&articleID=288&month=2&-day=14&year=2007*

Gardner, R.A. (1996). *Psychotherapy with Sex-abuse Victims: True, False, and Hysterical*. London: Creative Therapeutics.

Gates, K. (2000). *Deviant Desires: Incredibly Strange Sex*. New York: Juno Books.

Geberth, V.J. (1998). Anatomy of a lust murder. *Law and Order*, **45**(5).

George, A.A. & Richards, D. (2013). Tourism in Trinidad and Tobago: The evolving attitudes and behaviors and its implications in an era of HIV/AIDS epidemic. *Études Caribéennes*, **19**.

Gerbasi, K.C., Paolone, N., Higner, J., Scaletta, L.L., Bernstein, P.L., Conway, S. & Privitera, A. (2008). Furries from A to Z (anthropomorphism to zoomorphism). *Society and Animals*, **16**(3), 197–222.

Gerbasi, K.C., Scaletta, L.L., Plante, C.N. & Bernstein, P.L. (2011). Why so FURious? Rebuttal of Dr. Fiona Probyn-Rapsey's response to Gerbasi *et al*.'s Furries from A to Z (anthropomorphism to zoomorphism). *Society and Animals*, **19**, 302–304.

Gerber, A. (2005). Sex by numbers: Excerpts from 'The Book of Sex Lists'. In: R. Kick (Ed.), *Everything You Know about Sex Is Wrong* (pp. 340–344). New York: The Disinformation Company.

Giannini, A.J., Colapietro, G., Slaby, A.E., Melemis, S.M. & Bowman, R.K. (1998). Sexualization of the female foot as a response to sexually transmitted epidemics: A preliminary study. *Psychological Reports*, **83**, 491–498.

Gibbons, D. (2011a). *Does hypnophilia exist?* Hypnothoughts. Retrieved October 13, 2011 from *http://www.hypnothoughts.com/forum/topics/does-hypnophilia-exist*

Gibbons, D. (2011b). *Hypnosis, seduction and hypnophilia*. Hyperempiria. Retrieved October 28, 2011 from *http://hyperempiria.blogspot.co.uk/2011/10/hypnosis-seduction-and-hypnophilia.html*

Giles, F. (2003). *Fresh Milk – The Secret Life of Breasts*. New York: Simon & Schuster.

Giles, F. (2004). Relational, and strange: A preliminary foray into a project to queer breastfeeding. *Australian Feminist Studies*, **19**, 301–314.

Giles, F. (2005). The well-tempered breast: Fostering fluidity in breastly meaning and function. *Women's Studies: An Inter-disciplinary Journal*, **34**, 301–326.

Gillett, C.A., Griffiths, M.D. & Davies, P. (1989). The hypnotic suppression of conditioned electrodermal responses. In: D. Waxman, D. Pederson, I. Wilkie & P. Mellett (Eds). *Hypnosis* (pp. 60–66). London: Whurr Publishers.

Girl Friday (2010). *Pop culture: Piggyback rides.* Drama Beans. Retrieved July 11, 2010 from http://www.dramabeans.com/2010/07/pop-culture-piggyback-rides/

Goebel, J. (2012). *Zoophilia: Thinking through trans-species sexuality. A Geology of Borders.* Wordpress. Retrieved March 30, 2012 from http://ageologyofborders.wordpress.com/2012/03/30/zoophilia-thinking-through-trans-species-sexuality/

Goldberg, J.E. & Steele, S.R. (2010). Rectal foreign bodies. *Surgical Clinics of North America*, **90**, 173–184.

Goldstone, S.E. (1999). *The Ins and Outs of Gay Sex: A Medical Handbook for Men.* New York: Dell Publishing.

Gonzalez-Arnal, S. (1998). The ambiguous politics of petticoating. *International Journal of Transgenderism*, **2**(3).

Gordon, W.A. & Elias, J.E. (2005). Potentially lethal modes of sexual expression. Paper presented at the *2005 Western Region Annual Conference of the Society for the Scientific Study of Sexuality.*

Gosselin, C. & Wilson, G. (1984). Fetishism, sadomasochism and related behaviours. In: K. Howells (Ed.), *The Psychology of Sexual Diversity* (pp. 89–110). London: Blackwells.

Gosselin, C.C. (1987). The sadomasochistic contract. In: G.D. Wilson (Ed.), *Variant Sexuality: Research and Theory* (pp. 229–257). Baltimore, MD: Johns Hopkins University Press.

Gosselin, C.C. & Wilson, G.D. (1980). *Sexual Variations.* London: Faber & Faber.

Gould, G.M. & Pyle, W.L. (1901). *Anomalies and Curiosities of Medicine.* London: W.B. Saunders.

Gould, S.J. (1991). Toward a theory of sexuality and consumption: Consumer lovemaps. In: R.H. Holman & M.R. Solomon (Eds.), *Advances in Consumer Research*, Vol. 18 (pp. 381–383). Provo, UT: Association for Consumer Research.

Goulian, J-J. (2014). *In defense of hairy women: Searching for a fair standard of beauty.* Vice. Retrieved February 11, 2014 from http://www.vice.com/read/in-defense-of-hairy-women-0000222-v21n2

Graves, R.W., Allison, E.J, Bass, R.R. & Hunt, R.C. (1983). Anal eroticism: Two unusual rectal foreign bodies and their removal. *Southern Medical Journal*, **76**, 677–678.

Gravning, J. (2015). *The fetish for videogame characters trapped in quicksand.* Motherboard. Retrieved March 19, 2015 from http://motherboard.vice.com/read/quicksand

Grebowicz, M. (2010). When species me(a)t: Confronting bestiality pornography. *Humanimalia*, **1**(2), 1–17.

Greenhill, R. & Griffiths, M.D. (2014). The use of online asynchronous interviews in the study of paraphilias. *SAGE Research Methods Cases.* doi: 10.4135/978144627305013508526

Greenhill, R. & Griffiths, M.D. (2015). Compassion, dominance/submission, and curled lips: A thematic analysis of dacryphilic experience. *International Journal of Sexual Health*, **27**, 337–350. doi: 10.1080/19317611.2015.1013596

Greenhill, R. and Griffiths, M.D. (2016). Sexual interest as performance, intellect and pathological dilemma: A critical discursive case study of dacryphilia. *Psychology and Sexuality*, **7**, 265–278.

Greenhill, R. & Griffiths, M.D. (2022). Is there a place for sensory aspects and alternative representations in non-normative sexual interest research? Reflections from a study into dacryphilia. *Journal of Concurrent Disorders*, **4**(2), 1–15.

Greenspan, S. (2011). *Eleven unbelievably insane deaths during sex.* 11 Points. Retrieved November 8, 2011 from http://www.11points.com/Dating-Sex/11_Unbelievably_Insane_Deaths_During_Sex

Griffiths, M.D. (1995). Is there a role for psychology in podiatry teaching? *Journal of British Podiatric Medicine*, **50**, 59–60.

Griffiths, M.D. (1996). Internet addiction: An issue for clinical psychology? *Clinical Psychology Forum*, **97**, 32–36.

Griffiths, M.D. (1998a). Cak-watch (continued): A return to Animal Farm. *Headpress: The Journal of Sex, Death and Religion*, **17**, 65–66.

Griffiths, M.D. (1998b). Shrink rap: The Croft Report. *Arcade*, **1**(November), p. 49.

Griffiths, M.D. (1999a). Dying for it: Autoerotic deaths. *Bizarre*, **24**, 62–65.

Griffiths, M.D (1999b). Adam Ant: Sex and perversion for teenyboppers. *Headpress: The Journal of Sex, Death and Religion*, **19**, 116–119.

Griffiths, M.D. (2000). Excessive internet use: Implications for sexual behavior. *CyberPsychology and Behavior*, **3**, 537–552.

Griffiths, M.D. (2001a). Stumped! Amputee fetishes. *Bizarre*, **44**, 70–74.

Griffiths, M.D. (2001b). Sex on the internet: Observations and implications for sex addiction. *Journal of Sex Research*, **38**, 333–342.

Griffiths, M.D (2003). *Adam Ant: The king of sexual diversity.* AntLib Online. https://www.academia.edu/902509/Griffiths_M_D_2003_Adam_Ant_The_King_of_Sexual_Diversity_AntLib_Online

Griffiths, M.D. (2004). Sex addiction on the internet. *Janus Head: Journal of Interdisciplinary Studies in Literature, Continental Philosophy, Phenomenological Psychology and the Arts*, 7(2), 188–217.

Griffiths, M.D. (2010). Colour atmospherics and its impact on player behaviour. *Casino and Gaming International*, **6**(3), 91–96.

Griffiths, M.D. (2012a). The use of online methodologies in studying paraphilias: A review. *Journal of Behavioral Addictions*, **1**, 143–150.

Griffiths, M.D. (2012b). Internet sex addiction: A review of empirical research. *Addiction Research and Theory*, **20**, 111–124.

Griffiths, M.D. (2012d). The use of online methodologies in studying paraphilias: A review. *Journal of Behavioral Addictions*, **1**, 143–150.

Griffiths, M.D. (2013). Eproctophilia in a young adult male: A case study. *Archives of Sexual Behavior*, **42**, 1383–1386.

Griffiths, M.D. (2019). Salirophilia and other co-occurring paraphilias in a middle-aged male: A case study. *Journal of Concurrent Disorders*, **1**(2), 1–8.

Griffiths, M.D., Gillett, C.A. & Davies, P. (1989a). The hypnotic suppression of conditioned electrodermal responses. *Perceptual and Motor Skills*, **69**, 186.

Griffiths, M.D., Gillett, C.A. & Davies, P. (1989b). An experimental investigation of ideational and exteroceptive conditioning. *Perceptual and Motor Skills*, **69**, 494.

Grosskurth, P. (1980). *Havelock Ellis: A Biography*. Toronto: McClelland & Stewart.

Grubin, D. (1994). Sexual murder. *British Journal of Psychiatry*, **165**, 624–629.

Gubb, K., Segal, J., Khotal, A. and Dicks, A. (2006). Clinical vampirism: A review and illustrative case report. *South African Psychiatry Review*, **9**, 163–168.

Gurley, G. (2001). Pleasures of the fur. *Vanity Fair*, March, 174–196.

Halevy, A., Levi, Y., Ahnaker, A. and Orda, R. (1989). Auto-vampirism: An unusual cause of anaemia. *Journal of the Royal Society of Medicine*, **82**, 630–631.

Harlow, H.F. and Zimmermann, R.R. (1958). The development of affective responsiveness in infant monkeys. *Proceedings of the American Philosophical Society*, **102**, 501–509.

Harwood, W. (2011) *Dictionary of Contemporary Mythology* (Third Edition), Los Angeles, CA: World Audience Inc.

Hattenstone, S. (2005). When I was four, I knew I was weird. *The Guardian*, March 7.

Hazell, B. (2008). American caught having sex with picnic table. *Daily Telegraph*, March 28.

Hazell, K. (2012). *Dress becomes transparent when wearer is sexually aroused.* Huffington Post. Retrieved April 5, 2012 from http://www.huffingtonpost.co.uk/2012/04/05/intimacy-dress-transparent-aroused_n_1405917.html

Hazelwood, R.R. (1983). *Autoerotic Fatalities*. Lexington, MA: Lexington Books.

Hazelwood, R.R. & Douglas, J.E. (1980). The lust murderer. *FBI Law Enforcement Bulletin*, **49**, 1–5.

Hazelwood, R.R., Dietz, P.E. & Burgess, A.W. (1981). The investigation of autoerotic fatalities. *Journal of Police Science & Administration*, **9**, 404–411.

Health Explores (2011). *Hypnofetishism.* http://www.healthexplores.com/wiki/hypnofetishism

Hebdige, D. (1979). *Subculture: The Meaning of Style*. New York: Methuen & Co.

Hemandas, A.H., Muller, G.W. & Ahmed, I. (2005). Rectal impaction with epoxy resin: A case report. *Journal of Gastrointestinal Surgery*, **9**, 747–749

Hemphill, R.E. & Zabow T. (1983) Clinical vampirism: A presentation of three cases and a re-evaluation of Haigh, the "acid-bath murderer". *South African Medical Journal*, **63**(8), 278–281.

Hennessy, M. (2015). *Findom in Dublin: The Irish men who are turned on by women spending their money.* The Journal. Retrieved August 30, 2015 from http://www.thejournal.ie/findom-dublin-2296085-Aug2015/

Herbert, E. (2009). Sex: Weather-driven desire? *Elle,* July 28.

Hicinbothem, J., Gonsalves, S. & Lester, D. (2006). Body modification and suicidal behavior. *Death Studies*, **30**, 351–363.

Hickey, E.W. (Ed.) (2003). *Encyclopedia of Murder and Violent Crime*. London: Sage Publications.

Hickey, E.W. (2006). Paraphilia and signatures in crime scene investigation. In: E.W. Hickey (Ed.), *Sex Crimes and Paraphilias* (pp. 95–107). Saddle River, NJ: Pearson Prentice Hall.

Hickey, E.W. (2010). *Serial Murderers and Their Victims* (Fifth Edition). Pacific Grove, CA: Brooks/Cole.

Hill, C.A. & Preston, L.K. (1996). Individual differences in the experience of sexual motivation: Theory and measurements of dispositional sexual motives. *Journal of Sex Research*, **33**, 27–45.

Hill, D. (2000). *Cuddle time: In the world of plushophiles, not all stuffed animals are created equal.* Salon. Retrieved June 19, 2000 from *http://www.salon.com/2000/06/19/plushies/*

Hill, J.T. (1980). Penile injuries from vacuum cleaners. *British Medical Journal*, **281**(6238), 519.

Hingsburger, D. (1989). Motives for coprophilia: Working with individuals who had been institutionalized with developmental handicaps. *Journal of Sex Research*, **26**, 139–140.

Hirsch, A. & Gruss, J. (1999). Human male sexual response to olfactory stimuli. *Journal of Neurological and Orthopaedic Medicine and Surgery*, **19**, 14–19.

Hirsch, A.R. & Trannel, T.J. (1996). Chemosensory dysfunction and psychiatric diagnoses. *Journal of Neurological and Orthopaedic Medicine and Surgery*, **17**, 25–30.

Hirsch, A.R., Schroder, M., Gruss, J., Bermele, C. and Zagorski, D. (1999). Scentsational sex: Olfactory stimuli and sexual response in the human female. *International Journal of Aromatherapy*, **9**(2), 75–81.

Hirschfeld, M. (1948). *Sexual Anomalies and Perversions*. New York: Emerson.

Hocken, K. & Thorn, K. (2017). Voyeurism, exhibitionism and other non-contact sexual offences. In: B. Winder & P. Banyard (Eds.). *A Psychologist's Casebook of Crime: From Arson to Voyeurism* (pp. 243–263). London: Bloomsbury Publishing.

Holmes, A. (2003). In grossness and in health: Psycho-dermatology, female gorillas, and why women love to pick their boyfriends' zits. *Salon*, August 11.

Holmes, S.T. & Holmes, R.M. (2009). *Sex Crimes: Patterns and Behaviors* (Third Edition). Thousand Oaks, CA: Sage.

Howie, C. (2009). *Claustrophilia: The Erotics of Enclosure in Medieval Literature (New Middle Ages)*. Basingstoke, UK: Palgrave Macmillan.

Huang, W-C., Jiang, J-K., Wang, H-S., Yang, S-H., Chen, W-S., Lin, T-C. & Lin, J-K. (2003). Retained rectal foreign bodies. *Journal of the Chinese Medical Association*, **66**, 606–611.

Hucker, S.J. (2008). Sexual masochism: Psychopathology and theory. In: D.R. Laws & W.T. O'Donohue (Eds.), *Sexual Deviance: Theory, Assessment and Treatment* (pp. 250–263). New York: Guilford Press

Hucker, S.J. (2011a). Hypoxyphilia. *Archives of Sexual Behavior*, **40**, 1323–1326.

Hucker, S. (2011b). *Sexual sadism*. Located at *http://www.forensicpsychiatry.ca/paraphilia/sadism.htmhttp://www.forensicpsychiatry.ca/paraphilia/sadism.htm*

Huffington Post (2009). *Andre Thomas, Texas death row inmate, pulls out eye, eats it.* Retrieved September 9, 2009 from *http://www.huffingtonpost.com/2009/01/09/andre-thomas-texas-death-_n_156765.html*

Huffington Post (2013a). *46 sexual fetishes you've never heard of.* Retrieved October 23, 2013 from *http://www.huffingtonpost.com/2013/10/23/sexual-fetish_n_4144418.html*

Huffington Post (2013b). *Rafe Biggs' thumb has become his "surrogate penis" after accident left him paralyzed*. Retrieved April 22, 2013 from *http://www.huffingtonpost.com/2013/04/22/rafe-biggs-thumb_n_3132325.html?utm_hp_ref=weird-news*

Huffington Post (2014). *Woman tortured, killed animals while filming brutal fetish sex video: Cops*. Retrieved April 6, 2014 from *http://www.huffingtonpost.com/2014/04/06/woman-tortured-animals-fetish-video_n_5100535.html*

Hvozdık, A., Bugarsky, A., Kottferova, J., Vargova, M., Ondrasovicova, O., Ondrasovic, M. & Sasakova, N. (2006). Ethological, psychological and legal aspects of animal sexual abuse. *The Veterinary Journal*, **172**, 374–376.

Imami, R.H. & Kemal, M. (1988). Vacuum cleaner use in autoerotic death. *American Journal of Forensic Medicine and Pathology*, **9**, 246–248.

Intimate Medicine (2010). *Do you like to listen to others having sex?* Retrieved May 10, 2010 from *http://www.intimatemedicine.com/sex-in-society/do-you-like-to-listen-to-others-having-sex/*

Jaffe, P. & DiCataldo, F. (1994). Clinical vampirism: Blending myth and reality. *Bulletin of the American Academy of Psychiatry and the Law*, **22**, 533–544.

Jaiswal, A.K. (1992). An unusual foreign body in the preputial sac. *Genitourinary Medicine*, **68**, 334–335.

Jamison, P. & Morel, L.C. (2012). Man who had sex with dog won't be charged because of unusual reason. *Tampa Bay Times*, June 20.

Janssen, D.F (2014). How to "ascertain" paraphilia: An etymological hint. *Archives of Sexual Behavior*, **43**(7), 1245–1312.

Janssen, W., Koops, E., Anders, S., Kuhn, S. & Püschel, K. (2005). Forensic aspects of 40 accidental autoerotic death in Northern Germany. *Forensic Science International*, **147**, S61–S64.

Janus, S.S. & Janus, C.L. (1993). *The Janus Report on Sexual Behavior*. Chichester, UK: Wiley.

Japan Today (2008, September 2). Arrested uniform thief says he has sweat fetish.

Jiménez-Jiménez, F.J., Sayed, Y., García-Soldevilla, M.A. & Barcenilla, B. (2002). Possible zoophilia associated with dopaminergic therapy in Parkinson disease. *Annals of Pharmacotherapy*, **36**, 1178–1179.

Johansson, E. (2012). *Woman charged for sex with human skeleton*. The Local. Retrieved November 20, 2012 from *http://www.thelocal.se/44536/20121120/*

Johnston, M.A. (2011). *Beard Fetish in Early Modern England*. London: Ashgate.

Joshi, S. (2010). *Summer and intimacy: Feeling hot, hot, hot*. Complete Wellbeing. Retrieved May 11, 2010 from *http://completewellbeing.com/article/feeling-hot-hot-hot/*

Joyce, J. (1975). *Selected Letters of James Joyce* (edited by R. Ellmann). New York: Viking Press.

Kafka, M. (2010a). The DSM diagnostic criteria for fetishism. *Archives of Sexual Behavior*, **39**, 357–362.

Kafka, M.P. (2010b). The DSM diagnostic criteria for paraphilia not otherwise specified. *Archives of Sexual Behavior*, **39**, 373–376.

Kafka, M.P. & Hennen, J. (1999). The paraphilia-related disorders: An empirical investigation of nonparaphilic hypersexuality disorders in 206 outpatient males. *Journal of Sex and Marital Therapy*, **25**, 305–319.

Kafka, M.P. & Hennen, J. (2003). Hypersexual desire in males: Are males with paraphilias different from males with paraphilia-related disorders? *Sexual Abuse: A Journal of Research and Treatment*, **4**, 307–321.

Kahr, B. (2007). *Sex and the Psyche*. London: Penguin Books.

Kaul, A. & Duffy, S. (1991). Gerontophilia: A case report. *Medicine, Science and the Law*, **31**, 110–114.

Kaur, A.A. & Pankaj, G. (2009). Telephone scatologia: An aural assault. *Journal of Punjab Academy of Forensic Medicine and Toxicology*, **9**(2), 87–91.

Kayton, L. (1972). The relationship of the vampire legend to schizophrenia. *Journal of Youth and Adolescence*, **1**, 303–314.

Kelly, B.D., Abood, Z. and Shanley, D. (1999). Vampirism and schizophrenia. *Irish Journal of Psychological Medicine*, **16**, 114–117.

Kendall, P. (2010). Why ugly men always attract the prettiest women. *Daily Mail* (n.d.). http://www.dailymail.co.uk/news/article-70897/Why-ugly-men-attract-prettiest-women.html

Kenney, R.D. (1988). Adolescent males who insert genitourinary foreign bodies: Is psychiatric referral required? *Urology*, **32**, 127–129.

Keppel, R.D., Weis, J.G., Brown, K.M. and Welch, K. (2005). The Jack the Ripper murders: A modus operandi and signature analysis of the 1888–1891 Whitechapel Murders. *Journal of Investigative Psychology and Offender Profiling*, **2**, 1–21.

Kerekes, D. (2010). Looners. *Headpress: The Journal of Sex, Death and Religion*, **21**, 142.

Kesse, R. (2007). *The anatomy of a fetish*. Wordpress. Retrieved June 27, 2007 from http://haircutfetish.wordpress.com/2007/06/22/the-anatomy-of-a-fetish/

Kick, R. (2005). The sex list you probably haven't read: Obscure and expunged material dealing with everyone's favorite activity. In: R. Kick (Ed.), *Everything You Know about Sex Is Wrong* (pp. 260–267). New York: The Disinformation Company.

Kijak, R. (2013). The sexuality of adults with intellectual disability in Poland. *Sexuality and Disability*, **31**(2), 109–123.

Kim, E.D., Mory, A., Wilson, D.D. & Zeagler, D. (2002). Treatment of a complete lower urinary tract obstruction secondary to an expandable foam sealant. *Urology*, **60**, 164.

King, C. (2010). *The A to Z of sexual history: A – avisodomy: The act of a human engaging in sexual activity involving a bird*. Vice. http://www.vice.com/en_uk/read/the-a-to-z-of-sexual-history-a-avisodomy-the-act-of-a-human-engaging-in-sexual-activity-involving-a-bird

King, M.B. (1990). Sneezing as a fetishistic stimulus. *Sexual and Marital Therapy*, **5**, 69–72.

Kinkipedia (2013). Impregnation fetishes. Retrieved January 21, 2013 from http://kinkipedia.wikidot.com/wiki:impregnation-fetish

Kinkly (2015). *Pantyhose fetish*. http://www.kinkly.com/definition/6774/pantyhose-fetish

Kinky Kelley (2011). *Fetish: Zelophilia.* Wordpress. Retrieved January 26, 2011 from http://kinkykelleykicksthekurse.wordpress.com/2011/01/26/fetish-zelophilia/

Kinky Sex Questions (2012a). *Arachnephilia.* http://www.kinky-sex-questions.com/arachnephilia.html

Kinky Sex Questions (2012b). *Entomophilia.* http://www.kinky-sex-questions.com/entomophilia.html

Kinky Sex Questions (2012c). *Equinophilia.* http://www.kinky-sex-questions.com/equinophilia.html

Kinsey, A.C., Pomeroy, W.B. & Martin, C.E. (1948). *Sexual Behavior in the Human Male.* Philadelphia, PA: W.B. Saunders Company.

Kinsey, A.C., Pomeroy, W.B., Martin, C.E. & Gebhard, P.H. (1953). *Sexual Behavior in the Human Female.* Philadelphia, PA: W.B. Saunders Company.

Kirov, G.K., Losanoff, J.E. & Kjossev, K.T. (2002). Zoophilia: A rare cause of traumatic injury to the rectum. *Injury*, **33**, 367–368.

Kise, K. & Nguyen, M. (2011). Adult baby syndrome and gender identity disorder. *Archives of Sexual Behavior*, **40**, 857–859.

Klein, A.M. (1993). *Little Big Men: Bodybuilding Subculture and Gender Construction.* Albany, NY: State University of New York Press.

Klein, L.A. & Houlihan, D. (2010). Relationship satisfaction, sexual satisfaction, and sexual problems in sexsomnia. *International Journal of Sexual Health*, **22**, 84–90.

Kleist, E. & Moi, H. (1993). Transmission of gonorrhoea through an inflatable doll. *Genitourinary Medicine*, **69**, 322.

Klintschar, M., Grabuschnigg, P. & Beham, A. (1998). Death from electrocution during autoerotic practice: Case report and review of the literature. *American Journal of Forensic Medicine and Pathology*, **19**, 190–193.

Kochakarn, W. & Pummanagura, W. (2008). Foreign bodies in the female urinary bladder: 20-year experience in Ramathibodi Hospital. *Asian Journal of Surgery*, **31**, 130–133.

Krueger, R.B. (2010). The DSM diagnostic criteria for sexual masochism. *Archives of Sexual Behavior*, **39**, 346–356.

Krueger, R.B. & Kaplan, M.S. (1999). Evaluation and treatment of sexual disorders: Frottage. *Innovations in Clinical Practice: A Source Book*, **18**, 185–197.

Krueger, R.B. & Kaplan, M.S. (2000). The nonviolent serial offender: Exhibitionism, frotteurism, and telephone scatalogia. In: L.B. Schlesinger (Ed.), *Serial Offenders: Current Thought, Recent Findings* (pp. 103–118). Boca Raton, FL: CRC Press.

Krueger, R.B. & Kaplan, M. (2001). The paraphilic and hypersexual disorders: An overview. *Journal of Psychiatric Practice*, **7**, 391–403.

Krueger, R.B. & Kaplan, M.S. (2008). Frotteurism: Assessment and treatment. In: D.R. Laws and W.T. O'Donohue (Eds), *Sexual Deviance: Theory, Assessment, and Treatment* (pp. 150–163). New York: Guilford Press.

Kunjukrishnan, R., Pawlak, A. & Varan, L.R. (1988). The clinical and forensic psychiatric issues of retifism. *Canadian Journal of Psychiatry*, **33**, 819–825.

Kuriansky, J. (2011). *Piquerism pervert.* Dr. Judy. Retrieved August 16, 2011 from https://www.drjudy.com/latest-posts/2011/8/16/piquerism-pervert.html

Lady Izabelle (n.d.). *Hypnofetishism and erotic hypnosis.* http://erotichypnosis.ladyizzabelle.com/

Lake, C.R. (2008). Hypothesis: Grandiosity and guilt cause paranoia; paranoid schizophrenia is a psychotic mood disorder: A review. *Schizophrenia Bulletin*, **34**, 1151–1162.
Lam, J. (2017). Fifty shades of sexual offending – Part 1. *The Law Gazette,* July.
Lang, R.A., Langevin, R., Bain, J., Frenzel, R. & Wright, P. (1989). Sex hormone profiles in genital exhibitionists. *Annals of Sex Research*, **2**, 67–75.
Långström, N. (2010). The DSM diagnostic criteria for exhibitionism, voyeurism, and frotteurism. *Archives of Sexual Behavior*, **39**, 317–324.
Långström, N. & Seto, M.C. (2006). Exhibitionistic and voyeuristic behavior in a Swedish national population survey. *Archives of Sexual Behavior*, **35**, 427–435.
Långström, N. & Zucker, K.J. (2005). Transvestic fetishism in the general population: Prevalence and correlates. *Journal of Sex and Marital Therapy*, **31**, 87–95.
Larkin, M. & Griffiths, M.D. (2004). Dangerous sports and recreational drug-use: Rationalising and contextualising risk. *Journal of Community and Applied Social Psychology*, **14**, 215–232.
Lamberth, P. (1997). Urethral self-insertion case report and review of the literature. *Emergency Medicine*, 9(1), 15–19.
Laws, D.R. & O'Donohue, W.T. (2008), *Sexual Deviance: Theory, Assessment and Treatment* (Second Edition). New York: Guilford Press.
Lawson, L.A. (1994). The dream screen in "The Moviegoer". *Papers on Language and Literature*, 30(1), 25.
Leadbeatter, S. (1988). Dental anesthetic death: An unusual autoerotic episode. *American Journal of Forensic Medicine and Pathology*, **9**, 60–63.
Lehne, G.K. (1994). Brain damage and paraphilias treated with medroxyprogesterone acetate. *Sex and Disability*, **10**, 145–158.
Lehne, G.K. & Money, J. (2003). Multiplex versus multiple taxonomy of paraphilias: Case example. *Sexual Abuse: A Journal of Research and Treatment*, **15**, 61–72.
Lemma, A. (2010). *Under the Skin: A Psychoanalytic Study of Body Modification*. London: Routledge.
Levin, R.J. (2006). The breast/nipple/areola complex and human sexuality. *Sexual and Relationship Therapy*, **21**, 237–249.
Levin, R. & Meston, C. (2006). Nipple/breast stimulation and sexual arousal in young men and women. *Journal of Sexual Medicine*, **3**, 450–454.
Levy, D. (2017). Man's bizarre medical condition means he's in love with his CAR and even has sex with motor he calls Goldie. *Sunday Mirror*, July 29.
Lewis, A. (2011). Ageplay: An adults-only game. *Counselling Australia*, 11(2), 1–9.
Litman, L.C. (1999). A case of pyrophilia. *Canadian Psychological Association Bulletin*, February, 18–20.
Littlejohn, R. (2012). So that's why they're called the funny people. *Daily Mail*, May 3.
Live Journal (2007). *BDSM: Theory and practice of figging.* http://tacit.livejournal.com/225189.html
Live Nation (2003). *Eyeballs.* https://eyeballs.livejournal.com
Lo, S.F., Wong, S.H., Leung, L.S., Law, I.C. & Yip, A.W.C. (2004). Traumatic rectal perforation by an eel. *Surgery*, **135**, 110–111.
London Fetish Fair (2014). *Edgeplay Top 10 medical play kit.* http://www.londonfetishfair.co.uk/index.php/stands/137-top-10-essential-medical-play-items

London Fetish Scene (2009). *Nettle*. Retrieved February 5, 2009 from *http://www.londonfetishscene.com/wipi/index.php/Nettle*

Longhurst, R. (2006). A pornography of birth: Crossing moral boundaries. *ACME: An International E-Journal for Critical Geographies*, **5**(2), 209–229.

Lopez, D.A. & Godard, E. (2013). Nazi uniform fetish and role-playing: A subculture of erotic evil. *Popular Culture Review*, **24**(1), 69–78.

Lothstein, L.M. (1997). Pantyhose fetishism and self cohesion: A paraphilic solution? *Gender and Psychoanalysis*, **2**(1), 103–121.

Lovatt, P. (2012). Sex and dancing. *Psychology Today,* March 12.

Love, B. (2001). *Encyclopedia of Unusual Sex Practices*. London: Greenwich Editions.

Love, B. (2005). Cat-fighting, eye-licking, head-sitting and statue-screwing. In: R. Kick (Ed.), *Everything You Know about Sex Is Wrong* (pp. 122–129). New York: The Disinformation Company.

Lovegrove, K. (2000). *Airline: Identity, Design and Culture.* New York: Te Neues Publishing Company.

Lowenstein, L.F. (2002). Fetishes and their associated behaviour. *Sexuality and Disability*, **20**, 135–147.

Lum, S. (2012). Bogus cop jailed for sexually assaulting girl, 12. *Straits Times*, September 26

Lussier, P. & Piche, L. (2008). Frotteurism: Psychopathology and theory. In: D.R. Laws and W.T. O'Donohue (Eds), *Sexual Deviance: Theory, Assessment and Treatment* (pp. 131–149). New York: Guilford Press.

Lykins, A.D. & Cantor, J.M. (2014). Vorarephilia: A case study in masochism and erotic consumption. *Archives of Sexual Behavior*, **43**, 181–186.

MacCulloch, M., Snowden, P., Wood, P. & Mills, H. (1983). Sadistic fantasy, sadistic behavior, and offending. *British Journal of Psychiatry*, **143**, 20–29.

MacCulloch, M., Gray, N. & Watt, A. (2000). Britain's sadist murderer syndrome reconsidered: An associative account of the aetiology of sadistic sexual fantasy. *Journal of Forensic Psychiatry*, **11**, 401–418.

MacDonald, J.M. (1986). *The Murderer and His Victims* (Second Edition). Springfield, IL: Charles C. Thomas.

Mackenzie, J.N. (1898). The physiological and pathological relations between the nose and sexual apparatus of man. *Journal of Laryngology, Rhinology and Otology*, **13**, 109–123.

Maddy's Mansion (2010). *Catheterophilia*. Retrieved October 4, 2010 from *http://maddysmansion.blogspot.co.uk/2010/10/catheterophilia.html?zx=b5754ebdc388557b*

Mahony, P.J. (1989). Aspects of nonperverse scopophilia within an analysis. *Journal of the American Psychoanalytic Association*, **37**(2), 365–399.

Mai, F.M.M. (1968). A new psychosexual syndrome: Ecouterism. *Australian and New Zealand Journal of Psychiatry*, **2**, 261–263.

Malitz, S. (1966). Another report on the wearing of diapers and rubber pants by an adult male. *American Journal of Psychiatry*, **122**, 1435–1437.

Malmquist, C.P. (1996). *Homicide: A Psychiatric Perspective*. Washington, DC: American Psychiatric Press.

Mangan, M.A. (2004). A phenomenology of problematic sexual behavior occurring in sleep. *Archives of Sexual Behavior*, **33**, 287–293.

Mangan, M.A. & Reips, U. (2007). Sleep, sex, and the web: Surveying the difficult-to-reach clinical population suffering from sexsomnia. *Behavior Research Methods*, **39**, 233–236.

Mannion, R.A. (1973). Penile laceration. *Journal of the American Medical Association*, **224**, 1763–1763.

Mantegazza, P. (2001). *The Sexual Relations of Mankind*. Honolulu, HI: University Press of the Pacific.

Costa-Neto, E. & Marques, J.G.W. (2000). Faunistic resources used as medicines by artisanal fishermen from Siribinha Beach, state of Bahia, Brazil. *Journal of Ethnobiology*, **20**(1), 93–109.

Marsh, A. (2010). Love among objectum sexuals. *Electronic Journal of Human Sexuality*, **13**, March 1.

Marshall, W.L. & Kennedy, P. (2003). Sexual sadism in sexual offenders: An elusive diagnosis. *Aggression and Violent Behavior*, **8**, 1–22.

Marshall, W.L. & Yates, P.M. (2004). Diagnostic issues in sexual sadism among sexual offenders. *Journal of Sexual Aggression*, **10**, 21–27.

Marshall, J., Walker, B., Benford, S., Tomlinson, G., Egglestone, S.R., Reeves, S., Brundell, P., Tennent, P., Cranwell, J., Harter, P. and Longhurst, J. (2011). The gas mask: A probe for exploring fearsome interactions. *Proceedings of the 2011 Annual Conference Extended Abstracts on Human Factors in Computing Systems, New York* (pp. 127–136).

Marten, Z. (1986). Candaulerism: Case report. *Psychiatrica Polska*, **20**, 235–237.

Martins, Y., Tiggemann, M. and Churchett, L. (2008). Hair today, gone tomorrow: A comparison of body hair removal practices in gay and heterosexual men. *Body Image*, **5**, 312–316.

Massen, J. (1994). Zoophilie. *Die sexuelle Liebe zu Tieren* [in German]. Cologne: Pinto Press.

Masters, P. (2001). *Look into My Eyes: How to Use Hypnosis to Bring Out the Best in Your Sex Life*. Eugene, OR: Greenery Press.

Masters, P. (2011). *Look into my eyes.* Retrieved May 6, 2011 from http://www.peter-masters.com/hypno/index.php/Hypno_fetish

Masters, R.E.L. (1962). *Forbidden Sexual Behavior and Morality*. New York: Lancer Books.

Masters, R.E.L & Lea, A.E.E. (1963). *Perverse Crimes in History: Evolving Concepts of Sadism, Lust-Murder, and Necrophilia – From Ancient to Modern Times*. New York: The Julian Press.

Matek, O. (1988). Obscene phone callers. *Journal of Social Work and Human Sexuality*, **7**, 113–130.

Matson, T. A. & McNamara, P. (2012). *The Hospital Emergency Department: A Guide to Operational Excellence*. Chicago: American Hospital Publishing.

McAninch, J.W., Kahn, R.I., Jeffrey, R.B., Laing, F.C. & Krieger, M.J. (1984). Major traumatic and septic genital injuries. *Journal of Trauma-Injury, Infection, and Critical Care*, **24**, 291–298.

McCallum, E.L. (1998). *Object Lessons: How to Do Things with Fetishism*. New York: State University of New York Press.

McCary, J.L. (1967). *Human Sexuality*. New York: Van Nostrand Reinhold.

McCary, J.L. and McCary, S.P. (1982). *McCary's Human Sexuality* (Fourth Edition). Belmont, CA: Wadsworth.

McCasker, T. (2015). *The emerging fetish of laying alien eggs inside yourself.* Vice. Retrieved August 13, 2015 from http://www.vice.com/en_uk/read/the-emerging-fetish-of-laying-alien-eggs-inside-yourself

McClintock, M. (1971). Menstrual synchrony and suppression. *Nature*, **229**, 244–245.

McCombs, E. (2008). *Toonophilia: Is it porn?* Huffington Post. Retrieved October 1, 2008 from http://www.asylum.com/2008/10/01/toonophilia-is-it-porn/

McCormack, S. (2011). *Malcolm Brenner chronicles his sexual relationship with dolphin in "Wet Goddess".* Huffington Post. Retrieved September 29, 2011 from http://www.huffingtonpost.com/2011/09/23/malcolm-brenner-dolphin_n_974764.html

McDowell, C. (1989). *Shoes, Fashion and Fantasy*. London: Thames & Hudson Ltd.

McGuigan, S. (2023). "Freddie the dolphin hooked my arm with his penis, it was all perfectly normal": How bizarre scandal erupted over animal activist's alleged abuse in 1990. *Daily Mail*, September 23.

McGuire, B.E., Choon, G.L., Nayer, P. and Sanders, J. (1998). An unusual paraphilia: Case report of oral partialism. *Sexual and Marital Therapy*, **13**, 207–210.

McGuire, C. (1989). *Perfect Victim*. New York: Dell.

McIntyre, K.E. (2011). *Looners: Inside the world of balloon fetishism.* Berkeley Graduate School of Journalism, UC Berkeley. Retrieved 27 April, 2011 from http://escholarship.org/uc/item/40c3h6kk

McLennan, J.J., Sekula-Perlman, A., Lippstone, M.B. & Callery, R.T. (1998). Propane-associated autoerotic fatalities. *American Journal of Forensic Medicine and Pathology*, **19**, 381–386.

McNally, R.J. & Lukach, B.M. (1991). Behavioral treatment of zoophilic exhibitionism. *Journal of Behavioral Therapy and Experimental Psychiatry*, **22**, 281–284.

Meijer, H. (2000). Shibari: House of Japanese bondage. *Secret Magazine*, **18**, 23–46.

Metro (2006). *Man has sex with dead deer.* http://www.metro.co.uk/weird/25475-man-has-sex-with-dead-deer

Metro (2008). *Nun beauty contest won't become a habit.* Retrieved August 27, 2008 from http://metro.co.uk/2008/08/27/nun-beauty-contest-wont-become-a-habit-432891/

Miami Herald (2014, April 4). Miami woman charged with role in animal torture sex fetish porn video.

Miletski, H. (2000). Bestiality and zoophilia: An exploratory study. *Scandinavian Journal of Sexology*, **3**, 149–150.

Miletski, H. (2001). Zoophilia: Implications for therapy. *Journal of Sex Education and Therapy*, **26**(2), 85–89.

Miletski, H. (2002). *Understanding Bestiality and Zoophilia*. Bethesda, MD: East-West Publishing LLC (ebook).

Miletski, H. (2017). Zoophilia: Another sexual orientation? *Archives of Sexual Behavior*, **46**(1), 39–42.

Milner, J.S., Dopke, C.A. & Crouch, J.L. (2008). Paraphilia not otherwise specified: Psychopathology and theory. In: D.R. Laws and W.T. O'Donohue (Eds), *Sexual

Deviance: Theory, Assessment and Treatment (pp. 384–418). New York: Guilford Press.

Mintz, I.L. (1964). Autocannibalism: A case study. *American Journal of Psychiatry*, **120**, 1017.

Monasterio, E. & Prince, C. (2011). Self-cannibalism in the absence of psychosis and substance use. *Australasian Psychiatry*, **19**, 170–172.

Money, J. (1980). *Love and Love Sickness: The Science of Sex, Gender Difference and Pair-bonding.* Baltimore, MD: Johns Hopkins University Press.

Money, J. (1984). Paraphilias: Phenomenology and classification. *American Journal of Psychotherapy*, **38**, 164–179

Money, J. (1986). *Lovemaps: Clinical Concepts of Sexual/Erotic Health and Pathology, Paraphilia, and Gender Transposition in Childhood, Adolescence, and Maturity.* New York: Irvington.

Money, J. (1988) *Gay, Straight, and In-between: The Sexology of Erotic Orientation.* Oxford, UK: Oxford University Press.

Money, J. (1990a). Paraphilia in females: Fixation on amputation and lameness – two personal accounts. *Journal of Psychology and Human Sexuality*, **3**, 165–172.

Money, J. (1990b). Forensic sexology: Paraphilic serial rape (biastophilia) and lust murder (erotophonophilia). *American Journal of Psychotherapy*, **44**, 26–36

Money, J. (1994). *Principles of Developmental Sexology.* New York: Continuum.

Money, J., Jobaris, R. & Furth, G. (1977). Apotemnophilia: Two cases of self-demand amputation as a paraphilia. *Journal of Sex Research*, **13**, 115–125.

Money, J. & Simcoe, K.W. (1986). Acrotomophilia, sex and disability: New concepts and case report. *Sexuality and Disability*, **7**, 43–50.

Monroe, W. (2012a). *Fetish of the week: Dacryphilia.* ZZ Insider. Retrieved February 23, 2012 from *http://www.zzinsider.com/blogs/view/fetish_of_the_week_dacryphilia*

Monroe, W. (2012b). *Fetish of the week: Dendrophilia.* ZZ Insider. Retrieved January 6, 2012 from *http://www.zzinsider.com/blogs/view/fetish_of_the_week_dendrophilia*

Monroe, W. (2012c). *Fetish of the week: Schediaphilia (toonophilia).* ZZ Insider. Retrieved March 12, 2012 from *http://www.zzinsider.com/blogs/view/fetish_of_the_week_schediaphilia_toonophilia*

Monaghan, L. (2005). Big handsome men, bears, and others: Virtual constructions of "fat male embodiment". *Body and Society*, **11**, 81–111.

Montagu, A. (1986). *Touching: The Human Significance of the Skin.* New York: Harper & Row.

Monteseirin, J., Camacho, M.J., Bonilla, I., Sánchez-Hernández, C., Hernández, M. & Conde, J. (2001). Honeymoon rhinitis. *Allergy*, **56**, 353–354.

Moon, S.J., Kim, D.H., Chung, J.H., Jo, J.K., Son, Y.W., Choi, H.Y. and Moon, H.S. (2010). Unusual foreign bodies in the urinary bladder and urethra due to autoerotism. *International Neurourology Journal*, **14**, 186–189.

Morana (2008). *Burusera.* Heaven 666. Retrieved February 19, 2008 from *http://www.heaven666.org/burusera-24070.php*

Morgan, G. (2009). *8 Freakiest Fetishes.* Oddee. Retrieved June 18, 2009 from *http://www.oddee.com/item_96718.aspx*

Morris, D. (1967). *The Naked Ape*. London: Jonathan Cape.

Moser, C. (1992). Lust, lack of desire, and paraphilias: Some thoughts and possible connections. *Journal of Sex & Marital Therapy*, **18**(1), 65–69.

Moser, C. & Kleinplatz, P.J. (2002). Transvestic fetishism: Psychopathology or iatrogenic effect? *New Jersey Psychologist*, **52**(2), 16–17.

Moser, C. & Kleinplatz, P.J. (2006). DSM-IV-TR and the paraphilias: An argument for removal. *Journal of Psychology and Human Sexuality*, **17**, 91–109.

Moser, C. & Kleinplatz, P.J. (2007). Themes of expression. In: D. Langbridge and M. Barker (Eds), *Safe, Sane and Consensual: Contemporary Perspectives on SM* (pp. 35–54). Basingstoke, UK: Macmillan.

Moser, C. & Levitt, E.E. (1987). An exploratory descriptive study of a sado-masochistically oriented sample. *Journal of Sex Research*, **23**, 322–337.

Moser, C., Lee, J. & Christensen, P. (1993) Nipple piercing: An exploratory–descriptive study. *Journal of Psychology and Human Sexuality*, **6**(2), 51–61.

Moskowitz, D.A. & Roloff, M.E. (2007). The ultimate high: Sexual addiction and the bug-chasing phenomenon. *Sexual Addiction and Compulsivity*, **14**, 21–40,

Mundinger-Klow, G. (2009). *The Golden Fetish: Case Histories in the Wild World of Watersports*. Paris: Olympia Press.

Mundinger-Klow, G. (2010). *Pony Training: Five Case Studies on Pony Play, Ownership and Kinky Submission*. Paris: Olympia Press.

Munro, H.M.C. (2006). Animal sexual abuse: A veterinary taboo? *The Veterinary Journal*, **172**, 195–197.

Munro, H.M.C. & Thrusfield, M.V. (2001). Battered pets: Sexual abuse. *Journal of Small Animal Practice*, **42**, 333–337.

Murphy, W.D. & Page, I.J. (2008). Exhibitionism: Psychopathology and theory. In: D.R. Laws and W.T. O'Donohue (Eds), *Sexual Deviance: Theory, Assessment and Treatment* (pp. 61–75). New York: Guilford Press.

Music Banter (n.d.). *What is your fetish?* https://www.musicbanter.com/lounge/23897-what-is-your-fetish-10.html

Naish, D. (2008). Traumatic anal intercourse with a pig. In: *Tetrapod Zoology*. CFZ Press. Retrieved February 22, 2008 from http://scienceblogs.com/tetrapodzoology/2008/02/22/he-loved-pigs-too-much/

Nation Master (2005). *Glove fetishism*. http://www.statemaster.com/encyclopedia/Glove-fetishism

Nation Master (2008). *Veil fetishism*. http://www.nationmaster.com/encyclopedia/Veil-fetishism

Nation Master (2012a). *Mask fetishism*. http://www.statemaster.com/encyclopedia/Mask-fetishism

Nation Master (2012b). *Damsel in distress*. http://www.statemaster.com/encyclopedia/Damsel-in-distress

Nation Master (2012c). *Faunoiphilia*. http://www.nationmaster.com/encyclopedia/

Nation Master (2012d). *Mask fetishism*. http://www.statemaster.com/encyclopedia/Mask-fetishismhttp://www.statemaster.com/encyclopedia/Mask-fetishism

Nation Master (2012e). *Veil fetishism*. http://www.statemaster.com/encyclopedia/Veil-fetishism

References and Further Reading 309

Nation Master (2012f). *Endosomatophilia.* http://www.nationmaster.com/encyclopedia/Endosomatophilia

Nation Master (2012g). *Unbirthing.* http://www.nationmaster.com/encyclopedia/Unbirthing

Nation Master (2012h). *Queefing.* http://www.nationmaster.com/encyclopedia/Queefing

Nation Master (2013a). *Dental braces fetishism.* http://www.nationmaster.com/encyclopedia/Dental-braces-fetishism

Nation Master (2013b). *Lift and carry.* http://www.nationmaster.com/encyclopedia/Lift-and-Carry

Nation Master (2013c). *Scuba fetishism.* http://www.nationmaster.com/encyclopedia/Scuba-fetishism

Nation Master (2013d). *Stuck fetishism.* http://www.nationmaster.com/encyclopedia/Stuck-Fetishism

Nation Master (2013e). *Omorashi.* http://www.statemaster.com/encyclopedia/Omorashi

Nation Master (2014). *Breast expansion fetish.* http://www.statemaster.com/encyclopedia/Breast-expansion-fetish

Nattress, L.W. (1996). Amelotasis. Men attracted to women who are amputees: A descriptive study. Doctoral thesis, Walden University, Minnesota, USA.

Necromagickal (n.d.). *Alien sex. Girls and corpses.* http://www.girlsandcorpses.com/print11/print11_aliensex.html

Nelson, S. (2012). *Fetish spotlight: Mechanophilia.* http://www.thehoneybunnys.com/fetish-spotlight-mechanophilia/

Neustifter, R. (2008). *Tuesday's twisted fetish: Eye licking (oculingus).* Exploring Intimacy. Retrieved September 23, 2008 from http://exploringintimacy.wordpress.com/2008/09/23/tuesdays-twisted-fetish-eye-licking-oculingus/

Newring, K.A.B., Wheeler, J. & Draper, C. (2008). Transvestic fetishism: Assessment and theory. In: D.R. Laws and W.T. O'Donohue (Eds), *Sexual Deviance: Theory, Assessment and Treatment* (Second Edition, pp. 285–305). New York: Guilford Press.

New Zealand Herald (2007, July 30). "Deviant saliva fetish" led to attack, court told.

Noguchi, M. & Kato, S. (2004). [A case of Williams Syndrome who exhibited fetishism] [in Japanese]. *Seishin Shinkeigaku Zasshi,* **106**(10), 1232–1241.

Noll, R. (1992). *Vampires, Werewolves and Demons: Twentieth Century Reports in the Psychiatric Literature.* New York: Brunner/Mazel.

Norris, G. (2010). *Illustrated Sex Guides: Dominance and Submission.* New York: Brian Phillipe.

Ntumy, E.K. (2013). *The 6 most bizarre safe-for-work fetishes.* Cracked. Retrieved November 2, 2013 from http://www.cracked.com/article_20691_the-6-most-bizarre-safe-for-work-fetishes.html

Occult and Violent Ritual Crime Research Center (2012). *Renfield's syndrome.* http://www.athenaresearchgroup.org/renfieldsyndrome.htm

Oguz, N. & Uygur, N. (2005). [A case of diaper fetishism] [in Turkish]. *Turk Psikiyatri Derg,* **16**, 133–138.

Oh Internet (2012). *Unbirthing.* http://ohInternet.com/Unbirthing

Omasiali (2011). *Sick white devil repeatedly has sex with cow manure back in jail.* Wordpress. Retrieved May 15, 2011 from http://omasiali.wordpress.com/2011/05/15/sick-white-devil-repeatedly-has-sex-with-cow-manure-back-in-jail/

Opentopia (2013). *What is inflatable fetishism?* http://encycl.opentopia.com/term/Inflatable_fetishism

O'Reilly, J. (2014). *The New Sex Bible: The New Guide To Sensual Love.* London: Quiver.

Otto, S. (2009). Woman getting married to fairground ride. *Daily Telegraph*, August 5.

Özkan, A., Kaya, M., Okur, M., Küçük, A. & Turan, H. (2011). Three-year-old boy with swelling and ecchymosis of the penis. *Turkish Archives of Pediatrics*, **46**, 259–260.

Page Pulp (2014). *Sexual fetishes of famous authors.* http://www.pagepulp.com/2091/sexual-fetishes-of-famous-authors/

Paget, L. (2002). *The Big O: How to Have Them, Give Them, and Keep Them Coming.* London: Piatkus Books.

Pate, J. and Gabbard, J.O. (2003). Adult baby syndrome. *American Journal of Psychiatry*, **160**, 1932–1936.

Pearson, G.A. (1991). Insect fetish objects. *Cultural Entomology Digest*, **4**, November.

Penix, T.M. (2008). Paraphilia not otherwise specified: Assessment and treatment. In: D.R. Laws and W.T. O'Donohue (Eds), *Sexual Deviance: Theory, Assessment and Treatment* (pp. 419–438). New York: Guilford Press.

Person, E.S., Terestman, N., Myers, W.A., Goldberg, E.L. & Salvadori, C. (1989). Gender differences in sexual behaviors and fantasies in a college population. *Journal of Sex and Marital Therapy*, **15**, 187–198.

Persaud, R. (2003). *From the Edge of the Couch: Bizarre Psychiatric Cases and What They Teach Us about Ourselves.* London. Bantam Books.

Pet Abuse (2007). *Sex with dead dog, assaulting an ACO – Freeland, MI.* http://www.pet-abuse.com/cases/9867/MI/US/#ixzz22CLTh2Kx

Pettit, I. & Barr, R. (1980). Temporal lobe epilepsy with diaper fetishism and gender dysphoria. *Medical Journal of Australia*, **2**, 208–209.

Pond, M. (1985). *Shoes Never Lie.* New York: Berkley Publishing Group.

Potasman, I., Oren, A. & Srugo, I. (1999). Isolation of *Ureaplasma urealyticum* and *Mycoplasma hominis* from public toilet bowls. *Infection Control and Hospital Epidemiology*, **20**, 66–68.

Pranzarone, G.F. (2000). *The Dictionary of Sexology.* http://ebookee.org/Dictionary-of-Sexology-EN_997360.html

Pravda (2004, November 10). Cat rapes woman after performing oral sex on her.

Price, M., Kafka, M., Commons, M.L., Gutheil, T.G. & Simpson, W. (2002). Telephone scatologia: Comorbidity with other paraphilias and paraphilia-related disorders. *International Journal of Law and Psychiatry*, **25**, 37–49.

Prins, H. (1985). Vampirism: A clinical condition. *British Journal of Psychiatry*, **146**, 666–668.

Probyn-Rapsey, F. (2011). Furries and the limits of species identity disorder: A response to Gerbasi et al. *Society and Animals*, **19**, 294–301.

Psychology Dictionary (2014). *What is toucherism?* http://psychologydictionary.org/toucherism/

Purcell, C. and Arrigo, B. (2001). Explaining paraphilias and lust murder: Toward an integrated model. *International Journal of Offender Therapy and Comparative Criminology*, **45**(1), 6–31.

Quinsey, V.L., Chaplin, T.C. & Upfold, D. (1989). Arsonists and sexual arousal to fire setting: Correlation unsupported. *Canadian Journal of Behavior Therapy and Experimental Psychiatry*, **20**, 203–209.

Ramachandran, V.S. (1994). Phantom limbs, neglect syndromes, repressed memories, and Freudian psychology. *International Review of Neurobiology*, **37**, 291–333.

Randall, M.B., Vance, R.P. & McCalmont, T.H. (1990). Xenolingual autoeroticism. *American Journal of Forensic Medicine and Pathology*, **11**, 89–92.

Randall, C., Meethan, K., Randall, H. and Dobbs, F. (1999). Nettle sting of *Urtica dioica* for joint pain: An exploratory study of this complementary therapy. *Complementary Therapies in Medicine*, **7**, 126–131.

Reed, N. (2010). *Six depraved sexual fetishes that are older than you think*. Cracked. Retrieved March 30, 2010 from *http://www.cracked.com/article_18472_6-depraved-sexual-fetishes-that-are-older-than-you-think.html*

Rehor, J.E. (2015). Sensual, erotic, and sexual behaviors of women from the "kink" community. *Archives of Sexual Behavior*, **44**(4), 825–836.

Religious Sex (2012). *"Bizarre" fetishes (Part 1): Gothic fetish*. Retrieved May 8, 2012 from *http://www.religioussex.com/bizarre-fetishes/*

Ressler, R.K., Burgess, A.W. & Douglas, J.E. (1988). *Sexual Homicide: Patterns and Motives*. New York: Free Press.

Richardson, N. (2008): Flex-rated! Female bodybuilding: Feminist resistance or erotic spectacle? *Journal of Gender Studies*, **17**, 289–301

Right Diagnosis (2011). *What is homilophilia?* *http://www.rightdiagnosis.com/h/homilophilia/basics.htm*

Right Diagnosis (2012a). *Capnolagnia*. *http://www.rightdiagnosis.com/c/capnolagnia/intro.htm*

Right Diagnosis (2012b). *Catheterophilia*. *http://www.rightdiagnosis.com/c/catheterophilia/intro.htm*

Right Diagnosis (2012c). *Choreophilia*. *http://www.rightdiagnosis.com/c/choreophilia/intro.htm*

Right Diagnosis (2012d). *Ecouterism*. Retrieved February 1, 2012 from *http://www.rightdiagnosis.com/e/ecouteurism/intro.htm*

Right Diagnosis (2012e). *Knismolagnia*. *http://www.rightdiagnosis.com/k/knismolagnia/intro.htm*

Right Diagnosis (2012f). *Xenophilia*. *http://www.rightdiagnosis.com/x/xenophilia/intro.htm*

Right Diagnosis (2012g). *What is harmatophilia?* *http://www.rightdiagnosis.com/h/harmatophilia/basics.htm*

Right Diagnosis (2013a). *Arachnephilia*. *http://www.rightdiagnosis.com/a/arachnephilia/intro.htm*

Right Diagnosis (2013b). *Pecattiphilia*. *http://www.rightdiagnosis.com/p/pecattiphilia/intro.htm*

Rigney, T. (2012). *Abandoned couch sex: Man arrested for getting busy with furniture*. The Inquisitor. Retrieved September 27, 2012 from http://www.inquisitr.com/345157/abandoned-couch-sex-man-arrested-for-getting-busy-with-furniture/

Rogers, D.J. (2009). Adult sexual offences. In: W.D.S. McLay (Ed.), *Clinical Forensic Medicine* (Third Edition) (pp. 137–154). Cambridge, UK: Cambridge University Press.

Rogers, M.F. (1999). *Barbie Culture*. London: Sage Publications.

Rolnik, D. (2012). *Exploring the looner fetish – People who f*ck inflatable pool toys*. After Dark LA. Retrieved July 17, 2012 from http://blogs.laweekly.com/afterdark/2012/07/people_actually_hump_inflatabl_1.php

Rosenfeld, D.S. & Elhajjar, A.J. (1998). Sleepsex: A variant of sleepwalking. *Archives of Sexual Behavior*, **27**, 269–278.

Rosie, B. (2012). *Odontophilia: A fetish for teeth*. Billierosie. Retrieved November 30, 2012 from http://billierosie.blogspot.co.uk/2012/11/odontophilia-fetish-for-teeth_30.html?zx=e29fd1eddbccbd8c

Rosman, J.P. & Resnick, P.J. (1989). Sexual attraction to corpses: A psychiatric review of necrophilia. *Bulletin of the American Academy of Psychiatry and the Law*, **17**, 153–163.

Rossi, W.A. (1976). *The Sex Life of the Foot and Shoe*. Malabar, FL: Krieger Publishing.

Rossi, W.A. (1990a). Foot and shoe fetishism: Part 1. *Journal of Current Podiatric Medicine*, **39**(9), 9–23.

Rossi, W.A. (1990b). Foot and shoe fetishism: Part 2. *Journal of Current Podiatric Medicine*, **39**(10), 16–20.

Rossi, M., Cascini, F. & Torcigliani, S. (1991). [Penile injuries caused by masturbation with a vacuum cleaner: Description of a case and review of the literature] [in Italian]. *Minerva Urologica e Nefrologica*, **44**(1), 43–45.

Rubber Puppett (2012). *About Rubber Puppett*. http://rubberpupett.com/about.html

Rubber World Rendezvous (2013). *Frequently asked questions*. http://www.rubberdollworldrendezvous.com/faq.php

Rufus, A. (2010). *The red state sex fetish*. The Daily Beast. Retrieved March 21, 2010 from http://www.thedailybeast.com/articles/2010/03/21/the-red-state-sex-fetish.html

Rufus, A. (2012a). *Did claustrophilia kill U.K. spy Gareth Williams?* The Daily Beast. Retrieved April 30, 2012 from http://www.thedailybeast.com/articles/2012/04/30/did-claustrophilia-kill-u-k-spy-gareth-williams.html

Rufus, A. (2012b). Turned on by tight spaces. *Psychology Today*, May 2.

Rupp, J.C. (1973). The love bug. *Journal of Forensic Sciences*, **18**, 259–262.

Russo, A. (2008). *Vampire Nation*. Woodbury, MN: Llewellyn Worldwide.

Rust, D.J. (2001). *The sociology of furry fandom*. Visi. http://www.visi.com/~phantos/furrysoc.html

Sagan, C. (1995). *The Demon-haunted World: Science As a Candle in the Dark*. New York: Random House.

San-Joyz, N. (2004). *An acne fetish is no laughing matter*. E-Zine Articles. Retrieved December 4, 2004 from http://ezinearticles.com/?An-Acne-Fetish-is-No-Laughing-Matter&id=6684

Sancaktar, A. (2006). An analysis of shoe within the context of social history of fashion. Doctoral dissertation, İzmir Institute of Technology.

Sandnabba, N.K., Santtila, P. & Nordling, N. (1999). Sexual behavior and social adaptation among sadomasochistically oriented males. *Journal of Sex Research*, **36**, 273–282.

Sandnabba, N.K., Santtila, P., Alison, L. & Nordling, N. (2002a). Demographics, sexual behaviour, family background and abuse experiences of practitioners of sadomasochistic sex: A review of recent research. *Sexual and Relationship Therapy*, **17**, 39–55.

Sandnabba, N.K., Santtila, P., Nordling, N., Beetz, A.M. & Alison, L. (2002b). Characteristics of a sample of sadomasochistically oriented males with recent experience of sexual contact with animals. *Deviant Behavior*, **23**, 511–529.

Sangbleu (2012). *Wool fetish.* Retrieved June 7, 2012 from *http://sangbleu. com/2013/06/07/wool-fetish/*

Santtila, P., Sandnabba, N.K., Alison, L. & Nordling, G.N. (2002). Investigating the underlying structure in sadomasochistically oriented behaviour: Evidence for partially ordered scales. *Archives of Sexual Behavior*, **31**, 185–196.

Sattler, J.M. (1966). Embarrassment and blushing: A theoretical review. *Journal of Social Psychology*, **69**(1), 117–133.

Sauvageau, A. & Racette, S. (2006a). Aqua-eroticum: An unusual autoerotic fatality in a lake involving a home-made diving apparatus. *Journal of Forensic Sciences*, **51**, 137–139.

Sauvageau, A. & Racette, S. (2006b). Autoerotic deaths in the literature from 1954 to 2004: A review. *Journal of Forensic Sciences*, **51**, 140–146.

Schaupp, W.C. (1981). Commentary. *American Journal of Surgery*, **142**, 85–88.

Schedel-Stupperich, A. (2002). [Criminal acts against horses: Phenomenology and psychosocial construct] [in German]. *Dtsch Tierarztl Wochenschr*, **109**, 116–119.

Schenck, C.H. & Mahowald, M.W. (2005). Rapid eye movement and non-REM sleep parasomnias. *Primary Psychiatry*, **12**(8), 67–74.

Schenck, C.H., Arnulf, I. & Mahowald, M.W. (2007). Sleep and sex: What can go wrong? A review of the literature on sleep-related disorders and abnormal sexual behaviors and experiences. *Sleep*, **30**, 683–702.

Scherk, M.A. (2009). FIP: A disease full of curiosities. *Journal of Feline Medicine and Surgery*, **11**, 223

Schlesinger, L.B. (2003). *Mechaphilia: Sexual Attraction to Machines.* Portland, OR: Please Press.

Schlesinger, L.B. (2004a). *Sexual Murder: Catathymic and Compulsive Homicides.* London: CRC Press.

Schlesinger, L.B. (2004b). *Sexual Murder.* New York: CRC Press.

Schott, J.C., Davis, G.J. & Hunsaker, J.C. (2003). Accidental electrocution during autoeroticism: A shocking case. *American Journal of Forensic Medicine and Pathology*, **24**, 92–95.

Schwartz, T. (2009). *Mask and encasement fetish.* Mental Help. Retrieved April 29, 2009 from *http://www.mentalhelp.net/poc/view_doc.php?type=advice&id= 6613&at=7&cn=10&ad_7=1*

Scorolli, C., Ghirlanda, S., Enquist, M., Zattoni, S. & Jannini, E.A. (2007). Relative

prevalence of different fetishes. *International Journal of Impotence Research*, **19**, 432–437.
Semple, K. (2009). Bartender, make it a stiletto. *New York Times*, June 10.
Sergeant, M., Davies, M.N.O., Dickins, T.E. & Griffiths, M.D. (2005). The self-reported importance of olfaction during human mate choice. *Sexualities, Evolution and Gender*, **7**, 199–213.
Sergeant, M.J.T., Dickins, T.E., Davies, M.N.O. & Griffiths, M.D. (2007). Hedonic ratings by women of body odor in men are related to sexual orientation. *Archives of Sexual Behavior*, **36**, 395–401.
Serial Killer Calendar (2012). *Vorarephilia*. http://www.serialkillercalendar.com/VORAREPHILIA.html
Sex and the University (2008). *Sthenolagnia: Muscle fetishism*. http://sexandtheuniversity.wordpress.com/2008/05/28/sthenolagnia-muscle-fetishism/
Sex Obsessed (2009). *Dysmorphophilia*. Wordpress. Retrieved December 4, 2009 from http://sexobsessed.wordpress.com/2009/12/04/dysmorphophilia/
Sexy Tofu (2011). *Fetish Friday: Trichophilia*. Retrieved December 2, 2011 from http://sexytofu.com/2011/12/02/fetish-friday-trichophilia-hair-fetish/
Sexy Tofu (2012). *National Fetish Day: Interview with a trampler*. Retrieved January 20, 2012 from http://sexytofu.com/tag/trampling/
Shaffer, L. & Penn, J. (2006). A comprehensive paraphilia classification system. In: E.W. Hickey (Ed.), *Sex Crimes and Paraphilia*. Saddle River, NJ: Pearson Prentice Hall.
Shapiro, C.M., Fedoroff, J.P. & Trajanovic, N.N. (1996). Sexual behavior in sleep: A newly described parasomnia. *Sleep Research*, **25**, 367.
Shapiro, C.M., Trajanovic, N.N. and Fedoroff, J.P. (2003) Sexsomnia: A new parasomnia? *Canadian Journal of Psychiatry*, **48**, 311–317.
Sharma, T.C., and Kagan, H.N. (1980). Scrotal emphysema. *American Surgery*. **46**, 652–653.
Shaw, J.A., Campo-Bowen, A.E., Applegate, B., Perez, D., Antoine, L.B., Hart, E.L., Lahey, B.B., Testa, R.J. and Devaney, A. (1993). Young boys who commit serious sexual offenses: Demographics, psychometrics, and phenomenology. *Bulletin of the American Academy of Psychiatry and the Law*, **21**, 399–408.
Shaw-Garlock, G. (2011). Loving machines: Theorising human and sociable-technology interaction – Human–robot personal relationships. *Lecture Notes of the Institute for Computer Sciences, Social Informatics and Telecommunications Engineering*, **59**, 1–10
Steele, V. (1996). *Fetish, Fashion, Sex and Power*. Oxford, UK: Oxford University Press.
Shiwach, R.S. & Prosser, J. (1998). Treatment of an unusual case of masochism. *Journal of Sex and Marital Therapy*, **24**, 303–307.
Show, C. (2012). Man arrested for the fourth time for having sex with a teddy bear in public. *Daily Mail*, June 15.
Simons, I. (2009). On fetishes and clean pencil tips. *Psychology Today*, March 8.
Simpson, A. (2008). Woman with objects fetish marries Eiffel Tower. *Daily Telegraph*, June 4.

Singer, P. (2001). *Heavy petting.* http://www.utilitarian.net/singer/by/2001—-.htm
Singer, P.P. & Jones, G.R. (2006). An unusual autoerotic fatality associated with chloroform inhalation. *Journal of Analytical Toxicology,* **30**, 216–218.
Sir Bamm! (n.d.). *Edge play.* http://www.sirbamm.com/edgeplay.html
Sivaloganathan, S. (1981). Curiosum eroticum: A case of fatal electrocution during auto-erotic practice. *Medicine, Science and the Law,* **21**, 47–50
Sivaloganathan S. (1984). Aqua-eroticum: A case of auto-erotic drowning. *Medicine, Science and the Law,* **24**, 300–302.
Skinner, L.J. & Becker, J.V. (1985). Sexual dysfunctions and deviations. In: M. Hersen and S.M. Turner (Eds), *Diagnostic Interviewing* (pp. 211–239). New York: Plenum Press.
Sklar, J. & Sabbadini, A. (2008). David Cronenberg's spider: Between confusion and fragmentation. *International Journal of Psychoanalysis,* **89**, 427–432.
Skruff, J. (2012). *Britain's filthiest sex fiend strikes again.* Retrieved July 18, 2012 from *http//skruff.com/2012/07/britains-filthiest-sex-fiend-strikes-again/*
Skugarevsky, O., Ehrlich, E. & Sheleg, S. (2011). Accidental strangulation resulted from hypoxyphilia associated with multiple paraphilias and substance abuse: A psychological autopsy case report. *Romanian Journal of Legal Medicine,* **19**, 249–252.
Slade, J.W. (1984). Violence in the hard-core pornographic film: A historical survey. *Journal of Communication,* **34**, 148–163.
Slothrop, T. (2012). *The Bible and macrophilia: He Thong's goliath art.* Remnant of Giants. Retrieved February 6, 2012 from *https://remnantofgiants.wordpress.com/2012/02/06/the-bible-and-macrophilia-he-thongs-goliath-art/*
Smith, C. (2009). Pleasure and distance: Exploring sexual cultures in the classroom. *Sexualities,* **12**, 568–585.
Smith, L. (2012). *The alternative A–Z of sex: Xenophilia.* Rarely Wears Lipstick. Retrieved January 11, 2012 from *http://www.lori-smith.co.uk/2012/01/alternative-to-z-of-sex-xenophilia.html*
Smith, R.S. (1976). Voyeurism: A review of the literature. *Archives of Sexual Behavior,* **5**, 585–608.
The Smoking Gun (2008). *Kinky sex, shocking death.* Retrieved January 25, 2008 from *http://www.thesmokinggun.com/documents/crime/kinky-sex-shocking-death*
Smoking Sweeties (2010). *Women with coughing fetish.* http://smokingsweeties.2forum.biz/t298-women-with-coughing-fetish
Snopes (2000). *Lobster love.* Retrieved January 26, 2000 from *http://www.snopes.com/risque/juvenile/lobster.asp*
Snopes (2006). *Deerly beloved.* Retrieved February 26, 2006 from *http://www.snopes.com/risque/animals/deertongue.asp*
Soble, A. (1996). *Sexual Investigations.* New York: New York University Press.
Social Kink (2007). *Jeff Gord interview.* Retrieved October 24, 2007 from *http://www.socialkink.com/articles.php?do=view&id=92*
Social Kink (n.d.). *Coughing fetish.* http://www.socialkink.com/kinktionary/index.php/Coughing_Fetish
Solomon, R. (1997). Sexual paradigms. In: A. Soble (Ed.), *The Philosophy of Sex: Contemporary Readings* (Third Edition, pp. 21–29). Oxford: Rowman & Little.

Speaker, T.J. (n.d.). Psychosexual infantilism in adults: The eroticization of regression. Doctoral thesis, Columbia Pacific University, California, USA.

Spencer, P.N. (2007). *Bizarre allegations at pin fetish arraignment.* Staten Island Advance. Retrieved June 6, 2007 from *http://blog.silive.com/advance update/2007/06/bizarre_allegations_at_pinfeti.html*

Spectrum (2004). *The Toybag Guide to Hot Wax and Temperature Play.* Emeryville, CA: Greenery Press.

Spengler, A. (1977). Manifest sadomasochism of males: Results of an empirical study. *Archives of Sexual Behavior*, **6**, 441–456.

Sperling, M. (1964). A case of ophidiophilia: A clinical contribution to snake symbolism. *International Journal of Psychoanalysis*, **45**, 227–233.

Spiritual BDSM (2011). *What is sitophilia?* Retrieved December 6, 2011 from *http://www.spiritualbdsm.com/2011/12/what-is-sitophilia.html?zx=69b8151a4d2896e3*

Sportsman's Daily (2010, December 23). Belichick one-ups Rex Ryan; admits to rare ear fetish.

Srivastava A. (1980). Survival of gonococci in urethral secretions with reference to nonsexual transmission of gonococcal infections. *Journal of Medical Microbiology*, **13**, 593–596.

Stallybrass, P. & Jones, A.R. (2001). Fetishizing the glove in Renaissance Europe. *Critical Inquiry*, **28**, 114–132.

Steel, K. (2006). *101 uses for a dead deer.* In The Medieval Middle. Retrieved November 16, 2006 from *http://www.inthemedievalmiddle.com/2006/11/101-uses-for-dead-deer.html*

Steel, K. (2007). *101 uses for a dead dog.* In The Medieval Middle. Retrieved February 27, 2007 from *http://www.inthemedievalmiddle.com/2007/02/101-uses-for-dead-dog.html*

Steele, V. (1996). *Fetish, Fashion, Sex and Power.* Oxford, UK: Oxford University Press.

Steele, V. (1998). *Shoes: A Lexicon of Style.* London: Co & Bear Productions.

Steele, V. (2001). *Fashion, Fetish, Fantasy. Masquerade and Identities: Essays on Gender, Sexuality and Marginality.* London: Routledge.

Stein, M.L., Schlesinger, L.B. & Pinizzotto, A.J. (2010). Necrophilia and sexual homicide. *Journal of Forensic Science*, **55**, 443–446.

Stekel, W. (1952). *Sexual Aberrations: The Phenomena of Fetishism in Relation to Sex*, Vol. 1 (translated by S. Parker). New York: Boni & Liveright.

Stekel, W. & van Teslaar, J.S. (1925). *Peculiarities of Behavior: Wandering Mania, Dipsomania, Cleptomania, Pyromania and Allied Impulsive Acts.* New York: Boni & Liveright.

Stephens, P. & Taff, M. (1987). Rectal impaction following enema with a concrete mix. *American Journal of Forensic Medicine and Pathology*, **8**, 179–182.

Stephens, W. (2002). *Demon Lovers: Witchcraft, Sex, and the Crisis of Belief.* Chicago, IL: University of Chicago Press.

Strauss, R.S. (2012). I'm in love with a three-foot statue of Adonis: Carer, 40, spends every day with £400 moulding of the Greek god of desire she has dubbed "Hans". *Daily Mail*, March 23.

Stoller, R.J. (1971). The term "transvestism". *Archives of General Psychiatry*, **24**, 230–237.
Stoller, R.J. (1982). Erotic vomiting. *Archives of Sexual Behavior*, **11**, 361–365.
Stollznow, K. (2011). Paranormal paramours. *The Skeptical Inquirer*, March 14.
Stravodimos, K.G., Koritsiadis, G. & Koutalellis, G. (2009). Electrical wire as a foreign body in a male urethra: A case report. *Journal of Medical Case Reports*, **3**, 49
Sumitra (2012). *Girls licking doorknobs: More madness from Japan*. Oddity Central. Retrieved January 13, 2012 from *http://www.odditycentral.com/pics/girls-licking-doorknobs-more-madness-from-japan.html*
Summers, C. (2015). Wallet rape: Meet the men who get a kick out of giving away money. *Daily Star*, December 27.
Summers, J. (2003). A complication of an unusual sexual practice. *Southern Medical Journal*, **96**, 716–717.
Supervert (2001). *Extra-terrestrial Sex Fetish* (self-published book). *http://supervert.com/*
Swami, V. & Furnham, A. (2008). *The Psychology of Physical Attraction*. London: Routledge.
Swami, V. & Furnham, A. (2009). Big and beautiful: Attractiveness and health ratings of the female body by male "fat admirers". *Archives of Sexual Behavior*, **38**, 201–208.
Swami, V. & Tovee, M.J. (2006). The influence of body weight on the physical attractiveness preferences of feminist and non-feminist heterosexual women and lesbians. *Psychology of Women Quarterly*, **30**, 252–257.
Swami, V. & Tovee, M.J. (2009). Big beautiful women: The body size preferences of male fat admirers. *Journal of Sex Research*, **46**, 89–96.
Sydney Morning Herald (2010, April 17). "Truly bizarre" case of a man called Spink, his mice and a suspected bestiality farm.
Taktak, S., Karakus, M. & Eke, S.M. (2015a). The man whose fetish object is ejaculate: A case report. *Journal of Psychiatry*, **18**(3), 276.
Taktak, S., Karakus, M., Kaplan, A. & Eke, S.M. (2015b). Shoe fetishism and kleptomania comorbidity: A case report. *European Journal of Pharmaceutical and Medical Research*, **2**, 14–19.
Talerico, D. (2001). Interpreting sexual imagery in Japanese prints: A fresh approach to Hokusai's "The Dream of the Fisherman's Wife: Female Diver and Two Octopuses". *Impressions: The Journal of the Ukiyo-e Society of America*, **23**, 24–42.
Terry, L.L. & Vasey, P.L. (2011). Feederism in a woman. *Archives of Sexual Behavior*, **40**, 639–645.
Terry, L.L., Suschinsky, K.D., Lalumière, M.L. & Vasey, P.L. (2012). Feederism: An exaggeration of a normative mate selection preference? *Archives of Sexual Behavior*, **41**(1), 249–260
Thadeusz, F. (2007). Objectophilia, fetishism and neo-sexuality: Falling in love with things. *Der Spiegel*, November 5.
The Atlantic (2009). *Pogonophilia*. Busted. Retrieved July 12, 2009 from *http://www.theatlantic.com/daily-dish/archive/2009/07/pogonophilia-busted/198899/*

The Frisky (2012). *Five things you probably didn't know about witches.* Retrieved October 5, 2012 from *http://www.thefrisky.com/2012-10-05/5-things-you-probably-didnt-know-about-witches/*

The Independent (2010, March 30). Growing fetish trend: Pedal-pumping, revving and cranking.

The Smoking Gun (2006). *Can you get dear with a dead deer?* Retrieved November 16, 2006 from *http://www.thesmokinggun.com/documents/crime/can-you-get-dear-dead-deer*

The Smoking Gun (2012). *Man busted for curbside sex with old couch.* Retrieved September 24, 2012 from *http://www.thesmokinggun.com/documents/man-busted-for-couch-sex-684512*

The Sneaky Badger (2005). *Gerbil felching.* Badger Bob. Retrieved October 26, 2005 from *http://badgerbob.blogspot.co.uk/2005/10/gerbil-felching.html*

The Sun (2008, July 5). Man admits to octopus porn.

The Sun (2012, December 17). Swedish "skeleton sex" case woman convicted of "disturbing the peace of dead".

The Times of India (2007, April 15). The kinks of virtual men.

The Toilet Duck (2011). *Queening: Can this be enjoyable for both parties?* Retrieved August 7, 2011 from *http://thetoiletduck.com/20/queening-can-this-be-enjoyable-for-both-parties/*

Thibault, R., Spencer, J.D., Bishop, J.W. & Hibler, N.S. (1984) An unusual autoerotic death: Asphyxia with an abdominal ligature. *Journal of Forensic Science,* **29**, 679–684.

Thompson, H.S. (1966). *Hell's Angels: A Strange and Terrible Saga of the Outlaw Motorcycle Gangs.* London: Random House.

Thompson, S.L. (2000). The arts of the motorcycle: Biology, culture, and aesthetics in technological choice. *Technology and Culture,* **41**, 99–115.

Tipado, Z. (2015). *Exploring the vore fetish of game characters eating each other whole.* The Stoned Gamer. Retrieved October 25, 2015 from *http://thestonedgamer.com/features/item/351-exploring-the-vore-fetish-of-game-characters-swallowing-each-other-whole*

Tolba, A.M., Azab, A.A.H., Nasr, M.A. & Salah, E. (2014). Dartos fascio-myo-cutaneous flap for penile skin loss: A simple flap with an immense potential. *Surgical Science,* **5**, 6–9.

Torbati, J. (2007). Profs question students' Wikipedia dependency. *Yale Daily News,* February 27

Trajanovic, N.N., Mangan, M. & Shapiro, C.M. (2007). Sexual behaviour in sleep: An Internet survey. *Social Psychiatry and Psychiatric Epidemiology,* **42**, 1024–1031.

Trash Can Stories (2012). *FAQ page.* http://www.trashcanstories.net/trashcanstories_faq.html

Tremayne, T. (2009). Used condoms: A dangerous fetish? *Sexually Transmitted Infection,* **85**, 483.

Tuchman, W.W. & Lachman, J.H. (1964). An unusual perversion: The wearing of diapers and rubber pants in a 29-year-old male. *American Journal of Psychiatry,* **120**, 1198–1199.

Tungol, J.R. (2013). Paralyzed man Rafe Biggs has "orgasmic sensations" through his thumb, "surrogate penis". *International Business Times*, April 22

Turnbull, O.H., Lovett, V.E., Chaldecott, J. & Lucas, M.D. (2014). Reports of intimate touch: Erogenous zones and somatosensory cortical organization. *Cortex*, **53**, 146–154.

Twinn, F. (2007). *The Miscellany of Sex: Tantalizing Travels through Love, Lust and Libido.* London: Arcturus.

Volk, T. and Sagan, D. (2009). *Death/Sex.* White River Junction, VT: Chelsea Green Publishing.

Urban Dictionary (2012a). *Tamakeri.* http://www.urbandictionary.com/define.php?term=Tamakeri

Urban Dictionary (2012b). *Partial unbirthing.* http://www.urbandictionary.com/define.php?term=unbirthing

Urban Dictionary (2013). *Jarmel berries.* http://www.urbandictionary.com/define.php?term=Jarmel%20Berries&defid=1700690

Uva, J.L. (1995). Review: Autoerotic asphyxiation in the United States. *Journal of Forensic Sciences*, **40**, 574–581.

Vanden Bergh, R.L. & Kelly, J. F. (1964). Vampirism: A review with new observations. *Archives of General Psychiatry*, **11**, 543–547.

van Ophoven, A. & de Kernion, J.B. (2000). Clinical management of foreign bodies of the genitourinary tract. *Journal of Urology*, **164**, 274–287.

van Teslaar, J.S. (1922). *Sex and the Senses.* Boston, MA: The Gorham Press

Vātsyāyana, M. (4th century AD). *Kama Sutra.* New York: Lancer Books.

Veale, D. & Daniels, J. (2012). Cosmetic clitoridectomy in a 33-year-old woman. *Archives of Sex Behavior*, **41**, 725–730.

Vembu, V. (2008). On sale: Beijing cheergirls' dirty lingerie. *DNA India*, September 13.

Vitello, C. (2006). Hybristophilia: The love of criminals. In: E.W. Hickey (Ed.), *Sex Crimes and Paraphilia.* Saddle River, NJ: Pearson Prentice Hall.

Vivid Random Existence (2010a). *Cynosexuality (or cynophilia): The sexual attraction to dogs.* Wordpress. Retrieved November 14, 2010 from http://vividrandomexistence.wordpress.com/2010/11/14/cynosexuality-or-cynophilia-the-sexual-attraction-to-dogs/

Vivid Random Existence (2010b). *Delphinic zoosexuality (or zoophilia): The sexual attraction to dolphins.* Wordpress. Retrieved December 5, 2010 from http://vividrandomexistence.wordpress.com/2010/12/05/delphinic-zoosexuality-or-zoophilia-the-sexual-attraction-to-dolphins/

Vivid Random Existence (2010c). *Zoosexuality: Should it be considered acceptable?* Wordpress. Retrieved July 20, 2010 from http://vividrandomexistence.wordpress.com/2010/07/20/zoosexuality-should-it-be-considered-acceptable-or-not/

Vivid Random Existence (2011a). *Equinsexuality (or equinophilia): The sexual attraction to horses.* Wordpress. Retrieved July 26, 2011 from http://vividrandomexistence.wordpress.com/2011/07/26/equinosexuality-or-equinophilia-the-sexual-attraction-to-horses/

Vivid Random Existence (2011b). *Crocodilian zoosexuality (or zoophilia): The sexual attraction to alligators and crocodiles.* Wordpress. Retrieved December 5,

2011 from http://vividrandomexistence.wordpress.com/2011/12/05/crocodilian-zoosexuality-or-zoophilia-the-sexual-attraction-to-alligators-and-crocodiles/

Vivid Random Existence (2012). *Lizard zoosexuality (or zoophilia): The sexual attraction to lizards*. Wordpress. Retrieved January 13, 2012 from http://vividrandomexistence.wordpress.com/2012/01/13/lizard-zoosexuality-or-zoophilia-the-sexual-attraction-to-lizards/

von Krafft-Ebing, R. (1877). *Psychopathia Sexualis*. New York: Paperback Library (1965 reprint).

von Krafft-Ebing, R. (1886). *Psychopathia Sexualis* (translated by C.G. Chaddock). Philadelphia, PA: F.A. Davis.

von Sacher-Masoch, L. (2000). *Venus in Furs* (translated by J. Neugroschel). New York: Penguin.

Vorpagel, B. (1988). A rodent by any other name: Implications of a contemporary legend. *International Folklore Review*, **6**, 53–57.

Voorhoeve, A., During, E., Jopling, D., Wilson, T. & Kamm, F. (2011). Who am I? Beyond "I think, therefore I am". *Annals of the New York Academy of Sciences*, **1234**(1), 134–148.

Weinberg, M.S. & Williams, C.J. (2010). Men sexually interested in transwomen (MSTW): Gendered embodiment and the construction of sexual desire. *Journal of Sex Research*, **47**, 374–383.

Weinberg, M.S., Williams, C.J. & Moser, C. (1984). The social constituents of sadomasochism. *Social Problems*, **31**, 379–389.

Weinberg, M.S., Williams, C.J. & Calhan, C. (1994). Homosexual foot fetishism. *Archives of Sexual Behavior*, **23**, 611–626.

Weinberg, M.S., Williams, C.J. & Calhan, C. (1995). "If the shoe fits …": Exploring male homosexual foot fetishism. *Journal of Sex Research*, **32**, 17–27.

Weiss, M.D. (2006). Working at play: BDSM sexuality in the San Francisco Bay area. *Anthropologica*, **48**, 229–245.

Wenderoth, U. & Jonas, U. (1979). Curiosity in urology? Masturbation injuries. *European Urology*, **6**, 312–313.

Wheelchair Lifestyles (2011). *Disability fetish and medical fetish*. Retrieved August 12, 2011 from http://www.streetsie.com/disability-fetish-medical-fetish/

White, J.H. (2007). Evidence of primary, secondary, and collateral paraphilias left at serial murder and sex offender crime scenes. *Journal of Forensic Sciences*, **52**, 1194–1201.

White, M.J. (1978). The statue syndrome: Perversion? Fantasy? Anecdote? *Journal of Sex Research*, **14**, 246–249.

White, R.R. (2012). *Edgeplay isn't your grandmother's BDSM scene*. Vice. Retrieved September 12, 2012 from http://www.vice.com/read/edgeplay-isnt-your-grandmothers-bdsm-scene

White Watch (2011). *White man who repeatedly has sex with cow manure back in jail*. White Watch. Retrieved March 27, 2011 from http://whitewatch.info/2011/03/27/white-man-who-repeatedly-has-sex-with-cow-manure-back-in-jail.aspx

Whitty, M.T. & Fisher, W.A. (2008). The sexy side of the Internet: An examination of sexual activities and materials in cyberspace. In: A. Barak (Ed.), *Psychological*

Aspects of Cyberspace: Theory, Research, Applications (pp. 185–208). Cambridge, UK: Cambridge University Press.

Wiederman, M.W. (2003). Paraphilia and fetishism. *The Family Journal: Counseling and Therapy for Couples and Families*, **11**, 315–321.

Wiki (2024). Impregnation fetish. *http://psychology.wikia.com/wiki/Impregnation_fetish*

Wiki Answers (2013). What is a pedal pumping fetish? *http://wiki.answers.com/Q/What_is_a_pedal_pumping_fetish*

Wikibin (2012). Partial unbirthing fetishism. *http://wikibin.org/articles/partial-unbirthing-fetishism.html*

Wikifur (2009). Unbirth. Retrieved March 19, 2009 from *http://en.wikifur.com/wiki/Unbirth*

Wikifur (2010). Hypertrophilia. Retrieved November 11, 2010 from *http://en.wikifur.com/wiki/Hypertrophilia*

Wikifur (2012a). Microphilia. *http://en.wikifur.com/wiki/Microphilia*

Wikifur (2012b). Animal totem. *http://en.wikifur.com/wiki/Animal_totem*

Wikifur (2012c). Plushophilia. *http://en.wikifur.com/wiki/Plushophilia*

Wikipedia (2011). Insertion fantasies. Retrieved September 4, 2011 from *http://en.wikipedia.org/wiki/User:Xomic/Insertion_fantasy*

Wikipedia (2012a). Uniform fetishism. *http://en.wikipedia.org/wiki/Uniform_fetishism*

Wikipedia (2012b). Vaginal flatulence. *http://en.wikipedia.org/wiki/Vaginal_flatulence*

Wikipedia (2012c). Facesitting. *http://en.wikipedia.org/wiki/Facesitting*

Wikipedia (2012d). *Bukkake. http://en.wikipedia.org/wiki/Bukkake*

Wikipedia (2012e). *Gokkun. http://en.wikipedia.org/wiki/Gokkun*

Wikipedia (2012f). *Gerbilling. http://en.wikipedia.org/wiki/Gerbilling*

Wikipedia (2012g). Attraction to transgender people. *http://en.wikipedia.org/wiki/Attraction_to_transgender_people*

Wikipedia (2012h). Autagonistophilia. *http://en.wikipedia.org/wiki/Autagonistophilia*

Wikipedia (2012i). Oculophilia. *http://en.wikipedia.org/wiki/Oculophilia*

Wikipedia (2012j). Talk: Teratophilia. *http://en.wikipedia.org/wiki/Talk%3ATeratophilia*

Wikipedia (2012k). Penile subincision. *http://en.wikipedia.org/wiki/Penile_subincision*

Wipipedia (2012l). Veil fetishism. *http://www.londonfetishscene.com/wipi/index.php/Veil_fetishism*

Wikipedia (2012m). *Tamakeri. http://en.wikipedia.org/wiki/Tamakeri*

Wikipedia (2012n). Muscle worship. *http://en.wikipedia.org/wiki/Muscle_worship*

Wikipedia (2012o). Scrotal inflation. *http://en.wikipedia.org/wiki/Scrotal_inflation*

Wikipedia (2012p). Pregnancy fetishism. *http://en.wikipedia.org/wiki/Pregnancy_fetishism*

Wikipedia (2012q). Medical fetishism. *http://en.wikipedia.org/wiki/Medical_fetishism*

Wikipedia (2012r). Tickling game. *http://en.wikipedia.org/wiki/Tickling_game*

Wikipedia (2012s). Balloon fetish. *http://en.wikipedia.org/wiki/Balloon_fetish*

Wikipedia (2012t). Muscle worship. *http://en.wikipedia.org/wiki/Muscle_worship*

Wikipedia (2012u). Recreational hypnosis. *http://en.wikipedia.org/wiki/Recreational_hypnosis*

Wikipedia (2012v). Pelvis justo major. *http://en.wikipedia.org/wiki/Pelvis_justo_major*

Wikipedia (2012w). Kataptronophilia. *http://en.wikipedia.org/wiki/Katoptronophilia*

Wikipedia (2012x). Mechanophilia. *http://en.wikipedia.org/wiki/Mechanophilia*
Wikipedia (2012y). Sexual fetishism. *http://en.wikipedia.org/wiki/Sexual_fetishism#Psychological_origins_and_development*
Wikipedia (2012z). Sensation play. *http://en.wikipedia.org/wiki/Sensation_play_(BDSM)*
Wikipedia (2012aa). Temperature play. *http://en.wikipedia.org/wiki/Temperature_play*
Wikipedia (2012bb). Cannibalism. *http://en.wikipedia.org/wiki/Cannibalism*
Wikipedia (2012cc). Human sacrifice in Aztec culture. *http://en.wikipedia.org/wiki/Human_sacrifice_in_Aztec_culture*
Wikipedia (2012dd). Sexual cannibalism. *http://en.wikipedia.org/wiki/Sexual_cannibalism*
Wikipedia (2012ee). Stinging nettle. *http://en.wikipedia.org/wiki/Stinging_nettle*
Wikipedia (2012ff). Talk: Crush fetish. *http://en.wikipedia.org/wiki/Talk%3ACrush_fetish*
Wikipedia (2012gg). Trampling. *http://en.wikipedia.org/wiki/Trampling*
Wikipedia (2012hh). Cruising for sex. *http://en.wikipedia.org/wiki/Cruising_for_sex*
Wikipedia (2012ii). Xenophily. *http://en.wikipedia.org/wiki/Xenophily*
Wikipedia (2012jj). Spectrophilia. *http://en.wikipedia.org/wiki/Spectrophilia*
Wikipedia (2013a). Splosh! *http://en.wikipedia.org/wiki/Splosh!*
Wikipedia (2013b). Wet and messy fetishism. *http://en.wikipedia.org/wiki/Wet_and_messy_fetishism*
Wikipedia (2013c). Hentai. *http://en.wikipedia.org/wiki/Hentai*
Wikipedia (2013d). Cuckold. *http://en.wikipedia.org/wiki/Cuckold*
Wikipedia (2013e). Manga. *http://en.wikipedia.org/wiki/Manga*
Wikipedia (2013f). Tentacle erotica. *http://en.wikipedia.org/wiki/Tentacle_erotica*
Wikipedia (2013g). Sex magic. *http://en.wikipedia.org/wiki/Sex_magic*
Wikipedia (2013h). Wicca. *http://en.wikipedia.org/wiki/Wicca*
Wikipedia (2013i). *Urotsukidoji*. *https://en.wikipedia.org/wiki/Urotsukidōji*
Wikipedia (2013j). Hemorrhoid. *http://en.wikipedia.org/wiki/Hemorrhoid*.
Wikipedia (2013k). Haircut fetishism. *http://en.wikipedia.org/wiki/User:Kaldari/Haircut_fetishism*
Wikipedia (2013l). Clothing fetishism. *http://en.wikipedia.org/wiki/Clothing_fetish*
Wikipedia (2013m). Wet and messy fetishism. *http://en.wikipedia.org/wiki/Wet_and_messy_fetishism*
Wikipedia (2013n). Nazi chic. *http://en.wikipedia.org/wiki/Nazi_chic*
Wikipedia (2013o). Pecattiphilia. *http://en.wikipedia.org/wiki/Pecattiphilia*
Wikipedia (2013p). Uniform fetishism. *http://en.wikipedia.org/wiki/Nun_fetishism*
Wikipedia (2013q). Sensation play (BDSM). *http://en.wikipedia.org/wiki/Sensation_play_(BDSM)*
Wikipedia (2013r). Total enclosure fetishism. *http://en.wikipedia.org/wiki/Total_enclosure_fetishism*
Wikipedia (2013s). Mummification (BDSM). *http://en.wikipedia.org/wiki/Mummification_(BDSM)*
Wikipedia (2013t). Omorashi. *http://en.wikipedia.org/wiki/Omorashi*
Wikipedia (2014b). Oculophilia. *http://en.wikipedia.org/wiki/Oculophilia*

Wikipedia (2014c). F*** off, I'm a hairy woman. *http://en.wikipedia.org/wiki/F***_Off,_I'm_a_Hairy_Woman*

Wikipedia (2014d). Mummification (BDSM). *http://en.wikipedia.org/wiki/Mummification_(BDSM)*

Wikipedia (2014e). Sensation play (BDSM). *http://en.wikipedia.org/wiki/Sensation_play_(BDSM)*

Wikipedia (2014f). Total enclosure fetishism. *http://en.wikipedia.org/wiki/Total_enclosure_fetishism*

Wikipedia (2014g). Wax play. *http://en.wikipedia.org/wiki/Wax_play*

Wikipedia (2014h). Toucherism. *http://en.wikipedia.org/wiki/Toucherism*

Wikipedia (2015a). Dacryphilia. *http://en.wikipedia.org/wiki/Dacryphilia*

Wikipedia (2015b). Lip. *https://en.wikipedia.org/wiki/Lip*

Wikipedia (2015c). Glove fetishism. *https://en.wikipedia.org/wiki/Glove_fetishism*

Wikipedia (2015d). Body inflation. *http://en.wikipedia.org/wiki/Body_inflation*

Wikipedia (2015e). Underwear fetishism. *https://en.wikipedia.org/wiki/Underwear_fetishism#Panties*

Wikipedia (2015f). Shunga. *https://en.wikipedia.org/wiki/Shunga*

Wikipedia (2017). Mechanophilia. *http://en.wikipedia.org/wiki/Mechanophilia*

Williams, C.J. and Weinberg, M.S. (2003). Zoophilia in men: A study of sexual interest in animals. *Archives of Sexual Behavior*, 32, 523–535.

Williams, D.J. (2006). Different (painful!) strokes for different folks: A general overview of sexual sadomasochism (SM) and its diversity. *Sexual Addiction and Compulsivity*, **13**, 333–346.

Williams, L. (1991). Film bodies: Gender, genre and excess. *Film Quarterly*, **44**(4), 2–13.

Wilson, G.D. & Barrett, P.T. (1987). Parental characteristics and partner choice: Some evidence for oedipal imprinting. *Journal of Biosocial Science*, **19**, 157–161.

Wilson, G. & Gosselin, C. (1980). Personality characteristics of fetishists, transvestites and sadomasochists. *Personality and Individual Differences*, **1**, 289–295.

Wilson, N. (2000) A psychoanalytic contribution to psychic vampirism: A case vignette. *American Journal of Psychoanalysis*, **60**, 177–186.

Winder, B. & Banyard, P. (2017). *A Psychologist's Casebook of Crime: From Arson to Voyeurism.* London: Bloomsbury Publishing.

Wipipedia (2011). *Bride fetish. London Fetish Scene,* Retrieved September 6, 2011 from *http://www.londonfetishscene.com/wipi/index.php/Bride_fetish*

Wipipedia (2013a). Figging. *http://www.londonfetishscene.com/wipi/index.php/Figging*

Wipipedia (2013b). Pervertible. *http://www.londonfetishscene.com/wipi/index.php/Pervertable*

Wise, T.N. (1982). Urethral manipulation: An unusual paraphilia. *Journal of Sex and Marital Therapy*, **8**, 222–227.

Wise, T.N. (1985). Fetishism – etiology and treatment: A review from multiple perspectives. *Comprehensive Psychiatry*, **26**, 249–257.

Wise, T.N. & Goldberg, R.L. (1995). Escalation of a fetish: Coprophagia in a non-psychotic adult of normal intelligence. *Journal of Sex and Marital Therapy*, **21**, 272–275.

Wise Geek (2012). *What is vaginal flatulence?* Retrieved November 13, 2012 from http://www.wisegeek.com/what-is-vaginal-flatulence.htm

Wochner, M. & Klosinski, G. (1988). Child and adolescent psychiatry aspects of animal abuse: A comparison with aggressive patients in child and adolescent psychiatry. *Schweiz Arch Neurol Psychiatry*, **139**(3), 59–67.

Wohlrab, S., Stahl, J. & Kappeler, P.M. (2007). Modifying the body: Motivations for getting tattooed and pierced. *Body Image*, **4**, 87–95

Wonderland Burlesque (2011). *Acquired tastes: Armpits*. Retrieved January 22, 2011 from *https://wonderlandburlesque.blogspot.com/2011/01/acquired-tastes-chapter-2-armpits.html?zx=abdfff7185081eb6*

Yates, P.M., Hucker, S.J. & Kingston, W.A. (2008). Sexual sadism: Psychopathology and theory. In: D.R. Laws and W.T. O'Donohue (Eds), *Sexual Deviance: Theory, Assessment and Treatment* (pp. 213–230). New York: Guilford Press.

Yenisey, Z. (2016). *How the bizarre "overwatch" fetish is getting gamers hot and bothered.* Maxim. Retrieved May 11, 2016 from *http://www.maxim.com/entertainment/overwatch-pornhub-2016-5*

Yoganathan, K.G. & Blackwell, A.L. (2006). Unusual cause of acute scrotal cellulitis in an HIV-positive man. *Sexually Transmitted Infections*, **82**, A187–A188.

Young, L. & Alexander, B. (2012). *The Chemistry between Us: Love, Sex, and the Science of Attraction*. London: Penguin.

Zerubavel, E. (1991). *The Fine Line: Making Distinctions in Everyday Life*. Chicago, IL: University of Chicago Press.

Zucker, K.J. & Blanchard, R. (1997). Transvestic fetishism: Psychopathology and theory. In: D.R. Laws and W.T. O'Donohue (Eds), *Sexual Deviance: Theory, Assessment, and Treatment* (First Edition, pp. 253–279). New York: Guilford Press.

Zufall, R. (1973). Laceration of penis from hand vacuum cleaner. *Journal of the American Medical Association*, **224**, 630.